# THE RISE OF MODERN DIPLOMACY

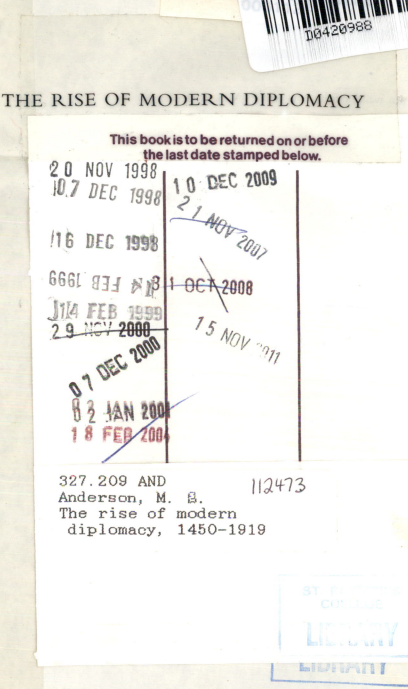

Also available from Longman by M.S. Anderson

*The Ascendancy of Europe 1815–1914* (second edition 1985)

*Europe in the Eighteenth Century 1713–1783*, (third edition 1987)

# THE RISE OF MODERN DIPLOMACY 1450–1919

*M.S. Anderson*

*Longman*
London and New York

**LONGMAN GROUP UK LIMITED**
Longman House, Burnt Mill,
Harlow, Essex CM20 2JE, England
*and Associated Companies throughout the world.*

Published in the United States of America
by Longman Publishing, New York.

© Longman Group UK Limited 1993

First published 1993

ISBN 0 582 21232 4 CSD
ISBN 0 582 21237 5 PPR

**British Library Cataloguing-in-Publication Data**

A catalogue record for this book is
available from the British Library

**Library of Congress Cataloging in Publication Data**

Anderson, M. S. (Matthew Smith)
    The rise of modern diplomacy, 1450–1919 / M.S. Anderson.
        p.   cm.
    Includes bibliographical references and index.
    ISBN 0–582–21232–4 (cased). -- ISBN 0–582–21237–5 (paper)
    1. Diplomacy--History. 2. International relations--History.
    I. Title.
    JX1635.A53 1993
    327.2'09--dc20                                        92–34237
                                                          CIP

Set by 7B in 10/12pt Bembo

Produced by Longman Singapore Publishers (Pte) Ltd.
Printed in Singapore

# Contents

# Contents

# Preface

This book, which is based in part on many years of teaching at the London School of Economics, attempts to supplement in some significant ways conventional histories of international relations for the period which it covers. It does this by concentrating on some aspects of the subject which tend in the normal undergraduate course to receive relatively little attention and to be forced to the periphery of what is discussed. It deals therefore with a number of topics which collectively cover a large area of historical ground and which are somewhat varied. Each has its own interest and importance: each has been written about extensively over this long period. I have attempted to use this large body of historical writing to paint a coherent picture, both of the developing framework of diplomacy which more and more bound the states of Europe together throughout much of the continent's modern history and of the parallel discussion of the meaning of these links and of the objectives to which they might or should be directed. Inevitably, given the length of the period and the many-faceted nature of the subject, the picture has been painted with a fairly broad brush. I hope, however, that what may have been lost in terms of the finer details has been counterbalanced by gains in scope and breadth.

A book such as this is impossible to write without access to rich library resources. It is a pleasure to acknowledge the indispensable help, with this and much other writing, which I have received over many years from the British Library, the London Library and, in my own college, the British Library of Political and Economic Science.

M.S. ANDERSON
London

vii

# Introduction

Any group of independent states with interests and ambitions of their own, living side by side and united by some basic community of outlook and traditions, must have some degree of formal and organised contact with one another. What has distinguished the states of Europe in this respect throughout modern history has been the increasingly close and wide-ranging nature of this contact, the growth of a network of institutions through which it has been carried on, and the way in which it has come to transcend, from the middle of the nineteenth century onwards, the merely governmental sphere and to spill over into a wide range of others, technical, intellectual and economic. During the middle ages the rulers of Europe could not avoid maintaining relations with one another, even though these often had a large element of symbolism and conspicuous display as much as of genuine political content. But there was then little or nothing in the way of institutions concerned solely or even mainly with the formulation and conduct of foreign policy. Professional diplomats and any idea of diplomacy as a career with a distinct nature and demands of its own did not exist. The ideal of some effective unity of Christendom against an alien and generally hostile outside world retained genuine power and popular appeal, however unreal it might now be becoming in practice; but beyond this there was little which could·be called international theory. Respect for the papacy as a potential arbiter in disputes between secular rulers, and perhaps for the Holy Roman Emperor as a monarch in some sense superior to others, were not enough to justify the use of such a term; and otherwise there was little rationale for the relations between states apart from the endless conflicting dynastic and other claims of individual monarchs. With the world outside Europe, indeed outside western and central Europe, relations were slight in the extreme, diplomatic contacts rare and usually marked by mutual suspicion and misunderstanding. Until at least the end of the sixteenth century an embassy even to Russia was a considerable and possibly dangerous adventure and one to the sultan in Constantinople or the shah of Persia even more so.

By the beginning of the twentieth century, as the generations which saw the formation of the modern Europe-shaped and Europe–dominated world drew to a close, all this had changed. Foreign policy was now a major preoccupation of every European government. Often, in a political environment marked by growing competition between states and by technological developments which made any conflict between them much more potentially destructive, it was their main preoccupation. The major states of the middle ages, in which power was normally diffused widely among the subordinate structures – provincial or noble assemblies, self-governing cities, corporate bodies of all kinds – which made them up, had the vitality and powers of survival of so many primitive and undeveloped organisms. Though they might suffer defeat on the battlefield they were difficult or impossible to conquer in any lasting sense. The much more sophisticated and centralised ones of the decades before 1914 were more vulnerable because they were so much more advanced. They were therefore forced to give more, and more continuous, attention to the activities and possible intentions of their neighbours. Diplomacy, moreover, was now, and had for generations been becoming, at least a kind of profession. Everywhere foreign offices, now rapidly becoming larger, more complex in their organisation and, with some reluctance, wider in their view of what constituted international relations, executed and sometimes planned foreign policy. A network of institutions which had grown up over a long period in response to practical necessities now provided the foundation for unprecedentedly close and continuous relations between the states. Moreover, this institutional framework was now being extended beyond Europe and beginning to embrace not merely her great independent offshoot in North America but the few other non–European states, notably Japan, which already conducted significant foreign policies of their own. The process which would soon extend this European system to the world in general was now under way.

The four centuries or more between the end of the middle ages and the First World War also saw the development of a body of generally accepted rules which defined and safeguarded the position and status of diplomats. At the same time their activities came increasingly to be seen in terms of ideas and ideals which gave unity and some underlying intellectual structure (if that is not too elevated a term) to the growing volume of diplomatic activity. A balance of power in some form is always likely to emerge in any grouping of independent and self-regarding states closely-knit enough to be called a state-system, as much of Europe at least had become by the sixteenth century. Whether or not the name is used the reality is always at least potentially present. During these centuries the amount and quality of the attention given to the concept by both statesmen and publicists varied greatly. First discussed with some clarity in late-Renaissance Italy, the idea of the balance as an inescapable and, to most observers, beneficial aspect of international relations reached its highest pitch in the eighteenth century, receded somewhat into the background of political comment during that which followed and was made by the disaster of 1914 the target of a chorus of criticism and condemnation. Yet throughout this long period it provided as no other idea could a guiding thread of attitudes and assumptions, a traditional and widely accepted way of seeing and making sense of the international world. Nevertheless, it was not without competitors. From the beginning it was challenged by the belief that its inevitable assumption of competing and therefore potentially conflicting forces within any state-system could not be accepted as an unchanging given, a law of political nature, but must be transcended. The fate of Europe, and later of the world, could not be left at the mercy of the unrestrained self-interest and aggressive impulses of individual states or rulers. They must be led to better things by the creation of an international order and international institutions which rose above selfishness and conflict, by concerted action to safeguard peace. At one extreme this might mean no more than measures designed to make it more difficult for rival states to go to war and to force on them a breathing-space during which their quarrels might be settled without conflict. At the other it meant highly ambitious schemes of supranational government. A recognised code of international law, some kind of international judiciary to interpret and apply it, disarmament, the fostering of the international cooperation on a wide range of practical issues which was growing rapidly from the 1860s onwards; all these might play a part in this process, which was essential if the wealth and happiness of humanity were not to be squandered in destructive internecine struggles.

All these, then, were threads in the complex tapestry of the 'old diplomacy', the system of regulated and organised contacts between states which Europe had evolved by the early twentieth century and which, with all its faults, was one of her more important gifts to the world. Its evolution is the subject of this book.

# CHAPTER ONE

# The 'New Diplomacy' of the Fifteenth and Sixteenth Centuries

## THE NEW DIPLOMATIC WORLD TAKES SHAPE

In western Europe during the fifteenth and sixteenth centuries the major states were becoming stronger, more united and more militarily effective than ever before. Side by side with this went a tendency for the relations between them, or more accurately between their rulers, to become closer and more continuous. It is hardly possible to trace the beginning of this process even to any approximate date. Perhaps it can be detected as early as the later twelfth century, when the Plantagenets in England, in their struggle with Philip Augustus of France, made alliances with Aragon and the Guelph dukes of Bavaria, while Philip had the support of the Holy Roman Emperor. It can be seen with greater certainty from the first decades of the fourteenth century. By then Anglo-French rivalry was drawing Scotland at one geographical extreme and the Spanish kingdoms at the other into its orbit. Moreover, the establishment of Angevin rule in Naples from the 1260s onwards had now brought the Italian world into a closer political relationship than before with France and, to some extent, with much of western Europe. The eastern and even central parts of the continent, it is true, were still remote from the west in their political concerns. Italy's political connections to the east centred largely around the complex struggles of the newly established Angevin kings of Hungary with Naples and Venice; while from the reign of the Emperor Charles IV (1346–78) the political centre of gravity in the Holy Roman Empire moved perceptibly eastwards, and the bonds linking the German world to the conflicts of its western neighbours slackened somewhat. Moreover, northern Europe was still a largely self-contained political sphere. The Scandinavian world was an inward-looking one, linked politically to the rest of Europe only by the tendency of Denmark and Poland to cooperate against the threatening power of the Hanse cities and by the desire of the Danes to protect their trade against the Dutch and English. Europe was therefore still far from being a unified political system; but by the outbreak of the Hundred Years War in the 1330s the continent was equally far from being a mere agglomeration of states, each indifferent to and unaffected by the actions of its neighbours. Europe was already divided into a number of fairly unified and effective regional state-systems – England and France with their allies or satellites in Spain, Scotland and the Netherlands; Italy; the Baltic; the German world – within each of which relations between monarchs were becoming closer and more continuous and between which political contacts, though looser and more intermittent, were tending to grow.[1]

A century and a half later, in the last decades of the fifteenth century, many of the fundamentals of this situation had not changed. Many of the same lines of alliance and cleavage were still visible – the readiness of France and Scotland to combine against England; the tendency of England to look to Flanders or Castile for allies against France; the French interest in Italy, particularly in Naples, and the opposition it aroused. There were still around the periphery of Europe many small or relatively underdeveloped states – the Scandinavian kingdoms, Poland, Scotland, Hungary, Portugal, not to mention the remote and almost unknown Russia – whose role in international relations was secondary, whose outlooks and interests were limited, and who often reacted to the initiatives of the greater states rather than taking any of their own. Even for the greater monarchies political horizons were still much narrower than they were soon to become. The best-known political and diplomatic memoirs of the later fifteenth century, those of Philippe de Commynes, show how limited as yet was the scope even of French foreign policy. In them Burgundy, the Netherlands, England and, in his later years, Italy figure prominently; but relations with Spain count for little and the Ottoman empire – the greatest political and military success-story of the age – hardly appears at all.

## Italian beginnings

Nevertheless, by the middle of the fifteenth century there were clearly taking root in Italy new diplomatic techniques and institutions. These formed the basis of a system of interstate relations recognisable as the

1. This paragraph is based largely on W. Kienast, 'Die Anfänge des europäischen Staatensystems im späteren Mittelalter', *Historische Zeitschrift*, cliii (1935–36), 229–71, which was reprinted as a pamphlet with the same title (Berlin, 1936).

direct ancestor of the one which exists today. That this system should appear first in any developed form in Italy is not surprising. By the mid-fourteenth century most of the Italian peninsula was divided between a fairly small number of relatively well organised states – the duchy of Milan, the Florentine republic, the kingdom of Naples, the Papal State, the Venetian republic, at a lower level of importance Mantua, Genoa and perhaps one or two others. These competed with one another intensely for power, for territory, in the last analysis for survival. It was therefore essential for their rulers to watch closely each other's doings and to be as well informed as possible about each other's policies and ambitions. Moreover, these states were geographically small compared to the great European monarchies, and they had at their disposal relatively large numbers of highly educated men. In Italy it was therefore possible to raise day-to-day government to a high pitch of efficiency, to control the territory of these states effectively from a single centre, in a way which was still quite impracticable in France, Spain or the growing Habsburg *Hausmacht*. One aspect of this type of government – unified, consistent, well-informed – was that its foreign policies were more continuous and better organised than any hitherto seen.

Fifteenth-century Italy, then, was in miniature what in the following hundred years most of western Europe and later the rest of the continent was to become. In the acuteness of its rivalries, and in the expression which it gave them in the new form of organised professional diplomacy, it pointed out the direction which the entire continent was later to take. By the last years of the fifteenth century can be seen the first clear signs that the sort of close and continuous interstate relationships already in existence in Italy for two or three generations were spreading beyond the Alps. The French invasion of Italy in 1494, that textbook dividing-line in the history of Europe, quite suddenly sharpened the rivalries and focused the ambitions of the major powers of the continent. When in 1495 fear of French power brought together the Spanish kingdoms, the Holy Roman Emperor and most of the important Italian states in the Holy League (which was joined by England in the following year), this was a new departure in the history of the continent. Though the league proved disunited and short-lived and rapidly betrayed the hollowness of the pompous verbiage with which it was surrounded, it was none the less a portent; there was no mediæval precedent for so ambitious and geographically wide-ranging a combination of states. Comparable alliances were soon to follow it, their composition changing with kaleidoscopic suddenness. All of them were more or less ineffective; but their very existence showed that Europe had now entered a new political age. These alliances, moreover, both demanded and were created by a new system of diplomacy and new techniques of diplomatic organisation, by a diplomatic network which, from its Italian roots, was now beginning to embrace more and more of Europe.

The relative modernity of this diplomatic network can be seen in several ways. In the first place it was now beginning to be generally, though slowly, recognised that the sending and receiving of diplomatic representatives was an attribute of sovereignty, a right to which only rulers were entitled. In the middle ages this had been very far from the case. Then 'all sorts of principals sent diplomatic agents to all sorts of recipients'.[2] Until far into the fifteenth century, and in many cases much later than that, diplomacy was still a game played not merely by sovereigns but by a wide range of people and institutions, many of them surprisingly humble. A procurator (essentially a representative empowered to negotiate on behalf of his principal) might well be sent by a group of merchants, or even a single one, to deal with a ruler against whom they had some claim or from whom they wished to extract some grant or concession. Thus in England Sir Thomas More gained his first diplomatic experience when in 1509 he negotiated with the municipal authorities of Antwerp on behalf of the Mercers Company of London. Such an agent might equally well be despatched by a ruling prince to deal with a private individual rather than a fellow-ruler. These relatively plebeian origins of much of the web of diplomatic representation which was beginning to cover Europe can be seen in the fact that until the seventeenth century the title 'ambassador and procurator' was very widely used. It was only in the age of Richelieu that the more dignified term 'plenipotentiary' drove 'procurator' out of use.[3] Throughout the fifteenth century, and even in Italy, then, a variety of individuals and entities continued to send and receive diplomatic agents – nobles, bishops, the college of cardinals (as distinct from the papacy) individual *condottieri*. There are numerous instances of a sovereign power receiving diplomatic representatives from its own subjects: Venice for example received many sent by dependent cities within its own territories.[4]

In France, until the accession of Louis XI in 1461, great feudatories continued on occasion to conduct diplomatic relations of their own with foreign states; and their right to do so seems to have been often at least tacitly recognised. Thus, under Charles VII, Louis' father, the duke of Orleans sent an ambassador to Venice, while the Comte de Foix sent others to Castile and Navarre and also received embassies from them.[5] By

2. D.E. Queller, *The Office of Ambassador in the Middle Ages* (Princeton, 1967), p. 11.
3. G. Mattingly, *Renaissance Diplomacy* (Harmondsworth, 1965), p. 29.
4. Queller, *The Office of Ambassador*, pp. 72–3.
5. A. Dezert, 'Louis XI et ses ambassadeurs', *Revue Historique*, cliv (1929), 4–5.

the later fifteenth century, however, this situation was under challenge. More and more, as they consolidated their control over their own territories, rulers in western Europe became unwilling to allow their subjects this sort of freedom, with the threat to their power and the security of their territories which it clearly involved. Louis XI, in one of his first acts as king, asserted firmly that he alone could send and receive ambassadors in France. The duke of Burgundy, the greatest of his vassals, was too powerful to be deprived of his former rights in this respect. So was the semi-independent duke of Brittany, though he was forbidden to have diplomatic relations with any enemy of France. Nevertheless, Louis was able to assert with considerable success his claim to a monopoly of French diplomatic relations, particularly as his control of the postal system gave him an important weapon against efforts by any noble, however great, to conduct a personal foreign policy.[6] After his death in 1483 the duke of Orleans, himself a member of the royal family, still negotiated on his own account with the pope and the duke of Brittany and corresponded privately with the imperial ambassador to France; the principle that only the king should have a foreign policy was not yet completely victorious. However, when in 1497 Orleans proposed to act in this way in Lombardy, Charles VIII, now of full age and as jealous as his father of his prerogatives, successfully threatened him with exile if he persisted.[7] The idea that non-sovereign individuals or entities could send and receive diplomatic representatives was thus still very much alive at the end of the fifteenth century. A hundred years later Alberto Gentili, in his *De Jure Belli libri tres* (1598), one of the first great works of international law, could still speak of those sent by rulers to their subjects or vice versa as forming a distinct class of diplomat (though he placed them in the lowest of the three categories into which he divided diplomatic agents).[8] Even as late as the early eighteenth century the duchy of Milan was sending *ambasciatori* to its ruler, the king of Spain.[9] From the end of the fifteenth century onwards, however, the idea that only sovereigns could play the great game of diplomacy was slowly crystallising and gaining acceptance.

The most striking characteristic of the new breed of diplomats was the fact that more and more of them were 'permanent'. In other words, many of them remained in post at the court of some foreign ruler for a considerable time, transacting business and transmitting information over a

6. Dezert, 'Louis XI . . .', 5–6.
7. M.A.R. de Maulde-la-Clavière, *La Diplomatie au temps de Machiavel* (Paris, 1892–3), i, 179–80.
8. O. Krauske, *Die Entwicklung der ständigen Diplomatie vom fünfzehnten Jahrhundert bis zu den Beschlussen von 1815 und 1818* (Leipzig, 1885), p. 150.
9. Krauske, *Die Entwicklung . . .*, p. 159.

period of at least months and often years. They did not, like almost all their mediæval predecessors, visit a foreign court merely to conclude a specific piece of business, to negotiate, sign or swear adherence to a particular treaty, or to add additional lustre to a coronation or a royal marriage. There is, inevitably, a certain grey area in discussion of this development. How long must a diplomat remain in any post for his mission to qualify as a permanent one? Also the position of a diplomat sent originally on some special and temporary mission could easily become difficult to distinguish from that of a permanent representative if conditions changed, new problems arose, and he had to be sent new instructions and his stay prolonged. Sometimes, again, at least in the early stages of this new development, a man might for quite a long period perform all the functions of a resident ambassador and even be addressed as such without any formal accreditation: in such cases he might himself be uncertain of his precise status. Sir Thomas Spinelly, for example, when he represented Henry VIII in the Netherlands in 1514–17, found himself in this position.[10] But of the reality and importance of the development there is no doubt. Occasionally, though rarely, it is recognised in contemporary terminology. The ambassador sent to Rome by the duke of Savoy in 1460 is apparently the first to be officially and explicitly described as permanent – '*orator et ambaxiator continuus et procurator*'.[11]

Permanent diplomatic representation was the invention of one or two states of north and north-central Italy: Florence, Venice and, most important of all, the duchy of Milan. Involved in active and rapidly changing mutual rivalries, and by the end of the fifteenth century more and more likely to be seriously affected by the actions of much greater powers, these states increasingly needed information.

> It was a situation which called for incessant alertness, a need to be constantly informed about the military strengths and intentions of rival powers, a determination to be prepared both to seize opportunities for minor gains and to counter such opportunistic moves by others. It was also a situation which was both fostered by, and itself encouraged, the growth of performance in regimes, bureaucracies, diplomatic activity, and military establishments.[12]

Knowledge of events outside, even far outside, their own frontiers might allow rulers to steer with some degree of safety through the rocks

10. Betty Behrens, 'The Office of English Resident Ambassador: Its Evolution as illustrated by the Career of Sir Thomas Spinelly, 1509–1522', *Transactions of the Royal Historical Society*, 4th series, xvi (1933), 176.
11. L. Weckmann, 'Les Origines des missions diplomatiques permanentes', *Revue internationale de droit international publique*, troisième série, lvi (1952), 170.
12. M. Mallett, 'Diplomacy and War in late Fifteenth-Century Italy', *Proceedings of the British Academy*, lxvii (1981), 268–9.

and shoals of an increasingly dangerous political environment. It is easy to
see why they should have felt the need for a network of permanent agents
abroad, negotiating and, most important of all, gathering information,
earlier than their more powerful counterparts north of the Alps. Different
historial roots have been suggested from which the permanent embassy
may have grown – the *baiulo*, the essentially commercial agent already
maintained by Venice in Constantinople for many generations; or more
plausibly the procurators maintained by many rulers at the papal curia,
who by the fifteenth century had evolved into something resembling
ambasssadors and were sometimes even given that title.[13] But it seems
more likely that it developed almost insensibly as, with the growth in scale
and intensity of diplomatic activity, the temporary and *ad hoc* embassies of
the middle ages became more frequent and lasted longer.[14] A changing
political environment gave birth to a new political institution to meet new
needs. Nicodemus of Pontremoli, who was representing Milan in Florence
in 1446, and who held this post for over twenty years (broken by a spell in
Rome) has strong claims to be regarded as the first true permanent
diplomatic agent. The duchy of Milan, with a permanent representative in
Naples and perhaps also one in Genoa from 1455, another in Rome
apparently from 1458 and more or less continuous representation in
Venice from the same year, was the first state in Europe to equip itself
with a diplomatic machine which had some of the major characteristics of
those which exist today. It may be significant that Milan, a monarchy,
seems to have had a clear policy of leaving its ambassadors in the same
post for long periods, indeed for as long as possible, whereas the republics
of Florence and Venice changed theirs much more frequently.[15] By the
1540s, however, all the largest secular states in Italy – Venice, Florence,
Milan, Naples – had established permanent embassies in each other's
capitals. Naples, the slowest to adopt the new methods, sent a resident
ambassador to Venice in 1457 and one to Milan by the end of the
following year.

Once established in Italy, the permanent embassy soon began to spread
north of the Alps. Filippo Maria Visconti, duke of Milan, had maintained
as early as 1425–32 a resident representative at the court of Sigismund,
king of Hungary and Holy Roman Emperor elect, while for most of the

13. Weckmann, 'Les Origines . . .', 177–83.
14. At least as early as 1269 Venetian ambassadors sent on temporary missions were
ordered to remain at their posts until given leave to come home; and it became increasingly
difficult to obtain such permission (Queller, *The Office of Ambassador*, p. 83). A good account
of the different theories regarding the possible origins of the resident ambassador can be
found in Mattingly, *Renaissance Diplomacy*, Chapter 6.
15. A. Schaube, 'Zur Entstehungsgeschichte der ständigen Gesandschaften,' *Mitteilungen
des Instituts für österreichischen Geschichtsforschung*, x (1889), 508–21.

7

same period Sigismund had a similar ambassador in Milan: this was probably 'the first clear case of the exchange of regularly accredited resident ambassadors in history'.[16] The Sforza dukes of Milan had an ambassador in France from 1463 onwards; and from 1474 there was a continuous series of Florentine representatives at the French court, while Venice sent her first permanent ambassador to Paris in 1479. London saw its first permanent Milanese ambassador in 1490 and its first Venetian one six years later. As early as 1450 the papacy had sent a permanent nuncio, the first of a new type, to Spain; and another who was clearly a diplomatic representative can be found in Venice by 1500. Under Leo X (1513–23) nunciatures to France, the emperor and Portugal were added and a relatively modern and largely secular system of papal diplomacy was clearly emerging (until about 1540 a number of papal nuncios were laymen). This was not systematised until 1585, during the great reforming pontificate of Sixtus V;[17] but by the early years of the sixteenth century the papacy, like the secular states of Italy (of which in many essentials it was now one) had obvious need of continuous diplomatic contact with the major rulers of Europe and of a continuous flow of information from their courts. In eight years Leo X appointed three nuncios in France, each of whom before leaving his post awaited the arrival of his successor and briefed him on the current state of business.[18] Simultaneously there was a development of the system of 'cardinal protectors' by which members of the college of cardinals undertook to safeguard at the papal curia certain interests of particular secular rulers. (Their main task was to refer to the curia the nominations to bishoprics made by their employer and to see that the appropriate papal bulls of provision were issued.) Though this arrangement was first explicitly recognised by Pope Julius II in the early years of the sixteenth century it had existed earlier: Cardinal Piccolomini, who became cardinal protector of England in 1492, was apparently the first officially approved holder of such a post.[19] Though they were not diplomats the cardinal protectors performed some quasi-diplomatic functions: their emergence was another, though minor, sign of the way in which much of Europe was now beginning to be more closely bound together politically than ever before.

For well over a generation after its appearance in Italy, however, the 'new diplomacy' found few imitators elsewhere. Permanent representatives

16. Mattingly, *Renaissance Diplomacy*, p. 71.

17. H. Biaudet, *Les Nonciatures apostoliques permanentes jusqu'en 1648* (Helsinki, 1910), pp. 15–20; I. Cardinale, *Le Saint-Siège et la diplomatie* (Paris–Tournai–Rome–New York, 1962), pp. 30ff.

18. P. Richard, 'Origines de la nonciature de France: débuts de la représentation permanente sous Leon X', *Revue des Questions Historiques*, xxxvi (1906), 112–80.

19. W.E.Wilkie, *The Cardinal Protectors of England* (Cambridge, 1974), pp. 10–11.

might go from the Italian states to France or England, Spain or the emperor; but for several decades these powers showed little desire to return the compliment. This is understandable. What France or the emperor might do mattered far more to Milan or Florence than the actions of any Italian principality normally could to the major rulers of Europe. But between themselves these rulers were by the end of the fifteenth century beginning to make use of the new device. Ferdinand of Aragon had a permanent diplomatic representative in London from 1488 onwards and the Emperor Maximilian one from 1493. France, however, whose great inherent strength *vis-à-vis* all her neighbours meant that her need for information about them and their plans was often not very pressing, was rather slow to adopt such methods. The same is true of England, protected by geography. France sent a permanent ambassador to the emperor only as late as 1509: from the same year dates the first permanent English embassy to a foreign court. It was only after a series of dynastic accidents and an imperial election had created, by 1519, an unprecedented concentration of territories in the hands of the Emperor Charles V, and the battle of Pavia had illustrated six years later the dangers which France might face in this new situation, that the French government really felt the need of permanent diplomatic representation abroad on a large scale. At the accession of Francis I in 1515 it had a single resident ambassador abroad: when he died in 1547 it had ten. During his reign twenty-five French embassies (most of them indeed still very short-lived) were sent to England in thirty-one years,[20] and by 1589, it has been claimed, in spite of a generation of devastating though intermittent civil war, France had 'the most extensive ambassadorial system in Europe'.[21] The Ottoman government also, in control of a huge territory and the greatest military resources in Europe and buttressed by an unshakeable sense of superiority to the entire Christian world, felt no need at all in the sixteenth century for organised diplomatic relations with that world. It was not seriously to feel any such need, indeed, for almost three centuries to come.

It was still sometimes possible for information about foreign courts and their activities to be obtained more cheaply and effectively through channels other than the diplomatic. Lorenzo de Medici, effective ruler of Florence until his death in 1492, thought himself better served in this respect by Florentine merchants and bankers in the great commercial and financial centre of Lyons, who had close connections with the French

---

20. M.N. Baudoin-Matuszek, 'Un Ambassadeur en Ecosse au xvie siècle: Henri Clutin d'Oisel', *Revue Historique*, 569 (1989), 78.

21. De Lamar Jensen, 'French Diplomacy and the Wars of Religion', *Sixteenth Century Journal*, v, No.2 (October, 1974), 44.

court, than by his ambassadors in Paris. Earlier in the century his father, Cosimo, had been able to exert great influence on Florentine foreign policy because of the information about events and personalities abroad which he drew from his partners and agents in the Medici bank.[22] Moreover, matters of the highest importance might still be transacted by sovereigns face to face, as when in 1475 Edward IV of England and Louis XI of France met on a bridge at Picquigny in Picardy (though their mutual distrust was so great that they were separated by a strong trellis-work through the bars of which they embraced each other).[23] The Emperor Maximilian I had a particularly strong belief in his own powers as a diplomat: in the imperial Reichstag of 1498 he spoke, apparently seriously, of going in person to France to make a face-to-face agreement with Louis XII for the settlement of their rivalries.[24] In 1501 and 1504 the same Louis XII met Philip the Fair, Maximilian's son and ruler of the Netherlands, on French soil; and in 1507 he had an interview with Ferdinand of Aragon at Savona on the Ligurian coast. Royal 'summit' meetings of this kind were far from uncommon in the early decades of the sixteenth century. Apart from the famous Field of the Cloth of Gold encounter between Henry VIII and Francis I in 1520, the English king met the Emperor Charles V twice, once in England and again in France, in the same year. The emperor visited Henry in 1522 and met Francis I during the captivity of the latter in Spain in 1525–26 and at Aigues-Mortes in 1538. In eastern Europe the Emperor Maximilian met Ladislas II of Hungary and Bohemia and Sigismund I of Poland in 1515 in Vienna; and the Archduke Ferdinand, the younger brother of Charles V, met Louis II of Hungary and Bohemia on two occasions in 1523. After the 1530s interviews of this kind became noticeably less frequent, perhaps because of their repeated failure to produce any lasting results; but until then they were always a factor of at least potential importance in international relations.

The network of diplomacy built up in Europe during the first decades of the sixteenth century was sharply disrupted from the 1560s onwards, as the Counter-Reformation gained strength and religious antagonisms became more bitter. In 1568 England, the most important Protestant state,

22. Schaube, 'Entstehungsgeschichte', 532–3; Maulde-la-Clavière, *Diplomatie*, i, 451; C.S. Gutkind, *Cosimo de Medici, Pater Patriae, 1389–1464* (Oxford, 1938), p. 140. In 1503 Machiavelli claimed that the great Italian banks were better and more quickly informed about foreign events than the Italian governments (Maulde-la-Clavière, *Diplomatie*, iii, 152). On this point see also F. Ohmann, *Die Anfänge des Postwesens und die Taxis* (Leipzig, 1909), pp. 273ff.

23. Philippe de Commynes, *Memoirs: The Reign of Louis XI, 1461–1483* (Harmondsworth, 1972), p. 255. On the need for precautions against treachery in such meetings see Maulde-la-Clavière, *Diplomatie*, i, 258ff.

24. H. Gollwitzer, 'Zur Geschichte der Diplomatie im Zeitalter Maximilians I', *Historisches Jahrbuch*, 74 Jahrgang (1954), 199.

ceased to have a resident ambassador in Madrid (though Spanish ambassadors remained in London until 1584, testimony to the slow growth of the idea that reciprocity was an essential characteristic of diplomatic contacts). For the next two decades the only embassy accredited by Elizabeth I to any Catholic country was that to France; and after 1589 even it ceased to exist for several years. During the same decades religious bitterness and distrust meant that there was a long hiatus in diplomatic relations between the Italian states and Protestant Europe, and that the creation of such relations between Catholic Europe and Scandinavia was seriously delayed. But this was only a temporary interruption, though a serious one, in the growing volume of contacts of this kind. The death of Philip II of Spain in 1598, the Franco–Spanish and Anglo–Spanish treaties of 1598 and 1604, the Spanish–Dutch truce of 1609, meant their fairly rapid reconstruction in the first years of the seventeenth century. English resident ambassadors then reappeared in Spain and Venice, Spanish and Venetian ones in London, Dutch ones in Venice and Paris, French and Spanish ones, though only intermittently, in Scandinavia. The forces of modernity, which in a limited but genuine way the new diplomatic machinery typified, had proved strong enough to resist the disruptive pressures of religious antagonism.

## A profession and its duties

Slowly and without deliberate planning on the part of any government, a group of men who can fairly be described as professional diplomats was taking shape during the sixteenth century. The emergence of the permanent embassy, which meant that an ambassador might well remain in post for long, even very long periods (an extreme example is Honoré de Caix, who was French resident in Portugal from 1518 to 1559 – though there were also six special and temporary French embassies to Lisbon during these years) aided this development. So, more fundamentally, did the natural tendency of governments to employ the same man, once he had proved his ability and readiness to serve, in a series of different embassies. Commynes is a well-known example. An even better one is Sigismund von Herberstein, who in thirty-eight years in the service of the Austrian Habsburgs was employed on as many as seventy different missions, most of them of course very short. Among the men who represented Henry VIII, Thomas Boleyn (later Earl of Wiltshire) served in 1512–34 on five missions to the Holy Roman Emperor, four to France and others to Spain and the Low Countries; while Dr John Clerk, who was rewarded with the bishopric of London, went in 1519–41 four times to France, as often to Rome and once to the duchy of Cleves. There is evidence, moreover, that such men were now beginning, however hesitantly, to feel members of a distinct professional group with its own traditions and standards. They could even see themselves, in an atmosphere saturated in classical precedents, as in some sense heirs of the heralds of the Roman republic, of the wanderer Odysseus and even of the messenger-god Hermes.[25] Moreover, although diplomatic nomenclature remained for long confused and arbitrary, a hierarchy of ranks was slowly emerging. By the middle of the sixteenth century a general distinction was established between special and *ad hoc* ambassadors, often though by no means always nobles, and the resident ambassador, of lower birth and very often a lawyer or churchman. There was also by that time a general feeling that only independent rulers of some real significance were entitled to send ambassadors, envoys of the highest rank, and that this right was denied to rulers whose sovereignty was limited by any kind of feudal tie or subjection.[26] Kings had the right of embassy. So, it was generally agreed, had the republic of Venice, whose doge could be regarded as a quasi-monarch and which ruled the mediæval kingdom of Cyprus until its conquest by the Turks in 1571. But the rights of the lesser states and rulers of Europe in this respect were much more debatable, and they were often expected to restrict themselves to sending abroad representatives of lower standing. There was also widespread agreement that the best ambassador, especially for a ceremonial or honorific mission, was the holder of some court or administrative appointment which gave him immediate personal contact with the monarch he represented. Such a man could claim to personify his master in a clear and unmistakable way; to choose him was therefore a compliment to the ruler to whose court he was sent.[27]

The resident diplomatic representative in the later fifteenth and early sixteenth centuries might be given any one of a bewildering variety of titles – *orator*, *procurator*, *commissarius*, *nuncius*, *deputatus*, *legatus*, *consiliarius*, or some combination of two or more of these. It was only during the sixteenth century that the terms *orator* and finally *ambassador* began to supplant the others. But however he was referred to, his most important function was the gathering and sending back to his government of

25. B. Picard, *Das Gesandtschaftswesen Ostmitteleuropas in der frühen Neuzeit* (Graz-Vienna-Cologne, 1967), p. 165.

26. Krauske, *Die Entwicklung*, pp. 155–6. Here again there were inevitably borderline cases, for example the grand master of the Knights of St John who, although he effectively exercised sovereign rights in Rhodes, the headquarters of the order, was normally considered in the early sixteenth century not to enjoy the right of embassy (Maulde-la-Clavière, *Diplomatie*, i, 170).

27. D. Starkey, 'Representation through intimacy: a study in the symbolism of monarchy and court office in early-modern England', in I. Lewis, ed., *Symbols and Sentiments* (London–New York–San Francisco, 1977), pp. 201–2.

information about the state in which he was stationed, its ruling personalities and their outlooks and plans. Compared to this, negotiation was as a rule secondary; when it was needed it was very often entrusted to a special envoy sent for the purpose who returned home when his work was done. A special mission of this kind would normally report only on the specific issues with which it was concerned; the provision of a steady flow of information, with all its implications for the making of policy, was the task of the diplomat established in some foreign capital on a permanent or semi-permanent basis.[28] By the second half of the fifteenth century one court in particular, the papal one in Rome, was established as the greatest centre of diplomatic gossip and exchange of news, since more diplomatic agents were gathered there than anywhere else in the world. The prominence of this information-gathering function meant inevitably that the diplomat was often regarded as little more than a licensed spy. He must therefore, it was felt, be kept under strict surveillance and preferably sent home, at least in the case of special missions, as soon as he had completed the business for which he had been sent. His movements and contacts must be carefully watched and recorded. Unless this were done he might well provide his master with military or strategic information of real value in case of war. More seriously, he might tamper with the loyalty of the subjects of the ruler to whom he was accredited and thus threaten his position. There were plenty of instances in which ambassadors behaved in the first of these ways,[29] and some at least in which they tried to behave in the second.

It is far from surprising, therefore, that many rulers of the late fifteenth and early sixteenth centuries were reluctant to receive foreign diplomats unless this were clearly necessary. Louis XI in France, Henry VII in England, Ferdinand II in Aragon and the Emperor Maximilian I all showed this feeling: Henry VII is said to have contemplated on his deathbed expelling all foreign ambassadors. For a long time much writing and even legislation reflected this mistrust. 'It is not safe', wrote Commynes,

> to have ambassadors coming and going so much because they often discuss evil things. . . . . For every messenger or ambassador sent to me I would send two in return, and if the princes become bored with them and say that no more should be sent I would still send them whenever I had a chance or

28. For contemporary stress on the importance of an ambassador providing all possible information to his principal , even that which might at first be unwelcome, see the 'Conseils à un ambassadeur' of Pierre Danès (1561), analysed in L. Delavaud, 'La diplomatie d'autrefois', *Revue d'Histoire Diplomatique*, xxviii–xxix (1914–15), 611–12.

29. See the long list, relating mainly to the Italian states, of instances in which late-mediæval ambassadors provided their governments with military information, in Queller, *The Office of Ambassador*, pp. 92–3.

the means. For no better or safer way is known of sending a spy who has the opportunity to observe and find things out. And if you send two or three people it is impossible to remain on guard so constantly that one or other cannot have a few words, either secretly or otherwise, with someone.[30]

Feelings of this kind were most extreme in eastern Europe, in Poland, the Ottoman empire and Russia. In the last of these, fears that foreign diplomats might foment disloyalty and sedition were more acute than anywhere else; and as a result the houses of ambassadors were closely guarded to prevent all unauthorised contact with natives.[31] In Venice, which had a long tradition of governmental secrecy, legislation of 1451 and 1481 forbade anyone in an official position to have any contact with foreigners involving state affairs, while in 1500 a Venetian ambassador to Maximilian I found his lodgings closely guarded by soldiers so that no one should talk to him. The same note of nervous suspicion sounds through much of the writing of the sixteenth century on diplomats and their functions. One author thought that ambassadors were so often sent to tamper with the loyalty of the subjects of the monarch who received them, and to tempt them to defect to his enemies, that 'they can by a change of name be more truly described as tempters and spies'. Another, writing as late as 1618, after a very strong warning of the danger of their collecting damaging military information, urged that when sent by an enemy ruler in time of war they should not only be deprived of any arms they were carrying but should also have their clothing searched to make sure that nothing was concealed in it.[32] It was only slowly that these attitudes disappeared or even appreciably softened.

N.B

The information transmitted by diplomats, however, was not always political or military. In an age without newspapers or learned societies and the periodicals they published, when the printed book was still rare and expensive, diplomats might sometimes be significant in the spreading of knowledge and culture in general. Thus the Greek exile Janus Lascaris, who became a diplomat in French service in the 1490s, had before that taught in Florence; his missions in Italy provided the manuscripts from

---

30. Commynes, *Memoirs*, pp. 198–9.

31. See the comments in Picard, *Gesandtschaftswesen*, pp. 102–3. There are many contemporary accounts of the suspicion with which foreign diplomats in Russia were regarded by its government and of the severity with which their activities were controlled. For the treatment of English embassies in the second half of the sixteenth century see, e.g. *Calendar of State Papers Foreign, 1584–5* (London, 1916), pp. 83–6; G. Tolstoi, *The First Forty Years of Intercourse between England and Russia* (St Petersburg, 1875), pp. 227–8, 231–5; *Russia at the Close of the Sixteenth Century*, ed. E.A. Bond (London, 1856), pp. 343–4. For that of a papal embassy in the early 1580s see *The Moscovia of Antonio Possevino, S.J.*, trans. and ed. H.F. Graham (Pittsburg, 1977), pp. 16–18, 49.

32. Krauske, *Die Entwicklung*, pp. 14–15.

which several editions of the Greek classics were printed. Johann Reuchlin, perhaps the greatest scholar of his age, was able to visit Italy in 1498 through being sent to Rome as representative of a German prince, the Elector Palatine, while the great French humanist Guillaume Budé visited Venice in 1501, apparently as a member of a French mission. In the 1530s French ambassadors there, Jean du Pins and Guillaume Pellicier, bought books and Greek manuscripts for the new royal library at Fontainebleau.[33] Diplomats also played some role in disseminating knowledge of the new Spanish and Portuguese geographical discoveries outside Europe (about which the Portuguese government at least was for long extremely secretive). Jean Nicot, French ambassador in Lisbon in 1559–61, gathered materials on the Portuguese empire, sent home lemon and banana trees from the East Indies, and suggested for the first time the use of indigo imported from Asia in the French dyeing industry. The Baron de Fourquevaux, French ambassador in Madrid during 1565–72, provided much information on the spice trade and Spanish and Portuguese activities in the Pacific.[34] Until well into the eighteenth century diplomats were to remain an important channel for the transmission from one part of Europe to another not merely of a wide variety of luxury goods (fine textiles, furniture, books, horses, etc.) demanded by friends or political associates at home, but also of fashions, scientific and technical information, skilled workmen and cultural innovations of all sorts.

## Ceremonial and precedence

From the beginning ceremonial had played a leading role in diplomacy. Religious ceremonies were in the middle ages an important ingredient in the conduct of relations between rulers. Negotiations were often begun with prayers, agreements signed in a church or abbey and holy relics displayed to add greater solemnity to the occasion.[35] It long remained normal practice, once a treaty had been signed, for the rulers party to it to take a solemn and public oath to observe it, almost always in a church and often sworn on some particularly venerated relic. Thus, after the peace of Cateau-Cambrésis between France, Spain and England in 1559, Philip II of Spain swore to observe it in the palace chapel in Brussels with his hand on an alleged fragment of the true cross, while Henry II of France and his son took an oath of the same kind in Notre Dame, and there was a

33. M. Lowry, *The World of Aldus Manutius: Business and Scholarship in Renaissance Venice* (Oxford, 1979), pp. 163, 245, 266, 281–2, 285.
34. D.F. Lach, *Asia in the Making of Europe*, ii, Pt.II (Chicago–London, 1977), 33–4, 276–7.
35. Queller, *The Office of Ambassador*, p. 191; Maulde-la- Clavière, *Diplomatie*, iii, 234–5.

similar exchange of solemn undertakings between Elizabeth I and the French king. The special and ceremonial embassies sent to observe the swearing of such oaths were among the most splendid and ostentatious of the age. All this was, in large part, a reflection of the very low prevailing standards of political morality. Such ceremonies, like much mediæval judicial procedure, reflected a belief, often only too well justified, that an ordinary promise, a seal or a signature unsupported by some specially solemn ceremony, was not to be relied on.

In the fifteenth and early sixteenth centuries, as the diplomatic network became more complex and the bonds it created between rulers more tightly drawn, diplomatic ceremonial became more significant and more anxiously scrutinised. It became increasingly the custom to send noblemen, high-ranking officials or sometimes even members of the ruling family, to greet special embassies from a foreign ruler and accompany their public entry, which usually involved much elaborate and self-conscious display, into the capital of the ruler receiving them. The size of the embassy, the number of horses and the amount of baggage it brought with it, the richness of the clothes worn by the ambassador and his suite (gold chains, as an ostentatious display of the wealth and importance of the monarch represented were particularly important in this respect) were all carefully scrutinised; and any appearance of parsimony was likely to arouse criticism and ridicule. The embassies of obedience, which before the Reformation virtually all European monarchs sent to the papacy, particularly on their accession, showed this preoccupation with appearances at its most extreme.[36] All this, however, applied only to special and usually short-lived embassies, normally headed by men of high, sometimes very high, social rank and including a large ceremonial element. The resident ambassador, of lower social standing than his special and *ad hoc* colleague and with more humdrum functions, was not usually accorded such honours. The same tendency towards greater formality and display can be seen also in the growing importance of the ceremonial oration pronounced by the special ambassador or one of his suite (who might have been brought simply for that purpose) when the ambassador was given his first formal audience by the ruler to whom he had been sent. Many of these speeches were tediously verbose, mere inflated displays of empty rhetoric, but they were by the later fifteenth century frequently printed. The wisespread use of the term 'orator' as a synonym for 'ambassador' or 'envoy' illustrates the importance attached to this particular aspect of display, an importance which certainly owed something to the humanist stress on pure and classical Latin style; and

36. Maulde-la-Clavière, *Diplomatie*, i, 113–4; ii, 183–4, iii, 235, 238.

ambassadors were sometimes appointed merely for their oratorical abilities (the choice of Lascaris as French ambassador to Venice in 1507 is a good case in point).[37]

But by far the most hotly-debated aspect of diplomatic ceremonial, and one which could have great practical importance, was that of the precedence claimed by the rulers of Europe and hence by the ambassadors who were their direct and personal representatives. Issues of this kind were to complicate and envenom international relations for 200 years or more. Every aspect of political life was still in the sixteenth and seventeenth centuries saturated in symbolism to an extent which today it requires a real imaginative leap fully to understand or sympathise with. The signature of a treaty, still more the entry of a monarch into a city (especially a capital city) in celebration of a military victory, or for his coronation or a meeting with another ruler, produced an outburst of ingenious and expensive political iconography, expressed in masques, *tableaux vivants* and triumphal arches.[38] Implicit in such ceremonies was very often a powerful element of competition, a wish to assert the greatness of a ruler against his rivals and a determination to resist any slight which they might offer to his standing or reputation. The intense anxiety of both sides at the Field of the Cloth of Gold over such things as the exact placing of the lists in which tilting was to take place, the order and position in which the shields of Henry VIII and Francis I were to be hung on the Tree of Honour in these lists and the need for the size of their retinues and bodyguards to be exactly the same when they met[39] shows these preoccupations at their most intense. In diplomatic relations it was above all on the perennial question of precedence that they became focused.

By the end of the fifteenth century it was generally recognised that papal representatives took precedence over all others of equivalent rank, and that those of the Holy Roman Emperor came in second place. But the right to occupy the other rungs on the ladder was the subject of endless, acrimonious and sometimes dangerous debate. 'The dignity and reputation of princes', said Philip II in the 1550s, 'is of no less importance to them than their states.' Half a century later an experienced observer could repeat this in almost the same words: 'Princes and sovereign states

37. I. Bernays, 'Die Diplomatie um 1500', *Historische Zeitschrift*, 138 (1928), 14. For illustrations of the prestige a Renaissance diplomat could acquire by the ability to make fluent speeches in Latin see W.G. and Emily Waters (eds.), *The Vespasiano Memoirs. Lives of Illustrious Men of the XVth Century* (London, 1926), pp. 150, 321, 387.

38. See in general S. Anglo, *Spectacle, Pageantry and Early Tudor Policy* (Oxford, 1969) and J. Jacquot (ed.), *Fêtes et cérémonies au temps de Charles Quint* (Paris, 1960).

39. Anglo, *Spectacle, Pageantry . . .* , pp. 149–51.

often hold more dear the conservation of their rank and dignity than that of their lands and possessions'.[40] Both were stating what had for generations been an accepted fact; and the grant of some much-desired enhancement of status could be a potent inducement in relations between rulers. Thus in 1519 Francis I tried to buy the vote of the Elector Joachim I of Brandenburg in the forthcoming imperial election by offering him, among more material advantages, royal status in diplomatic ceremonial. The first organised scheme governing the precedence of the different rulers of Europe was drawn up by Pope Julius II in 1504. It gave third place to the King of the Romans, the title assumed by the son of the Holy Roman Emperor once his right of succession to the imperial throne had been recognised by the diet of the empire; but even this had until recently been hotly challenged. In 1488 the claims of the French ambassador at the papal court to precedence over the representative of the King of the Romans had led to an undignified scuffle in which the Frenchman was forcibly ejected by his rival from the coveted place in a public procession.[41] Until well into the sixteenth century quarrels of this kind were confined largely to special and temporary ambassadors. The resident diplomatic representative, with less ostentatiously public functions, was less likely to be involved in them, especially as it was still not always clear that he was in fact the direct and personal representative of his sovereign in the same way as the special ambassador. As, however, the importance of the resident ambassador grew and his representative character became undeniable, he too became more and more involved in questions of this peculiarly sensitive sort.

The crux of the matter was that appearances – the right to a place of honour in public ceremonies of any kind; coats of arms; the grant by one ruler to another of a particular title; the use of specific forms of address; the right to receive rather than make the first visit when two diplomats had to deal with each other; the right of a diplomat to sign his name to a treaty above that of another – clearly and indeed brutally symbolised power and status. Any change in ceremonial indicated a rise or fall in the standing of a state or its ruler: diplomats therefore watched with a jealous eye the formalities observed on any great public occasion. When, for example, the Emperor Charles V visited the French court in 1540 the representative of the duke of Mantua sent his secretary to observe the festivities merely so that he could take careful note of the order of

40. M.J. Rodriguez-Salgado, *The Changing Face of Empire. Charles V, Philip II and Habsburg Authority* (Cambridge, 1988), p. 25; J. Hotman, Sieur de Villiers, *De la charge et dignité de l'ambassadeur*, 2nd edn. (Paris, 1604), pp. 58–58v.

41. Queller, *The Office of Ambassador*, p. 202. For other examples of such disputes in the later fifteenth century see Maulde-la-Clavière, *Diplomatie*, iii, 276–89.

precedence observed.[42] For intangible objectives of this kind rulers were often willing to sacrifice considerable material advantages. Thus when Ivan IV of Russia was negotiating peace with King Stepan Bathory of Poland in 1582, at the end of a long and unsuccessful war, one of his major preoccupations was to ensure that in the treaty and associated documents he was given the title of tsar of Kazan and Astrakhan, ' for in his eyes none of the fortresses he was preparing to surrender to the King remotely compared in importance with this salutation'.[43] The quarterings on a coat of arms could carry the same implications as the grant or refusal of a title. Thus a long dispute was set off when, in the 1550s, Christian III of Denmark began to incorporate in his coat of arms the three crowns of Sweden, since this implied a reassertion of Danish claims to suzerainty which had been repudiated by Gustavus Vasa in 1523 (later Erik XIV of Sweden retaliated by including the Danish lions in his own arms).[44] An ambassador who gave way on some disputed point of this kind accepted by implication a position of inferiority for the monarch he represented. He thus neglected one of his most essential duties and might expose himself to severe punishment. By the same token an ambassador who successfully asserted a disputed claim felt a sense of achievement which no other victory could bring: perhaps the most spectacular triumph in the eyes of contemporaries won by the conde de Gondomar, one of a group of brilliant Spanish diplomats of the early seventeenth century, was his success, as ambassador to England, in asserting precedence over his French rival.

What constituted the greatness of a state or a monarchy and therefore the basis of its claims to rank high in any scheme of precedence? Clearly sheer physical resources, power and wealth, were important. But all sorts of other factors could be thrown into the balance by an ambitious ruler assisted by ingenious lawyers and imaginative historians. Did, for example, a state which had allegedly been converted to Christianity earlier than a rival derive from this fact legitimate claims to precedence over it? How much weight should be given to some traditional and now completely obsolete claim to a feudal superiority over some other ruler, or to having received the sacred unction as part of a coronation ceremony, or (as was sometimes argued in the case of England) to the power of the royal touch to cure the King's Evil? Was a concession made by any ruler on such

42. M. Smith, 'Familiarité française et politesse italienne au xvie siècle. Les diplomates italiens juges des manières du cour des Valois', *Revue d'Histoire Diplomatique*, 1988, 216.

43. *The Moscovia of Antonio Possevino*, p. 128.

44. M. Roberts, *The Early Vasas. A History of Sweden, 1523–1611* (Cambridge, 1968), pp. 152, 210.

matters necessarily binding on his successors? The possibilities of dispute, and dispute of a peculiarly wounding sort, were almost endless. Very often claims of this kind were couched in terms so grandiloquent that they were certain to arouse bad feeling; and the withdrawal of marks of respect given in the past because of subsequent changes in the material strength and importance of the states concerned could be a particularly bitter pill to swallow. Thus from 1558 onwards the Tsar Ivan IV began to deny the kings of Denmark the title of 'brother' which earlier rulers of Russia had used for almost three generations when writing to them. A few years later he began a violent quarrel with Erik XIV of Sweden over the latter's temerity in adressing him in this way in diplomatic documents, claiming that 'the (Holy) Roman Emperor and other great sovereigns are our brothers, but it is impossible to call you a brother because the Swedish land is lower in honour than those states'.[45] By the 1570s, indeed, Ivan had become unwilling to regard any rulers except the sultan in Constantinople and the Holy Roman Emperor as his equals: he may even have had doubts about the latter, who was after all formally only an elective monarch. Such attitudes, often as aggressively expressed, were widespread. It is easy to understand the resentment they could generate.

## PRACTICALITIES AND ARCHAISMS

The day-to-day processes of this new diplomacy reflected its growing intensity, continuity and professionalism. Diplomats now corresponded with their own governments more regularly and copiously than ever before. Frequent letters giving information of any important development at the court where he was stationed were the minimum now expected of any resident ambassador. In the Italian states, where the premium on being well informed was greatest, a marked improvement in the flow of such news is clearly visible in the second half of the fifteenth century. When the Milanese ambassador to Venice is found complaining that as long as eight days has gone by without his having received a despatch from home[46] it is clear that we are entering an era in which communication and guidance, on an almost modern scale, are beginning at least in a few states to be taken for granted. By the early decades of the sixteenth century it seems to have been quite normal for diplomats of the

---

45. R. Yu Wipper, *Ivan Grozny* (Tashkent, 1942), p. 130; A.Yanov, *The Origins of Autocracy: Ivan the Terrible in Russian History* (Berkeley, 1981), p. 209.
46. Queller, *The Office of Ambassador*, p. 136fn.

Austrian Habsburgs to write to Vienna as a matter of course every second or at least every third day. One who allowed as long as a week to elapse between despatches had to justify the omission to the Archduke Ferdinand, the effective ruler under his brother Charles V of the Habsburg territories in central Europe.[47] Similar standards were now being set by several of the great monarchies. One important result of this was a rapid growth of several impressively large diplomatic archives. Those of Milan, not surprisingly in view of its leading role in the creation of quasi-modern diplomacy, are the fullest for the later fifteenth century; but even those of a smaller principality such as the duchy of Mantua are very rich.[48] Already in Florence and Venice at least, and perhaps in other Italian capitals, registers were kept in which all despatches sent to ambassadors and all those received from them were listed and summarised. The greater states beyond the Alps were, in these as in other respects, slow to follow the Italian example; but even they learned by experience that without well-organised archives the effective conduct of foreign policy was very difficult. The French government began from the beginning of the sixteenth century to keep copies in a fairly systematic way of correspondence with its representatives at foreign courts, while the great Spanish collection at Simancas, the most important of all for the historian of later sixteenth- and early seventeenth-century international relations, began to take shape from the 1560s onwards.

The growing importance of diplomacy and the persisting view of the diplomat as no more than a licensed spy meant that his correspondence, perhaps more than ever before, was now the target of efforts to intercept and read it. Measures to protect it against being interfered with in this way or against its being lost through the accidents of travel were by the later fifteenth century widespread and systematic. Important despatches were always, if at all possible, carried by diplomatic courier and not entrusted to the normal postal services, such as these were, or to messengers hired locally. The Gonzaga dukes of Mantua were perhaps the first rulers to command specifically that their diplomatic correspondence be protected in this way. But the risk of a courier being forcibly intercepted and robbed of the letters he carried was a real one. At least one case is known of one being waylaid while himself carrying despatches seized in the same way from the messenger of a rival power, and it was not very unusual for such couriers to travel disguised as merchants or wandering scholars in an effort to protect themselves against such

47. Picard, *Das Gesandtschaftswesen*, pp. 130–1.
48. V. Ilardi, 'Fifteenth-Century Diplomatic Documents in Western European Archives and Libraries, 1450–1494', *Studies in the Renaissance*, ix (1962), 68, 99.

attacks.[49] Despatches were also often sent in duplicate or even triplicate and by different routes,[50] or sometimes even sewn into the clothing of the messenger who carried them. There was also a rapid growth in the use of cyphers as a means of protecting information against prying eyes. Simple substitution cyphers had begun to be used in Italy at least as early as the middle of the thirteenth century. The earliest Venetian diplomatic document in such a one dates from 1411; and another of only three years later can be found in the Florentine archives. The first to survive in those of Milan appears only in 1454; but in this respect as in others the duchy was clearly playing a major role in the development of new techniques, for the *Nationalbibliothek* in Vienna possesses a list of no fewer than 200 cypher keys used by the Milanese chancery in the years 1450–96.[51] (The simplicity of early cyphers meant that their effectiveness depended on their being frequently changed.) In 1555 one of the papal secretaries was made officially responsible for the cyphering and decyphering of despatches; but it seems likely that he had already been performing this function for some time,[52] and by the middle of the sixteenth century governments all over Europe were making use of such methods. Cyphers began to be used in the diplomatic correspondence of the Austrian Habsburgs, for example, shortly before the death of Maximilian I in 1519 and spread rapidly under his successor.[53] By the mid-sixteenth century the first book on the subject, the *Polygraphiae libri sex* of Johann von Trittenheim (1502: dedicated to the Emperor Maximilian), was about to be followed by the more important *De furtivis litterarum notis* of Giovanni Battista della Porta (1563). This in turn led on to the *Traité des chiffres* of Blaise de Vigenère (1586). The growth in the subtlety and sophistication of cyphers during the century was marked: by its end, at least in terms of possibilities, they had come a long way from the elementary techniques of the age of Commynes. De Vigenère proposed a method of encryption which for almost three centuries was thought to be unbreakable; and by the second

49. E. John, B. Allen, *Post and Courier Service in the Diplomacy of Early Modern Europe* (The Hague, 1972), pp. 23–4, 28, and 'Les courriers diplomatiques à la fin du XVIe siècle (1560–1600)', *Revue d'Histoire Diplomatique*, 1972, 230.

50. See, for example, the insistence on the importance of this of an early seventeenth-century writer in E. Griselle, 'Un manuel du parfait diplomate au dix-septième siècle', *Revue d'Histoire Diplomatique*, xxxviii–xxxix (1914–15), 777–8. In the later 1560s the Spanish ambassador in Paris, Alava, began sending his despatches in triplicate because of the danger of interception (Allen, *Post and Courier Service*, p. 93).

51. Queller, *The Office of Ambassador*, pp. 140–1; Ilardi, 'Fifteenth-Century Diplomatic Documents', 71fn. 22. A French cypher from the end of the fifteenth century is reproduced in Maulde-la-Clavière, *Diplomatie*, iii, 34fn.

52. R. Ancel, 'La Secrétairerie pontificale sous Paul IV', *Revue des Questions Historiques*, N.S., xxxv (1906), 431.

53. Picard, *Das Gesandtschaftswesen*, p. 132.

half of the century many rulers were employing experts to read the cyphers used by their rivals, as a little later Henry IV of France used François Viète, one of the greatest mathematicians of the age.[54]

Codes and cyphers were still not being used to full effect. In particular there was, as for many generations to come, a marked tendency for governments, through inertia or economy, to continue to use the same ones over long periods. Often they remained in use for years after they had been broken by a rival power. Chapuys, the Spanish ambassador in London, for example, used only one cypher in his correspondence throughout the whole period 1529–41, though it was broken by the English government at least as early as 1535.[55] Nevertheless, by the later decades of the sixteenth century the use of codes and cyphers was more widespread and systematic than ever before. Moreover, they were now shaking off some of the association with numerology, number-mysticism and magical and semi-magical studies in general which had been marked in the earlier part of the century. Trittenheim was to his contemporaries essentially an author of magical and cabbalistic works; but two or three generations later cryptography had become a science, albeit a minor one.

In other respects also diplomacy was slowly and uncertainly becoming more efficient. As information about foreign courts and their policies became more essential, many governments increasingly required from their diplomats not merely a regular day-to-day flow of despatches but also a long and comprehensive report at the end of each mission. As early as 1269 Venetian ambassadors were required by law to submit such reports in writing within fifteen days of their return: registers of *Relazioni* of this kind began to be kept from 1425, and their publication from 1839 onwards has provided historians with a rich and heavily exploited source of information on many aspects of late mediæval and early modern Europe. (It has probably also helped to give them too favourable a view of the efficiency of Venetian diplomatic machinery as compared with that of other Italian states of the period.) In Florence too similar reports were demanded of ambassadors, though not as early as in Venice.[56] North of the Alps the practice took much longer to establish itself, and in some states, notably England, never took root at all. It illustrates once more, however, how relations between many states of western Europe were becoming more organised and continuous, more based on systematically collected information, than ever before.

54. *Encyclopédie de la Pléiade: l'Histoire et ses Méthodes* (Paris, 1961), pp. 620–3.
55. Mattingly, *Renaissance Diplomacy*, pp. 237–8.
56. Queller, *The Office of Ambassador*, pp. 142–3.

## Diplomatic immunity

Another important characteristic of modern international relations, the freedom of the diplomat from legal action in both civil and criminal cases, was beginning to be established, though this process was patchy and uneven. By the later middle ages some immunity of both the persons and the goods of ambassadors had become fairly generally recognised; but this was by no means universally admitted, and certainly not always a complete protection against an angry monarch. In 1510 Pope Julius II threw into prison the representative in Rome of the duke of Savoy because the unfortunate diplomat had offered to mediate in the struggle which Julius, the most warlike of all occupants of the papal throne, was then carrying on with France. In the following year Henry VIII had the papal envoy in London arrested for allegedly revealing secret information to the French ambassador; and in 1516 his successor was not merely arrested and had his papers seized but (according to the Venetian ambassador at least) was threatened with the rack.[57] In 1529 Henry threatened to punish the imperial ambassador for throwing doubt in his reports to Charles V on the genuineness of Henry's friendship; and in the previous year Granvelle, the ambassador of Charles in Paris, had spent almost six weeks in prison after angering Francis I.[58] In 1540, in a more spectacular incident, the house of the French ambassador in Venice was surrounded by soldiers and threatened by cannon to force him to give up three Venetians who had taken refuge there after allegedly disclosing state secrets to him.

Moreover, although it was generally agreed that ambassadors and their retinues had some sort of immunity, there was still plenty of scope for argument about its exact nature and limits. The exemption from taxes and customs duties enjoyed by diplomats, for example, varied widely between different states; and all sorts of other and more important questions arose to which there was no clear or generally accepted answer. Did a diplomat have complete immunity from legal proceedings in respect of wrongs committed against a private individual? Such a principle was slowly developing, but even by the end of the sixteenth century it was by no means undisputed. Until well into the eighteenth century it could still be argued that if accused of a serious crime the diplomat was subject to the law and courts of the state in which he was serving.[59] How far, again, did

57. Joycelyne G. Russell, *The Field of the Cloth of Gold: Men and Manners in 1520* (London, 1969), p. 93.

58. E.R. Adair, *The Exterritoriality of Ambassadors in the Sixteenth and Seventeenth Centuries* (London, 1929), pp. 205–06.

59. See below, p. 54.

the immunity enjoyed by the ambassador cover other members of his mission? Did his entire household form a little island entirely under his own control, completely protected against the surrounding municipal law of the host country? Were his secretary and interpreter in this respect different from ordinary servants, since they were essential to the carrying-on of his work and, it could be argued, served the embassy rather than the ambassador as an individual?[60] The lack of any generally agreed answer to such problems meant that they were often settled on an *ad hoc* basis. A weak ruler might well be driven by political pressure or even the threat of outright force to grant humiliatingly wide immunities to the representatives of a more powerful one.

The most acute problems of all were caused by ambassadors who encouraged or took part in plots, even attempts at rebellion or assassination, directed against the ruler to whom they were accredited. The series of Spanish-backed conspiracies aimed at Queen Elizabeth from the 1560s onwards provide the clearest and best-known examples of this kind of difficulty. Activities of this kind led to the Spanish ambassador in London being for a time in 1569 confined to his house; and three years later his share in the Ridolfi plot led to his expulsion from the country. The bishop of Ross, who represented Mary Queen of Scots at the English court, was imprisoned in 1571–73 for his part in the same plot; while in 1584 another Spanish ambassador was expelled after the unmasking of the Throckmorton conspiracy. Nor was conduct of this kind by any means confined to the representatives of Catholic rulers. The English ambassador to France, Sir Nicholas Throckmorton, intrigued in 1559–60 with the growing Huguenot faction against the government and was arrested for such behaviour in 1563, while a few years later one of his successors, Sir Henry Norris, did his best to help the Huguenot rebels in the civil war which was by then dividing the country.

Nevertheless the sixteenth century saw a slow consolidation and strengthening of diplomatic immunities. Theorists could still argue that an ambassador who plotted against the ruler to whom he was accredited could be punished as a criminal; but by the later decades of the century, as the Elizabethan cases show, usually the worst he could expect was mere expulsion. The freedom of worship within their embassies of Catholic ambassadors and their households in Protestant states and their Protestant counterparts in Catholic ones was never seriously challenged except in Spain under Philip II. The question of how far an embassy building was immune from entry and search by the authorities of the host country and

---

60. Hotman, *De la Dignité*, pp. 70v., ff., discusses all these questions in terms which show how debatable they still remained at the end of the sixteenth century.

could thus act as a sanctuary for criminals, particularly political ones, was for long to be hotly debated; but the general tendency of the period, in spite of some well-known incidents to the contrary such as that in Venice in 1540, was towards strengthening and extending diplomatic immunities in this respect also.

## The ideal ambassador

The new significance of diplomats was reflected in a considerable literature which discussed the way in which they should carry out their duties and the qualities and qualifications they should possess. These descriptions of the 'ideal ambassador' are for the most part remarkably stereotyped and repetitive, and sometimes plagiarised.[61] Their view of the abilities and characteristics needed in an ambassador was very high: one writer of the 1570s demanded that he be 'adorned with all virtues required, and commendable, in a good man, and unfurnished of any vice to blemish his credit, or that may win him the Surname of a wicked man'.[62] He must have, it was agreed, appropriate training and experience: in academic terms this meant some knowledge of law, particularly of Roman Law, and also it was increasingly argued of history. He must be eloquent, equipped with 'apt words, ready tongue, sweet voyce, and speedy deliverance to discharge his Message'.[63] It was usually agreed that it was an advantage for him to speak the language of the country to which he was sent, though some writers pointed out that at times it might be useful for him to conceal this knowledge: also an ability to negotiate in Latin was still essential for diplomats despatched to Poland or one of the German courts. He must be at least moderately rich, and thus able to bear the financial sacrifices which this sort of service usually imposed. He must be physically presentable, with if possible an impressive presence and manner. He must maintain the standing of the ruler he personified by keeping a large household, a fine equipage of horses and coaches, and a lavish and hospitable table. The last was particularly useful in the gluttonous and hard-drinking countries of northern Europe; in the more

61. Thus Hotman's book, one of the best-known, was largely a plagiarism of an earlier work. See the very detailed criticisms in Colazon, Gentil-homme Breton, *Notes sur un petit livre premièrement intitulé l'Ambassadeur . . . par le Sieur de Villiers Hotman* (Paris, 1604). Mattingly, *Renaissance Diplomacy*, Chapter 22, gives a good summary of the main features of this dreary body of writing.

62. F(rancis) T(hynne), *The Perfect Ambassador, treating of the Antiquitie, Priviledges and Behaviour of Men belonging to that Function* (London, 1652), p. 14. This run-of-the-mill little book was in fact completed in 1578.

63. T(hynne), *The Perfect Ambassador* pp. 18–19. Thynne backs up this assertion in very typical style by quoting a long string of biblical and classical examples to illustrate the quasi-miraculous powers of oratory.

abstemious Mediterranean states it was often thought less important. If an ambassador was agreeable and easy to get on with, resolute in his refusal to give offence to anyone, he would acquire more influence. He must therefore be prudent, self-controlled, invariably polite and, most important of all, impenetrably discreet.

On all this agreement was unanimous. To one fundamental question, however, these writers could give no clear answer. How far was the ambassador, and particularly the resident ambassador with all the ambiguities which still clouded his information-gathering and reporting functions, obliged to be honest in the performance of his duties? What indeed did honesty mean in this context? Was he obliged to obey instructions from the ruler he represented when these seemed to infringe some fundamental moral law or to impugn his personal honour? To these and similar questions, which bulk large in this literature, writers on the ideal ambassador spoke with more than one voice. The Venetian Ermolao Barbaro, whose *De officio legati* (1490) was the first book to be concerned entirely with resident ambassadors, had no doubt that the duty of a diplomat was first and foremost to further the interests of his own state and its ruler; and in general hard-headed views of this kind were more widespread and more clearly expressed in Italy than elsewhere. But there was no unanimity. Many writers confronted with such moral difficulties took refuge in generalities or in the sort of barely relevant illustrative examples drawn from the classics or the Bible which are tediously frequent in writing of this type.

## The diplomatic periphery: eastern and northern Europe

Sixteenth-century Europe was thus struggling slowly towards arrangements for the conduct of international relations in many ways recognisably similar to those of the present day. The modernity of the situation, however, even at the end of the century, can easily be exaggerated. Many practices and assumptions of the middle ages were still very much alive. Some of them were to survive for generations.

This was particularly the case in eastern and northern Europe. With them the states which were leading the way in the new diplomatic methods – the Italian principalities, Spain, France, England – had relations which were still slight, intermittent and often non-existent. At the beginning of the seventeenth century Europe was still divided between a core of western states, in which permanent diplomatic representation was well rooted and between which diplomatic relations were active and more or less continuous, and a periphery of less developed ones – the Scandinavian countries, Poland, Russia and in the west Scotland and

Portugal – where diplomacy was less important and diplomatic organisation more primitive. Between these two Europes there were as yet only slender links. Both the western core states and the peripheral ones had limited political horizons. Each was diplomatically active only where it saw some need for such action. Poland, territorially the largest state in Europe and a formidable military power, sent abroad no fewer than ninety-five embassies, all temporary and *ad hoc* ones, in the years 1492–1506. However, of these a fifth went to one state, Hungary, with which Poland's relations were particularly close and generally harmonious. About ten each went to Moldavia, to the Teutonic Knights in East Prussia, to the Tatar khanate of the Crimea and to the Ottoman empire, while the papacy and the Holy Roman Emperor each received eight embassies. But beyond this there were no contacts at all with western Europe, though there were apparently some very tenuous and indirect ones through Hungary with France, Venice and even England, and the king of Portugal was written to in 1495 on behalf of the merchants of Danzig.[64] Just as western Europe was still of little importance to Poland, so Poland attracted little interest in western Europe and thus few western diplomatic initiatives. Not until late in the seventeenth century did France begin to take a sustained interest in the east-European state which was for the next hundred years or more to bulk so large in her foreign policy; and when in 1572 Philip II of Spain hoped to engineer the election of the Archduke Maximilian as king of Poland his only means of doing so was through his ambassador to the Holy Roman Emperor, as he had no representative of his own in the country.

Russia, more remote and inaccessible, received even less attention from most of the west-European states. The Emperor Maximilian I signed an alliance with the Grand Duke Ivan III of Muscovy in 1490 which was revived in 1514; and three years later Ivan made an agreement with the king of Denmark. This made specific provision, among other things, for the personal safety of any envoys the two rulers might send to each other – a good indication of how embryonic their relations still were. The first Russian treaty with Sweden had been signed in 1482; and intermittent contacts with the papacy began about the same time. Some parts of Burgundian court ceremonial, which became predominant in both Madrid and Vienna during the sixteenth century, were also occasionally used in Russia, mainly in the reception of imperial ambassadors.[65] Throughout

---

64. M. Biskup, 'Die polnische Diplomatie in der zweiten Hälfte des 15. und den Anfängen des 16. Jahrhunderts', *Jahrbücher für Geschichte Osteuropas*, Neue Folge, 26 (1978), 177.

65. W. Kirchner, 'Russia and Europe in the Age of Reformation', *Archiv für Reformationsgeschichte*, 1952, Heft ii, 176.

the century, moreover, there were intermittent hopes in western Europe that Russian military strength, which was often grossly overrated, might somehow be used as a weapon against the Turks.[66] There was even momentary discussion of the possibility of Ivan IV being invited to send representatives to the Council of Trent.[67] But all this meant little in practice. Rulers of Russia were forced by the facts of geography to maintain some diplomatic relations with Sweden, Denmark and Poland. It has been claimed that the treaty of 1562 with Denmark was the first ever negotiated by Russia with any western state on a basis of complete equality.[68] But of the major west-European states only England had anything like the same practical significance in her eyes. The arrival in Moscow in 1553, via the White Sea, of a small group of Englishmen led by Richard Chancellor, and the appearance in London four years later of the first Russian envoy ever seen there, began a connection between the two countries which for the rest of the century was surprisingly close and harmonious. But this, on the English side, was a purely commercial relationship. English ambassadors appeared in Russia fairly frequently and sometimes stayed there for quite long periods. But they went there to protect and if possible extend the trading interests of the Muscovy Company merchants, and discussed political issues only when necessary to serve this purpose. No other major west-European state had any significant diplomatic relations with Russia during the sixteenth century. The first French ambassador to Moscow (significantly a mere Dieppe merchant) appeared only in 1586; and no Russian ambassador reached France until 1615. Philip II thought in the 1570s of sending an envoy in an effort at alliance with Ivan IV against the Turks; but nothing came of this. So far as western Europe's relations with Sweden and even Denmark (given some international importance by her physical control of the Sound and thus of seaborne trade through it) are concerned the picture is not very different. The Baltic still formed to a considerable extent a distinct and self-contained political world; and to western Europe in general its states seemed too poor and remote to be of much interest. In 1604 a

66. S.M. Seredonin, *Sochinenie Dzils'a Fletcher'a 'Of the Russe Commonwealth' kak istoricheskii istochnik* (St Petersburg, 1891), pp. 336–41. See also, for example, the discussion of this possibility in 1576–77 in *Calendar of State Papers, Rome, 1572–1578* (London, 1926), pp. 263, 271, 293, 311.

67. *Calendar of State Papers, Rome, 1558–1571* (London, 1916), pp. 31–2.

68. W. Kirchner, 'A Milestone in European History: The Danish–Russian Treaty of 1562', *Slavonic and East European Review*, xxii (1944), 44. On Russian lack of interest in western Europe during this period see K. Rassmussen, 'On the information level of the Posolskiy Prikaz in the sixteenth century', *Forschungen zur Osteuropäische Geschichte*, 24 (1978), 87–99.

French writer could still speak of Denmark as 'so distant a country where we have scarcely any business'.[69]

The Ottoman empire occupied a peculiar and ambiguous position. It was unquestionably a great power, very arguably the greatest of all. Not only its immediate neighbours but most Europeans saw it as a dangerous and imminent threat. In 1481 the Turks had captured Otranto in southern Italy; in 1499 they penetrated as far as Vicenza in the north of the peninsula; in 1529, when they laid siege to Vienna, their forces raided far into Bavaria; in 1565 they threatened to take Malta and with it mastery of the whole Mediterranean. They were therefore inevitably a weighty factor in the political calculations of many European rulers, some of them attracted by the idea of using Turkish power for their own purposes. In 1494, faced by the first French triumphs in Italy, Naples and the papacy itself negotiated with the sultan for help against Charles VIII. In 1500 a Turkish ambassador offered Pope Alexander VI Ottoman military support in return for the cession of the port of Taranto, while in the same year the Emperor Maximilian sent an ambassador to Constantinople. In the 1530s Francis I seriously attempted to use Ottoman strength, and particularly the Turkish fleet, against his arch-rival Charles V; this was an effort hitherto unparalleled at effective cooperation between a great Christian state and an infidel one. A generation or more later, fear of the Counter-Reformation and of Spanish power meant that the Protestants of England and the Netherlands, and the French Huguenots, became willing to see the Turks as an ally. There were suggestions in 1574 that they should subsidise William of Orange and benefit from the increasing diversion of Spanish resources to the struggle in the Netherlands which would result from this; and in 1612 the emerging Dutch Republic opened formal diplomatic relations by sending a resident ambassador to Constantinople. The English, who in the last decades of the sixteenth century became significant suppliers to the Turks of some essential military raw materials, had already sent an ambassador of their own in 1583.

Yet nothing could get round the fact that the Turks were militantly anti-Christian, a continual menace to all Christendom. Throughout the sixteenth century an essentially mediæval attitude of hostility and distrust was never abandoned by the statesmen of Europe. For them, as for their predecessors, 'the Turk was a species different *in kind* from Christian states whether Catholic or Protestant, a political pariah excluded by his very nature from membership in the family of European states'.[70] It might, as a

69. Hotman, *De la charge et dignité de l'ambassadeur*, p. 57.

70. F.L. Baumer, 'England, the Turk, and the Common Corps of Christendom', *American Historical Review*, 1 (1944–45), 27.

matter of practical politics, be necessary to make use of him; but there was a deep-rooted feeling that this was unnatural, indeed downright immoral. European unity in a crusade against the Ottoman empire, an ideal which inspired the Emperor Charles V, was an increasingly impractical dream; but the slackening of active hostility between Catholic and Protestant states in the first two decades of the seventeenth century saw some revival of schemes of this kind.[71] The Ottoman empire, therefore, in spite of its resources and achievements, was very far from being a part of the European state-system, especially as the Turks showed not the slightest interest in developing any kind of effective diplomatic representation in the capitals of Europe.

In diplomacy then, as in other spheres, the idea of two Europes – a richer, stronger and more rapidly developing centre and a poorer, weaker (with the great exception of the Ottoman empire) and less developed periphery – corresponds in general to the facts of the sixteenth century. In terms of diplomatic organisation the most important result of this contrast was the slowness with which the idea of the resident ambassador as opposed to the temporary and *ad hoc* one took root in the states of the periphery. Other contrasts, however, at least of degree and emphasis, can also be seen in the way in which the two Europes conducted their diplomacy.

Thus in eastern Europe collective embassies carried by a number, often a considerable one, of individuals acting as a body continued to be common. They were also, and long continued to be, far from uncommon in the west, especially when a large element of ceremonial and appearances or some issue such as an important royal marriage was involved. The French mission to England in 1581, to quote only one example, which tried to negotiate a marriage between Elizabeth I and the duke of Anjou, consisted of thirteen ambassadors led by a minor member of the French royal family: it numbered in all about 700 people.[72] But the idea that a diplomatic mission normally meant the accrediting of an individual diplomat to an individual ruler was slower to establish itself east of the Elbe and the Adriatic than in western Europe. A typical example is the negotiations carried on in 1530 for an agreement between the Archduke Ferdinand and John Zapolyai, who had been elected king of Hungary in 1526, which involved groups of six representatives on the Habsburg side and seven on the other.[73] Collective embassies of this kind

---

71. Baumer, 'England, the Turk . . .', pp. 43ff.

72. N.M. Sutherland, *The French Secretaries of State in the Age of Catherine de Medici* (London, 1962), p. 226.

73. Picard, *Das Gesandtschaftswesen*, pp. 50–1.

had obvious potential shortcomings, since they risked quarrels and rivalries between their members and delays in assembling them before they set out. They were sometimes, however, preferred by diplomats, since they divided the work involved and might, it was felt, carry more weight and offer better chances of success than a mission entrusted to a single ambassador. Generally the sending of a large embassy with multiple membership of this kind was seen as a sign of respect to the ruler to whom it was accredited; by the same token a reduction in the size of an embassy or the sending of an obviously small one signified the reverse. Again, an embassy might be accredited not merely to a monarch but also to influential individuals at his court or in his government, another survival of the mediæval assumption that a wide variety of people and institutions were entitled to send and receive such representatives. This particular legacy of the past, though by no means unknown in the west, was again more visible in eastern and central Europe. A typical case is the accrediting in 1531, for a projected mission to Poland which did not in fact take place, of a Habsburg ambassador not merely to King Sigismund I and his son, Sigismund Augustus, but also to the queen, the *voevode* of Cracow, the chancellor, the bishop of Przemysl and a number of other prominent men, ten in all.[74]

## Recruitment and payment

The weaknesses of the early modern state were inevitably reflected in those of its diplomatic machinery. Even the most successful and experienced diplomats seldom spent more than a part, usually a fairly small one, of their working lives in diplomacy. Herberstein's imposing total of seventy missions occupied only about a quarter of his entire career.[75] When circumstances demanded it, moreover, a diplomat could well combine with his diplomatic functions others of a completely different kind. The French ambassador to Scotland, who in 1548–49 played a leading role in controlling and supplying the French expeditionary force sent there, and who from the end of 1550 personally commanded it,[76] is merely a rather extreme example of what was possible. Service as a diplomat, with the discomforts and even dangers it often involved and the heavy personal expenses usually associated with it, was normally undertaken as a stepping-stone to preferment at home, as giving the diplomat a claim to some more comfortable and lucrative court or

74. Picard, *Das Gesandtschaftswesen*, pp. 50–4.
75. Picard, *Das Gesandtschaftswesen*, p. 37.
76. M.-N. Baudoin-Matuszek, 'Un ambassadeur en Ecosse au XVIe siècle: Henri Clutin d'Oisel', *Revue Historique*, 569 (1989), 94, 97.

administrative appointment, and not for its own sake.[77] There now existed, scattered throughout western and central Europe, a considerable number of experienced diplomats; but no state as yet had anything that deserved the name of a diplomatic service. Rulers, particularly in the later fifteenth century and the early decades of the sixteenth, often showed a striking indifference (which was to continue, with slowly diminishing effect, for another 200 years) to the nationality of those they employed in this way. Thus an Italian, Spinelly, served as English ambassador in the Netherlands and Spain, and a Frenchman, Machado, also as ambassador to Spain; while the Emperor Maximilian sent an Italian to England and an Aragonese to Spain. Francis I tried to use only Frenchmen in the states geographically close to France; but he sent many foreigners to represent him in more distant countries. Of the forty-eight different ambassadors sent by Poland to Charles V and the Holy Roman Empire during 1518–56 (many of them in collective embassies with several members) six were German, three Italian and one was from the Netherlands.[78] Remnants of this cosmopolitanism, which was marked particularly in the frequent employment as diplomats by many states of Italians and later of Swiss, were to be seen down to the French Revolution.

Moreover, the payment of diplomats continued throughout the sixteenth century and for long afterwards to be disorganised and arbitrary. There were inevitably variations between different states in this respect, and between the situations prevailing in the same state at different times. Queen Elizabeth, in spite of her well-attested meanness, seems to have paid her diplomats better and more punctiliously than her contemporaries Henry III and Philip II. But shortage of money, sometimes serious shortage, was the rule rather than the exception for most ambassadors at most times. The majority of them, certainly of those representing the states of western Europe, received salaries. These, however, were usually inadequate to meet the often very heavy expenses which diplomats had to face. They also tended to be paid irregularly and with long delays. Even when money was available, the mechanics of transferring it over considerable distances could create difficulties. The £300 paid by bill of exchange to the English ambassador in Madrid in October 1561, for instance, did not reach him until April of the following year.[79] Sometimes, especially in the fifteenth and early sixteenth centuries, arrangements for the transfer of funds might be very primitive indeed. In

---

77. This point is well illustrated with regard to the ambassadors of Elizabeth I in G.M. Bell, 'Elizabethen Diplomatic Compensation: Its Nature and Variety,' *Journal of British Studies*, xx, No.2 (1981), 1–25.

78. Krauske, *Die Entwicklung*, pp. 225–6; Picard, *Das Gesandtschaftswesen*, pp. 16–17.

79. G.M. Bell, 'John Man: the last Elizabethan Resident Ambassador in Spain', *Sixteenth Century Journal*, vii, No.2 (1976), 77.

1516 an English agent (admittedly an unofficial and semi-secret one) sent to arrange a treaty between Henry VIII and the Swiss cantons suggested that if necessary money might be sent him sewn into the coats of messengers 'after the manner of Italy'.[80] Like their mediæval forerunners the diplomats of the early modern period complained loudly and frequently of lack of money and arrears of payment, and of the bad effect these had on their efficiency.[81] Thus, to take a rather extreme case, in 1580 the French ambassador in Copenhagen, who had long been irregularly paid, was in fear of imminent imprisonment for debt, and in the following year was unable for months on end to appear at court because of the amount he owed. In 1589, still in post, he died bankrupt and all his papers were seized by his creditors.[82] It is not surprising that it was often difficult to find suitable men willing to accept such potentially ruinous appointments. A diplomat who was driven to borrow in order to defend the position and interests of the state he represented might find himself very heavily in debt and have much difficulty in securing repayment from an empty or overburdened treasury: the French ambassador to Scotland who incurred such debts to pay the French forces there in 1558–60 was owed over 129,000 livres when he returned to France.[83]

More important as an index of the continuing strength of traditional assumptions, diplomatic salaries (and expense allowances where the latter were granted) were hardly ever governed by fixed scales. What an ambassador received depended on the skill and pertinacity with which he and his supporters at court or in government office urged his claims, on the other sources of income available to him, of course on the state at any given moment of the treasury from which he was paid and, particularly in the late fifteenth and early sixteenth centuries, on his social status as distinct from his diplomatic rank. Papal diplomacy, one of the best organised, is a good example of the possible difficulties. Nuncios, though they received a monthly allowance, were expected to supplement this with what they received from the sale of indulgences and from the benefices they held. Only under Gregory XIII (1572–85) were they assigned fixed salaries; and even then these were not regularly paid, while the nuncios in Naples and Spain still received as payment a percentage of the papal taxes they collected.[84] It should be remembered, moreover, that the ability and effort which a diplomat brought to the performance of his

---

80. J. Wegg, *Richard Pace, a Tudor Diplomat* (London, 1932), pp. 71, 82.

81. For examples see Maulde-la-Clavière, *Diplomatie*, i, 341– 2.

82. G. Baguenault de Puchesse, 'Un ambassadeur de France au Danemarck au seizième siècle', *Revue d'Histoire Diplomatique*, 1911, 192–3.

83. Baudoin-Matuszek, 'Un ambassadeur . . .', 123.

84. Biaudet, *Les Nonciatures apostoliques*, pp. 71–87.

duties would very often have made him much richer if they had been used in other ways at home, in some administrative post or in the care of his own estates. 'Opportunity costs' of this kind are impossible to measure and were not very often used as arguments by the diplomats themselves; but they must sometimes have been substantial.[85]

There was still, indeed, no clear rule that the cost of maintaining a diplomat should fall exclusively on the ruler whom he represented. The practice of acquiring suitable houses as ambassadorial residences was adopted only very slowly even by the major states to which a network of permanent representatives was becoming more and more essential. Gregory XIII again seems to have been the first pope to make any effort of this kind; but its effects were limited.[86] In the later fifteenth century it was quite common for ambassadors to receive from rulers to whom they were accredited not merely accommodation but allowances, sometimes very substantial ones, for the maintenance of themselves and their retinue. In Italy, in this as in other respects in the forefront of change, this was increasingly frowned on: in 1466 the Venetian senate forbade its representatives to receive such payments in either money or kind from the rulers to whom they were sent and also tried to end any obligation of Venice to maintain representatives sent to it.[87] It was only slowly and patchily, however, that such practices died away. In England the principle that resident ambassadors of foreign states must pay for their own lodging seems to have been asserted from 1556 onwards; but those on temporary and extraordinary missions continued sometimes for the next half-century to be given free quarters. Some rulers, such as those of Spain and the Holy Roman Empire, continued on occasion, as a mark of respect to a fellow-monarch, to pay the entire expenses of an extraordinary embassy, though this was now definitely unusual. Practice varied widely, however. In the Dutch republic even resident envoys were housed at public expense until as late as 1649; and representatives of peripheral and semi-European countries continued to expect free maintenance long after the practice had been generally abandoned in western Europe.[88]

There was one way in which a diplomat, poorly and irregularly paid, might hope to benefit quite substantially by undertaking an embassy. This was by receiving a present from the ruler to whom he had been

---

85. See the comments on the long service to the Venetian republic in the sixteenth century of Leonardo Dona in J.C. Davis, *A Venetian Family and its Fortune, 1500–1900: The Dona and the Conservation of their Wealth* (Philadelphia, 1975), pp. 55–7.

86. Biaudet, *Les Nonciatures apostoliques*, pp. 89–90.

87. D.E. Queller, *Early Venetian Legislation on Ambassadors* (Geneva, 1966), p. 22.

88. The best general discussion of this question remains the appendix on 'Entertainment of Ambassadors' in Adair, *The Exterritoriality of Ambassadors*.

accredited when he departed for home at the end of his stay: indeed the giving of such presents had become a well-established tradition long before the emergence of the permanent embassy. The most common form they took was that of a gold chain, the weight and value of which was carefully proportioned to the rank and importance of the recipient. Thus in 1519 the French ambassador to Venice was given a parting present of such a chain valued at 700 ducats, while a decade later the more important of two English ambassadors sent to the Emperor Charles V at Bologna received one worth 2,000 ducats and his junior colleague a smaller one worth half as much.[89] But such a present might well take other forms. Rich and expensive garments were sometimes given, at least in the early sixteenth century, as were silver plate, horses, furs, jewels and even cash. One French ambassador to England at the end of the century, for example, was given by Elizabeth 'a cupboard of plate' worth 4,000 crowns.[90] A successful or lucky ambassador might benefit very substantially in this way. The more valuable the gift the more emphatic the demonstration of munificence by the giver; here again the pervasive emphasis on status and status-symbols came into play. A lavish present which could be sold or used as security for a loan when the diplomat concerned returned home might compensate for a good many privations endured during his embassy.

## The physical difficulties

Finally, the limits imposed on the workings of the diplomatic machine by the crass physical facts of distance and difficulty of movement should not be forgotten. A diplomat accredited to a ruler whose court was still peripatetic in the mediæval style was condemned to incessant, exhausting and expensive travel: a Venetian ambassador to the Emperor Maximilian complained in 1507 that during the twenty months he had spent in Germany he had been almost permanently on horseback.[91] Such a state of affairs was now exceptional, however. A more serious and widespread problem was posed by the slowness and unreliability of communications. Governments might struggle against this: the creation at the beginning of the sixteenth century of a Spanish postal system centred on Barcelona was

89. J. de Pins, 'Autour des guerres d'Italie', *Revue d'Histoire Diplomatique* (1947), 246; R.J. Knecht, (ed.), *The Voyage of Sir Nicholas Carewe to the Emperor Charles V in the year 1529* (Cambridge, 1959), p. 43.

90. G.B. Harrison and R.A. Jones, (eds.), *A Journal of all that was accomplished by Monsieur de Maisse, ambassador in England from King Henri IV to Queen Elizabeth Anno Domini 1597* (London, 1931), p. 89. A list of the presents given to English ambassadors by foreign rulers in 1569–86 can be found in Bell, 'Elizabethan Diplomatic Compensation . . .', p. 25.

91. Maulde-la-Clavière, *Diplomatie*, iii, 7.

largely a product of the growing need for good diplomatic communications with Italy, and by the time of Leo X, France, Spain and the Holy Roman Emperor each had in Rome a postmaster of their own. But the physical problems were insoluble. Journey times were long, especially in bad weather and in the more unfavourable seasons. Even a courier carrying only despatches took in the second half of the sixteenth century on average eleven days to go from Madrid to Paris in summer and seventeen in winter, while from Madrid to Vienna might take twenty-five days and from London to Paris four.[92]

Journeys were not merely long but could be unpredictable. Bad weather, difficulty in procuring horses, all sorts of accidents could mean unforeseeable delays. In the early sixteenth century a despatch from Florence to Naples might in winter take six weeks to reach its destination (though this must have been abnormally slow); but in 1513 news of the election of Leo X reached Florence from Rome in a mere ten hours. A courier from Rome to Venice usually took five days; but those of the great German banking house of Fugger could do the journey in less than two.[93] At the end of the century papal couriers normally needed about fifteen days to travel from Rome to Paris; but the journey could be done in nine. In 1581–82 ordinary couriers between Lyons and Rome, organised and paid by the bankers and merchants of the two cities, averaged twenty days for the journey; but the longest time was thirty-four days and the shortest only nine.[94] For a complete embassy, encumbered with servants and baggage, travel was far slower; an English one in 1529 needed forty-two days to get from the Channel coast of France to Bologna, though a courier travelling post could move more than four times as fast.[95] Movement was often slowest of all in east and east-central Europe, where even the poor roads of the west scarcely existed. There an embassy on horseback could hope to average little more than twenty miles a day, rather more on sledges in winter, rather less in wagons; the journey from Vienna to Moscow took Herberstein not far short of four months.[96] One of the most convincing and down-to-earth accounts of the discomforts which had to be faced by diplomats travelling in eastern Europe was provided by Antonio Possevino, the Jesuit sent by the papacy in 1582 to mediate between Russia and Poland. An envoy to Russia, he

92. Allen, 'Les courriers diplomatiques', 234; *Post and Courier Service*, Chapter iv, passim. For examples of the difficult journeys often made by diplomats, especially in winter, see Maulde-la-Clavière, *Diplomatie*, ii, 158–60.

93. E. Rodocanachi, 'Les couriers pontificaux du quatorzième au dix-septième siècle', *Revue d'Histoire Diplomatique*, 1912, 412.

94. Allen, *Post and Courier Service*, p. 82.

95. Knecht, *The Voyage of Sir Nicholas Carewe*, pp. 39–40.

96. Picard, *Das Gesandtschaftswesen*, pp. 84–5.

wrote, must have a tent to sleep in when there was no lodging available and also a bed which, when unrolled, could be completely encased in leather or cotton. He needed this 'to prevent soot falling down from the roof of his chamber on his face when he is asleep, as happens in Muscovy and Lithuania, and to protect him from the flies, which bite fiercely and, unlike elsewhere, are active at night, working their way through the linen to cause intense discomfort'. He must also, Possevino went on, have plain black curtains which could be used to divide a room into sections, since the entire staff of the embassy might well be forced to spend the night together in a single room together with their horses for the sake of warmth in winter, and this created great problems of privacy and decency.[97] The difficulty and hardship of movement east of the Elbe is shown in the prominence there, during much of the sixteenth century at least, of the *praecursor*, a member of the mission who travelled two or three days journey ahead of it making arrangements for its reception and feeding.

The security from attack which an embassy offered, and still more the exemption from customs-duties which its members normally enjoyed, offered a powerful inducement for travelling merchants and other hangers-on to attach themselves to it if they could. This again applied particularly in eastern Europe where, it was claimed, the embassies exchanged between Russia and Poland were often swollen in this way to 800–1200 horsemen in all.[98] The same phenomenon was by no means unknown in the west, however, at least in the first half of the sixteenth century: the use of merchants as diplomatic or quasi-diplomatic agents was, after all, still fairly common. Thus, the French embassy sent to England in 1518 was 'supported by a host of gentlemen, archers, wrestlers, musicians and tennis-players' and its entry into London was spoilt by the fact that it was accompanied by a great number of pedlars and dubious petty traders who brought with them, in the words of a contemporary, 'diverse merchandise uncostomed, all under the colour of the trussery of the Ambassadors'.[99]

## The limits of accomplishment

By the end of the sixteenth century, therefore, Europe presented the picture of a continent evolving, in a quite unplanned way, a network of official contacts between states more extensive, continuous and

97. *The Moscovia of Antonio Possevino*, p. 40.
98. Picard, *Das Gesandtschaftswesen*, p. 63. Possevino (*Moscovia*, p. 20) also commented on the large number of merchants normally attached to Russian and Polish embassies.
99. Anglo, *Spectacle, Pageantry . . .* , pp. 128–9.

professional than anything hitherto known. The picture, however, was not a simple one. There were still great variations between different parts of the continent, marked inconsistencies and irrationalities, large survivals of past attitudes and practices. Moreover, the new diplomatic structure had done little or nothing to improve the tone and atmosphere of interstate relations. A pervasive distrust, a universal assumption that no state would keep a promise longer than suited its interests, a readiness to disregard quite brutally on occasion what embryonic international law existed, characterise the entire century. The best-known meeting of sovereigns, that of Henry VIII and Francis I at the Field of the Cloth of Gold in 1520, in spite of all the declarations of friendship and brotherhood which marked it, was surrounded by fear and suspicion. There were rumours that the English contingent was to be attacked by the French fleet as it crossed the Channel; and artillery was moved for its protection to the English garrison-town of Calais, whose governor reported on French troop-movements in the area. Until the moment of the meeting there were fears of treachery on both sides, while each suspected that the other had more soldiers in the area than had been agreed.[100] Fears of this kind, and also the universal preoccupation with appearances and prestige, are reflected in the fact that a high proportion of such royal meetings took place in frontier areas (the Field of the Cloth of Gold was carefully sited halfway between Guines, in the English enclave around Calais, and Ardres in French territory) so that neither participant would have to travel far through the lands of the other. An ambassador might even find himself taken prisoner while passing through the territory of one state *en route* for another if his captors thought his activities likely to be dangerous to them: in the 1550s the Spanish governor of the Netherlands, the formidable Margaret of Hungary, tried to capture a French envoy returning from a mission to England, while a little later a Turkish one was arrested in Venice on his way to France. Earlier, in the later fifteenth century and the first decades of the sixteenth, the situation in this respect had been a good deal worse. An unfortunate French ambassador *en route* to Scotland, who was shipwrecked on the English coast in 1455, remained in prison for three years until Charles VII paid the ransom demanded for his release (the salt tax in Normandy had to be increased to raise the money). More than eighty years later, in the most striking case of this kind, French envoys on their way to Constantinople to negotiate an alliance with the sultan were murdered by Spanish soldiers when they entered Milanese territory. It is not surprising that in 1509 the Florentine government instructed its envoy to the Emperor Maximilian to take the precaution of

100. Russell, *The Field of the Cloth of Gold*, pp. 64–5, 101.

returning home disguised as a merchant.[101] Even at the end of the sixteenth century and in the greatest states of western Europe an ambassador could not be confident of physical security: in 1601 the French ambassador in Madrid, the comte de Rochepot, had his house forcibly broken into after a serious scuffle between members of his household and a number of Spaniards. Diplomacy had developed considerably during the century. But it had done so as an instrument of the aggressive, distrustful and untrustworthy monarchies which now completely dominated European political life, not as a restraint upon them.

101. Rosemary Devonshire-Jones, *Francesco Vettori, Florentine Citizen and Medici Servant* (London, 1972), p. 32.

# CHAPTER TWO

# Old Regime Diplomacy at its Height, c1600–1789

## THE LEGACY OF THE PAST

Many aspects of the diplomatic organisation of western and central Europe as it existed by the beginning of the seventeenth century continued with little essential change down to the French Revolution and indeed beyond. The core of diplomacy continued to be the resident diplomat, concerned largely with the collection of information and reporting home relatively frequently in despatches of which particularly important or delicate parts were usually in cypher. He was still supplemented by special ambassadors sent for short periods for particular purposes, though their functions became more and more purely formal. A preoccupation, though a slowly waning one, with precedence and ceremonial still bulked very large: the safeguarding by the ambassador of the honour and standing of the monarch he represented continued for long to be widely seen as the most fundamental of all his duties. There were still many unanswered questions, though these became progressively fewer, about the nature and extent of diplomatic immunities.

Slowly, however, this system was changing and developing. Gradually it became more institutionalised as something resembling organised diplomatic services emerged. By the eighteenth century foreign offices, departments of state concerned simply or mainly with the making and execution of foreign policy, could be seen in embryo in many parts of Europe. The geographical scope of these quasi-modern international relations was widened as, from the end of the seventeenth century onwards, a new factor in the European balance, the hitherto unimportant Russian empire, was incorporated in it. The mechanisms of international relations from the age of Richelieu to that of Robespierre thus show a mixture of the old and the new, of old methods and assumptions working in and gradually being adapted to, new situations. But the persisting strength of the old and the traditional, the slowness of change, is a dominant theme of the period.

## The diplomat: duties and rewards, difficulties and immunities

In one fundamental respect there had, by the end of the seventeenth century, been a final break with the legacy of the middle ages. By then it was clear that diplomatic representation was the prerogative of sovereigns alone. The ambiguities of the sixteenth century, when a mediaeval vagueness as to who had the right to send and receive ambassadors still to some extent persisted, were now a thing of the past. Entities, however powerful, which were non-sovereign or merely quasi-sovereign, were now generally agreed not to possess such rights. In the first half of the seventeenth century the Dutch East India Company, for example, still sent representatives of its own to negotiate with European powers; but by its end any diplomatic activity in Europe carried on by non-sovereign entities was a curiosity without practical significance. François de Callières, the French diplomat who wrote in the 1690s the best-known diplomatic manual of the period, pointed out that the cities of Bologna and Ferrara, now incorporated in the papal state, still sent 'diplomatic deputations' to the pope and that in Spanish-ruled Sicily Messina, until the rising of 1674 there, had been able to send similar deputations to Madrid; but he rightly saw these as unimportant hangovers from the past.[1] However, the diplomacy which really mattered had always been that of sovereign states; this final withering away of the claims of other entities to conduct some sort of foreign relations of their own was merely a kind of necessary tidying-up, the clearing of an undergrowth of quasi-diplomacy.

The most essential function of the diplomat resident for a substantial period of time in some foreign capital remained what it had always been: the collecting and sending home of information. Normally this duty was spelt out explicitly in the instructions he received at the beginning of his embassy. Thus Sir William Trumbull, when he was sent as English ambassador to Paris in 1685, was told that:

> You shall constantly correspond with our ministers in other foreign courts, for our better service, and your mutual information and assistance in your respective negotiations; and you shall also maintain a good correspondence and intercourse with all the other ambassadors, envoys and ministers of princes and

1. F. de Callières, *The Art of Diplomacy*, ed. H.M.A. Keens-Soper and K.W. Schweizer (New York, 1983), p. 104.

states in amity with us, and as far as you can penetrate into the designs of their respective superiors, and of what you can discover of this nature you shall give us a constant account by one of our Principal Secretaries of State.

Two decades earlier Louis XIV had put it more succinctly: 'Nothing happens in the world which does not come under the cognizance of . . . . a good ambassador', while in the early eighteenth century a leading international lawyer wrote flatly of resident diplomats that 'it is precisely for the purpose of getting information that they are maintained in the courts of friendly powers'.[2] As in the past, this normally involved a process of barter: to obtain information the ambassador had to be able and willing to give it in return. It was therefore important for him to be well informed about events in his own country and in the political world generally; and ambassadors sometimes asked in their despatches for news which they could trade with their colleagues from other states since, as one of them told the French foreign minister in 1674, 'You know that in [diplomacy] as in other ordinary transactions it is necessary to give in order to receive'.[3]

As in the past, governments also attempted, with varying degrees of success, to obtain information by opening and reading the correspondence of foreign diplomats. Codes and cyphers still gave some protection against this, and in one or two cases at least cryptography was carried in the seventeenth century to a level which was not to be surpassed for generations to come. The *grand chiffre* devised in mid-century by Antoine Rossignol, a member of the greatest family of French cryptographers, was not broken, after the key to it had been lost, until the 1870s.[4] But clearly a great many despatches were intercepted and read in many different parts of Europe. By the 1650s those to and from all foreign diplomats in London were being opened and copied in the Post Office; and in 1665 the French ambassador acknowledged that the English 'have tricks to open letters more skilfully than anywhere in the world'.[5] In the eighteenth century such practices, at least in Great Britain, became still more professional. The Jacobite threat, which until the middle of the century seemed to all British statesmen very real, led to intensified efforts of this kind, with attempts to obtain keys to the cyphers used by foreign governments and to gather information from postal centres on the

2. P. Fraser, *The Intelligence of the Secretaries of State and their Monopoly of Licensed News, 1660–1688* (Cambridge, 1956), p. 65; J.J. Jusserand, *A French Ambassador at the Court of Charles II* (New York, 1892), pp. 198–9; C. Van Bynkershoek, *In Foro Legatorum tam in causa civili, quam criminali, liber singularis* (Oxford–London, 1946; first published 1721), p. 9.
3. W.J. Roosen, 'The Functioning of Ambassadors under Louis XIV', *French Historical Studies*, vi, No. 3 (Spring, 1970), 319.
4. *Encyclopédie de la Pléiade; L'Histoire et ses Méthodes*, p. 627.
5. Fraser, *Intelligence*, pp. 24–5.

continent such as Danzig, Brussels, Leyden, Antwerp and Hamburg.[6] The Post Office Act of 1741 gave legal backing to the opening and copying of letters on the orders of one of the Secretaries of State; and in 1765 a general warrant ordered that all diplomatic correspondence passing through London should be treated in this way. The 'Secret Office' in which this skilled and highly confidential work was done dated back to 1653 and was an unpublicised aspect of the new efficiency which the Cromwellian period brought to much government activity; by the end of the eighteenth century it had a staff of ten.[7]

France also had an active *cabinet noir* which was often headed by the foreign minister (in the eighteenth century at least four, Torcy, Fleury, Rouillé and Choiseul, combined the two appointments). Here also the opening and copying of letters was carried to a high level of professionalism.[8] Even in the 1660s Charles II had been complaining in London that his correspondence with his sister, the Duchess of Orleans, was being regularly opened in the French post,[9] while from about 1748 Louis XV himself began to take a good deal of interest in work of this kind. Indeed the *cabinet noir* had a considerably wider scope than its British counterpart. On occasion it interfered with the correspondence of French ministers or former ministers (Choiseul after his fall in 1770 and Turgot during his period in office in 1774–76), and even with that of members of the royal family. It was also a slightly larger organisation than that in London, and certainly a more costly one. Its activities were well enough known to provoke widespread protest in the *cahiers* of 1789. A similar organisation of the Habsburg government, the *Geheime Kabinets-Kanzlei*, operated not merely in Vienna but in Brussels, Liège, Frankfurt and Regensburg and enjoyed a high reputation for its technical skill. Under the Emperor Charles VI it took the form it was to retain, with some reorganisation in the 1750s, until the 1848 revolution swept it away. Joseph II in the 1780s attached great importance to its work (not surprisingly for a ruler of his suspicious and autocratic temperament) and it was claimed that in the single year 1780–81 alone no fewer than fifteen foreign diplomatic cyphers were broken in Vienna.[10]

These efforts at information-gathering by fair means or foul were merely an intensification of something visible from the very beginnings of

6. P.S. Fritz, 'The Anti-Jacobite Intelligence System of the English Ministers, 1715–1745', *Historical Journal*, xvi, (1973), 265ff.

7. K. Ellis, *The Post-Office in the Eighteenth Century* (London, 1958), pp. 62–9.

8. See the description, written c.1725–30, in F. Vaillé, *Le Cabinet Noir* (Paris, 1950), pp. 99–104.

9. Jusserand, *A French Ambassador*, p. 50.

10. F. Stix, 'Zur Geschichte und Organisation der Wiener Geheimen Ziffernkanzlei', *Mitteilungen des Österreichischen Instituts für Geschichtsforschung*, 51 (1937), p. 142.

organised diplomacy. They had nothing essentially new about them. The same is true of the view of the ideal ambassador taken by writers of the seventeenth and eighteenth centuries. The literature which discussed his duties and the personal qualities which he needed to perform them successfully became in the seventeenth century more copious than ever before. It even grew as the century went on. The most complete bibliography available lists thirty-three works of this kind published in the quarter-century 1626–50, sixty-six in 1651–75 and seventy-seven in 1676–1700.[11] Much of this writing, however, remained essentially the same as in earlier generations – inevitably so, since most of the characteristics of a successful diplomat have not changed over centuries. Antoine Pecquet, a writer of the early eighteenth century who was also a senior official in the French foreign ministry, is typical of much of what was still being said on the subject. The diplomat, he wrote, must be modest, self-controlled and discreet. He must be sagacious and have good judgement, be patient and yet at the same time firm in maintaining the interests of the ruler he represented. He must be a fluent and persuasive speaker, if possible with an attractive personal appearance, and must understand that liberality in entertainment and general style of life could be an important help in negotiation.[12] No sixteenth-century writer on the subject would have disagreed with any of this.

In one important respect, however, the attitudes reflected in this uninspiring and repetitive body of writing were changing. By the last decades of the seventeenth century a much heavier emphasis than ever before was being placed on the need for honesty, for the diplomat to behave in a way which inspired confidence in those with whom he dealt. This, it was now increasingly argued, would be far more effective in the long run than any amount of sharp practice. In 1684 Colbert de Croissy, the French foreign minister, urged his son, the Marquis de Torcy, then embarking on an embassy to Portugal, to make every effort 'to gain the reputation of a perfectly honourable man, and to deserve it' . Some decades later Pecquet asserted flatly that deceit in diplomacy was positively dangerous and that 'truth and probity are . . . . the two qualities most essential to the success of a public minister'. Personal virtue, he went on, was indispensable, for 'nothing is so dangerous as intelligence when it is guided by a corrupt heart'.[13] In this new, or at least much heavier, emphasis on fair dealing can be seen a genuine movement away from the

11. V.E. Hrabar (Grabar), *De Legatorum jure tractatum catalogus completus ab anno MDCXXV usque ad annum MDCC* (Dorpat, 1918).

12. A. Pecquet, *Discours sur l'art de négocier* (Paris, 1737), pp. 14–18, 39–40, 42–60.

13. Quoted in P. Gerbore, *Formen und Stile der Diplomatie* (Reinbeck bei Hamburg, 1964), p. 69; *Discours*, pp. 6–8, 13, 41.

*Honesty*

*N.B*

primitive assumptions of the age of Commynes and Machiavelli. In place of an unbridled power struggle in which almost anything was permissible and extreme instability in relations between states was the norm, it was now being asserted that the task of diplomacy was not to deceive or even perhaps to defeat an opponent, but rather to reconcile conflicting ambitions and help different states to coexist, at least for considerable periods, in a reasonable degree of amity. Callières stressed more than any of his predecessors the role of the diplomat as a moderating influence and the extent to which, through prudence and common sense, apparently divergent state interests could be at least partially harmonised.[14] It would be absurd to make high claims for the international morality of the later seventeenth and eighteenth centuries. In the 1680s, when Colbert de Croissy was preaching honourable behaviour to his son, the theft or attempted theft of despatches was still a commonplace of diplomacy.[15] But the states of western Europe were now being driven by harsh experience if by nothing higher to aim at something more than the chaotic free-for-all which had marked the Italian wars and the Habsburg–Valois struggles of the first half of the sixteenth century.

Many of the rituals and formalities of diplomacy changed only slowly, sometimes hardly at all, during the two centuries before the French revolution. Some change there was, however. A whole series of practices and expedients which had been widely used as an organised diplomatic system began to take shape fell into disuse as it became better established. Collective embassies with a number of members often of formally equal rank, which had been common in the sixteenth century, rapidly ceased to be so. It was generally agreed that republics were now much more likely than monarchies to use them; and this belief seems to be borne out by the facts. In the seventeenth century the new Dutch republic was the only important power to make extensive use of this method of representation. When the States-General had particular items of important business to transact with a foreign state it continued until late in the century to send abroad for this purpose missions recruited from its own members: sometimes as many as sixteen were accredited. Until the second half of the century even the greatest powers still occasionally made use of multi-member embassies and there was still some surviving feeling that a ruler was particularly honoured by receiving a group of ambassadors rather than an individual. Louis XIV, for example, accredited three to negotiate jointly with the English government in 1665. But this was now increasingly unusual: the individual ambassador or envoy leading and

14. M. Keens-Soper, 'Francois de Callières and Diplomatic Theory', *Historical Journal*, xvi, (1973), 485–508.
15. C. Picavet, *La Diplomatie française au temps de Louis XIV* (Paris, 1930), pp. 187–9.

controlling a mission whose other members were clearly his subordinates was established as the norm.

Another practice fairly common in the sixteenth century, that of the 'circular' embassy which visited a series of different states, negotiating with each in turn, also persisted into the first half of that which followed. Thus in 1629 the Baron de Charnacé represented France on a mission to Denmark, went from there to several of the German states, and from Germany to help negotiate a truce between Sweden and Poland. In the same year Sir Thomas Roe went as English representative in turn to The Hague, Copenhagen and Königsberg (where the Elector of Brandenburg then was) before also helping with the Swedish–Polish negotiations. But this sort of arrangement too became rarer as the century went on.

Other practices normal in the past were also now disappearing. One of the most curious of these was the knighting of ambassadors at the end of their mission by the monarch to whom they had been accredited and the grant to them of augmentations to their coats of arms. Those of Venice were particularly favoured in this way. In England Henry VII granted such an augmentation to a Venetian representative as early as 1506, and the practice was not abandoned in London until 1763.[16] France, the papacy, Poland and perhaps other states, also honoured Venetian ambassadors in these ways, while in 1603 the doge in Venice knighted a group of seven ambassadors sent to him by the Grisons league in Switzerland, and in 1621 James I did the same for six deputies sent to London by the Dutch republic. But this was no more than a politeness with little political meaning, and one which disappeared, though slowly, during the seventeenth and eighteenth centuries.

More important, the practice of rulers or their representatives, in circumstances charged with religious symbolism, swearing solemn and public oaths to observe a treaty was now also disappearing. It was slow to vanish. Abraham de Wicquefort, when in 1681 he published the best-known and most widely read work on diplomacy produced anywhere in early modern Europe, could still speak of the formal witnessing of a royal oath to keep a treaty of peace or alliance as one of the obvious reasons for the sending of an extraordinary ambassador.[17] However, after the end of the sixteenth century provision for ceremonies of this kind becomes rarer and is found mainly in treaties to which Spain was a signatory. The last case of the taking of such an oath seems to be the despatch in the 1770s of a group of representatives of the Swiss cantons to Paris to swear to the

16. A.R. Wagner and A.C. Cole, 'The Venetian Ambassador's Augmentation', *The Coat of Arms*, iii (1954–5), 80–3, 130–5. I am indebted to Dr David Starkey for this reference.

17. A. de Wicquefort, *L'Ambassadeur et ses fonctions* (Cologne, 1720; first published 1681), i, 443.

observance of an agreement just made with the French government. But long before this the custom, in an atmosphere with a much lower religious charge than in the past and an age when, for all their obvious defects, standards of international conduct were higher than in the mêlée of the early sixteenth century, had lost any real significance. In rather the same way the practice of giving hostages for the due execution of a treaty, quite common in the distrustful atmosphere of the sixteenth century, was last seen in operation in 1748, when two British peers were sent to Paris as guarantees of the restitution by Britain of the conquests she had made in north America at the expense of France.

The maintenance of diplomats by the states to which they were sent, still common in the sixteenth century, ebbed away in western Europe in that which followed. Here again the ideas and practices of the past showed considerable vitality. The most important English writer of the seventeenth century on international law still thought in its middle years that 'the reception of ambassadors further requires that hospitality should be provided befitting their rank, and necessaries supplied to them',[18] and practice varied considerably between different states. The Dutch showed themselves remarkably conservative in this respect; but elsewhere in the west the practice fairly rapidly died out. In England Charles I decided soon after his accession no longer to provide for the 'diet' of foreign diplomats in London. In the Ottoman empire and Russia, states very much on the periphery of European diplomacy and seen still as un-European, such traditions proved much more tenacious. In Constantinople the Porte, until far into the eighteenth century, paid to representatives of the western states a maintenance allowance (*ta'in*) graduated according to their rank.[19] Russian diplomats in west-European capitals until the end of the seventeenth century expected to be maintained by the rulers to whom they were accredited, and often complained vociferously when they were treated less generously than they had expected. In 1662 the English government allocated £2,000 to meet the costs of maintaining a Russian ambassador during his short stay in London; and two decades later another, after much argument, forced his hosts to allow him £100 a week – twice as much as he had originally been offered. His embassy cost £3,000 in all. Another in 1687 was less lucky and was obliged to be satisfied with only £50 a week.[20] This obligation to maintain visiting

18. R. Zouch, *Juris et judicii fecialis . . . explicatio* (Washington, 1911; first published 1650), ii, 21.

19. B. Spuler, 'Europäische Diplomaten in Konstantinopel bis zum Frieden von Belgrad (1739)', *Jahrbücher für Geschichte Osteuropas*, i (1936), 212–13.

20. *Calendar of State Papers Domestic, 1660–1661* (London, 1860), p. 505; I. Vinogradoff, 'Russian Missions to London, 1569–1687', *Oxford Slavonic Papers*, New Series, xiv (1981), 52, 59–60, 65.

embassies was a mutual one, however. Those which went to Moscow from the west were fed by the Russian government; and the ceremonial presentation each day of food to the foreigners was considered of such symbolic importance that it was kept up even during the terrible famine of 1601–03, the worst in all Russian history.[21] But arrangements of this kind were always liable to generate disputes. An English observer much involved in these problems complained of Russian diplomats in 1673 that 'it is their Custome, to think, whatsoever they get, too little, and whatever they give, too much', while in 1698 an embassy sent by the Emperor Leopold I to Moscow argued that in future, to avoid such disagreements, the tsar and the Holy Roman Emperor should each be responsible for the maintenance of their own embassies in the way now generally accepted in Europe.[22] After the revolution in relations with western Europe produced by Peter I the undignified haggling over money which had marked so many of the short-lived Russian embassies of the past disappeared. Nevertheless, as late as the 1740s, the British government was still contributing to the cost of housing the now permanent Russian representatives in London at a rate proportional to their diplomatic rank – £200 a year for ministers-resident, £400 for envoys or ambassadors.[23] However, this was merely a hangover from the past; and after the middle of the century even these payments ceased.

Many of the tangible rewards of diplomatic life changed little, at least in the seventeenth century. An ambassador could still expect, at the end of his mission, to receive from the ruler to whom he had been accredited a farewell present which was often, particularly for special ambassadors of high social rank, of considerable value. This was an area where susceptibilities could be all too easily hurt and bad feeling aroused. Venice, intensely touchy about its international status[24], was particularly liable to take umbrage if one of its representatives were not offered such a present or were offered one of less value than expected: the failure of the duke of Savoy to make a gift to a departing Venetian ambassador in 1603, for example, aroused notably bad feeling in the republic. On the other hand an ambassador might refuse a present because he thought it insultingly small, because his mission had been unsuccessful, or because it seemed that the monarch he represented was about to go to war with the one whose

---

21. R.E.F. Smith and D. Christian, *Bread and Salt; A Social and Economic History of Food and Drink in Russia* (Cambridge, 1984), pp. 117–8, 121.

22. Vinogradoff, 'Russian Missions', 54; J.-G. Korb, *Diary of an Austrian Secretary of Legation at the Court of Peter the Great* (London, 1863), i, 12.

23. I. Vinogradoff, 'Russian Missions to London, 1711–1789', *Oxford Slavonic Papers*, New Series, xv (1982), 54–5.

24. See below, p. 59.

court he was leaving. In 1665 Lord Holles, when he left Paris, rejected for this reason a valuable diamond offered him by Louis XIV.

The leaving present given to an ambassador could still take a variety of different forms. During the seventeenth century in England 'gilt plate', its weight carefully graded to accord with the importance and traditional status of the ruler who, through his representative, was being honoured in this way, was the most normal gift. Thus, in 1614 James I, believing that he was making presents more valuable than his ambassadors at foreign courts were receiving, ordered that in future the French and Spanish resident ambassadors, who had hitherto been given 4,000 ounces of plate on their departure, should in future receive only half as much and that the representatives of lesser states should also have their customary allowance cut by half.[25] Presents of this kind to resident heads of mission were everywhere more standardised and governed by tradition than those to the more glamorous extraordinary ambassadors, whose duties and length of stay were so extremely variable. For minor members of foreign missions, of whom ambassadors' secretaries were the most important, gold chains continued during much of the seventeenth century to be a very common form of gift all over Europe. But such presents varied greatly. An extraordinary ambassador of particularly high standing, or one whom it was desired to honour markedly, could be given very valuable jewels and other luxury goods. The Maréchal de Cadenet, a French ambassador on a special mission who stayed in London for only a few days in 1621, was given by James I jewellery said to be worth £2,500, while the duke of Buckingham, the king's favourite, presented him with ponies and four albino falcons, the latter much prized by huntsmen. The Maréchal de Bassompierre, again a military man, after another brief embassy to London five years later, was given by Charles I 'four diamonds set in a lozenge, and a great stone at the end': this was said to be worth £7,000 and was perhaps the most valuable present ever given by any English ruler to a foreign diplomat. Moreover, Bassompierre also received from the new French-born queen, Henrietta Maria, 'a very fine diamond'.[26] These were both embassies with a large symbolic and ceremonial element: envoys of this kind were often given presents whose significance was also purely symbolic and which bore no relationship to the length of their stay or to the importance of the issues with which they were concerned. An imperial ambassador who in 1622 spent only eleven days in London and

25. Sir John Finett, *Finetti Philoxenis: Som Choice Observations . . . touching the Reception . . . of Forren Ambassadors in England* (London, 1656), pp. 30–1.

26. C.H. Carter, *The Secret Diplomacy of the Habsburgs, 1598–1625* (New York–London, 1964), p. 191; *Memoirs of the Embassy of the Marshal de Bassompierre to the Court of England in 1626*, ed. J.W. Croker (London, 1819), pp. 107, 111.

achieved nothing of significance nevertheless received a present worth £1,600 on his departure.[27] Resident ambassadors were usually less generously treated. Occasionally presents to them took a peculiar and inconvenient form. It was not uncommon for foreign representatives in Sweden to be given a quantity of copper, the only Swedish product for which there was a ready international market, which they could sell on their return home. Bulstrode Whitelocke, English ambassador there in 1653–54, was given £2,500 worth of the metal which was eventually cast into guns for the navy (though he also received a miniature of Queen Christina in a diamond setting and the heir to the throne, the future Charles X, gave him a gold box set on one side with diamonds and with Charles's portrait on the other).[28]

The second half of the seventeenth century saw a distinct movement away from the erratic lavishness which had marked much of this aspect of international relations in earlier decades. As diplomacy became more of a distinct profession, with standards more clear-cut than in the past, the feeling grew that present-giving should be regulated and kept within reasonable limits. In 1651 the Dutch republic forbade its diplomats to accept gifts from foreign governments; and in 1692 regulations were issued in Sweden which for the first time specified the value of those to be given to foreign representatives on their departure. In England P.I. Potemkin was the last Russian ambassador, in 1681, to arrive in London bearing gifts to be presented in semi-oriental style to the king; he was also the last to receive a present in the traditional manner when he left.[29] However, the role of gifts and 'gratifications' of many different kinds in international relations remained substantial throughout the later seventeenth and eighteenth centuries. The States-General might have reservations about presents to departing diplomats; but none the less it gave 'the usual respect' of 6,000 guilders to an English ambassador when he left The Hague in 1670, with 600 more for his secretary. Three years earlier, on the conclusion of an Anglo-Dutch peace treaty, it had already voted the same man a gold chain and a medal worth another 6,000.[30] A diplomat who helped to bring peace between two belligerent states by mediating between them might be particularly well rewarded. A century later John Murray, the British ambassador in Constantinople, bitterly

27. *Finetti Philoxenis*, p. 101.

28. *Journal of the Swedish Embassy in the Years 1653 and 1654. Impartially written by the Ambassador Bulstrode Whitelocke*, ed. H. Reeve (London, 1855), ii, 181, 198.

29. Ragnhild Hatton, 'Gratifications and Foreign Policy: Anglo-French Rivalry in Sweden during the Nine Years War', in Ragnhild Hatton and J.S. Bromley (eds), *William III and Louis XIV: Essays 1680–1720 by and for Mark A. Thomson* (Liverpool, 1968), p. 69fn.; Vinogradoff, 'Russian Missions to London, 1569–1687', 51.

30. K.H.D. Haley, *An English Diplomat in the Low Countries: Sir William Temple and John de Witt* (Oxford, 1986), pp. 181, 280.

regretted that in 1774 he had not been able to act as mediator in the making of the Russo-Turkish peace of Kutchuk–Kainardji and thus gain the valuable presents from both sides which would have been his reward. This feeling was shared by his Prussian and Habsburg colleagues, who had cherished the same hopes.[31] As late as 1792, Sir Robert Ainslie, Murray's successor, complained that by not being called on to mediate in the peace negotiations which had just produced the Russo-Turkish treaty of Jassy he had lost the opportunity to make about £30,000 in presents from both sides,[32] though this was probably a great exaggeration.

Diplomacy could still be made an uncomfortable and even dangerous profession by the slowness and physical difficulty of communications and by the inconveniences of life in the smaller and more remote capitals. This was, as before, most obvious in eastern and northern Europe, a world of long distances and often almost non-existent roads. But even contacts between the most developed states of the west could on occasion, as in previous generations, demand from diplomats a good deal of physical hardihood. Part of the suite of a French special ambassador to London in 1626, on their return journey to Paris, spent no less than five days on the Dover–Calais crossing in very bad weather. During it they were forced to throw into the sea both the ambassador's carriages, containing more than 40,000 livres worth of his clothes, while twenty-nine of his horses died of thirst. Moreover, the fact that the embassy had already been delayed in Dover for a fortnight had cost him 14,000 crowns even before these further disasters.[33] Almost seventy years later the English envoy to Savoy was shipwrecked off the coast of Sardinia and very nearly drowned, with the loss of all his papers and equipage. These are merely two of many illustrations of the dangers of travel by sea, even though this was often easier, especially over long distances, than movement by land. It was normal, moreover, as in earlier generations, for a diplomat going to one of the more out-of-the-way capitals, if he expected to stay for any length of time, to equip himself with a mass of essentials which might be difficult or impossible to obtain at his destination. Thus an English ambassador going to Stockholm in the mid-seventeenth century took with him a great quantity of household goods and even food 'hard to be met with in Sweden', as well as enough horses to fill a ship hired specially to carry them. His precautions were justified, for when he reached Sweden it proved difficult even to find accommodation for his servants.[34] A

---

31. Public Record Office, State Papers Foreign, S.P.97/50, Murray to Lord Rochford, 3 August, 1774, No. 17.

32. British Library, Additional MSS 38229, f.161.

33. *Memoirs . . . Bassompierre*, p. 119.

34. Whitelocke, *Journal*, i, 79, 278.

generation later, another, bound for so great a centre of civilisation as Paris, still found it necessary to take with him sixty boxes of household goods and twenty of food, seven or eight dozen chairs and armchairs, a coach, a chaise and twenty horses.[35] Courts which were still in constant movement and countries with little in the way of a fixed capital, such as Sweden, were particularly uncomfortable and trying. Perhaps the most difficult of all was Poland where, as a French secret agent complained in the 1670s, the court 'ran about like a troop of gipsies'.[36]

As time went on, the slow growth of Europe's wealth, and the even slower improvement of its communications, did something to reduce this sort of inconvenience, expense and even physical danger. But at the outbreak of the French revolution there were still capitals where life for a diplomat was uncomfortable and unattractive. Physical discomforts, however, were now partially offset by the fact that the legal immunities of diplomats were becoming more clearly defined and generally recognised than in the past. The questions about their nature and extent which had exercised lawyers in the sixteenth century were not completely answered in the seventeenth and eighteenth. But the position did become clearer in various respects; and the problems and disputes which arose were seldom so acute or threatening as they had sometimes been in the past. From Grotius onwards there was increasing agreement that diplomats were entitled to a high degree of immunity from civil or criminal proceedings of any kind. There was now no doubt that an ambassador and his suite had an absolute right to the free practice of their religion, even though it differed from that established in the country where they were stationed. Sometimes diplomats stretched or abused this right to support dissident religious minorities, to the annoyance of the governments with which they had to deal. In the 1650s the Venetian representative in London maintained more than twenty Catholic priests who ministered to the numerous English Catholics who filled the embassy chapel to overflowing. Later French Huguenots were to use the Dutch embassy in Paris in much the same way. The anger generated by this sort of situation among English Protestants underlay the mob destruction of the chapels attached to the Bavarian and Sardinian legations during the Gordon Riots of 1780; but in general religious frictions of this kind were not a serious source of difficulty. Legal opinion moved steadily in favour of the absolute immunity of anyone with diplomatic status from the jurisdiction of the host state. 'I deny', wrote the most important eighteenth-century commentator on the subject, 'that anyone can reach a decision through

35. Ruth Clark, *Sir William Trumbull in Paris, 1685–1686* (Cambridge, 1938), pp. 18–19.
36. Martine Rémusat, 'Un ambassadeur de France en Pologne', *Revue de Paris*, Sept.–Oct., 1919, 569.

duly constituted judicial procedure in regard to the life, property, and reputation of the ambassador except the prince who sent him or the magistrate to whose jurisdiction he was formerly subject'.[37] This was not yet a universally accepted point of view. As late as the 1760s an influential theorist could still argue that an ambassador who, on his own initiative, encouraged sedition within the state to which he was accredited, could be punished by it even with death, while if he had acted on the orders of his master he could be held as a hostage until the latter had given satisfaction.[38] There were still eighteenth-century examples, some of them politically important, of the arrest of diplomats for alleged plotting against the state in which they were stationed. Counts Gyllenborg and Görtz, the Swedish ministers in London and The Hague, suffered this fate in 1717. So, two years later, did the Prince de Cellamare, the Spanish ambassador in Paris: his arrest was followed by an effort by the Spanish government to seize his French counterpart in Madrid (who was forewarned and escaped). But by the later decades of the century such conduct was becoming increasingly unthinkable.

The immunity of diplomats from civil proceedings was also being more and more clearly asserted. This was a process which extended over a long period, and in the seventeenth century the extent of their privileges in this respect was still far from clear. In 1666 the Portuguese minister-resident in the Dutch republic had his household goods seized for debt; and when, two years later, he attempted to leave for Portugal his creditors secured a court order for his arrest.[39] The most important and spectacular case, however, came in London when, in September 1708, A.A. Matveev, the Russian minister, was arrested on the complaint of a number of tradesmen to whom he owed money. He spent only a few hours in prison; but when he was released the heads of all the foreign missions in London (except that of Sweden, which was then at war with Russia) accompanied him to his house in a demonstration of solidarity and next morning visited him to promise their support. The following year saw the passing by Parliament of legislation protecting foreign diplomats against criminal and civil proceedings – the most explicit undertaking of this kind hitherto given by any state – and a special mission to Moscow to apologise to Peter I for the insult offered to his representative. It was still possible, however, for the issue of civil immunity to cause difficulties. A generation or more later, Baron Cederhielm, the Holstein envoy in Paris and chamberlain to the king of Sweden, was sent to the Châtelet prison at the

---

37. Bynkershoek, *De foro legatorum* . . . , pp. 132–3.

38. J.-J. Burlamaqui, *Suite des principes du droit politique* (Geneva–Copenhagen, 1764), iii, 213–15.

39. Bynkershoek, *De foro legatorum* . . . , p. 65.

demand of his creditors, while in 1772 the Hessian minister in the French capital was officially warned that his furniture could be seized and he himself refused a passport to leave the country if he failed to pay what he owed.[40] Moreover, there were still jurists prepared to justify such action.[41] But the whole drift of events was towards a widening and consolidation of the immunities claimed by diplomats in the performance of their duties. ABUSE OF IMMUNITIES

These diplomats, as in earlier generations, were by no means always scrupulous in their use of their privileges. Everywhere they enjoyed exemption from customs duties on goods to be used by themselves and their households. It was therefore tempting, and usually easy, to import excessive quantities of goods and then resell them at a profit to local merchants, 'from whom', wrote Callières in 1697, 'they receive a tribute, for lending their names to defraud the Sovereign of his dues'. Two generations later Horace Walpole complained that in London the Spanish ambassador was 'almost the only envoy from a foreign court who disdained to turn his exalted office to trading purposes'.[42] More serious was the way in which, in one or two capitals, foreign envoys used their rights of immunity not merely to shelter criminals in the embassy or legation but also to exclude the local police from a considerable area around it. They could thus create, ostensibly in defence of their rights, islands of lawlessness in which criminals could take sanctuary and defy the forces of law and order. This was seen at its most extreme in Rome. There an unsuccessful effort in 1687 by Innocent XI to end such rights claimed by the French ambassador, the Marquis de Lavardin, led to a bitter dispute. (The pope may have been influenced by the fact that three years earlier the Spanish government had limited the right of asylum in Madrid, where it had also been quite unjustifiably extended, to the houses of foreign ambassadors.) Lavardin entered the city with 800 armed men, repossessed his embassy by force and was then excommunicated: these events produced the most active controversy on diplomatic immunities of the entire early modern period.[43] By the eighteenth century the position in Rome had become so impossible (since not merely considerable areas around foreign embassies but also churches and the houses of cardinals offered refuge to criminals) that the papal police had to be equipped with special maps to show them which streets they were permitted to pass

40. Th. Funck-Brentano, 'Le droit des gens et les immunités diplomatiques au XVIIIe siècle', *Revue d'Histoire Diplomatique* (1892), 550.
41. For example, Burlamaqui, *Suite des principes*, iii, 218.
42. *The Art of Diplomacy*, pp. 118–19; *Journal of the Reign of George III* (London, 1859), i, 112–13.
43. Hrabar, *De legatorum jure tractatum* . . . , pp. 197–229, refers to twelve publications on it which appeared in various languages in 1688 and prints long extracts from two of them.

through.[44] Similar, though less extreme, French claims in Venice, where the ambassador demanded that any holder of a 'patent de familiarité' signed by him must be considered a member of his household, led to a long breach between the two states in 1710–23 and renewed friction in the later 1720s. Excesses of this sort, however, did not alter the fact that in most respects the legal status of diplomats was, by the eighteenth century, more securely and satisfactorily established than ever before.

## The great preoccupation; ceremonial and procedure

A more significant legacy of the past was the continuing intense sensitivity over diplomatic ceremonial and appearances of all kinds. One obvious aspect of this was the attention which continued to be given throughout the seventeenth century to the public entry of a newly arrived ambassador to the capital in which he was taking up his post. This remained, as in previous generations, an ostentatious display of the greatness and wealth of the ruler he represented. Sometimes for this reason civic dignitaries or merchants trading with the country from which the ambassador came would turn out to swell the column of men and vehicles and deepen the impression made on those who watched. This was, again as in the past, a genuine form of public entertainment; printed programmes giving details of the time and place of the entry and of the carriages and costumes were sometimes sold to potential spectators.[45] Elaborate descriptions, usually illustrated with engravings showing the sumptuous costumes and the carving and gilding of the coaches, might be published to commemorate the event.[46] In eastern Europe organised ostentation of this kind remained important on occasion until late in the eighteenth century, well after it had ceased to have much significance in the west. In 1775, for instance, there were extremely elaborate entries into each other's capitals by the Russian and Turkish ambassadors charged with the ratification of the peace-treaty between the two states signed in the previous year.[47] But more important, and certainly more divisive, than such occasions was the endlessly controversial and emotionally potent question of precedence.

Throughout the seventeenth century, and far into the eighteenth, the issue of precedence continued to arouse strong feeling and generate

44. G. Maugain, 'Rome et le gouvernement pontifical au XVIIIe siècle, d'après les voyageurs français', in H. Bedarida and others (eds), *L'Italie au XVIIIe siède* (Paris, 1929), p. 64.

45. See the general discussion in W.J. Roosen, *The Age of Louis XIV: The Rise of Modern Diplomacy* (Cambridge, Mass., 1976), pp. 114–16.

46. The best English example is probably J.M. Wright, *An Account of . . . Roger, Earl of Castlemaine's Embassy . . . to His Holiness Innocent XI* (London, 1688).

47. They are described in *Mubadele – An Ottoman–Russian Exchange of Ambassadors*, annotated and translated by N. Itzkowitz and M. More (Chicago–London, 1970), pp. 91–5, 157–62.

disputes as it had done in earlier generations. 'Points of honour, rank, precedence, are the most delicate articles of political faith', wrote a well-informed commentator as late as 1746. 'Princes cede towns, even provinces, but all the ability of the most adroit negotiators cannot decide them to give up a rank which they believe to be their right'.[48] This scale of values, he went on, was justified by both history and necessity. Sharp hereditary inequalities between the different social orders were essential to the existence of any society. But if a recognised and accepted scale of ranks were needed within a particular society it was just as essential within the international one made up of different states which Europe was increasingly becoming. In this greater society 'there must be in the first place a certain order of ranks between the chiefs of these particular ones. Without this they could not communicate with one another, if each claimed to take the first place'.[49] This was an unusually clear and succinct statement of assumptions which had been current for generations. Few writers, however, wasted much time on theoretical justifications of this sort. Instead they produced a copious literature on more or less specific issues, highly legalistic, repetitive and partisan, very frequently inspired merely by the need to justify some particular national or dynastic claim. 'Every state', wrote a historian at the end of the eighteenth century when such questions had lost much of their earlier emotional charge, 'while contending for this high and delicate point, has brought forward every sort of argument, however weighty, or however trivial, which could apply exclusively to itself'.[50] In all this writing the emphasis was usually very heavily, as in the past, on the obligation of the diplomat to defend jealously the honour of the sovereign he represented against any claim, any change in ceremonial, which might be construed as the slightest threat to it. This was still universally seen, at least until well into the eighteenth century, as one of his most important duties, perhaps the most important of all. 'An ambassador', wrote an anonymous author of the early seventeenth century, 'must not permit or allow anyone to challenge or in any other way offend the honour of his Prince on any subject at all', while more than sixty years later Wicquefort could still assume that ceremonial niceties must be an essential preoccupation of any diplomat.[51] Such assumptions, and the need for perpetual watchfulness which they implied, inevitably had an inhibiting effect. 'An ambassador', wrote a

---

48. J. Rousset de Missy, *Mémoires sur le rang et la préséance entre les souverains de l'Europe* (Amsterdam, 1746), Aux lecteurs.

49. Rousset de Missy, *Mémoires*, p. 4.

50. R. Ward, *An Enquiry into the Foundation and History of the Law of Nations in Europe* (London, 1795), ii, 381.

51. E. Griselle, (ed.), 'Un manuel du parfait diplomate au dix-septième siècle', *Revue d'Histoire Diplomatique* 1915, 775; Wicquefort, *L'Ambassadeur*, i, 416.

member of the staff of the Spanish embassy in London in the 1690s, 'should be specially careful to maintain the authority of his position and assert his prerogatives, as for instance in not giving the door or the right hand to any minister or individual, whether of his own country or another. . . . I refer to the ceremony of offering the door, the chair or the right-hand seat in the coach'.[52] When any number of heads of diplomatic missions were assembled in one place, even on the most innocent social occasion, there was always in the seventeenth century, as much as in the preceding one, a likelihood of trouble. When in 1619, to take an illuminating example, all the foreign ambassadors in London were invited to watch a display of tilting on the birthday of James I the occasion provided a remarkable exhibition of the complications which could arise. Elaborate precautions were taken to avoid disputes over precedence between the representatives of France and Spain (the long-standing rivalry between these two states was the most serious potential source of this kind of friction) by placing them both on the king's right and at the same distance from him. However, the Frenchman complained that the Spaniard could be seen by the king whereas he could not; and in any case, he argued, the rulers of France claimed precedence over those of Spain, not merely parity with them. He therefore refused to attend or to allow his wife to. The Venetian ambassador complained that though the republic had always been treated as the equal of the kingdoms of Europe he had been offered a place which did not fully reflect this. Then the Dutch representative in his turn alleged that he was being asked to accept a position implying mere equality with that of the duke of Savoy, which was contrary to his instructions: he therefore also refused to attend. The Savoyard himself did not appear on the day, apparently because he was unsure whether to give precedence to the representative of the king of Bohemia (the 'Winter King' Frederick of the Palatinate); but his absence at once made the Venetian ambassador fear that Savoy, perhaps with French or Spanish help, was intriguing to threaten the precedence claimed by the republic.[53] Such a chapter of accidents, however ridiculous in modern eyes, epitomised a genuinely important aspect of international relations. Its importance was institutionalised in the emergence from the later sixteenth century onwards in many states of officials whose duty it was to supervise the reception of foreign diplomatic representatives and smooth out differences between them on questions of ceremonial and precedence. Such were the *conducteur des ambassadeurs* and *maître des*

52. H.J. Chaytor, 'Embajada espanola. An anonymous contemporary Spanish guide to diplomatic procedure in the last quarter of the seventeenth century', Royal Historical Society, *Camden Miscellany* xiv (London, 1926), 7.
53. *Finetti Philoxenis*, pp. 64–6.

*cérémonies* in France, the *conductor de los embajadores* in Spain, and the master of ceremonies in England.[54]

A number of well-established general principles were accepted as regulating precedence. It was still widely agreed that, as laid down in the papal ranking of 1504, the Holy Roman Emperor came first of all secular rulers, and this pre-eminence all emperors jealously guarded: it was only after considerable resistance that Ferdinand III (1637–57) agreed to address Louis XIV as 'Majesté Royale'.[55] There was also general, though not complete, agreement that hereditary monarchs ranked above merely elective ones (in spite of the fact that the Holy Roman Emperor was himself elected, at least in form) and that republics ranked lower than any kind of monarchy. But this left many problems unsolved and in the prevailing state of feeling insoluble. In particular the emergence as significant factors in international relations of new or growing states with new or heightened claims to precedence raised difficult questions. Venice was generally agreed to be a sort of honorary kingdom. Nevertheless, the Venetian government always felt its position to be somewhat ambiguous and was correspondingly sensitive to anything that seemed even remotely to challenge it. Venetian diplomats were likely to demand every ceremonial honour to which they could assert any shred of claim, and to be very touchy when faced with any apparent threat, however slight, to their status. The three special ambassadors sent to James II in 1685, for example, to congratulate him on his coronation and ask for English help against the Turks, unsuccessfully demanded privileges which were regarded as quite unjustified – to be 'conducted' at their audience with the king by a duke rather than as usual a mere earl and for their coaches to be allowed to enter the courtyard of the royal palace.[56] The position during the seventeenth century of the duchy of Savoy was much more uncertain than that of Venice. Its ruler was not, until in 1713 he acquired the title of king of Sicily as part of the Utrecht settlement, formally entitled to royal honours. In the 1620s the Danish ambassador in London, representing a monarch, refused to pay a courtesy call on his Savoyard colleague; this he felt would be demeaning in view of the difference in rank between their principals.[57] Yet by then the duchy was already becoming a power of some significance because of its position astride several of the most important routes across the Alps and its growing,

54.  See in general A.J. Loomie, 'The Conducteur des Ambassadeurs of Seventeenth-Century France and Spain', *Revue Belge de Philologie et d'Histoire*, 52 (1975) 333–56.
55.  Rousset de Missy, *Mémoires*, p. 13.
56.  'Embajada espanola', p. 23.
57.  *Finetti Philoxenis*, pp. 232–3.

though still limited, military strength. There was thus a discrepancy between the increasing importance of the dukes in international affairs and the position to which they were relegated in terms of formal honours; and as the seventeenth century progressed many governments became willing to regard them as *de facto* royal. When Charles Emmanuel II died, in 1675, special envoys bringing news of his death were treated in both Paris and London as the representatives of a king: both Charles II and Louis XIV wore violet mourning, the colour appropriate for a royal death. In 1696 Louis agreed to give the duke the title of 'Royal Highness' in all public acts and to treat his representatives in France as those of a monarch.[58]

The most striking and important example of a conflict between the real significance of a state and the ceremonial treatment to which its representatives were entitled, however, was that of the Dutch republic. By the beginning of the seventeenth century it was the greatest commercial and financial power in Europe, as well as a very significant military one. Yet, in spite of the leading position in its political life of the Orange family, it was also clearly not a monarchy in the normal sense of that term: its representatives were therefore not entitled to be treated as those of a crowned head. But as time went on, the new state, conscious of its strength and achievements, became less and less willing to accept this situation. The instructions given to the Dutch negotiators at the Munster peace congress which began its work in 1645 insisted on their being treated on the same footing as those of Venice; and by the end of the century Dutch ambassadors in Paris were claiming royal honours. In his last years even Louis XIV was giving the Dutch republic the treatment in this respect which it demanded.[59] England suffered to some extent from a similar gulf between her real power and her ceremonial status during the Interregnum of 1649–60, a gulf in this case deepened by the widespread hostility aroused by the execution of Charles I. For several years the standing of the representatives abroad of the various Commonwealth governments was seriously weakened by the disappearance of the monarchy: in 1654, for example, the Danish ambassador in Sweden claimed precedence over his English equivalent since the latter was acting for Cromwell, a mere protector, not for an anointed king.[60] Yet here again political realities asserted themselves. Whitelocke, the English

58. W. Roosen, 'Early Modern Diplomatic Ceremonial: A Systems Approach', *Journal of Modern History*, 52 (September, 1980), 464.

59. R.M. Hatton, 'Louis XIV and his Fellow-Monarchs', in *Louis XIV and the Craft of Kingship*, ed. J. Rule (Columbus, Ohio, 1969), p. 157.

60. Whitelocke, *Journal*, ii, 107–9.

ambassador, found his treatment by the Swedes and his ability to negotiate with them unaffected by ceremonial niceties.

In other words the rules of precedence and other aspects of diplomatic ceremonial were not immutable. However slowly, the forms tended over time to reflect the facts. A government which wished to show goodwill, or the reverse, to another could send the appropriate signals by variations, sometimes subtle ones, in its attitude to ceremonial matters. The symbolism which these involved, and which was indeed their essence, was frequently manipulated for political purposes.[61] When in 1732, to quote only two British cases, the representative of George II in Turin was promoted from minister plenipotentiary to full ambassador, this was a clear indication of a desire in London to improve relations between the two states (especially as the diplomat in question was an earl), while simultaneously the strained Anglo-Prussian relations of the 1730s were reflected in the fact that Britain was represented in Berlin throughout the decade by a mere secretary (and he a humble army captain).

Many of the manifestations of this passionate interest in ceremonial and precedence were not particularly dangerous. They could be seen in constant arguments in every European court, as in the past, about the relative positions of diplomats on formal and even informal occasions, their placing at table at meals where more than one was present, the precise way in which they were conducted to their first audience with the ruler to whom they were accredited, when and whether they stood or sat at such audiences, the precise moment when they or the ruler removed their hats, and a variety of such tremendous niceties. There was no necessary relationship between the real importance of a state and the willingness of its ruler and his representatives to make a fuss over things of this sort. Seventeenth-century Russia, poor, remote, deeply xenophobic, was not generally seen as part of the European political system at all. Not until the exhausting struggles with Sweden and Poland in 1654–67 did she show real signs of growth and expansion. Only after the truce of 1686 with the Poles was it clear that she might well be the force of the future in eastern Europe. Yet throughout the seventeenth century no diplomats were more pertinacious than those of Russia in asserting what they claimed as the honorific rights of their master. The 'ceremonious stomachs' of Russian ambassadors 'whose Nation stands so much on Ceremony' were the subject of comment in England in the early years of the century, as they had already been in the reign of Elizabeth.[62]

---

61. This aspect of the subject is explored in some detail in Roosen, 'Early Modern Diplomatic Ceremonial', passim.

62. *Finetti Philoxenis*, p. 46.

Certainly, some of the claims they advanced were extreme even by the standards of so punctilious an age. In 1614 the Prince of Wales himself had to be excluded from a dinner at which the Russian ambassador was to be present, since it was feared that the latter would refuse to accept a place on the king's left if the prince were seated on his right. Sixty years later, in a yet more striking case, the newly arrived Russian ambassador to Denmark, finding that the king, Christian V, was in bed and too ill to receive him, insisted on having another bed provided on which he could lie side by side with the king so that they could talk.[63]

The same intensity of punctilio was to be seen in the treatment of foreign diplomats in Russia. There the government even lent ceremonial costumes from the treasury to poor members of the tsar's council, the *boyarskaya duma*, so that they could make a suitably impressive show when an envoy from the west was officially received in Moscow.[64] When, in another striking instance, the earl of Carlisle reached the capital in 1664 as ambassador from Charles II, he had a long argument with the official deputed to receive him as to which should first descend from his sledge when they met formally. Finally it was agreed that both should get down at the same moment. However the Russian 'tooke occasion to deceive his Excellence, and falsify his word, hanging in the aire betwixt the armes of his servants, and but touching the earth with his tiptoes, whilst the Ambassador came out freely'.[65] Moreover, no ruler had a title longer or more complex than that of the tsar; and none was more ready to resent the omission of even the smallest part of it. In 1629 the Tsar Mikhail severely reproved Louis XIII himself for failing to use his full title in official letters and warned him that 'We cannot approve your habit of wishing to be our friend and yet denying and taking from us the titles and qualities which almighty God has given us and which we so justly possess.' If France wanted good relations with Russia his full title (which he carefully recited) must be used in all future letters, for it was the duty of friends 'rather to augment reciprocally their titles and qualities than to diminish or curtail them'.[66] Even the size of the sheets of paper on which the tsar's letters were written varied, at least in the early seventeenth century, according to the status of the ruler to whom they were addressed. The Holy Roman Emperor, the shah of Persia and the sultan in Constantinople were honoured with large sheets (the fact that two of the

63. *Finetti Philoxenis*, p. 25; Vinogradoff, 'Russian Missions to London, 1569–1687', 52.

64. R.O. Crummey, *Aristocrats and Servitors: The Boyar Elite in Russia, 1613–1689* (Princeton, 1983), pp. 42, 59–61.

65. (G. Miège), *A Relation of Three Embassies from His Sacred Majestie Charles II . . . Performed by . . . The Earle of Carlisle in the Years 1663 and 1664* (London, 1669), pp. 131–2.

66. *Recueil des Instructions données aux ambassadeurs et ministres de France . . . Russie*, i, ed. A. Rambaud (Paris, 1890), 29.

three were non-European illustrates how large a role Asia still played in Russian foreign policy), while the kings of Sweden, Poland, England and Denmark had to be content with smaller ones. The official seals attached to these letters were protected by cases; but these were decorated when the letter was being sent to one of the greater rulers and merely plain when a less important one was being addressed.[67]

Contemporaries, even the men themselves involved in heated arguments over matters of ceremonial, were often well aware that most of these questions were trivial. Such disputes, wrote a successful English diplomat in the 1670s, 'seem to me but so many impertinencies that are grown this last age into the character of Ambassadors; having been raised and cultivated by men, who, wanting other talents to value themselves upon in those employments, endeavoured to do it by exactness or niceties in the forms'.[68] There were even occasional suggestions that relations between states be eased and simplified by abandoning the whole idea of an order of precedence betwen sovereigns. The Swedish king Gustavus Adolphus in the early 1630s, faced with a struggle between rival English and French ambassadors, dismissed such contests as futile since all kings had their authority directly from God and thus were equal in status.[69] But ceremonial and precedence none the less remained until well into the eighteenth century a factor of importance in international relations. They could even bring major states to the brink of war. The best and best-known example of this is the battle fought in the streets of London in 1661 between the retinues of the French and Spanish ambassadors, the culmination of two centuries of bitter competition of this kind. The official entry to the English capital of a new Swedish ambassador became the occasion for a struggle over which of the two rivals should give way to the other; in this almost fifty men were killed and wounded. The Spaniards were heavily outnumbered (the French ambassador, d'Estrades, had prepared for a struggle by bringing to London a number of officers from regiments commanded by himself and his son as well as soldiers from the garrison of Gravelines, on the northern coast of France); but they none the less won the immediate contest by cutting the traces of the horses pulling the French ambassador's coach. Louis XIV, young, anxious to assert his personal and dynastic prestige and conscious of ruling the most powerful state in Europe, reacted vigorously. (He claimed in his memoirs that the Spanish ambassador had planned the incident and had spent almost 500,000 livres in organising and arming a mob of 2,000 men

67. W.E.D. Allen, ed., *Russian Embassies to the Georgian Kings (1589–1605)* (Cambridge, 1970), i, 413fn.

68. Sir William Temple, *Works* (London, 1754), i, 287.

69. F. Dickmann, *Der Westfälische Friede* (Munster, 1959), p. 210.

to attack d'Estrades and his retinue.)[70] Spain, exhausted and virtually bankrupt, was forced by the threat of war to give way. In March of the following year her ambassador in Paris publicly apologised and promised that in future she would recognise French claims to precedence. This was the most spectacular humiliation suffered by any major European state during the seventeenth century; and Louis did not hesitate to turn the knife in the wound. All the representatives in Paris of foreign states were invited to witness the Spanish apology and were asked to inform their courts of it, while a medal was specially struck to commemorate the French triumph. It was, in fact, far from being a complete victory. The Austrian branch of the Habsburgs continued to give precedence to the representatives of its Spanish relatives, the pope insisted on treating the French and Spanish ambassadors in Rome as equals, and the Spanish government ordered its diplomats not to appear in public with a French one of equal rank, and thus avoid giving way to him. But the whole incident shows well how issues of this kind could envenom international relations and even threaten international peace.

At sea the question of the salute allegedly owed by vessels, both merchant and naval, of one power to those of another, by firing a salvo, by lowering their colours, or more rarely by half-lowering some of their sails, was the equivalent of these struggles for precedence on land. Until the 1660s it was, at least in its most acute and dangerous form, mainly an Anglo-Dutch contest. In the treaties with the States-General of 1654 and 1667 the English government succeeded in having its claims accepted by its rival; and so sensible a man as Sir William Temple felt that nothing had ever given him greater pleasure than forcing the Dutch to give way once more on this point in the peace negotiations of 1674.[71] From the 1660s, however, Louis XIV began to press very intransigently pretensions of this kind which had already been raised unsuccessfully by Cardinal Richelieu more than a generation earlier. Once again the threat of outright war was brought into play. In 1678 and again in 1684 the republic of Genoa was forced by destructive naval bombardments to recognise French claims of this kind. In 1685, in time of peace, a Spanish fleet was forced to salute a French one after fighting which involved considerable casualties; and in 1688 French and Dutch squadrons fought off the Spanish coast, again in time of peace, over the same issue.

All this testifies to the extreme importance attached to every status-symbol in an avidly status-conscious age. Less dangerous, but still a

70. *Memoirs for the Instruction of the Dauphin*, ed. and trans. P. Sonnino (New York–London, 1970), pp. 69, 71.
71. Sir William Temple, *Works*, i, 170.

potential irritant, was the way in which this passionate interest in ceremonial could protract and complicate negotiations between states, especially when a number were involved. No peace congress of the seventeenth and early eighteenth centuries was unaffected by considerations of this kind. The formal opening in December 1644 of the congress at Munster was delayed for six months, at least partly by quarrels over ceremonial. Indeed, well before it assembled, the governments involved had been quite aware that quarrels over precedence would be the first obstacle to peace-making and by no means the least serious.[72] Its work, once it had got under way, was slowed and complicated by disputes of this kind between the French and Spanish and French and imperial representatives, while the Venetian one, Contarini, threatened to withdraw altogether from the negotiations unless the comte d'Avaux, the leader of the French delegation, treated him on a basis of complete equality. When in January 1645 the French agreed to give the Dutch representatives the coveted title of 'Excellency' this at once led to demands from the imperial electors that theirs must be given it also. This in its turn provoked similar claims from several of the Italian princes, so that 'before long Munster swarmed with Excellencies'.[73]

It was taken for granted, therefore, in the major peace conferences of the later seventeenth century that the arrangements must ensure that no important state was placed in a position of apparent inferiority to a rival. When France and Spain made peace in 1659 after a struggle which had lasted for almost a quarter of a century it was agreed that their representatives, Cardinal Mazarin and Don Luis de Haro, should meet on a small island in the River Bidassoa, which separated their territories in the Pyrenees. On it a pavilion was built, joined by separate bridges to the French and Spanish banks of the river, so that neither minister should have to pass through foreign territory. In this way the appearance of complete equality could be preserved and the *amour-propre* of both satisfied. At Ryswick in 1697 the building in which the two sides met was arranged so that the Swedish diplomat who acted as mediator had a central position, with the French representatives and those of the anti-French coalition each occupying an identical wing. Even here, however, status still reared its head, for Louis XIV clearly thought it derogated from his dignity as a ruler by divine right to be referred to in the final treaty in the same terms as William III, the mere constitutional

---

72. See, for example, the warnings on this point in the instructions of the French government to its representatives at the abortive peace congress at Cologne in 1637 and those of 30 September 1643, to the negotiators about to leave for Munster, in F. Dickmann et al (eds), *Acta Pacis Westphalicae*, Serie 1, Band 1 (Munster, 1962), 38, 64–5.

73. Dickmann, *Westfälische Friede*, pp. 208–10.

king of a parliamentary state. In the final stages of the peace-making at Utrecht in 1713 the representatives of the different powers avoided many of the difficulties and delays which had marked earlier such conferences by entering the meeting-place in the town hall *pêle-mêle* (i.e. in no particular order) and then seating themselves at a round table which had no head.

It is possible to make too much of all this. Just as ideas of precedence between states could be adjusted in practice to cope with the growing importance of the Dutch republic or Savoy, so governments which really wanted to negotiate could always find ways of doing so which side-stepped difficulties of ceremonial and procedure. Very often, as in all ages, the achievements of an international congress merely reflected the outcome of earlier and less formal negotiations. The war of 1689–97 saw a long series of such contacts between the belligerents almost from its outbreak; and the final settlement stemmed from protracted discussions between French and Dutch emissaries in 1694–96. Secret negotiations of this kind could occasionally be at a very high level. In 1709, when the position of France in the war of the Spanish Succession appeared desperate, the foreign minister himself, the marquis de Torcy, went incognito to The Hague to explore the possibility of making peace on acceptable terms. Sometimes commanders in the field could be used as negotiators: in 1714 the treaty of Rastadt which ended the struggle between Louis XIV and the Emperor Charles VI was based on personal contacts between the commanders of the opposing armies, Marshal Villars on the French side and Prince Eugene on the imperial one.

Quibbles over ceremonial therefore did not necessarily impede effective contact and negotiation between states. But they were always, until far into the eighteenth century, a potentially negative factor. They could always be used when any government wished to drag out proceedings or in some way be obstructive. Moreover, it must be stressed, they reflected deep and genuine preoccupations of the age. Rulers and governments might well be willing when it suited their own purposes to overlook the difficulties which precedence, titles and formal procedures in general so often caused. But anything which seemed to offer a challenge to what they regarded as their rightful status was certain to cause resentment. This can be seen in their reaction to the most striking change of this kind during the whole early modern period – the assumption by Tsar Peter I in 1721 of the new title of Emperor (*Imperator*). This clearly symbolised Russia's new strength and the international position to which she had now raised herself with spectacular speed. As such it could not be welcome to many of Peter's fellow monarchs. The smaller Protestant states of northern Europe – Brandenburg-Prussia, Sweden, Denmark – which were all to varying extents anxious to conciliate Russia, had little hesitation in recognising the new title. Nor had the Dutch republic, still a great commercial force in the Baltic. But Britain and the Austrian Habsburgs did not follow suit until 1742, and France and Spain not until three years after that. Indeed Franco-Russian disputes on this issue flared up briefly once more in the 1760s and were not finally laid to rest until 1772. In Vienna the new status of the Romanov dynasty was particularly resented. A second imperial title in Europe seemed to devalue that of Holy Roman Emperor, still a symbol of the unity of Christendom, endowed with great prestige and held continuously by members of the Habsburg family for almost three centuries. The result was controversy between Vienna and St Petersburg which dragged on for two decades.

By the mid-eighteenth century, and probably earlier, the power of ceremonial, precedence and titles to arouse intense feeling was none the less clearly in decline. When in 1769 at a ball in St James's palace the French ambassador in London, the comte du Châtelet-Lomont, risked provoking a diplomatic incident by pushing forward to assert precedence over his Russian colleague, Count Chernyshev, he was felt by most contemporaries to have been rude and indiscreet rather than to have shown a proper concern for the honour of Louis XV. Half a century earlier his behaviour would have seemed much more normal and aroused much less criticism.[74] Other signs of a relaxation of the extreme punctilio of earlier generations were now clearly to be seen. A striking one came in 1760 when, at the marriage of the Princess of Brazil, the daughter of King Joseph I, the masterful Portuguese chief minister, the marques de Pombal, announced that though the papal nuncio and the imperial ambassador would take precedence over all other foreign envoys this would be governed so far as the rest of them were concerned simply by the dates on which they had presented their credentials.[75] This principle, that within each diplomatic rank (ambassador, minister-resident, etc.) precedence should be decided merely by seniority, was to lead more than half a century later, by the international convention of 1818, to a final solution of most of the issues on which for generations so many energies had been expended and so much ink spilt. Where non-European states and rulers were concerned there were still sometimes considerable efforts to impress by ostentatious display and pompous ceremonial. In 1778, for example, envoys from the Indian state of Mysore (a potentially valuable ally of France against British power in India) were conducted, when they were

---

74. For a detailed account of this dispute by an expert contemporary observer, Sir Charles Cottrell-Dormer, the master of the ceremonies, see Vinogradoff, 'Russian missions to London, 1711–1789', 64–6.

75. I. Cardinale, *Le Saint-Siège et la diplomatie* (Paris–Tournai–Rome–New York, 1962), p. 111.

received by Louis XVI at Versailles, by a deliberately circuitous route through a very long series of rooms all of which were filled with stands and spectators in a demonstration of French power and greatness.[76] A hundred years earlier such an expedient might well have been used to impress envoys from some European state; but by the later eighteenth century it showed merely that the Indians were exotic visitors from outside the European diplomatic system who might be influenced by such essentially childish devices. At sea, also, time produced more realistic and utilitarian attitudes. By the eighteenth century salutes were normally given merely by the firing of guns, not by the more humiliating lowering of the flag or striking of sails.[77] After Trafalgar, Admiralty instructions to the commanders of British men-of-war no longer ordered them to demand a salute from foreign naval vessels in the waters where Britain had for so long claimed such a right.

By the outbreak of the French revolution sensitivities on such matters were still not dead; but they were a much less obtrusive element in international relations than at any time since quasi-modern diplomacy began to emerge three centuries earlier. More and more, in an intellectual atmosphere increasingly sympathetic to utilitarian rationalism, such preoccupations now seemed trivial, even contemptible. 'Our ancestors', complained an English commentator in the 1790s, 'gave themselves up, without even seeming to feel the folly of their conduct, to an immoderate and perpetual contest for rank and pre-eminence, often as destructive, as in general it was ridiculous'.[78] But attitudes of this kind took time to gain the upper hand: the past relaxed its grip only slowly. As late as 1812 the French representative in Naples fought a duel with his Russian colleague over a question of precedence; and his doing so was officially approved in Paris.[79] Even in the 1830s the most influential work on international law could assume that salutes at sea were still a significant aspect of the subject.[80]

76. H. Murray Baillie, 'Etiquette and the Planning of the State Apartments in Baroque Palaces', *Archaeologia*, 101 (1967), 189.

77. T. Ortolan, *Règles internationales et diplomatie de la mer* (Paris, 1845), i, 365 fn.

78. Ward, *Enquiry*, ii, 360.

79. *Les affaires étrangères et le corps diplomatique français*, ed. J. Baillou (Paris, 1984), i, 470.

80. G.F. von Martens, *Précis du droit des gens moderne de l'Europe* (Paris, 1831), i, 348–56.

# CHANGE AND DEVELOPMENT

The picture painted in the preceding pages is in the main one of stability, or at least of change which was usually slow and almost unconscious. But this is only one side of the story. By the beginning of the eighteenth century several important new developments were beginning to be visible. The web of diplomatic contacts which had developed in western and central Europe over the last 200 or more years was now being extended further east by the full incorporation in it for the first time of the great new emerging state of Russia: henceforth events in eastern Europe were to be far more significant in the calculations of statesmen in the west than ever in the past. At the same time, in a much slower and less spectacular process, foreign offices, departments of central government specialising in the formulation and conduct of foreign policy, were emerging in many European states. Even more slowly, professionalism in diplomacy was becoming more marked. By the end of the seventeenth century the chaotic medley of titles which had been used in earlier generations to describe diplomats of different ranks had been reduced to a simpler system which in its main lines was accepted by most states. During the eighteenth century diplomats were less irregularly paid than had hitherto been the case and there can be seen the first efforts, though very limited and ineffective ones, to provide them with some systematic professional training.

## *The diplomatic network extends*

In the seventeenth century, almost as much as in the sixteenth, Russia was a very marginal part of the evolving network of diplomacy. Embassies still went from Moscow to the states of Europe at irregular and often long intervals and stayed only briefly. Very often they were essentially ceremonial or symbolic, with little real political business to transact. A Russian representative stayed for about a year in Stockholm in 1635–36, and another spent four years in western Europe, mainly in the Dutch republic, in the early 1660s; but both of these were sent for mainly commercial purposes and the second was an Englishman long resident in Russia. It was only in 1673 that a Russian diplomat, V.I. Tiapkin, was established in Warsaw. He remained in post for four years and can thus be considered Russia's first permanent diplomatic representative; and though he had no successor until 1688 there was continuous Russian representation in the Polish capital from that time on. Both Sweden and Poland by the later seventeenth century had established and important places in Russian foreign policy. Russian representatives sent to them normally had the rank of Great Ambassador (*Velikii Posol*) and their complaints over ceremonial were less intrusive than in other capitals.[81] But further west the picture remained the traditional one of short-lived Russian embassies whose maintenance by their hosts frequently led to embarrassing disputes. Moreover, these often troublesome missions did little to make the Russian government better informed about the countries to which they went. They were strictly controlled by the instruction (*nakaz*) which they were given when they set out, whose emphasis was heavily on ceremonial, particularly on the use by foreigners of the tsar's full title. The report (*stateinyi spisok*) on his mission which a Russian ambassador wrote on his return was devoted in the main to showing that he had strictly observed these instructions. It usually contained very little general information on the country he had visited. Russian statesmen were therefore often badly informed about the politics of the outside world; and though in 1672 there was an effort to compile for their guidance an official manual of the available information about foreign states this was not published for well over a century.[82] Nor were foreign diplomats as yet much more welcome in Russia than during the sixteenth century. They continued to be closely guarded and severely restricted in their movements. A.L. Ordyn-Nashchokin, one of the more forward-looking Russian statesmen of the seventeenth century, objected in the 1660s to any permanent foreign diplomatic representation in the country because it would 'bring harm to the Muscovite state and embroil it with other nations' and because foreign diplomats would 'find out everything that went on in Moscow and tell it abroad'.[83]

This position changed with almost revolutionary speed during the first two decades of the eighteenth century. By 1701 the young Tsar Peter I had added to the resident representative in Warsaw others in The Hague, Copenhagen, Vienna and Constantinople. There was more or less permanent Russian representation in London and Berlin from 1707, in Paris from 1720, in Madrid from 1724. When the tsar died at the beginning of 1725 there were twelve Russian diplomatic missions at work in different European capitals, a figure which was not to be significantly exceeded for the rest of the eighteenth century. A considerable proportion of this first generation of Peter's representatives in western Europe were

81. Crummey, *Aristocrats and Servitors*, pp. 42, 59–61; D. Altbauer, 'The Diplomats of Peter the Great', *Jahrbücher für Geschichte Osteuropas*, 28 (1980), 1, fn, 2; Avis Bohlen 'Changes in Russian Diplomacy under Peter the Great', *Cahiers du monde russe et sovietique*, vii, (1966), 342.

82. Bohlen, 'Changes in Russian Diplomacy', 345; W.E. Butler, Introduction to P.P. Shafirov, *A Discourse Concerning the Just Causes of the War between Sweden and Russia: 1700–1721* (Dobbs Ferry, N.Y., 1973), p. 5.

83. Quoted in Bohlen, 'Changes in Russian Diplomacy', 342.

foreigners in Russian service; but by the 1720s these had been replaced by native-born Russians. Moreover, this growth of diplomatic contacts was a two-way process. In 1702 there were only four foreign diplomatic missions established in Russia on a long-term basis (apart from some unofficial agents of the hospodar of Wallachia and of some dissident Serbian groups): by 1719 there were eleven.[84] The entire ethos of Russian diplomacy was now rapidly changing. The new diplomats, often members of important noble families (Golitsyns, Dolgorukiis, Kurakins) were now increasingly citizens of a European world of high aristocratic culture. Unlike their predecessors they were at home in French, now establishing itself as the pre-eminent diplomatic language, and cultivated contacts with foreigners. The conventions of west-European international relations were now fully accepted in Russia, a process helped forward by the appearance there of translations of western works on international law and diplomacy. When Peter died his country had been irrevocably launched into the mainstream of international relations in Europe.[85]

The other great semi-Asiatic state on Europe's eastern frontier, the Ottoman Empire, behaved quite differently. There relative seclusion and indifference to most of the doings of the western powers continued to hold sway: this threw into sharper relief the completeness of the change in Russia. Such lack of interest in any active Turkish diplomatic relationship with the European states stemmed from a deap-seated view of the world. This drew a clear dividing-line, one impossible to cross, between the 'abode of Islam' and the outside non-Muslim world, the 'abode of war'. Between these different worlds relations must always be those of actual or at least potential hostility. It was the duty of the ruling sultan, at least in principle, to extend so far as he could the area controlled by true believers at the expense of that ruled by Christian infidels. An attitude of this kind, backed by all the great weight of Islamic religious conservatism, made diplomatic relations of what was now the normal European kind impossible. By sending permanent representatives to the courts of Europe the Ottomans would have been accepting a kind of regular and established contact with the west which denied their most deeply held assumptions, which implied an at least partial renunciation of the inherent superiority to the Christian world which they claimed, and which for a surprisingly long time, even after the balance of military strength had turned decisively against them, seemed to almost all of them unnecessary and to promise no

84. *Ocherk istorii Ministerstva Inostrannykh Del', 1802–1902* (St Petersburg, 1902), p. 38.

85. On the emergence of Russia as a major power see in general G.A. Nekrasov, 'Mezhdunarodnoe priznanie rossiskogo velikoderzhaviya v XVIIIv', in *Feodal'naya Rossiya vo vsemirnoe-itoricheskom protsesse* (Moscow, 1972).

real advantage. By early in the seventeenth century several of the states of Europe – France, England, the Dutch republic, Venice – already had permanent diplomatic representatives more or less securely established in Constantinope (though the English and Dutch ones at least were for long concerned above all merely with the fostering of their countries' trade: the former continued to be paid not by the British government but by a group of merchants, the Levant Company, until as late as the 1820s). In the eighteenth century they were joined by others – from Sweden after 1734, from Prussia after 1758. But Turkish missions to any part of Europe remained rare and exotic visitors. In Ottoman eyes, envoys from the rulers of the Kalmuck and Uzbek tribes of western Siberia and central Asia were, at least until the great defeats of the 1680s and 1690s at the hands of the Habsburgs, more important than those from most European states; and this attitude was slow to change. The 'Tulip Era' of the early eighteenth century saw a brief spurt of interest in the western world and its technological accomplishments: under the Grand Vizier Damad Ibrahim Pasha (1717–30) five short-lived diplomatic missions were sent to Europe – two to Vienna, one each to Paris, Moscow and Warsaw. But none of these stayed long or was meant to begin any sort of permanent relationship. They were intended merely to acquire enough western technical knowledge, particularly in military matters, to help strengthen the defensive powers of an empire increasingly threatened by European armies. Not until 1793 did Sultan Selim III make the first serious effort to establish permanent Turkish diplomatic missions in the main European capitals; and these were unsuccessful and short-lived. Moreover, throughout the eighteenth century such Ottoman diplomacy as there was remained largely untouched by European ideas and values. This was most clearly seen in the complete absence of any concept of the personal security and inviolability of the diplomats accredited to the sultan. When the Ottoman empire declared war on a foreign state its unfortunate representative in Constantinople was very often immediately thrown into the Seven Towers prison there, where he might stay for a considerable time. This was the fate of the French ambassador in 1658, the Venetian one in 1714, the Habsburg internuncio in 1716, the Russian minister in 1768 and the French chargé d'affaires in 1798. Until early in the eighteenth century, moreover, foreign diplomats when given audience by the sultan were expected to wear a Turkish-style robe over their normal clothing in order to spare him the repellent sight of European dress. Habsburg representatives at least continued to do this until 1719; and the Emperor Charles VI felt it necessary to insist in an article of the treaty of Belgrade which he signed with the sultan in 1739 on the right of his representatives to appear at such audiences in European clothes. In the seventeenth century Russia and the Ottoman empire had seemed to many European observers not altogether dissimilar; and of the two the latter appeared until the 1680s or 1690s clearly the more powerful. The very sharp difference in their relationship to western Europe which had developed by the death of Peter I was pregnant with implications for the future.


## The beginnings of foreign offices

Foreign ministers and foreign offices, an administrative apparatus exclusively or at least mainly concerned with the formulation and carrying-out of foreign policy, developed much more slowly than the diplomats whom they were to control. Their evolution was an unplanned and rather haphazard process whose speed and nature differed considerably in different parts of Europe. Some signs of their emergence can be seen even in the first days of the 'new diplomacy'. A papal *Secretaria Apostolica* in Rome for carrying on official correspondence had its functions defined by Pope Innocent VIII in 1487; and by the early sixteenth century a quite extensive and well-organised papal secretariat concerned largely with relations with the secular states of Europe had developed. It was from the *secretarius intimus* or *secretarius papae* of this period that the later papal secretary of state evolved, though that title was first used only in 1644. Almost simultaneously, under Ferdinand of Aragon, Miguel Perez de Alamàn began to specialise in the control and direction of relations with other states in a way which made him probably the nearest approach to a minister of foreign affairs hitherto seen anywhere in Europe.[86] In sixteenth-century Spain there was usually a secretary of state with particular responsibility for carrying out the decisions of the king in foreign policy matters. Gonzalo Perez was appointed by Philip II to this position in 1556; and from 1567 the work was controlled by two secretaries, one handling relations with the imperial, French and English courts, the other the Italian affairs which bulked so large in the Spanish scheme of things. In France, at the accession of Henry II in 1547, each of the four *secrétaires des finances* was given the task of overseeing the administration of a group of French provinces and also of relations with the foreign states which bordered on these; thus for example the secretary who supervised Burgundy and Champagne was normally also responsible for relations with the Swiss cantons and the states of west Germany. These secretaries also began to attend meetings of the royal council, though

---

86. J.M. Headley, *The Emperor and his Chancellor: a study of the imperial chancery under Gattinara* (Cambridge, 1983), p. 23.

merely as clerks, not as members, and in 1559 were given the title of secretaries of state. It was not until 1589 that a single secretary, Louis de Revol, was entrusted with the supervision of foreign affairs in general; and he was still an administrator, not a policy-maker. From the 1620s onwards, however, there was an unbroken line of French secretaries of state for foreign affairs.

In England the rapid increase in the amount of diplomatic correspondence from the beginning of the sixteenth century accelerated the development of the secretary of state, originally an officer of the royal household who drafted the king's letters and kept his private seal. After 1540 there were normally two such secretaries; and though they handled an enormously wide range of business, domestic, Irish and later colonial, 'the care of foreign affairs was their most important duty'.[87] In the sixteenth century, and to a considerable extent in the seventeenth also, their function, like that of the French secretaries under the last Valois kings, was merely executive. England's foreign policy was made by the privy council committee of foreign affairs, and in the last analysis by the king himself, aided by whichever minister or favourite had his ear at a given moment. But the sheer range and volume of business with which the secretaries of state dealt made them important officers of government. Russia equipped herself surprisingly early with one of the most ambitious of these early approaches to a foreign office. The *posolskii prikaz* (department of embassies), founded in 1549, had by the end of the sixteenth century become a substantial organisation employing almost a score of clerks. But this again was an administrative rather than a policy-making body. Its first head, I.M. Viskovaty, and his successors for over a century, were bureaucrats (*dyaki*); not until 1667 was it led by a boyar, a nobleman of the highest rank. Moreover, it was not concerned purely with diplomacy and foreign policy. Like some of its west-European counterparts it had responsibility also for a number of domestic or quasi-domestic concerns such as relations with the Don Cossacks and with foreign merchants in Russia.

By the early seventeenth century, therefore, foreign offices, in so far as they existed, were still for the most part embryonic. They were usually small. Their organisation and internal structures were normally fluid, even amorphous. Their heads, none of whom was of high noble birth and some of whom were of relatively humble origins, were officials rather than statesmen. Their responsibilities often included areas which had little or nothing to do with foreign policy. This slow process of evolutionary growth continued in the generations which followed. The Dutch

87. Florence M.G. Evans, *The Principal Secretary of State* (Manchester, 1923), p. 8.

republic, the greatest economic and political success story of the age, had at least in form some of the most incoherent and inefficient arrangements of all for the conduct of foreign policy. In the first half of the seventeenth century it was controlled by a secret committee of the States-General, usually with the stadtholder himself as its chairman. In the second half of the century decisions continued to be taken by a series of similar committees and indirectly by the seven provinces which sent delegates to the States-General. This system worked very slowly and made secrecy virtually impossible: it has been calculated that in all some 2,000 people may have had some influence, direct or indirect, on the functioning of this cumbersome machinery.[88] In practice real power was largely in the hands of Holland, much the richest and most important of the seven provinces, and particularly in those of its chief official, the Grand Pensionary. For three-quarters of a century from the 1650s successive holders of this post, John de Witt, Gaspar Fagel and Anthonie Heinsius, acted in effect as foreign ministers, and were thus among the most important figures on the European political stage.

Elsewhere some of these embryonic foreign offices were developing and growing, though this was still often a slow process. In Russia the *posol'skii prikaz*, which employed fewer than twenty clerks at the beginning of the seventeenth century, had almost twice as many by 1701: it also had a remarkably large number of interpreters and translators.[89] More importantly, it was now divided into five departments on an essentially geographical basis, three of them handling relations with distinct groups of European states and the other two those with Asiatic ones (China, Persia, the khanates of central Asia and the little Georgian kingdoms in the Caucasus). A relatively clear-cut organisation of this kind, later to become the typical form of internal structure of all foreign offices, had already been introduced in 1661 in Sweden, where the small machine for the control of foreign policy was still part of the royal chancery and hardly an independent entity at all; but it is interesting that it should also have evolved relatively early in a country still so isolated and underdeveloped as Russia. In England, by the later seventeenth century, there had emerged a fairly clear-cut distinction where foreign affairs were concerned between a northern and a southern department, with each of the two secretaries handling relations with the foreign states which fell into one of these geographical divisions. But each could and did act for

88. M.A.M. Franken, 'The general tendencies and structural aspects of the foreign policy and diplomacy of the Dutch Republic in the latter half of the 17th century', *Acta Historiae Neerlandica*, iii (Leiden, 1968), 22, fn. 2.

89. B. Meissner, 'Die zaristische Diplomatie. A. Der Gesandtschafts-Prikaz (Posolskij Prikaz)', *Jahrbücher für Geschichte Osteuropas*, Neue Folge, Band 4 (1956), 242–3.

the other when necessary; and English diplomats abroad frequently corresponded with both. This arrangement, flexible but strikingly unmodern, was to last until nearly the end of the eighteenth century. In France the secretary of state for foreign affairs had now become one of the greatest of government ministers. During the personal reign of Louis XIV from 1661 onwards the post was held by a succession of distinctly able men – Lionne, Pomponne, Colbert de Croissy, Torcy – and the administrative machine which they controlled grew substantially in size and complexity. Early in the seventeenth century, moreover, the post of *premier commis* had begun to emerge. These high-ranking bureaucrats, of whom there were normally two or three at any one time and who had always long practical experience of international relations, controlled the day-to-day working of the machinery of French diplomacy and were of critical importance to its effectiveness. By the end of the century they were dividing its work betwen them in a systematic and efficient way. The machine was still not a completely specialised one. The secretary of state for foreign affairs still retained, as did his fellow secretaries for war, the navy and the *maison du roi*, ultimate responsibility for the administration of a group of French provinces; and each of the four still acted as general secretary to the king, in the drawing up and despatching of official documents of all kinds, for three months in the year. But France, by the beginning of the eighteenth century, had gone far towards creating a modern foreign office, and the prestige of French diplomacy and diplomatic organisation, bolstered by the military successes of Louis' armies until the 1690s, was very high.

The three generations before the revolution of 1789 saw more of the same process of slow institutional adaptation. Great Britain, now reluctantly more and more involved in the politics of continental Europe, had at length to equip herself with more effective machinery for the conduct of foreign policy. Even before the end of the seventeenth century James II, in exile in France, had advised his son, should he ever rule in England, to have a single minister with undivided control of relations with other states.[90] A few years later there was a proposal to set up a council, composed exclusively of professional diplomats who had served abroad for at least seven years, to advise the king on foreign affairs. As time went on, moreover, there was an increasing tendency for one of the two secretaries of state clearly to dominate the other and become in effect foreign minister. Bolingbroke in 1711–14, Stanhope in 1714–21, the elder Pitt in 1756–61, were all clear cases of this; and in 1771, and again ten years later, George III – the most efficiency-minded English ruler for three

90. J.S. Clarke, *James the Second* (London, 1816), ii, 640.

centuries – pressed for the conduct of foreign policy to be unified in the hands of a single secretary.[91] Suggestions of this kind culminated in the creation of the foreign office which began its life in 1782. It was for a long time a small and cheap organisation. For most of the 1780s it numbered, apart from the secretary of state himself, merely an under-secretary and less than a dozen clerks. Nor was it particularly efficient, even by the elastic standards of that age. The British ambassador to Vienna complained in the 1780s that he had not received a line in reply to fifty despatches he had sent home; and when he returned to London he 'was under the utmost Astonishment at having been twice to the Secretary of State's Office without finding a single Soul there'.[92] But its existence meant that Britain had joined the other major states of Europe in providing herself with a minister and an administrative machine designed to conduct and control foreign policy.

In Russia change came earlier and was, at least in form, more striking. By 1720 Peter I had reorganised the *posolskii prikaz*, whose importance had declined sharply in the last two decades, as a new college of foreign affairs. This was a committee, modelled closely on the Swedish example, consisting of a president, a vice-president and two chancery counsellors: its creation was part of a far-reaching overhaul of Russian central government in Peter's last years which involved, among other changes, the eventual creation of nine colleges of this type. (It is interesting, however, that the tsar seems at first to have intended to give the college some jurisdiction over aspects of Russia's internal administration; and for a considerable time it did in fact handle quasi-internal issues such as relations with the Kalmuck tribes and with the Cossack hetman in the Ukraine. The idea of a department of state concerned solely with foreign affairs had clearly still to fight for acceptance.) This break with the past was in some ways more apparent than real, for the first members of the college had all served in its predecessor. Whether it was even much of an improvement is open to question; like many committees it was cumbersome and slow-moving and by the 1750s it had become notably disorderly and inefficient.[93] It grew rapidly, however: the 120 employees of its first days had become 261 at the accession of Catherine II in 1762. Of all the administrative colleges created by Peter in 1718–22 it, together with those of war and admiralty, was the most important and successful.

Elsewhere in Europe there were also significant eighteenth-century

91. D.B. Horn, *The British Diplomatic Service, 1689–1789* (Oxford, 1961), p. 2.

92. *Memoirs and Correspondence . . . of Sir Robert Murray Keith*, ed. Mrs Gillespie Smyth (London, 1849), ii. 228; J. Ehrman, *The British Government and Commercial Negotiations with Europe, 1783–1793* (Cambridge, 1962), p. 202 fn.

93. *Ocherk istorii Ministerstva Inostrannykh Del'*, p. 63.

developments. In Spain, as part of the administrative reorganisation under the first Bourbon king, Philip V, a new secretariat of state was created in 1714 for the handling of foreign affairs. Until after Philip's death in 1746 it was still an administrative and not a policy-making body; but in the second half of the century it acquired greater power and independence. Here again, however, can be seen the persisting tendency to link the conduct of foreign policy with miscellaneous internal functions; for the First Secretariat of State, as it was usually known, acquired in 1782 control of the Madrid police. In the Habsburg territories in central Europe, which because of their exposed geographical position and limited economic strength greatly needed an effective and well-controlled foreign policy, the Emperor Joseph I in 1709 set up a new committee of nine officials for this purpose. It was reorganised in 1721; and from the 1750s onwards the foreign policies of the monarchy were given greater continuity by a purely personal factor – the very long tenure of the post of Court and State Chancellor, for over forty years from his appointment in 1753, by Prince Wenzel von Kaunitz-Rietberg. In 1773 he succeeded, with the backing of Maria Theresa, in resisting a proposal for the dilution of his power by the creation of a collegiate-type administration, such as that in Russia, for the conduct of foreign affairs.[94] The *Staatskanzlei*, which controlled the day-to-day administration of foreign policy, had already been reorganised and made rather more efficient at the beginning of his period in office. There was, however, a complicating factor here which did not exist in any other European state. The ruler of the Habsburg territories was also Holy Roman Emperor, in theory at least the suzerain of hundreds of German states and rulers. As well as the *Staatskanzlei* in Vienna administering the foreign policy of the monarchy there was therefore also the *Reichskanzlei*, the imperial chancery headed by the Archbishop of Mainz, *ex officio* imperial chancellor, and concerned with the interests and representation of the empire as a whole. The rivalry between these two, which went far back into the seventeenth century, was ended only by an agreeement of 1790. This provided that Habsburg diplomats should have credentials from both chanceries. They were to receive instructions on imperial issues from the *Reichskanzlei* and on those affecting only the Habsburg territories from the *Staatskanzlei*, and would divide their reports between the two bodies on the same principle.[95] This agreement (which gave formal recognition to what had for several decades been becoming established practice) brings out well the complexities and

94. G. Küntzel, *Furst Kaunitz-Rittberg als Staatsmann* (Frankfurt–am–Main, 1923), p. 70.

95. I. Gross, *Die Geschichte der deutschen Reichshofkanzlei von 1559 bis 1806* (Vienna, 1933), pp. 41–96.

ambiguities inherent in much of the administrative structure of old–regime Europe.

In Sweden Charles XI and Charles XII kept control of foreign policy firmly in their own hands. Any influence on the part of the College of Chancery was further weakened by a reorganisation which Charles XII personally carried through in 1713–14. However, the constitution of 1720, and the collapse of royal power which underlay it, placed control for the next half-century in the hands of the Diet (*Riksdag*). A secret committee of this sometimes negotiated directly with foreign diplomats; and the work of the College of Chancery was largely reduced to preparing foreign policy questions for discussion by the Senate. The revolution of 1772 changed the situation once more. Gustavus III recovered control and became in effect his own foreign minister. The powers of the College of Chancery were increased by an ordinance of 1773 and in 1791, just before his assassination, Gustavus set up the King's Office for Foreign Correspondence. This was a very small organisation. At its foundation it employed only eight officials; and this number did not increase much for the next half-century. Nevertheless, it was the nearest approach to a foreign ministry which the country had as yet possessed. Even in the Ottoman empire there was some sign of change. There the *Reis-ul-Kuttab*, or *Reis Effendi* as he was usually called by foreigners, the head of the grand vizier's chancery, showed some signs of becoming at least an approximation to a foreign minister. From the Carlowitz peace negotiations with the Habsburgs in 1699, successive grand viziers began to leave him a good deal of control over foreign affairs, though he again was also entrusted with a wide variety of other and quite different functions. European observers very often exaggerated his importance, however; and the fact that he was expected to accompany the grand vizier on campaign in wartime often drastically reduced his influence on negotiations with foreign diplomats in Constantinople.[96]

It was in France, however, that during the eighteenth century a well-organised foreign ministry of a recognisably modern sort could most easily be found. The details of its internal structure varied somewhat from time to time, but the main lines remained fairly stable. A political department, which handled correspondence with French diplomats abroad, was usually divided along geographical lines into two sections each concerned with a distinct group of foreign states. Side by side with this grew up a number of smaller specialised departments – a *bureau des fonds* which dealt with the ministry's own internal finances, the surveillance of

96. C.V. Findley, 'The Legacy of Tradition to Reform. Origins of the Ottoman Foreign Ministry', *International Journal of Middle East Studies*, i (1970), 336–8.

foreigners in France, questions of diplomatic privilege and a wide variety of other relatively minor issues; a *bureau des interprètes* which took shape in the 1750s and 1760s and was given definitive form in 1768; a department concerned with codes and cyphers; and a geographical one which by the 1780s had a remarkable collection of about 10,000 maps. These and the other sources of expert knowledge which the ministry could call upon (the first of a series of legal advisers was appointed in 1723, for example) suggest a professionalism which it would be hard to equal elsewhere in old-regime Europe. It is not surprising to find the Russian government in 1784 asking officially for information on the organisation of the ministry; and the memorandum drawn up in response to this request by one of the *premiers commis* paints, even allowing for some gilding of the lily, an impressive picture of the efficiency with which, at least in theory, correspondence was classified, answered and indexed.[97]

## The growth of professionalism

Clearly diplomacy in the seventeenth and eighteenth centuries was still far from modern. It lacked the impersonality and regularity of the highly organised machines which conduct present-day international relations. It was often difficult to persuade able men to accept diplomatic posts in distant capitals. As in the sixteenth century there was a persistent and widespread feeling that an administrative or, better still, court appointment at home provided much rosier prospects. Men offered a diplomatic post could not be blamed, as one writer put it, for 'choosing rather to fix themselves near to the person of the Prince; because the recompences for that service are much greater, and much more frequent, and because those that are absent are commonly forgotten, which makes them look upon an embassy as a sort of an honourable exile'. Almost at the same moment an English observer put it more succinctly: 'Foreign service may sometimes provide a good stirrup but never a good saddle'.[98] In England and the Dutch republic difficulties of this kind were particularly acute: one result of this was a tendency from the 1660s onwards to give influential figures in Dutch public life, as an inducement to accept a mission abroad, the highest diplomatic rank of ambassador extraordinary, even if the mission in question were a run-of-the-mill one. Even so, important posts in Dutch

---

97. This very brief account is based mainly on J.-P. Samoyault, *Les Bureaux du secrétariat d'état des affaires étrangères sous Louis XV* (Paris, 1971). The memorandum of 1784 can be found in H. Doniol, *Politiques d'autrefois: le Comte de Vergennes et P.M. Hennin* (Paris, 1898). pp. 53–67.

98. Callières, *The Art of Diplomacy*, p. 177; H.L. Snyder, 'The British Diplomatic Service during the Godolphin Ministry', in *Studies in Diplomatic History: Essays in Memory of David Bayne Horn* (London, 1976), p. 51.

diplomacy had sometimes to be filled by second-rate men or go unfilled for long periods. In England, also, complaints of the difficulty of finding capable diplomats can be heard until far into the eighteenth century; and many agreed to serve only to put the government under a moral obligation to find some acceptable post for them at home on their return.[99] Sometimes the difficulties were really acute. In 1705–06, a striking case, the very important Vienna embassy was vacant for months, repeatedly turned down by a series of those to whom it was offered. When at last a reluctant taker was found he asked to be recalled almost as soon as he had arrived at his post. This situation meant that sometimes a completely unsuitable man was entrusted with an important appointment merely because, for some private reason of his own, he was willing to accept it. A good seventeenth-century example is Thomas Howard, second earl of Arundel, a great collector of pictures, who volunteered in 1636 for a special embassy to the Emperor Ferdinand II simply because he wished to see and perhaps buy a number of art treasures about which his agents in Germany had sent him glowing reports. In spite of his total lack of previous diplomatic experience, and a reserve and arrogance which alienated many of those he had to deal with, he was sent on this important and, in the event, quite fruitless mission.[100]

The slow growth of the idea of diplomacy as a distinct profession meant that appointments could still, down to the French revolution, sometimes be made in a remarkably haphazard way on the basis of family connections and sheer luck. In the early years of the 'new diplomacy' in the fifteenth and early sixteenth centuries it had not been unusual for a diplomat who died in post to be immediately succeeded by a relative, often a close one, who had been attached to his mission with this possibility in mind. Thus in 1506 the Spanish representative in Venice was succeeded by his son, who presented to the doge on the day after his father's death credentials prepared in advance; and when about the same time a French ambassador to Hungary died, his duties immediately passed to his nephew, who completed the work of the embassy.[101] Almost two centuries later it was being proposed that in much the same way every Spanish ambassador should have assigned to him a son or younger brother 'to assist him as a comrade in his work', be instructed in the conduct of embassy business and handle matters the ambassador himself could not spare time for, with the implication that he might well succeed to the post

99. On problems of this kind immediately after the revolution of 1689 see Viscount Lonsdale, *Memoir of the Reign of James II* (York, 1808), Introduction, pp. viii–ix.

100. F.C. Springell, ed, *Connoisseur and Diplomat. The Earl of Arundel's Embassy in Germany in 1636* (London, 1963), p. 3.

101. M.A.R. de Maulde-la-Clavière, *La Diplomatie au temps de Machiavel* (Paris, 1892–3) i, 367.

if it fell vacant.[102] The casual and amateurish character of much British diplomacy in particular, even in the eighteenth centry, is reflected in the fact that when an appointment, especially a relatively minor one, fell vacant without any suitable new holder of it being immediately available, it was sometimes filled merely by a casual volunteer. Thus in 1786, on the death of Sir Horace Mann, the British envoy to the grand duke of Tuscany, the post was filled for over six months by his nephew, who had no recognised diplomatic status at all.[103] In 1793, in a more striking case, a boy of seventeen was left at the beginning of the struggle with the French revolution as the sole British representative at the military headquarters of the king of Prussia.[104] On an even higher level of importance, the Habsburg representative at the Teschen peace negotiations with Prussia in 1779, Count Philip Cobenzl, owed his position to the accident of his cousin Ludwig, Maria Theresa's first choice, being crippled by gout when the time came to set out. 'Couldn't I go instead?', Count Phillip asked. 'I've never worked in diplomacy, but I've worked in other affairs. I can use my cousin's servants, his furniture and his carriages, it's not even necessary to send an announcement. Cobenzl has been announced and a Cobenzl will go.'[105]

This happy-go-lucky attitude, with its underlying assumption that diplomacy was not a career in itself but an interlude in other and often more attractive ones, was slowly dying as system, method and organisation became more pervasive in all branches of government. This change can be seen in several ways. In the first place, by the eighteenth century a hierarchy of diplomatic ranks more clear-cut than ever before had emerged, though this process was still incomplete. Until the mid-seventeenth century the essential distinction (oversimplifying somewhat) was that between ambassadors, either ordinary ones resident for some length of time or extraordinary ones sent for some special and limited purpose, and lesser diplomatic representatives referred to by a variety of different titles – resident, minister, agent, etc. It was still widely accepted that only major rulers (kings and the republic of Venice) could send and receive ambassadors; and it was not clear until at least the later sixteenth century that the status of a diplomat depended on his position in this still embryonic hierarchy of ranks and not, irrespective of his title, on the standing of the ruler he represented. The French writer Charles Paschal, in his *Legatus . . . Accessit Graecarum dictionum interpretatio*

102. 'Embajada espanola', p. 5.
103. Horn, *British Diplomatic Service*, p. 162.
104. K.L. Ellis, 'British Communications and Diplomacy in the Eighteenth Century', *Bulletin of the Institute of Historical Research*, xxxi (1958–9), 163.
105. D. Beales, *Joseph II*, i, *In the Shadow of Maria Theresa* (Cambridge, 1987), 426.

(Rouen, 1598), appears to have been the first theorist to state clearly what now seems so obvious a fact.[106] In any case many rulers were for long reluctant to send ambassadors to foreign capitals if a lower-ranking representative would suffice. This was partly to save money (since an ambassador had to live in a style and with an expense which was not expected of lesser mortals) and partly to minimise the risk of quarrels over precedence. As late as 1779 Russia maintained a full ambassador (*posol*) only in Warsaw: in all the other European capitals she had only 'ministers of the second rank'.[107]

By the age of Louis XIV, however, the diplomatic ladder was acquiring more rungs and they were more clearly defined. There was by then a growing feeling that the title 'resident' conferred a higher status than the older term 'agent' which was in any case dropping out of use. More important, 'envoy' (known from the fifteenth century in its Latin form *ablegatus*) was beginning to be widely used. It was usually taken, particularly when combined as it often was with the adjective 'extraordinary', as indicating a status superior to that of the resident: it became rapidly in many states during the later seventeenth century the most widely used of all diplomatic titles. The action of Louis XIV in sending for the first time, in 1679, an envoy extraordinary to the imperial court in Vienna probably helped to accelerate this process. William III in England, for example, appointed during his reign forty-two envoys extraordinary, as opposed to twelve ambassadors and a mere six residents.[108] At the same time, the distinction between ambassadors resident and those who were genuinely extraordinary, in the sense in which that term had hitherto been used, began to break down. More and more they were now given the title of 'extraordinary', even when they remained for long periods at the courts to which they were sent: increasingly the term, applied to either an ambassador or an envoy, became a mere title of honour. In the eighteenth century it was more and more usual for an ambassador accredited to any of the greatest European courts to be given it, irrespective of how long he stayed there or what his duties were. The term 'plenipotentiary', which by the later seventeenth century was also being widely used in diplomatic titles, mainly in the form 'minister plenipotentiary', was even more of a verbal decoration.[109] As the eighteenth century went on the combination of the two into 'envoy extraordinary and minister plenipotentiary' became the most usual way of

---

106. O. Krauske, *Die Entwicklung der ständigen Diplomatie vom fünfzehnten Jahrhundert bis zu den Beschlüssen von 1815 und 1818* (Leipzig, 1885) p. 156.
107. *Ocherk istorii Ministerstva Inostrannykh Del'*, p. 70.
108. Horn, *British Diplomatic Service*, p. 43.
109. Wicquefort, *L'Ambassadeur*, i, 73.

designating diplomatic representatives of the second rank, those below that of ambassador but still having the right of audience with the rulers to whom they were accredited.

These changes were complex and often confused.[110] Different courts had different customs and traditions in these matters which they usually changed only with reluctance. As the eighteenth century drew to a close, however, the situation was undoubtedly clearer and more regulated than in earlier generations. By the time of the French revolution three main classes of diplomat were generally recognised: the ambassador, with or without the title of 'extraordinary'; the envoy or envoy extraordinary, often with the additional designation of 'minister plenipotentiary'; and the resident, or now more commonly minister resident (the term 'minister' as a somewhat vague diplomatic title went back to at least the mid-sixteenth century). The humble agent had now virtually disappeared, and where he survived was not seen as having any diplomatic status; but relatively new categories of chargé d'affaires and secretary of embassy or of legation were appearing. Already in the later seventeenth century, moreover, the designation of chargé d'affaires had begun to be given to secretaries who thus acquired a representative character, either on appointment or on the death or departure of the head of the mission of which they were part. It would be a mistake to follow early modern Europe in the importance it attached to titles; but the emergence of a more clearly defined diplomatic hierarchy had some significance, both as cause and result, for the parallel emergence of diplomacy as at least a kind of profession.

The same growth of professionalism can also be seen in the increasingly regular and systematic payment of diplomats. In the seventeenth century they were still often paid very irregularly. When a government was poor, as for example that of Stuart England almost always was, its representatives abroad often had great difficulty in getting what it owed them. In 1612 the ambassador in Paris took the desperate step of writing directly to James I to ask for money and persuaded the duc de Bouillon, one of the greatest French nobles, to back his request. A year or two later his colleague at The Hague asked his friends in London to bribe an Exchequer official to obtain more regular payment of what he was owed.[111] More than half a century after that, Sir William Temple, one of the outstanding English diplomats of the seventeenth century, had to struggle repeatedly in the 1660s and early 1670s to obtain arrears of salary

110. The best fuller discussion is probably still that in Krauske, *Die Entwicklung*, pp. 150–86.

111. M. Lee, Jnr, 'The Jacobean Diplomatic Service', *American Historical Review*, 72 (1966–67), 1277–8.

and repayment for the expenses he had incurred,[112] and he is merely the best-known of many similar cases. By 1679 it was estimated that such payments were six or seven years in arrears; and in the 1690s English diplomats were still very often paid merely in Exchequer tallies which could be cashed only after long delay and at ruinous discounts to their face value.[113] Even before the end of the century, however, the situation, which was near its worst in England, was improving in many states. Already in 1669 there had been an effort to systematise the payment of salaries to English diplomats; and a fixed scale based on formal diplomatic rank (ambassador, envoy, minister or resident) was adopted in 1690 and remained largely unchanged for the next hundred years.[114] In Sweden, again, there was a series of efforts during the eighteenth century to regulate more rationally the salaries paid to different ranks of diplomat, though there as elsewhere it was easier to do this than to pay the salaries regularly.[115]

None of this meant that diplomats were well paid, if the financial demands still often made on them by their position are considered. The expense allowances they received often failed, sometimes by a long way, to cover the costs they had to meet. It was still easy, particularly in a post where lavish public display and expensive entertainment were essential, for them to incur heavy personal debts. In the eighteenth century at least one French nobleman refused the offer of the St Petersburg embassy because of the warning example of others who had ruined themselves by accepting it.[116] Of the Catholic states, that in Rome, in spite of the rapid decline in the political importance of the papacy, was still the pre-eminent example of such a post. In the later seventeenth century a French duke turned it down on the grounds that his father, by holding it, had accumulated debts of 200,000 livres.[117] Several decades later another French ambassador had in Rome a male staff of 145, including 'a theologian from the Sorbonne, two French secretaries and two Italian, eleven gentlemen of the chamber, a surgeon, sixty-two valets and lackeys of various kinds, four trumpeters, a French chef and his minions, plus coachmen, postillions and pages'. His successor spent immediately on appointment almost half a year's salary on

112. Haley, *An English Diplomat*, pp. 92, 108, 212–15, 238–9, 257, 292–3.

113. Phyllis S. Lachs, *The Diplomatic Corps under Charles II and James II* (New Brunswick, N.J., 1965), pp. 92–3; M. Lane, 'The Diplomatic Service under William III', *Transactions of the Royal Historical Society*, 4th ser., x (1927), 99.

114. Lachs, *Diplomatic Corps*, pp. 83–5; Horn, *British Diplomatic Service,* Chapter iii, passim.

115. S. Tunberg et al. *Histoire de l'administration des affaires étrangères de la Suède* CUpsal, 1940), pp. 338, 356, 358–9, 361.

116. *Les Affaires Étrangères* . . ., i. 193.

117. W.J. Roosen, 'The True Ambassador: occupational and personal characteristics of French ambassadors under Louis XIV', *European Studies Review*, 3 (1973), 136.

table-linen alone.[118] These were exceptional cases. But it remained true, as a very experienced commentator pointed out, that 'any man filled with an excessive desire of fortune or riches should abandon the calling of negotiator', while the most successful English diplomat of the eighteenth century claimed that after fourteen years in several highly important posts he found himself £20,000 worse off.[119] Nevertheless, the general direction of change is unmistakable. Salaries were now arranged in a more systematic hierarchy and paid more regularly than in the past. In this respect again, diplomacy, if not yet clearly a distinct profession, was on the way to becoming one.

The slowly growing organisational efficiency of most European states in the conduct of foreign policy can be illustrated in yet other ways. From the beginning heads of missions had had secretaries who often played an important role; but these had been recruited and paid by the diplomats themselves and had been merely their personal servants. This arrangement had obvious disadvantages. A secretary inevitably had access to highly confidential information: as Pecquet wrote in the early eighteenth century, 'silence, loyalty and secrecy should reign in every secretariat'.[120] Yet a disgruntled secretary, or one left unemployed by dismissal or the death or recall of his master, might easily be tempted to profit by the information he had acquired in his work. Under Louis XIV, when the reputation of French diplomacy was at its height, a good many of those employed by French diplomats betrayed secrets and sold cyphers.[121] One at least, abandoned in Madrid at the end of a mission, was immediately engaged by the representative of one of the states then leagued against Louis.[122] The best way to avoid such dangers was to make the secretary a government appointee and give him some official status and the modicum of job security which it brought. It could also be argued that this would help to build up a body of men with substantial diplomatic experience from which the diplomats of the future might be drawn. Moreover, a secretary attached to a legation or an embassy and not to an individual minister or ambassador, and remaining at his post over a fairly long period, could become a valuable source of information about local conditions: this might be of great help to a new head of mission coming to a strange country of which he knew little. These arguments were not

118. R.d'O. Butler, *Choiseul* (Oxford, 1980), i, 1044, 1046.

119. Pecquet, *Discours sur l'art de négocier*, p. 20; *Diaries and Correspondence of James Harris, first Earl of Malmesbury* (London, 1844), i, 457–8.

120. *Discours sur l'art de négocier*, p. 73.

121. W.J. Roosen, 'La Diplomatie du XVIIe siècle: fût-elle française ou européene?', *Revue d'Histoire Diplomatique*, 1979, pp. 10–11.

122. J. Klaits, 'Men of letters and political reform in France at the end of the reign of Louis XIV', *Journal of Modern History*, 43 (1971), 581.

universally accepted. In particular most French diplomats continued to appoint their own secretaries until the end of the old regime. In 1710 the marquis de Torcy, the reforming last foreign minister of Louis XIV, managed to secure that six should be paid annual pensions of 1,000 livres while they were unemployed between missions, and thus given some financial security; but this was a gesture with limited effect.[123] Even in 1788 there were only eight such appointed and paid by the government.

In some other states, however, the movement towards greater system and central control in this respect was more marked. In Sweden *secrétaires de commission* began to be appointed to some missions in foreign capitals from 1669 onwards, mainly it seems to provide for greater continuity in the event of the death or recall of the head of the mission. This arrangement was made more systematic in 1688; and after 1719 there was a good deal of discussion of the status and powers of secretaries of this kind. They were normally attached, however, only to the more important Swedish missions abroad: a mere minister resident, if he needed a secretary, had still himself to find and pay him. None the less, they could on occasion have considerable importance. Sometimes at least they seem to have reported to Stockholm independently of the chief under whom they served; and in the later years of the eighteenth century Gustavus III sometimes tried to use them in this way as agents of a secret personal diplomacy.[124] In Great Britain change was later and perhaps less systematic; but by the reign of George III British ambassadors were always provided by the government with a secretary of embassy, while by the later 1780s the more important legations were also being included in this arrangement. From the 1760s, moreover, some of the British secretaries of embassy in Paris and Madrid were also accredited as minister plenipotentiary: they could thus carry on the business of the mission quite effectively in the absence of its head.[125]

## Training and its limitations

Perhaps the clearest of all criteria of a true profession is the requirement of some systematic training for entry to it. By this test old-regime diplomacy never approached professional status. The early eighteenth century saw a number of assertions that its quality could be raised substantially by providing suitable training. Pecquet even claimed that good diplomats needed to be prepared from childhood for the work.[126] There was

123. Klaits, 'Men of letters . . .', 582.
124. S. Tunberg, et al., *Histoire* . . ., pp. 335–7.
125. Horn, *British Diplomatic Service*, pp. 45–6.
126. *Discours sur l'art de négocier*, Preface, pp. xxxiii–xxxiv.

general agreement that the education provided by schools and universities, mere book-learning, was of little use here. The qualities a diplomat needed – quickness of wit, courtly manners and an impressive appearance, social polish and *savoir-faire* – were not to be acquired in classrooms and libraries. A British ambassador expressed a widely accepted attitude when, in 1779, he dismissed his Neapolitan colleague at St Petersburg as 'merely a man of letters, unacquainted with and unfit for business'.[127] Proposals for the training of diplomats therefore took in the main two forms. Young men with such ambitions should, it was universally agreed, travel widely and thus gain a personal acquaintance with at least some of the major European states, their problems and resources. The best way of doing this was by attaching themselves to one of their country's missions abroad, serving in it in a junior and normally unpaid capacity and thus acquiring experience of diplomatic methods and routines as well as of a foreign country. This on-the-job training might be supplemented (though here agreement was less widespread) by study of past negotiations and of the achievements of successful diplomats and statesmen: the best way of doing this was by analysing the despatches and memoranda these had written. For this purpose suitable young men, it was sometimes proposed, might be attached for a period at the beginning of their careers to their country's foreign ministry.

All proposals for any kind of training, however, were subject to severe limitations; and the most important of these was rooted in the nature of old-regime society. It was a society completely dominated by inherited rank and status. There was, therefore, a strong and general assumption that the highest diplomatic appointments, and particularly those in the major capitals or in which a strong ceremonial and symbolic element was still involved (notably the embassies of the Catholic powers to the papacy) should normally be given to great aristocrats. But such men were totally unwilling to embark on a diplomatic career by doing humdrum routine work or studying documents, and then rising step by slow step through a hierarchy of ranks. For them a progress of this kind might be acceptable, at least to some extent, in the army. Fighting, after all, was by its very nature a noble occupation. It was no disgrace to a great nobleman to serve even in a junior capacity in a good regiment. But if he entered diplomacy at all he expected to do so at or near the top. To him an important embassy was a perquisite of birth rather than the culmination of years of painstaking effort. The strength of these attitudes varied considerably between different countries. The aristocratic grip on the most important diplomatic appointments was weaker in Great Britain, and probably in

127. Malmesbury, *Diaries*, i, 260.

Russia, than in France, Spain or the Habsburg territories. But everywhere it was still a factor inhibiting the growth of systematic training and the professionalism it symbolised.

On the desirability of travel as a preparation for diplomacy there was virtual unanimity. Callières urged that young Frenchmen, if they could not meet the cost themselves, should be able to see other countries as members of the entourages of French ambassadors or envoys 'according to the practice of the Spaniards and Italians who look upon it as an honour for them to accompany the ministers of their master in these sorts of voyages'.[128] But few governments made any systematic or sustained provision for helping young men to travel abroad and gain a knowledge of foreign language and countries. Russia, from the first years of the eighteenth century onwards, is the most important exception to this generalisation. In 1697 Peter I sent groups of Russian nobles to Venice, the Dutch republic and England, essentially to study seamanship; but though their training was intended to be purely technical they none the less provided when they returned home a nucleus of mainly young men with experience of foreign countries and a grasp of foreign languages. This was an asset of a kind which Russia had never hitherto possessed. These men supplied many of the first generation of Russian permanent representatives in western Europe: of the twelve of these accredited in the first decade of the eighteenth century five had been members of the group of students sent to Venice in 1697.[129] Moreover, the initiative of that year was followed up. When A.A. Matveev went as Russian minister to The Hague in 1699 eight young Russians were attached to his mission to gain the experience which would fit them for future diplomatic careers; and during the next decade members of several important noble families studied in Europe for this purpose with government backing. In the last years of Peter's reign a considerable number of students of lower social standing were sent to Königsberg, the United Netherlands and elsewhere to learn foreign languages, though not all of these were destined to become diplomats. By 1724, just before the tsar's death, Count A.I. Ostermann, the head of the new college of foreign affairs, could even hope that in future adequate teaching of the main west-European languages might be provided within the college itself.[130] The process which Peter had set in motion persisted to a considerable extent after his death. In mid-century the college of foreign affairs had 139 employees (not counting those engaged in minor routine clerical work). Of these

---

128. *The Art of Diplomacy*, p. 98.
129. Altbauer, 'The Diplomats of Peter the Great', 8.
130. D.J. Taylor, *Russian Foreign Policy, 1725–1739*, Ph.D. thesis, Univeristy of East Anglia, 1983, p. 17.

forty-five had received some sort of special training for a diplomatic career, and a good many had studied outside Russia. Another twenty-seven had been students in the imperial cadet corps, the naval academy, the mathematical-navigation school or the Slav–Greek–Latin academy. It is notable, however, that although titled nobles were very prominent in the highest ranks in the college it still had to make extensive use of commoners, since even in the 1750s it was impossible to find enough *dvoryane* (members of the privileged landowning class) with an adequate knowledge of foreign languages.[131] Under Catherine II the sending abroad of budding Russian diplomats for study and experience was placed on a more formal and permanent footing than hitherto. The official table of appointments in 1779 for the college of foreign affairs, which lasted until it was slightly modified by Catherine's son Paul in 1800, provided for each mission abroad to have two students regularly attached to it for these purposes.[132]

No other state went so far as this; but then none needed to, for none started from the same position of isolation and estrangement from the outside world. In England in the early part of the eighteenth century the crown occasionally gave some help, in a haphazard way, to suitable young would-be diplomats to travel in preparation for a career in government service. The writer Joseph Addison is the best-known of the few who benefited from this. But nothing sustained and organised of this kind was ever contemplated in London. The French government gave similar help to some young Frenchmen, but on the same unsystematic basis and small scale. In Sweden the new post of *secrétaire de commission* was intended in part to provide opportunities of this sort; but its holders also were few. In Spain, in the later 1780s, the foreign minister, Count Floridablanca, began attaching youths in their late teens to missions abroad to be given there some grounding in diplomatic skills: this again does not appear to have gone very far. In Brandenburg-Prussia Frederick II suggested in 1776 that young men fitted for a diplomatic career be sent, on leaving university, as secretaries to the Prussian missions in Vienna, London, Stockholm and St Petersburg (in that order of preference). This would give them a period of study and experience abroad after which it could be decided whether to offer them permanent appointments.[133] But these were to be men of non-noble birth or at best only from minor junker families, destined merely for posts such as Warsaw or The Hague where real aristocrats were

131. S.M. Troitskii, 'Russkie diplomaty v seredine XVIIIv.', in *Feodal'naya Rossiya vo vsemirno-istoricheskom protesse* (Moscow, 1972), pp. 404–06, 400.

132. *Ocherk istorii Ministerstva Inostrannykh Del'*, p. 70.

133. *Politische Correspondenz Friedrichs des Grossen* (Berlin, 1879–1936), xxxviii, 314–15.

not needed. Again the same point emerges: high social standing and systematic training did not mix.

Linguistic ability posed special problems where one particular geographical area was concerned. This was the Near East. Several states felt the need for a supply of men with a knowledge of Turkish to ease the conduct of diplomatic, and still more commercial and consular, relations with the Ottoman empire. As early as the 1550s the Venetian government had begun sending young men to Constantinople to learn the language: this seems to have continued for about a century but then faded away. In 1670 Colbert, the greatest of all the finance ministers of Louis XIV, organised the despatch to the Turkish capital of a number of very young French boys for the same purpose, while Greek Christian youths were brought to Paris to be educated in the Collège de Louis-le-Grand.[134] Some of the *jeunes de langue*, the young Frenchmen sent to Constantinople in this way, played a role of some significance in the slender intellectual contacts between the two countries: the first book printed in Turkey in the Latin alphabet, the Turkish grammar compiled by the Jesuit priest J.B. Holdermann (Constantinople, 1730) was intended for their use. The Austrian Habsburgs had made efforts in the same direction from the end of the sixteenth century, when the custom developed of sending with each internuncio to Constantinople a small number of boys (*Sprachknabe*) to learn Turkish. From the 1640s onwards one of the functions of the Habsburg representatives in the Turkish capital was to oversee their training; and by the early eighteenth century a number of these representatives were themselves former *Sprachknabe*. In 1754 this system was changed when the Empress Maria Theresa set up in Vienna the *Orientalische Akademie* to train young men for consular and diplomatic work in the Near East.[135] This was the first effort by any European power to provide systematic training at a relatively high academic level for the conduct of relations with any part of the non-European world; and the academy became an element of some significance in Habsburg diplomacy as a whole. Before the end of the century one of its graduates had risen to be chancellor (Baron Thugut, who succeeded Kaunitz in 1793) and in the later nineteenth and early twentieth centuries several others (Haymerle, Burian and Czernin) reached similar heights.

Russia, to whom the Near East was almost if not quite as important as to the Habsburgs, also made considerable though less systematic efforts to provide herself with men competent in Turkish. The Russian minister

134. Fatma Muge Goçek, *East Encounters West: France and the Ottoman Empire in the Eighteenth Century* (New York–London, 1987), pp. 99–101.

135. K.A. Roider, *Austria's Eastern Question, 1700–1790* (Princeton, 1982), pp. 9–10; H. Wildner, *Die Technik der Diplomatie: L'Art de Négocier* (Vienna, 1959), p. 62.

sent to Constantinople in 1724 was ordered to choose four students to be attached to his staff to learn the language; while the establishment of 1779 for the college of foreign affairs, which provided for two students to be attached to each Russian mission abroad, allowed that in the Turkish capital to have as many as eight. Even in England there were occasional signs that the usefulness of having available at least a few men with a knowledge of oriental languages was understood. In 1699 the government began to pay the professor of Arabic at Oxford an annual allowance of £100 to enable him to train 'young students in the modern Arabick and Turkish languages' who could translate letters from Muslim rulers. However, the money was used (rather typically for the English universities of this period) to help finance an additional chair of Arabic rather than an increased number of students.[136] For most of the eighteenth century a translator of oriental languages was attached to the office of one of the secretaries of state; but to obtain an English version of a letter in Turkish or Arabic was often far from easy. One to George II from the pasha of Tripoli in the 1750s had to be sent to the Netherlands to be translated; and another from the sultan of Morocco to George III in 1779 was still awaiting translation several months after reaching London.[137] Oriental languages, however, were a special and limited problem. Except to some extent in the Habsburg territories, the men who gained a knowledge of them were destined to remain translators, interpreters or at most consuls, auxiliaries rather than actors at the centre of the diplomatic stage. The languages which the young aspirant to diplomacy needed to acquire were those of western Europe, of which French was now by far the most important.

Travel and practical experience abroad were not the only possible ways of preparing for a career in diplomacy. There were also efforts to train suitable young men at home. The best-known example of this, and probably the most ambitious, was the political academy set up in Paris in 1712 by the Marquis de Torcy.[138] Cramped accommodation was found in the Louvre for six students, each of whom was to be paid an annual stipend of 1,000 livres, a director and later a secretary. These, with a further six unpaid students who joined in 1714, constituted the academy. It was from the first bound up with the establishment of a foreign ministry

136. P.J. Marshall and G. Williams, *The Great Map of Mankind: British Perceptions of the World in the Age of Enlightenment* (London, 1982), p. 71.

137. M.S. Anderson, 'Great Britain and the Barbary States in the eighteenth century', *Bulletin of the Institute of Historical Research*, xxix (1956), 106.

138. A good deal has been written on this. Three useful articles are: Klaits, 'Men of Letters . . .'; H.M.A. Keens-Soper, 'The French Political Academy, 1712: A School for Ambassadors', *European Studies Review*, ii, No. 4 (October, 1972); and G. Thuillier, 'L'Académie Politique de Torcy', *Revue d'Histoire Diplomatique* (1983).

archive. Torcy had himself been prepared to succeed his father, Colbert de Croissy, as foreign minister, by studying the diplomatic correspondence of Richelieu, Lionne and several of the most successful French diplomats of the early seventeenth century. The students of the academy were therefore to begin by arranging and cataloguing the papers of the foreign ministry as well as studying foreign languages and history. From this they would graduate to reading and summarising the records of past negotiations and finally to preparing detailed memoranda on various aspects of French foreign policy. There were regular seminars at which these papers were discussed and at which Torcy, whose personal interest in the scheme is clear, was sometimes himself present. This was an interesting and well-designed experiment; but its practical results were small. The academy was handicapped from the beginning by shortage of money; and Torcy's fall from office in October 1715 dealt it a severe blow. By 1721 it had been abolished as useless.

However, the idea that archive work might be used in the training of embryo diplomats still surfaced from time to time in France. The Abbé Leroy, a former pupil of the academy, put forward suggestions of this kind to Chauvelin, the foreign minister, in 1737. Pecquet made others in the following year. About 1770 there was quite an elaborate proposal to create at Versailles another school for diplomats with thirty-six pupils, while others were to be given practical training by travel abroad or work, in preparation for careers as consuls, in the main French ports. Nothing came of any of these suggestions. Occasionally young men with diplomatic ambitions were allowed, if strongly enough recommended, to study in the foreign ministry archives. Pierre-Michel Hennin, later as *premier commis* an important figure in French foreign policy, was given such permission in 1749. Moreover, by the 1780s each of the two departments of the ministry handling correspondence with French diplomats abroad included two or three men being trained for diplomatic work, though the training seems to have been more directly practical than anything Torcy had had in mind.[139] But none of this had much importance.

Elsewhere in Europe achievements were modest. In England the creation in 1724 of the Regius chairs of modern history at Oxford and Cambridge was meant, at least in part, to provide training for young men with diplomatic ambitions. Twenty in each university were to be taught modern history and languages and, if they reached the required standard, given suitable employment at home or abroad. But this scheme very quickly petered out with little result.[140] Frederick II in Prussia set up in

139. Doniol, *Politiques d'autrefois*, p. 56.
140. Horn, *British Diplomatic Service*, pp. 130–2.

1747 a 'séminaire d'ambassadeurs' where twelve young 'hommes de condition' were to study, with the title of counsellors of legation, under the supervision of high-ranking officials. It does not seem to have been very attractive to young Prussians, however: the king from the beginning envisaged recruiting students if necessary outside his own territories, in Meckleburg or Swedish Pomerania. In any case it succumbed within a few years to the stresses of the Seven Years War, and was not revived until 1775.[141] This too was a small-scale and short-lived experiment rather than a serious innovation.

So far as systematic training of diplomats was concerned, therefore, the eighteenth century saw projects and suggestions, but little lasting achievement. In two other aspects of modernisation more was achieved. These were the growth of organised and comprehensive diplomatic archives and the publication of the first great printed collections of international treaties. The first of these went back as far as the second half of the sixteenth century. Philip II began in 1567 the building up of a great Spanish archive at Simancas, the earliest of all major modern state archives. In England papers of the secretaries of state began to be deposited in the State Paper Office from 1578. For generations to come, nevertheless, most collections of this kind remained very patchy and incomplete, largely because ministers and diplomats tended to look on their papers as their personal property and to retain them when they gave up office. In France, in spite of its widespread reputation for diplomatic skill, the situation was for long more unsatisfactory than in several other states. When the future Cardinal Richelieu entered government service for the first time in 1616 he found available so little essential documentation on foreign policy that he had to ask French representatives abroad to send him copies of the instructions they had been given: without this he could not know even what the policies of his immediate predecessor had been. In 1628, now established as chief minister, he drew up proposals for the systematic preservation of official papers of all kinds, including those relating to foreign affairs; but nothing came of this.[142] The death in 1671 of Hugues de Lionne, the first foreign minister of Louis XIV's personal reign, began a new era. His papers were at once sealed by order of the king; and in the 1680s Colbert de Croissy built up a large working archive covering the years from 1660 onwards. Considerable efforts were made to fill the gaps which existed for earlier

---

141. *Politische Correspondenz Friedrichs des Grossen*, v, 340; xxxvii, 198–9; Ergänzundsband, 54.

142. L. Battifol, 'Le Charge d'ambassadeur au dix-septième siècle', *Revue d'Histoire Diplomatique* (1911), 347; A. Baschet, *Histoire du dépôt des archives des affaires étrangères* (Paris, 1875), p. 27.

decades, notably by the acquisition of a large collection of Richelieu's papers in 1705, while in 1710 Torcy had most of the archive moved from Versailles, where it had hitherto been, to the Louvre (the papers covering the years since 1698 remained at Versailles to be used in the daily business of the ministry). In 1763 the now very substantial collection in the Louvre (even in 1715 it had amounted to 2,000 bound volumes) returned to Versailles to be kept there in a new foreign ministry building. By then it amounted to 8,000 volumes; and by 1792, at the outbreak of war between revolutionary France and most of Europe, this figure had risen to 12,000.[143] The archive still left a good deal to be desired. In 1779 the correspondence relating to the Family Compact agreement of 1761 with Spain could not be found there, so that copies of it had to be obtained from Madrid, though the comte de Vergennes, as foreign minister in 1774–87, seems to have made efforts to achieve greater efficiency.[144] But this was by then certainly one of the finest collections of its kind, if not the finest, in existence.

Elsewhere the eighteenth century saw developments of comparable importance. In Vienna the Haus-Hof-und Staatsarchiv was founded in 1749, while in Russia the new college of foreign affairs had an archivist from 1720, almost the moment of its foundation. In 1724 Peter I ordered that all papers relating to foreign policy should be brought together in the college archive; and work on this continued for the next two decades.[145] In Spain the Archive of the Indies, which had great importance for some aspects of foreign policy, was set up in Seville in 1781. None of these collections was well catalogued or well arranged by present-day standards, and none was accessible to the general public. But their creation meant that a foundation was being laid upon which the detailed and scholarly study of diplomacy could later be built.

Very many of the disputed questions in international relations in old-regime Europe contained large elements, larger than would be the case today, of history and law. Generations of intermarriage between ruling families had covered the continent with a web of dynastic ties which generated numerous and complex claims to territories, titles and rights of all kinds. These had always bulked large in the history of diplomacy. Now, from the mid-seventeenth century onwards, they were more than ever in evidence, as pamphleteers and propagandists ready to justify them grew in numbers. International law, even though much of

---

143. Baschet, *Histoire du dépôt* . . ., p. 434.

144. Doniol, *Politiques d'autrefois*, pp. 38–42. A short account of the archive in the last years of the old regime can be found in Samoyault, *Les Bureaux du secrétariat d'état*, pp. 96–105.

145. Taylor, *Russian Foreign Policy*, pp. 31 fn., 37.

95

the writing about it was still almost a form of antiquarianism, was developing. Public interest in it, and in international relations in general, was growing over much of Europe. All this produced a growing demand for printed collections of the treaties between the European states on which so many claims and counter-claims were based.

Many early treaty collections, nevertheless, were not intended to be available to the general public at all. They were for use by statesmen and diplomats, working aids for the men engaged in the conduct of international affairs. The earliest of all were no more than small collections of handwritten copies of the agreements concerned. The peace-treaties of 1648, however, were published in three separate editions, two in Germany and one in the United Netherlands; and from the end of the seventeenth century large collections began to appear. One, published in Paris in 1693, brought together in six volumes all the treaties made since 1435 by the kings of France, while simultaneously Leibniz, the most complete intellectual of the age, tried in his *Codex Juris Gentium Diplomaticus* (1693) and *Mantissa Codicis* (1700) to provide collections which would form the legal basis for improved international relations and a more united society of states in Europe. Clearly the need for works of this kind was now being felt in foreign offices. It was proposed that the students of Torcy's academy should be employed in making 'a more complete and exact collection of peace-treaties', with an accompanying commentary; while the largest such enterprise hitherto, the *Corps universel diplomatique du droit des gens* of J. Dumont de Carlscroon (twelve volumes: Amsterdam–The Hague, 1726), an assembly of documents reaching back to the age of Charlemagne and drawn from sources all over Europe, was designed mainly as a help in policy-making and a kind of portable archive for the use of diplomats.[146] Works of this kind were another aspect of the way in which diplomacy was slowly becoming more systematic and institutional. They were also, since they were increasingly used by a small but important educated public, a link between diplomacy and the wider social world in which it operated.


## DIVISIONS AND UNITIES: FRONTIERS AND LANGUAGE

By the eighteenth century, therefore, the machinery of international relations in Europe combined old and new in the way inevitable in any form of organisation undergoing slow and unplanned change. The

146. Keens-Soper, 'The French Political Academy', p. 337. The best short discussion of printed treaty-collections in the seventeenth and eighteenth centuries is M. Toscano, *The History of Treaties and International Politics* (Baltimore, 1966), pp. 48–73.

traditional elements were still very important. But side by side with them had now appeared other and forward-looking ones. Moreover, the intellectual environment in which diplomacy functioned was also changing. Governments were becoming increasingly unwilling to tolerate many of the ambiguities, compromises and uncertainties which in the fifteenth, sixteenth and even seventeenth centuries had often been the essence of relations between them. This blurring of distinctions which to modern eyes seem self-evidently clear-cut was most evident in the lack of clearly-defined linear frontiers between states; and the two or three generations before the French revolution saw growing pressures for greater clarity in this respect.

Until the seventeenth century many, even most, European frontiers were very vague, zones in which the claims and jurisdictions of different rulers and their subjects overlapped and intersected in a complex and confusing way. This was especially true in eastern Europe, where many states were larger and central governments usually less effective at the peripheries of their territories than in the west. The most striking example of this is perhaps the frontier in the Danubian plain between the Ottoman empire and the Habsburg territories in central Europe. After the Turkish conquest of most of Hungary in the 1520s and 1530s the Hungarian nobles who had then fled westwards often still maintained claims to their former lands and even asserted their right to live tax-free on them for a limited period and to levy feudal dues in them. On their side the Turks taxed when they could areas which were formally outside their territory but which were accessible to the border-guards which they, like the Habsburgs, maintained all along this hazy frontier. Claims and counter-claims of this kind were to figure prominently for generations in Ottoman–Habsburg negotiations.[147] Even in western Europe it was normal for boundaries between states to be overlain by a mass of traditional rights, claims to exercise jurisdiction or to collect dues and taxes of various kinds, which made the modern idea of a frontier scarcely applicable. The importance of such rights, and the feeling that they were fundamental to the workings of society, is reflected in the fact that when one ruler ceded territory to another it was usually defined in terms of jurisdictions and local administrative divisions (on the French frontiers, for example, *baillages*, *prévotés*, *sénéchaussées* or *communes*) and not, as would now be the case, in those of lines laid down in precise geographical terms and illustrated by a map. Indeed, until cartography had reached a certain level of development it was very difficult to think of frontiers at all in

---

147. P.F. Sugar, *Southeastern Europe under Ottoman Rule, 1354–1804* (Seattle–London, 1977), p. 91.

these linear terms. There was a general assumption that traditional rights of all kinds were too fundamental to be overridden by a mere change in formal political allegiance. When territory changed hands, therefore, existing privileges and immunities were very often explicitly confirmed by the ruler under whose sway they had now fallen. In this way the territorial gains in the Spanish Netherlands and Franche Comté made by Louis XIV in the 1660s and 1670s were careful to leave private and corporate rights there untouched. Sometimes, as with the French annexation of Lille and Tournai, the king took an oath to respect the rights of the newly acquired cities even before their magistracies took one of allegiance to him.[148] In the same way many of the cities of the Swedish Baltic provinces, such as Riga and Dorpat, received promises to respect their existing position and rights when they were conquered by Russia in the second decade of the eighteenth century (though these promises were not always kept).

The most complex of all major west-European frontiers, and the one most studied by historians, was the eastern and north-eastern boundary of France. This was the product of centuries of historical accidents: indeed until the treaties of Madrid in 1526 and Cambrai in 1529, which ended for several generations to come any vestiges of French sovereignty over Amiens and the Vermandois, it is hardly possible to speak of a state frontier at all between France and the Low Countries. Even in 1659 the Peace of the Pyrenees still left 350 *terres contentieuses* scattered along it, with isolated enclaves on both sides, little islands of French or Spanish territory in a surrounding sea of foreign-ruled land. By the outbreak of the revolution in France this confused situation with all its potentialities for dispute and conflict had been largely rationalised. A series of agreements in 1769, 1770, 1772 and 1779, for example, ended by a process of exchange many of these enclaves on both sides of the border with the Austrian Netherlands. The same was true of the French frontier on the east with the territories of the Holy Roman Empire. There a long series of rectifications, again often based on exchanges carefully adjusted to make sure that neither side too obviously gained or lost by them, meant that by 1789 the boundary was essentially a modern linear one. The growing need for a clear dividing-line of this sort was often explicitly mentioned in eighteenth-century treaties between France and her eastern and north-eastern neighbours,[149] while the detailed work of rectification

148. Nelly Girard d'Albissin, *Genèse de la frontière Franco-Belge: Les variations des limites septentrionales de la France de 1659 à 1789* (Paris, 1970), p. 375.
149. J.-F. Noel, 'Les Problèmes des frontières entre la France et L'Empire dans la seconde moitié du XVIIIe siècle', *Revue Historique*, ccxxxv (1964), 346. There is at pp. 336–7 of this

and tidying-up absorbed much time and energy in the French foreign ministry: in 1734, as part of the frontier settlement at the end of the war of the Polish Succession, a *premier commis des limites* was appointed to handle the complex legal and other details involved. Fifteen years later a treaty ended French frontier controversies with the city-republic of Geneva, while in 1760 another signed in Turin (which incorporated a series of eight maps) greatly simplified in the same way France's south-eastern frontier.

The French case was merely the most striking example of a general process. Elsewhere also there was an increasing tendency to demarcate frontiers on the ground more clearly than ever before, as when at the end of the Thirty Years War that in Pomerania between Swedish and Brandenburg territory was marked out with boundary-stones.[150] Seventy years later the treaty of 1718 between the Emperor Charles VI and the Dutch republic, which fixed the boundaries of their territories in the southern Netherlands, provides what is probably the first example of a frontier being defined not merely in the text of a treaty but also on a map attached to it.[151] Negotiations in the middle years of the eighteenth century clarified the frontier between the Habsburg lands and the Venetian republic. Even the Ottoman empire began for the first time in its history to acquire some more or less clearly defined boundaries when, after the treaty of Carlowitz of 1699, joint commissions were set up to demarcate its frontiers with Habsburg territory. By the end of the eighteenth century the idea of the clear-cut linear frontier was accepted not merely by governments but by peoples as well. In 1789 the *cahiers* (statements of grievances) submitted to the newly summoned States-General from the Béarn and Bigorre areas in the Pyrenees included demands for clearer delimitation of the frontier with Spain, and those from Bresse, in south-eastern France, for further tidying-up of the boundary with Savoy.[152] In part such changes of attitude were the outcome of military necessities: as early as 1673 the great French military engineer Vauban had urged strongly that France's frontiers be rationalised to make them easier and cheaper to defend. They were probably helped also by the progress of cartography and a growing general familiarity with

---

article a useful map illustrating the process of frontier rationalisation. A long list of the treaties signed by France in 1718–89 with the aim of clarifying and simplifying her borders in the east and north-east can be found in P. de Lapradelle, *La Frontière: étude de droit international* (Paris, 1928), p. 45, fn, 1.

150. G. Parker, *The Thirty Years War* (London, 1984), p. 217.
151. Sir G. Clark, *The Seventeenth Century*, 2nd edn (Oxford, 1966), p. 144.
152. Lapradelle, *La Frontière*, p. 49.

maps: the great Cassini one of France, begun in 1750, was completed at the outbreak of the revolution. But most of all they were underlain by an intellectual transformation, by the victory of the modern idea of territorial sovereignty over the far older one of feudal dependence.

The feeling that Europe was bound together, in spite of all its internal rivalries, in some kind of underlying unity, was strengthened by the increasing predominance in the later seventeenth and eighteenth centuries of French as the language of international relations. Its status in this respect as the successor of Latin had by then already been developing for generations. By the end of the fifteenth century Louis XII was already using French in his letters to other monarchs (the only significant exception was Poland, whose ruler he wrote to in Latin), while at the same time it was the language of the imperial court under Maximilian I.[153] The century or more which followed saw a tendency for it to be used increasingly as the language of diplomacy. Though most of the negotiations of 1558–59 which culminated in the peace of Cateau-Cambrésis were still conducted in Latin it is clear that French was also extensively used.[154] The fact that a growing proportion of diplomats were now laymen whose fluency in Latin was often limited helped to accelerate this process, as did the fact that different nations pronounced the same Latin words in markedly different ways;[155] but as the language of treaties, especially those which involved a large number of states or in which the German states were concerned, Latin survived longer than as the language of negotiation. The first half of the seventeenth century was in this respect a period of somewhat confused transition. A listing made in Paris in 1640 shows that by then the rulers of England and Savoy, the States-General and many German princes, especially those of west Germany, corresponded with Louis XIII in French. But the king of Spain wrote in Spanish and almost all the Italian rulers in Italian, while the Scandinavian states, Poland, the Holy Roman Emperor, the Hanse cities and the elector of Saxony used Latin, and the Protestant Swiss cantons wrote in German.[156] In the protracted negotiations at Munster in 1645–48 the French representatives had their credentials drawn up in French and always used their own language in discussion. In May 1647 they even prepared a draft peace-treaty in French; and if this had been accepted by the other powers involved it would have marked an important stage in the establishment of the language as that of international relations, at least in western and central Europe. In fact, the treaty of Munster was in Latin

153. Maulde-la-Clavière, *Diplomatie*, ii, 80.
154. Joyceleyne C. Russell, *Peacemaking in the Renaissance* (London, 1986), pp. 147–9.
155. F. Brunot, *Histoire de la langue française des origines à 1900*, v (Paris, 1917), 389.
156. Brunot, *Histoire*, v, 391–2.

and in the negotiations 'Latin, French, Spanish and Italian seem to have been indiscriminately used . . . often in the same conversation'.[157]

But the triumph of French was delayed by only one or two decades. The Franco–Spanish treaty of 1659 was drawn up in both French and Spanish versions; but that of Aix–la–Chapelle in 1668 was in French alone, as was the Franco–Dutch peace settlement of 1678 (though the treaty of the same year between France and Spain was in both French and Spanish versions, and that of 1679 between France and the Holy Roman Empire was in Latin). In June 1682 Louis XIV, now at the height of his power, explicitly asserted his right to correspond with all foreign sovereigns in French and not to use Latin; and though the treaty of Ryswick between France and the Holy Roman Empire in 1697 was still in Latin most of the discussion which produced it was in French, as was the Franco–Dutch agreement of the same year. The Anglo–French treaty of Utrecht in 1713 was in Latin (the British copy) as well as French (the French one), but that of Rastadt in the following year in French alone. From the Aix–la–Chapelle peace of 1748 onwards every major international agreement involving the states of western and central Europe was in French; and from the peace settlement of 1763 the hitherto frequent provision that this was not to be taken as a precedent was dropped.[158] The victory of French was still not total. Callières at the end of the seventeenth century could still speak of 'Latin, ignorance of which would be a disgrace and a shame to any public man, for it is the common language of all Christian nations'.[159] But this was now an outdated view, or on the verge of being so.

In relations between the German states, in which legalistic considerations so often bulked large, Latin held its ground longer than in Europe generally. In the Near East Italian remained until as late as 1820 or so the most important diplomatic language, though there interpreters and translators were indispensable as nowhere else.[160] The treaty of Kutchuk–Kainardji was drawn up in 1774 in both Russian and Turkish versions but with a master copy, which was to be authoritative in case of dispute, in Italian. However, these were relatively minor qualifications to the pre-eminence of French. More and more it came to be used in relations between states which were not themselves French-speaking: in 1664 the new imperial ambassador to England addressed Charles II in it at

157. M. Bernard, *Four Lectures on Subjects connected with Diplomacy* (London, 1868), p. 18.

158. A general discussion of the emergence of French as the main language of international relations can be found in A. Ostrower, *Language, Law and Diplomacy*, i (Philadelphia, 1965), 275–97, on which this paragraph is largely based.

159. *The Practice of Diplomacy*, p. 98.

160. Spuler, 'Europäische Diplomaten in Konstantinopel', 206–7.

his first audience and in 1677 the king of Denmark, when addressed by a Polish ambassador in Latin, replied to him in French. By the later seventeenth century, therefore, it was clearly becoming the language of diplomacy in general, though perceptibly more slowly in eastern Europe than in the west.

Its emergence as the pre-eminent international language was not something forced by France upon a reluctant continent. When in 1665 Charles II complained that his ministers did not understand French the ambassadors sent to London by Louis XIV at once offered to negotiate in Latin. In 1714 Louis himself was ready to sign a treaty with the Holy Roman Empire drawn up in Latin: French was chosen by the imperial representatives as a time-saving device. It was the immense prestige of French culture and the status of the French monarchy as a model for much of Europe which gave the language its dominant position in diplomacy. As its great historian pointed out, 'French became the language of states because it had become the language of courts and aristocracies'.[161] The nineteenth century was to see its status as the language of diplomacy grow still further as it became even more a symbol of some underlying European unity which, however vague, was genuinely felt to exist by most of those who decided the continent's destinies.

---

161. Brunot, *Histoire*, v, 431.

# CHAPTER THREE

# Coming to Terms with a Changing World, 1789–1919

## THE STRUGGLE TO MODERNISE

Between the outbreak of the French revolution and the meeting of the Paris peace conference Europe's diplomatic organisation changed in many ways more radically than in the preceding 300 years. The nineteenth and twentieth centuries saw the continuation of trends already clearly visible – a consolidation of the network of diplomatic links between the European states and a further growth and elaboration of foreign offices. It also saw one very important new development; its extension far more than in the past to bind Europe to other continents. Some issues which had bulked large in previous generations now faded into the background. Ceremonial and precedence notably lost most of the power to agitate rulers and governments which they had hitherto possessed. Most significant of all, diplomacy by the later nineteenth century was beginning radically to change its character. It was ceasing to be overwhelmingly political in a narrow sense and acquiring new dimensions which, even well before the First World War, were clearly destined soon to become very important. The character of international relations was now broadening and their essential nature altering.

### The changing diplomatic map

Between the peace settlement of 1814–15 and the death of the old monarchical and aristocratic Europe after 1914 there was some growth in the size and a more marked one in the geographical scope of diplomatic services; but this was slow and largely confined to the major states. The continent approached the cataclysm of 1914 with a formal apparatus for the conduct of international relations which now seems strikingly small. Just before the outbreak of war the British diplomatic and consular services numbered only 446 in all, and of these fewer than 150 were career diplomats.[1] Though there had been some growth during the previous hundred years this was slow and unspectacular. The twenty heads of British missions abroad in 1816, when the effects of the country's long political isolation during the Napoleonic wars were still being felt, had increased to thirty-seven by 1860 (mainly because of the emergence of new independent states in Latin America); but the changes of the 1860s swept away many of the smaller legations in Germany and Italy, and the establishment of diplomatic representatives in China, Japan and one or two other non-European countries in the second half of the century did not compensate for these losses. The same small numbers and slow increase in them can be seen in the services of the other major powers. The 250 or so French diplomats of all ranks of the 1860s, for example, had increased surprisingly little by 1914, though from the 1880s their numbers began to grow rather more rapidly. Many important missions still functioned with what now seem tiny numbers: in 1860 those of Prussia in London and St Petersburg each had only six salaried employees in all, and those in Paris and Vienna only four apiece.[2] Moreover, any growth in numbers was often much less apparent, sometimes totally lacking, in the smaller states. The half-century after the Vienna settlement saw the development in several of them – Holland, Denmark, Sweden and the Swiss cantons – of a psychology of neutrality, a deliberate avoidance of involvement in international disputes and controversies, which became steadily stronger. This led to a feeling that while representation abroad for trade purposes was desirable and indeed essential, this could be achieved satisfactorily through consuls alone. Diplomats and diplomatic representation, it could be argued, were for these states a doubtfully necessary luxury and perhaps even a dangerous one. Thus Denmark, which had forty-four career diplomats in its service in 1797, had only twenty-eight fifty years later, and a mere twenty in 1914. In Holland opposition to the ambitious and unsuccessful foreign policy of King William I meant that in the quarter-century 1825–50 the number of missions abroad was reduced by five, while four others were downgraded and the salaries of Dutch diplomats cut by an average of a quarter.[3] Until the era of revolutions which began in the 1780s these secondary states had sometimes carried real weight in international affairs. In the seventeenth

1. Lord Strang, *The Foreign Office* (London, 1955), p. 30.
2. 'Report of the Select Committee on the Diplomatic Service', *Accounts and Papers*, 1861, vi, Appendix I, pp. 408–9.
3. *The Times Survey of Foreign Ministries of the World*, ed. Zara Steiner (London, 1982), pp. 171, 371.

century at least both the Dutch republic and Sweden could claim to rank as great powers in their own right. Their increasing withdrawal from the mainstream of European politics was a significant aspect of one of the most important changes of the nineteenth century – the clear emergence of a group of great powers in whose hands alone the political future of the continent was recognised to lie, and the relegation of all the other European states more clearly than in the past to varying degrees of political unimportance.[4] Not only did diplomatic services grow slowly in size: there was also none of the inflation of titles and wholesale upgrading of missions which was to develop after 1918 and still more after 1945. Already in the eighteenth century all the European states had shown themselves reluctant to appoint full ambassadors without substantial reasons of expediency or tradition. In the nineteenth and early twentieth centuries this attitude still held sway. In 1914 Britain maintained only nine embassies; and two of these were outside Europe and had been upgraded from legation status relatively recently (Washington in 1889 and Tokyo in 1905). There had been no British embassy in Rome until 1876 and none in Madrid until 1887. France, which had seven embassies in 1871, had still only ten in 1914. Even in Berlin the French legation was not raised to an embassy until 1862; and in the aftermath of the defeat of 1870–71 it was seriously proposed to save money by appointing only ministers and no ambassadors at all in future, though nothing came of this.[5]

That nineteenth-century diplomatic services should have remained small and unambitious, confined until late in the century to traditional functions and with no desire to expand their horizons or the scope of their activities, is not surprising. Foreign policy was in some ways still remarkably simple. The number of states actively involved in international relations was very small by the standards of the present day and the relationships between them relatively clear-cut. There was much less to be known about the broader background against which policy had to be made. Reasonably complete and reliable economic statistics of any kind became available only slowly even in many of the more developed European states; and in any case economic issues usually played only a subordinate role in policy-making. Public opinion, whatever that vague and difficult term may mean, was not often a serious consideration until very late in the nineteenth century, if then. International organisations, though on a bread-and-butter level becoming from the 1860s rapidly more important and active,[6] were still very much on the fringes of conventional diplomacy. In international relations, in a broader sense of

4. See below, pp. 186–8.
5. E. Hippeau, *Histoire diplomatique de la Troisième République* (Paris, 1889), p. 301.
6. See below, pp. 251–2.

the term, they were beginning to play an increasing part, and one with immense potentialities for the future; but even in 1914 they had only a secondary role in the thinking of diplomats or foreign offices. By the 1880s this situation was beginning slowly to change. The demands of a more and more complex economic life, and of an increasingly vocal and often volatile public opinion within each nation-state, were beginning to make some impression on the structure of traditional diplomacy.[7] Great changes were in prospect in the way in which for four centuries the states of Europe had been formally linked together. But at the outbreak of the First World War these were only in their early stages. The essence of European diplomacy was still political, still what it had been to Metternich or even to Richelieu. The mechanism could still be operated satisfactorily by diplomatic services which were small and content to remain so.

Certainly the geographical scope of European and European-style diplomacy expanded strikingly during the nineteenth century. The growth of empires in Africa and Asia, and of Europe's trade with the rest of the world, underlay a process which, by its later decades, had begun to bring China, Japan, Persia and even one or two independent or quasi-independent parts of Africa into what was now becoming a world system of diplomatic contacts. At least in Britain, the greatest of the imperial powers, this development was visible to some observers relatively early in the century. 'An English minister', wrote a pamphleteer in 1836,

> ought never to forget that the map of the British empire is the map of the world, and that if the ministers of other countries have only to study surrounding nations, he has to know the wants and interests of every people under the sun, from the savage Caffres of the Cape, to the civilized inhabitants of France and Germany.[8]

The significance of this should not be exaggerated, however. Until the end of the nineteenth century, or even later, most foreign offices adapted their internal structures, for so many generations designed to meet demands which were entirely European, only slowly and reluctantly to cope with new problems which increasingly embraced the entire world.[9]

One important non-European or only partly-European state whose position had long been ambiguous, the Ottoman empire, was now finally and firmly incorporated into European diplomacy. The resident Turkish missions sent to the major European capitals in 1793 by Selim III rapidly lost most of what practical significance they had ever possessed. From

7. See below, pp. 131–4; 136–40.
8. *A Few Remarks on our Foreign Policy* (London, 1836), pp. 53–4.
9. For some comments on this in the French context see A. Outrey, 'Histoire et principes de l'administration française des affaires étrangères', *Revue Française de Science Politique*, 1953, 508, 510.

1811 onwards they were in the care of mere chargés d'affaires, all of whom were Greeks, and controlled only skeleton staffs. The outbreak of the struggle for Greek independence in 1821 dealt them a death-blow: soon after it began they ceased to exist. However, the advantages for an increasingly enfeebled and menaced Ottoman empire of representation in the capitals of Europe were now too obvious to be disregarded. In the eighteenth century it had still been possible for Turks to feel that the empire, inherently superior to the infidel states which threatened it, had no need to stoop to such devices; but such an attitude was now no longer practicable. In 1835 a permanent Ottoman embassy reappeared in Paris. In the following year others appeared in Vienna and London. A legation was set up in Berlin in 1837 and another in St Petersburg twenty years later. In 1847 the ambassador in Vienna was sent on a special mission to the papacy. Perhaps an even more significant index of changing attitudes was the sending of a Turkish ambassador to Teheran in 1849: this formed part of 'probably the first exchange of permanent diplomatic missions by two Muslim states'.[10] By the end of the century there were fifteen Ottoman missions abroad and the empire was an integral (and in a negative sense, because of its growing weakness, important) part of the European system of international relations.

But with the non-European world in general, with Asia and whatever independent states could be said to exist in Africa, with Latin America and even to a large extent with the United States, Europe's relationship was still very largely an economic one based on the increasing flows of intercontinental trade. Diplomatic relations with states outside Europe and the Near East were needed (with the important exception of Anglo-American ones, in which territorial questions often bulked large) mainly to provide suitable conditions for the growth and security of that trade. Such a relationship could be fostered effectively and relatively cheaply by efficient consuls. It is significant that in the mid-century the French government paid its minister in Washington less than a seventh (20,000 francs against 150,000) of the salary of its ambassador in London.[11] There was thus from the 1850s a sharp growth of European consular representation in the outside world, particularly in Asia. But for decades to come the countries in which this happened were politically important as fields for the rivalries and ambitions of the European imperial powers rather than in their own right. Not until the Sino-Japanese war of 1894–95, perhaps not until the Russo-Japanese one of a decade later, did any Asiatic state become a true actor on the stage of world affairs, a

10. J.C. Hurewitz, 'Ottoman Diplomacy and the European State System', *Middle East Journal*, 15 (1961), 148.

11. *Les Affaires Étrangères et le corps diplomatique français*, ed. J. Baillou (Paris, 1984), i, 660.

subject rather than an object in international relations at the highest level. The growth of consular representation in Asia, however, was striking, especially in the crucial generation 1840–70, which saw the effective 'opening' of both China and Japan. France, for example, which also equipped herself with consuls in India and Malaya (Singapore, 1839; Calcutta, 1846; Bombay, 1866) established one in Canton, after some earlier unsuccessful attempts, in 1843 and others in Hongkong, Hankow and Tientsin from 1862. She had one in Bangkok from 1857 and in Tokyo from the following year.[12] The importance of east Asia in the general consular picture is especially marked in the case of Britain: by the end of the nineteenth century, when there were rather less than 200 salaried members of the British general consular service spread across the world, the more specialised and highly trained one which operated in China alone numbered seventy-five (including student interpreters and assistants).[13]

On the diplomatic level the picture was less impressive. In Persia, the first purely Asiatic state to attract serious European political attention, a British legation was established in Teheran in 1809, a Russian one in 1828 and a French one in 1855. But the main function of the British and Russian ministers was to observe and counter each other's activities; it was the rivalries of these two great imperial powers which kept alive their interest in Persia and made them establish and maintain relations with it. Though its ruler, Nasr-ed-Din Shah, visited Europe several times from the early 1870s onwards, and also established diplomatic representatives there, until the end of the nineteenth century Persia was not really part of the contemporary world. An English scholar who visited it in 1887–88 found that

> the atmosphere was mediæval; politics and progress were scarcely mentioned, and the talk turned mostly on mysticism, metaphysics and religion; the most burning political questions were those connected with the successors of the Prophet Mohammed in the seventh century of our era; only the most languid interest in external affairs was aroused by the occasional appearance of the official journals.[14]

In China the situation was not altogether dissimilar. Britain and France were able in 1860 to force the government to receive their representatives in Pekin; and Russian and American ones immediately followed. China,

---

12. M. Degros, 'La création des postes diplomatiques et consulaires français de 1815 à 1870', *Revue d'Histoire Diplomatique* (1986), 219–73.
13. D.C.M. Platt, *The Cinderella Service: British Consuls since 1825* (London, 1971), p. 202.
14. Quoted in *Near Eastern Culture and Society*, ed. T.C. Young (Princeton, 1959), pp. 136–7.

after some tentative experiments and with a good deal of reluctance, sent ministers of her own to London in 1877 and to Washington, St Petersburg and Tokyo in the following year. But the country remained for long a backwater in international relations. Western trade and investment there were rapidly growing; but the duties of western diplomats in Pekin remained essentially those of fostering these economic interests and seeing that no imperial power stole a march on its rivals in this respect. Chinese envoys in Europe and America did little negotiating: they were concerned mainly with the protection of Chinese abroad and with the collection of information and the purchase of guns, ships and machinery for their government.

Japan was a different matter. At first her potentialities were quite unseen in Europe. After the series of treaties in 1854–58 which helped to launch her on a rapid and irreversible process of change it could even still be questioned whether full-scale diplomatic representation there was worth what it cost. The French government tried to save money by accrediting the consul-general it sent to Japan in 1858 also as chargé d'affaires (a device quite often used outside Europe, mainly in minor Latin-American states where it was expected that political relations would be very much subordinate to commercial ones). In London there were doubts as to whether the likely trade justified the expense of full diplomatic representation: it still seemed possible that Japan's ports would be used mainly by whaling ships in the north Pacific rather than by merchantmen.[15] Japanese adaptability and dynamism soon ended such doubts; and this ability to adjust to new demands and enter the modern world was before long visible on the diplomatic level. By 1873 there were already nine Japanese legations abroad, in Washington and the major capitals of Europe. In 1906, in a sign of growing national confidence in the aftermath of victory over Russia, seven of these were raised to the status of embassies. Simultaneously several of the European powers upgraded their Tokyo legations to embassy rank – Britain and France in 1905 and Germany in the following year. Japan was now clearly a great power, at least in the Pacific. But apart from the United States she was the only non-European state which could claim anything like this status. The growth of western power and activity in Asia had done a good deal to extend the geographical scope of European-type diplomacy. So, in a very minor way, had similar activity in Africa; the first continuous French and British representation in Addis Ababa began in 1897 and 1898 respectively. Of the forty-one states in which Britain had permanent diplomatic representation in 1914 only twenty-two were in Europe

15. W.G. Beasley, *Great Britain and the Opening of Japan* (London, 1951), p. 192.

(twelve others were in the Americas, four in the Middle East and three in the Far East). The distribution for France and Germany was not very different, though that for the Habsburg empire and to a lesser extent Russia showed a greater preponderance of European interests. But the major posts, with very few exceptions, were still European ones. When the First World War broke out diplomatic services were still markedly concentrated in Europe and still thought predominantly in terms of European problems and rivalries.

## Foreign offices and their organisation

Foreign offices were also growing larger, though, like the diplomatic services they controlled, only gradually. Most of the growth was concentrated in the later decades of the nineteenth century and still more in the first years of the twentieth. Thus the French foreign ministry, which had in 1814 some seventy employees with functions directly related to foreign policy (i.e. excluding messengers, doorkeepers, etc.) had still only ninety in 1870; but by 1914 this figure had grown to 170.[16] In the Habsburg dominions the *Staatskanzlei* in 1848, the last year of its life, had thirty-nine officials with some degree of authority – departmental heads, ministerial advisers, departmental counsellors, ministerial secretaries and clerks. The foreign ministry which took its place in that year had fifty-one in 1895, ninety-two in 1911 and 146 when the monarchy collapsed in 1918.[17] In Russia a proposed reform of the ministry in 1910 suggested that there should be 187 established posts in all, an increase of forty-nine on the number fixed only thirteen years earlier.[18] Even in the small and neutrally-minded states the same process of growth in the later nineteenth and early twentieth centuries can be seen. The staff of the Dutch foreign ministry swelled from twenty-three in 1849 to forty-five in 1914; and the tiny Danish one grew from a mere nine in 1848 to twenty-one in 1900 and a remarkable fifty-eight in 1919. In Sweden an even more striking increase in face of the intensified pressures and dangers of the early twentieth century took place, from nineteen in 1905 to eighty-eight in 1918.[19]

These were still everywhere small numbers, especially if they are compared with the very much bigger ones in the other great ministries of all the major states. In 1870 the ninety serving in the French foreign

16. P. Bury, 'La Carrière diplomatique au temps du Second Empire', *Revue d'Histoire Diplomatique*, 1976, 280; *Les Affaires Etrangères . . ., ii, 1870–1980*, 108.

17. *Times Survey of Foreign Ministries*, p. 51.

18. G.H. Bolsover, 'Izvol'sky and Reform of the Russian Ministry of Foreign Affairs', *Slavonic and East European Review*, 63 (1985), 37.

19. *Times Survey of Foreign Ministries*, pp. 172, 371, 373, 461, 463.

ministry, for example, were dwarfed by the 1,500 employed in the ministry of finance, the largest of all French central government departments. In one or two cases there were even sharp reductions in staffs which had been inflated by patronage and the need to provide posts for young members of the ruling class. The emerging Turkish foreign ministry, a case in point, had about 200 salaried officials working in it in the early 1870s, at the end of the *Tanzimat* period of attempted administrative and legal reform. But the whole Turkish diplomatic and consular establishment, which was further swollen for political reasons by Sultan Abdul Hamid in the 1880s and 1890s, was considerably reduced by the revolution of 1908–09 which overthrew him, so that by 1914 the foreign ministry staff had fallen to probably no more than 150.[20] Russia until well into the second half of the nineteenth century is a more striking example. The foreign ministry in St Petersburg was in the first decades of the century ludicrously overstaffed: under Alexander I it gave ostensible employment to well over 700 people (including the poet Pushkin), many of whom had no real duties whatever. A former Russian ambassador in London complained in 1803 that it had 'more people than the offices of all the secretaries of state in Europe combined'.[21] Even in 1868 when the foreign minister, Count A.M. Gorchakov, sharply reduced the numbers, there were still 306 established posts: he cut this figure to 134.[22]

The essential conclusion, however, is clear. In 1914 or even 1918 foreign ministries everywhere were still by present-day standards very small institutions staffed by socially homogeneous élite groups but the pressures making for growth, and in the decade or more before 1914 rapid growth, were now irresistible. As the scope of foreign policy expanded to embrace areas hitherto regarded as unimportant or completely ignored, and as the geographical scope of the diplomatic network widened, the sheer amount of business to be handled grew correspondingly. The recognition in the 1820s of the new Latin-American republics as independent states is said to have increased the workload of the British foreign office by a half,[23] while in the later decades of the nineteenth century commercial and economic diplomacy and the need to influence the new force of mass public opinion were making new and unprecedented demands.[24] In the mid-1820s the total number of

20. C.V. Findley, *Bureaucratic Reform in the Ottoman empire; The Sublime Porte, 1789–1922* (Princeton, 1980), pp. 190–324.

21. Patricia Kennedy Grimstead, *The Foreign Ministers of Alexander I* (Berkeley–Los Angeles, 1969), p. 27.

22. Bolsover, 'Izvol'sky and Reform . . .', 23.

23. C.R. Middleton, *The Administration of British Foreign Policy, 1782–1846* (Durham, N.C., 1977), p. 187.

24. See below, pp. 132–3; 138–40.

despatches sent and received each year by the foreign office was about 12,000. Little more than a generation later, in 1857, it was almost 60,000. By 1916, the busiest wartime year, over 265,000 documents were entered in the central registry and over 90,000 more in that of the new foreign trade department.[25] Comparisons of this kind are difficult to make with accuracy over long periods of time; but the direction and size of the change are beyond doubt. A roughly similar pattern, especially as regards the rapid growth in business in the years before 1914, can be seen everywhere: the unit of the Russian foreign ministry which duplicated papers concerned with relations with the European states, for example, trebled its output in 1893–1906.[26]

In their internal organisation the foreign offices of the nineteenth and early twentieth centuries, in spite of frequent changes in detail, had a general similarity. Everywhere the most important element was a department or more usually a series of departments divided along geographical lines, which handled correspondence with missions abroad, of which those in the major European capitals were by far the most significant. There was usually a good deal of flexibility in the organisation of these political departments: their number and scope altered easily and often to meet changing demands. The British foreign office, for example, had in 1835–41 a short-lived China department, the result of the ending in 1833 of the East India Company's monopoly of trade with China and of the growing tensions which erupted in the 'Opium War' of 1839–42. By the 1880s it had three main departments of this kind: Eastern, Western and American (the last also covering China, Japan and Siam). By 1900, however, a Far Eastern department had been created and most of the business relating to African questions had been given to a new African department: in other words the administrative subdivisions were adapted to the changing political importance of different parts of the world. Much the same adaptability can be seen elsewhere. The German foreign ministry, for instance, set up in 1890 a colonial department in response to the Reich's acquisition a few years earlier of a largely valueless empire in Africa and the Pacific.

Around this central structure of political departments others were grouped. Often there was a consular and commercial one. This reflected the fact that although in almost every country men moved between the diplomatic and consular services the latter was still everywhere distinct from the former, with different duties and a much lower status. Usually again there was a department which controlled the internal administration

25. *Accounts and Papers*, 1870 (382) vii, p. 417; *The Records of the Foreign Office, 1782–1939* (Public Record Office Handbooks, No. 13; London, 1969), p. 67fn.

26. Bolsover, 'Izvol'sky and Reform . . .', 31.

of the ministry and its finances; sometimes this was also involved in the appointment and promotion of diplomats. Even the Turkish foreign ministry, very belatedly, acquired one such in 1871. Frequently, as the nineteenth century went on, there was also a department concerned with essentially legal issues such as naturalisation and extradition, and international legal disputes; the French ministry had such a *bureau des contentieux* for much of the century and the Sardinian and later Italian one had a *consiglio del contenzioso diplomatico* from 1856 onwards. As a movement in the same direction the German foreign office set up a legal and commercial department in 1885 and the British one acquired a legal adviser in 1893 (a post of Legal Assistant Under-Secretary had already been created in 1876). In several states the personal staff of the foreign minister, chosen by him and handling his correspondence and interviews, was a formally distinct entity. This often acted as his main link with and control over the permanent officials of the ministry and could have great practical importance in its day-to-day running. In France the *cabinet du ministre* throughout much of this period and in Italy the *gabinetto particolare* set up in 1855 were often extremely influential. That in France, about which most information is available, had at various times responsibility for a wide variety of technical services – couriers, diplomatic bags, codes and, much more significantly, personnel and appointments. To give details of the internal organisation of each of the foreign offices of Europe, and of the endless changes in detail which took place over more than a century, would be wearisome and repetitive.[27] There was, however, a clearly marked tendency for this organisation to become more complex as time went on. The number of departments within each major foreign ministry grew with the growing complexity of the work to be done. That of the Habsburgs in Vienna had five such departments in 1849 but seventeen by 1914, while by 1918 the division of the French foreign ministry which now handled both political and commercial policy was split into eleven sub-divisions. Even the German *Auswärtiges Amt*, the organisation of which was always relatively simple, was divided into five main departments in 1919 as against only two in 1871.

The growing professionalism of both diplomats and foreign office officials during this period is seen most clearly in changes in the ways in which they were recruited. Now, for the first time, fixed though often not very stringent criteria for appointment began to play a significant role.[28] But apart from this an increasingly professional tone can be

27. It can be followed in general terms in *The Times Survey* . . ., and in more detail for France in *Les Affaires Etrangères* . . .; for Italy in L.V. Ferraris, *L'amministrazione centrale del Ministero degli Esteri Italiano nel suo sviluppo storico (1848–1954)* (Florence, 1955); and for Germany in L. Cecil, *The German Diplomatic Service, 1871–1914* (Princeton, 1976).

28. See below, pp. 123–5.

detected in two other ways. A consciousness of belonging to a coherent professional group was both expressed and strengthened by the appearance, from the mid-nineteenth century onwards, of guides and yearbooks which for the first time listed the diplomats and foreign office officials in the service of most of the European states. This also gave the general public for the first time some information, though in a summary and superficial way, about the men who carried out their country's foreign policy. At the same time diplomatic archives, inevitably growing in size, became better organised, as did some of the libraries which were now a part of all major foreign offices. More and more, in other words, these now possessed the means not merely to carry out foreign policy but also to study foreign policy questions in some depth. In the eighteenth century none, with the possible exception of that of France, had carried out much that could be called research. Now all the larger ones were beginning to have at least some capacity of this kind.

Of the first of these developments one of the earliest examples was the publication in Sweden from 1824 onwards of a list of the country's consuls and vice-consuls. Until 1860 this was the work of the college of commerce; but in that year it was taken over by the foreign ministry and ten years later replaced by an annual list of Swedish diplomats and ministry officials.[29] In Britain the *Foreign Office List* made its first appearance in 1852, while France began to produce its *Annuaire Diplomatique* from 1858. Italy first published a similar list in 1865, and from 1888 a bulletin in which the foreign ministry provided information on promotions and transfers of officials and diplomats as well as condensed versions of consular and diplomatic reports. Publications of this sort broke sharply with the anonymity and complete immunity from public scrutiny which had hitherto marked foreign offices, and were therefore at first greeted in them with doubt or hostility. When the *Foreign Office List* made its first appearance 'it was strongly objected to in certain quarters, as likely to afford information to the general public with regard to the office, which they thought it advisable they should not possess, and much information was for a time withheld'.[30] But the wave of publications of this kind which began in the 1850s could only gather strength as the century went on and public interest in foreign policy questions grew.

The development of organised diplomatic archives and of foreign office libraries is perhaps best seen in Britain. There, from January 1801 onwards, correspondence covering the years since 1780 was systematically assembled from the State Paper Office and elsewhere and taken to the

29. S. Tunberg et al. (eds), *Histoire de l'administration des affaires étrangères de la Suède* (Upsal, 1940), p. 468.

30. Sir E. Hertslet, *Recollections of the Old Foreign Office* (London, 1901), p. 246.

foreign office – an obvious response to the need frequently to refer to it in the conduct of daily business and the resulting inconvenience if it were stored anywhere else. The first foreign office librarian had been appointed in 1800: when he retired a decade later he had organised this mass of papers into a systematic and usable collection.[31] The library itself was less lucky. Until the move in the 1860s to a new building with adequate space, it was dispersed on shelves scattered all over the old one, with the books crowded three rows deep on the shelves so that only those in the front row were visible, and no catalogue of it existed.[32] Yet the office now had as never before the means to produce serious analyses and discussions of foreign policy questions, and to use large masses of materials in the process. When in 1850 a radical member of parliament, J.A. Roebuck, moved a famous and extremely detailed vote of censure on Palmerston's foreign policy over a period of two decades, 2,000–3,000 volumes of manuscript correspondence were consulted by officials in the government's attempt to produce a convincing rebuttal.[33] An effort of this kind would have been quite beyond the office's powers at any time until well into the nineteenth century. Everywhere diplomatic archives were becoming more complete and more carefully arranged. Even in Constantinople the creation of one was begun in the 1850s (though in this case it was very poorly organised), while a Records Director was appointed at the end of the 1860s in an effort to control the tide of paper which, in the Turkish foreign office as in all others, was now flowing more and more strongly.[34]

In many ways, then, Europe's machinery for the conduct of international relations was moving into a new era. It now had to use new resources to meet new challenges. But the past and its legacy still bulked very large in many ways – in the aristocratic and socially exclusive makeup of both diplomatic services and foreign offices, in their continuing smallness and in their concentration on traditional and narrowly political aspects of policy. More specifically, in most offices the interception and reading of correspondence which seemed a possible source of useful information still continued. Public opinion, in an age which increasingly liked to think itself morally superior to its predecessors, was sometimes less willing than in the past to tolerate activities of this kind. In Britain the revelation that the correspondence of Mazzini, the Italian nationalist leader then a refugee in London, was being opened and read in this way produced strong criticism in parliament and the press. The result was the

31. Middleton, *The Administration of British Foreign Policy*, pp. 173–4.
32. Hertslet, *Recollections . . .*, p. 27.
33. Hertslet, *Recollections . . .*, pp. 72–3.
34. Findley, *Bureaucratic Reform . . .*, p. 188.

115

abolition in February 1844 of the Secret Office which for generations had been intercepting letters of possible interest to the government. A few months later the deciphering organisation which had existed for not far short of two centuries also disappeared. In the second half of the century British governments seem to have gathered no intelligence at all in this way. Indeed so high was their reputation for self-denial in this respect that in the first years of the twentieth century the brothers Paul and Jules Cambon, French ambassadors in London and Berlin respectively, entrusted their private correspondence regularly to the British diplomatic bag rather than sending it through the French ministry of foreign affairs or the French post office: if either of these channels had been used it would almost certainly have been opened and read.[35] Such rectitude, however, was very much the exception rather than the rule among the great powers. In Vienna the interception of letters became under Metternich more frequent than ever before. The head of the deciphering branch of the foreign ministry there claimed in 1823 that he had personally broken eighty-five foreign codes, at a time when eighty to a hundred letters were being opened on each working day.[36] The Austrian revolutionaries of 1848, flushed with liberal and democratic idealism, swept away the entire organisation. But this fit of morality hardly survived their short-lived victory over the old regime. By the end of the century France, Russia and the Habsburg empire all had flourishing *cabinets noirs*. Under the Third Republic coded diplomatic telegrams were passed as a matter of course to the French foreign office by the postal authorities to be decoded and read; and this activity reached a climax in the first years of the twentieth century. In 1902 the letters of Lord Lansdowne, the British foreign secretary, to the ambassador in Paris were clearly being opened in this way.[37] But in spite of all this it seems likely that during much of the nineteenth century this subterranean aspect of international relations was less important, and less prominent in the minds of both diplomats and policy-makers, than at any time in the last 300 years.

By the beginning of the twentieth century the attitudes and ambience of many foreign offices were altering quite rapidly. Far-reaching organisational changes were being forced upon many of them by the sheer growth of business, the sharpening of international rivalries and the accelerating pace of events. In Britain a considerable reorganisation got under way in 1903. Three years later the introduction of a new

35. C. Andrew, *Secret Service: The Making of the British Intelligence Community* (London, 1985), p. 85.
36. F. Stix, 'Zur Geschichte und Organisation der Wiener Geheimen Ziffernkanzlei', *Mitteilungen des Österreichischen Instituts für Geschichtsforschung*, 51 (1937), 142, 140.
37. Andrew, *Secret Service*, pp. 6–7.

registration system for despatches and telegrams played a crucial role in changing the position of the more senior officials, the first-division clerks, and giving them, far more than in the past, a share in policy-making. The British foreign office also showed itself more forward-looking than almost any other in the adoption of the typewriter: it appointed its first typist in 1889 and had eight by 1900. In France also, in 1907, there was an effort to reorganise work more rationally and effectively, in particular by bringing political and economic diplomacy together in a single *direction*. But adjustment to changing circumstances went deeper than formal organisation. The spirit too was often changing. Methods were becoming more businesslike. Officials worked harder, or at least more consistently. New technical aids were increasingly used. A young Frenchman, when in 1896 he entered his country's diplomatic service, found himself trained as in the past, largely by being made to copy as models of style despatches dating from the pre-revolutionary monarchy. No typewriters were as yet in use, and the young recruits were taught the 'diplomatic' style of handwriting, designed for maximum legibility. As a member of one of the two departments into which the *direction politique* of the foreign ministry was then divided, he found that he and his colleagues spent much of their time playing draughts and that there was considerable rivalry between the two as to which could make the better 'five o'clock tea'. But when he returned to the ministry in 1913, after a long spell of service in Rome, a great deal had changed. Work was much harder. Tea was taken, if at all, at one's desk. Each office now had a telephone. Female typists and even female secretaries were now employed. Only the building on the Quai d'Orsay was inadequate and the old lift often refused to work.[38] Similarly a young Russian diplomat, serving in a junior post in London during the very first years of the twentieth century, found that the embassy possessed only one typewriter, and that so old that it was difficult to use. However, when he returned in 1908 to the foreign ministry in St Petersburg he was struck by finding there a considerable number of women typists who 'filled the offices, walked arm in arm in the corridors, and flirted with everybody'.[39]

This spirit of change was not universal. The Italian foreign ministry and diplomatic service remained among the most overstaffed and inefficient in Europe. One foreign ministry clerk in the early years of the twentieth century 'soon decided that it was not worth the trouble to go to the office to sleep when I could sleep more comfortably in my own bed or pass my

38. J. Laroche, *Au Quai d'Orsay avec Briand et Poincaré, 1913–1926* (Paris, 1957), pp. 10–12.

39. *Revelations of a Russian Diplomat: The Memoirs of Dmitrii I. Abrikossov*, ed. G.A. Lensen, (Seattle, 1964), pp. 105, 143.

time in more interesting or more amusing tasks', while an Italian ambassador is said to have spent only fifteen days of a year in residence in a post which he disliked.[40] But in many of the major foreign offices of Europe things were changing very perceptibly in the years before 1914. They were ceasing to be the almost monastic institutions of the past. Their efficiency was growing, their outlook becoming wider and less bound by tradition. The increasing amount of business to be handled meant that more and more decisions were now taken by officials, even merely middle-ranking ones: it was no longer possible for almost every question to go to the minister himself for final decision, as had hitherto been normal. Increasingly officials helped to make policy, sometimes with decisive effect. The vast amount of routine clerical labour which had made up so much day-to-day activity in the past had been lightened by the coming of the woman typist and sometimes also of clerks recruited specifically for this sort of work. In 1890 all foreign ministries had been, to varying extents, tradition-bound and backward-looking. By 1914 some at least were becoming modern policy-making organs with efficient administrative and clerical underpinnings.

Whether, as is sometimes asserted, the development of more rapid communications, above all the telegraph, greatly increased the control of foreign ministries over diplomats in the field is at least debatable. Certainly the telegraph was more and more relied on. The first use of it in British diplomacy seems to have been by the Paris embassy in December 1852: by the middle of the following year the missions in Vienna, Berlin and Florence could also communicate in this way with London, and from 1878 British diplomatic telegrams were numbered in the same way as despatches. However, for long their cost helped to restrict their number. In 1860 the foreign secretary urged British diplomats not to use unnecessarily 'this very costly channel of communication',[41] and until at least the end of the nineteenth century the ministers in China and Japan, to save money, were still guided, except in serious emergencies, by despatches which took five weeks to reach them via the Suez Canal, or four if they were sent across Canada. Quite soon, none the less, complaints began to be heard that the coming of the telegraph had tilted the balance dangerously towards inflexible central control of all diplomatic activity. What one old-school diplomat called 'the telegraphic demoralisation of those who formerly had to act for themselves and are now content to be at the end of the wire'[42] had, it was claimed, given

---

40. R.J.B. Bosworth, *Italy the Least of the Great Powers: Italian Foreign Policy before the First World War* (Cambridge, 1979), p. 98.

41. *Accounts and Papers*, 1861 (459), vi, Appendix I, p. 465.

42. Sir H. Rumbold, *Recollections of a Diplomatist* (London, 1902), i, 111–12.

greater effect to the instinctive dislike felt by all foreign ministries for diplomats who showed initiative and were not afraid of responsibility. It is doubtful whether such charges were justified. One foreign secretary argued in the 1860s, with some force, that the coming of the telegraph meant that often diplomats were no longer sent, as in the past, long and detailed despatches with full instructions. This, he claimed, meant that they sometimes had to act more rather than less on their own initiative. It was growing uniformity of organisation, the growth of more professional diplomatic services with the relatively fixed standards and procedures which are the essence of any true profession, which were the main force limiting the independence and personal initiative of diplomats. The more highly organised and consciously efficient foreign offices became, the less scope there was for the individual who did not fit easily into these bigger and more complex machines. Even in pre-telegraph days, when instructions could be sent no faster than a horse could trot or a ship sail, it is far from clear that this meant greater independence for diplomats. Very often slow communications meant merely a slowing-down in the whole pace of events, an acceptance of the fact that important negotiations were bound to be protracted. It is also relevant here that in the seventeenth and eighteenth centuries meetings between rulers were exceedingly rare (Louis XIV never met William III, the Emperor Leopold I or Charles II of Spain, the rivals against whom he struggled for so long) and negotiations between them had therefore to be conducted entirely through their diplomats. In the nineteenth century, on the other hand, there was a significant amount of direct personal contact between them, or at least between their chief ministers. The congresses of 1814–21 are the most obvious example of this; but Napoleon III negotiated directly with Cavour at Plombières in 1858 and with Bismarck at Biarritz in 1865, while the peace preliminaries of 1871 were settled face-to-face between Bismarck and Thiers and the first *Dreikaiserbund* alliance of 1872–73 took shape from personal meetings between the rulers of Germany, Austria–Hungary and Russia. Any move of this kind towards the 'summit diplomacy' of our own day was likely to undermine somewhat the position formerly enjoyed by the heads of great diplomatic missions.

## Recruitment and training

Diplomacy remained throughout this period, especially in the major states, an aristocratic pursuit. In its higher reaches in particular it was still, as generally in the eighteenth century, the preserve of a social élite. It was also a profession, or quasi-profession, in which family connections, sometimes verging on downright nepotism, counted for much. There was a strong hereditary element in its recruitment patterns. A high proportion of diplomats everywhere still began their careers, until well into the second half of the nineteenth century, by serving as unpaid attachés; and it was not unusual for the head of a mission to ask for a son or a nephew to be assigned to it in this capacity. Few could go so far as Musurus Pasha, who during his thirty-five years as Turkish ambassador in London staffed the embassy entirely with his sons, nephews and sons-in-law; but even in the most developed states of western Europe and on the eve of the 1914 conflict family influences could still be important.[43] Foreign offices were affected by them just as much as service abroad. In the Habsburg empire, under the most snobbish and conservative regime of all, 'once a new family had gained a foothold in the foreign ministry it was almost a rule that the sons, and even the grandsons, remained in the profession'.[44] In London successive generations of the Hertslet family served in the foreign office continuously for well over a hundred years from 1795 onwards. Aristocratic influences were at their height during the first half of the nineteenth century and in any diplomatic service were always most marked at the highest levels. Of the twenty-three men who achieved the rank of British ambassador in 1815–60 twenty were aristocrats. Of the remaining three, George Canning, the future prime minister, was only briefly ambassador in Lisbon in 1814–15, when his political career at home was at a low ebb; and the two others, Robert Liston and Stratford Canning, represented Britain in Constantinople, a very important post but one in which high social rank was not the advantage it was in the other great capitals. Of the sixty-six British envoys extraordinary and ministers plenipotentiary during the same period forty-seven can be classed as aristocrats; while of the sixty-four French ambassadors and ministers who served in 1814–30 (admittedly a period when aristocratic influences were untypically strong in France) only ten were non-noble.[45] Even in the early twentieth century, except perhaps in France, now a republic formally at least grounded in a history of revolution, the tradition of a diplomacy conducted by aristocrats was still dominant. The German empire, down to the collapse of 1918, continued to give very marked preference in diplomatic appointments not merely to noblemen but to members of old Prussian families. It was also a distinct advantage there to have been, in one's university days, a member of an aristocratic student fraternity.[46] The

43. See, for example, the details on the newest and in some ways the most progressive great state of all in Cecil, *German Diplomatic Service,* pp. 21–3. For France earlier in the century see the examples given in Bury, 'La Carrière diplomatique . . .', 280–1.

44. *Times Survey of Foreign Ministries*, p. 51.

45. R.A. Jones, *The British Diplomatic Service, 1815–1914* (Gerrards Cross, 1983), pp. 16–17; *Les Affaires Etrangères . . .*, i, 535.

46. Cecil, *German Diplomatic Service*, pp. 63–4, 79–85.

few non-noble heads of German missions abroad were nearly always tucked away in very minor capitals far from Europe. At one point there were as many as four of them; but these were stationed respectively in Colombia, Venezuela, Peru and Siam. There is nothing surprising in this continuing emphasis on noble birth and high social rank. There was still a general assumption that the self-confidence and *savoir-faire* they conferred were essential in any aspirant to one of the major embassies. Even in 1914 there was still widespread agreement with Drouyn de Lhuys, one of the foreign ministers of Napoleon III, that aristocratic diplomats were 'very useful if not indispensable' for the éclat of our embassies, provided that merit is not altogether absent'.[47] Society in every great state of Europe was still dominated, to varying degrees, by landowning aristocracies. Everywhere inherited rank and titles were still an integral part of social life. Usually diplomatic services and foreign offices in this respect merely reflected the societies they served. This was not invariably the case. Both the Habsburg monarchy and the Bismarckian empire were represented by services more snobbish and restrictive than the societies which employed them. But it is pointless and unhistorical to condemn the absence of 'democracy' in the recruitment of diplomats when Europe in general was still so far from being democratic.

High and assured social status helped to keep diplomats, especially high-ranking ones, as in the past distinctly cosmopolitan in outlook. The aristocracies which ruled so much of Europe could still see themselves even in 1914 as in some sense parts of a social order which transcended national boundaries. They were united across these dividing-lines by fundamental similarities of outlook and often of education. A diplomat who spent most of his working life in foreign capitals could easily feel himself part of an aristocratic international to which national feeling was hardly more than a vulgar plebeian prejudice. These attitudes were far from new; but in the nineteenth century, in an age of increasingly strident nationalism, they stand out more clearly than ever before. They are seen most clearly in the marked tendency for diplomats to acquire foreign wives (and sometimes with them significant amounts of property in foreign countries). Thus, under the Second Empire, at least three heads of important French diplomatic missions had British wives, and others had American, Italian and Polish ones.[48] In the German service in 1891 there was only one ambassador (Prince Reuss in Vienna) who had a German wife. In Britain Sir Horace Rumbold, who ended his career as ambassador to Vienna in 1896–1900, is a striking individual case of the same

47. *Les Affaires Etrangères* . . ., i, 719.
48. Bury, 'La Carrière diplomatique . . .', 289.

cosmopolitanism. Born in India, brought up mainly in France and speaking both French and German perfectly, he thought seriously as a young man of entering Habsburg service and married an American, while his brother took a Russian wife, one of the Nelidov family which was prominent in tsarist diplomacy. Sir Robert Morier, perhaps the most successful British diplomat of the later nineteenth century, was partly French: in 1870 he had six cousins fighting in the French army. Many other such examples could easily be found.

Side by side with aristocratic influences went, at least in the great states of continental Europe, often very significant military ones. The use of soldiers as diplomatic representatives was far from unknown before the nineteenth century. During the great cycle of wars in 1689–1713 both Louis XIV and his English opponents employed military men to fill many of the most important diplomatic appointments, while under Napoleon I they were even more extensively used. In 1789–1814 twenty French missions abroad were headed by generals.[49] But during the nineteenth century soldiers were perhaps more continuously prominent in this way than ever before. The militarism which had begun to take root in Europe during the eighteenth century[50] was now steadily gaining strength. In the great conservative monarchies of Prussia, Russia and the Habsburg empire military influences, reflected in such small but highly significant things as the habitual wearing by their rulers of army uniforms, pervaded the atmosphere of the court and many of the upper reaches of government. Very often in them high-ranking officers had easier and more direct access to the ruler, and sometimes more influence over him, than any civilian minister, however important. Quite frequently therefore a soldier might be appointed to head a mission in Berlin or St Petersburg in the justified belief that military men were especially welcome there and likely to be effective representatives. Even in France soldiers often received high diplomatic appointments, especially under a regime in which military influences were strong, such as the Second Empire. Napoleon III sent a soldier, Baragueys d'Hilliers, as ambassador to Constantinople in 1853 and another, Pélissier, to London in 1858, though neither of these achieved much. More important was the appointment of one of his aides-de-camp, General Fleury, as ambassador in St Petersburg in 1869; and his successors, Le Flô and Chanzy, were both soldiers as well. In Italy also high diplomatic posts were often filled by generals and occasionally admirals.[51]

49. *Les Affaires Etrangères* . . ., i, 416, 422.

50. See M.S. Anderson, *War and Society in Europe of the Old Regime, 1618–1789* (London, 1988), pp. 170ff.

51. G. Negri, *La direzione ed il controllo democratico della politica estera in Italia* (Milan, 1967), p. 34.

The military influences which were so strong in diplomacy in central and eastern Europe were therefore by no means unknown in the great western states as well. In the later decades of the nineteenth century these influences were being institutionalised in the new appointment of the military attaché;[52] but this was merely one aspect of their significance. At the highest diplomatic level they were now more consistently important than ever before.

By the middle decades of the century the 'old diplomacy' as it had evolved over the last three hundred years, with its easy-going and cosmopolitan atmosphere, its often short hours of work, its extensive use of unpaid or inadequately paid diplomats, its almost complete immunity from effective public scrutiny, was under increasing pressure. More and more governments now demanded diplomatic services systematically and even rigidly organised, in which efficiency carried more weight and merit could expect to be rewarded more effectively. If heads of mission were allowed largely to choose their own subordinates central control was weakened. If young attachés were unpaid this made it more difficult to treat them as cogs in a bureaucratic machine. As one of them wrote in retrospect: 'The . . . taxpayer could owe them no grudge: they were unpaid. Society could expect nothing of them but amusement and a disposition to enjoy themselves; and they had no responsibilities unless it was that of not misleading the chief by wrong deciphering or an incorrect translation.'[53] If promotions were decided largely by social rank or family connections this impeded the growth of an efficient service. By mid-century, therefore, almost every European government was making efforts to control more effectively the recruitment and promotion of its diplomats. In this respect again diplomacy was becoming more organised and efficiency-minded.

In Britain from the 1820s all attachés had to have a letter of appointment signed by the secretary of state; and from 1815 a number of them began for the first time to be paid. These were only small and tentative steps, however, towards more effective central selection and control of young diplomats. Even in 1860 well under half the seventy-eight attachés in the British service were paid, however inadequately; and the unpaid ones were still regarded as being scarcely real members of the service at all. Nevertheless, a beginning had been made. Another way of improving quality and excluding obviously unsuitable candidates was to insist on some minimum formal academic qualification. Thus in France decrees of 1853 and 1856, which repeated an earlier one

52. See below, pp. 129–31.
53. H.E.H. Jerningham, *Reminiscences of an Attaché* (Edinburgh–London, 1886), p. 37.

of 1844, demanded that recruits to the diplomatic service hold a *licence en droit*, while the Belgian government in 1858 made a university degree essential for admission. But the most effective way of controlling recruitment was by an officially-organised entrance examination; and from the 1850s this device was being used by more and more states. Spain tried as early as 1852 to establish the principle of entrance by competitive examination. In 1856 qualifying examinations were introduced in Great Britain for both the foreign office and the diplomatic service; and in the same year the Sardinian government specified a similar test (three written papers, one of them in French, and three oral examinations). From 1860 young Frenchmen without a *licence en droit* could also gain appointment by taking an examination in diplomatic history, international law and languages. In the same year the Dutch government began to subject would-be diplomats to a test of this kind: a year earlier Gorchakov had tried to establish something similar in Russia. In Greece recruits to the diplomatic service, who had already to hold a law degree, were subjected, at least in theory, to a competitive entrance examination from 1868 onwards. In Japan a qualifying examination (which seems to have worked well and produced very good recruits) began in 1894, a minor but significant aspect of the extraordinary process of change which the country was now undergoing. Even in the Ottoman empire a commission was set up in 1885 to examine candidates for entry to Turkish diplomacy.

The immediate effect of these changes can be easily exaggerated. In some cases – Spain and Greece for example – the examinations were very irregular in their application and for long existed largely on paper. In Russia that introduced in 1859 had been sat two years later by a mere five candidates in all. Sometimes examinations, where they did take place, were not a very searching test of ability. This was at first the case in Britain, though the entrance examination for the foreign office was made considerably tougher in 1871 and that for the diplomatic service became more competitive from the 1880s onwards. Often there was a marked persistence of the traditional tendency to regard external polish and *savoir-faire*, good appearance and manners, as much more important than the ability to do well in examinations. This attitude remained strong in Germany, where the entrance examination was formally quite strict; and in Russia it was even stronger. There 'the entrance examinations were a simple formality. Entrance into the service and the whole subsequent diplomatic career depended entirely on the connections of the man in the ministry itself and at Court. As a result there were many badly prepared and incompetent people in the diplomatic service.' In the 1890s a well-connected young man could still enter the Russian foreign ministry on the strength of 'an oblong letter signed by a well-known titled name' and a short interview with Count Kapnist, the head of the Asiatic department of the ministry: there was no examination of any kind.[54]

Moreover, even in states where entrance examinations were testing and strictly applied, many of the highest diplomatic posts continued to be given to men who were not professional diplomats. France, a striking case of this, had from 1880 onwards a compulsory examination for all entrants to its diplomatic and consular services which was hedged around with precautions against favouritism or unfairness (all scripts were anonymous and double-marked; the five-man jury which ranked the candidates contained two members from outside the foreign ministry). This was followed by a three-year trial period for successful candidates, who had then to sit a second examination (*examen de classement*). Only after surmounting this final hurdle were they given permanent appointments. No other state imposed tests of such severity; of the sixty-six candidates who sat the entrance examination in 1913 only five achieved permanent posts. Yet this did not prevent a considerable proportion of headships of French missions going to outsiders – senators, prefects, colonial governors, soldiers (again notably in the case of appointments to St Petersburg) and even journalists.[55]

Most important of all, diplomacy remained an expensive and, except in the highest ranks, underpaid profession, one which only the well-to-do could hope to enter. This, coupled with its socially exclusive ambiance, restricted it as effectively as in the past to a small group at the top of society. Many states specified a minimum private income which recruits to their diplomatic services had to have (for example the 6,000 lire demanded by the Sardinian government in 1856 which continued to apply in the new united Italy, or the £400 required in Britain). But formal requirements of this kind were merely a recognition of reality, of the fact that few diplomats could hope to live on their salaries. That for an income of 10,000 marks as a condition of entry to the German diplomatic service was abolished in 1908; but this left the real position completely unchanged. In 1912 the foreign ministry calculated that a minimum of 15,000 marks was needed.

The First World War thus engulfed a Europe in which diplomatic services were still very far from being meritocracies. None the less, much of the inheritance of previous centuries was clearly being discarded. Extraordinary embassies of an essentially ceremonial kind, so frequent in the past, involving the sending of a great aristocrat on a mission of

54. I.V. Bestuzhev, *Borba v Rossii po voprosam vneshnei politiki 1906–1910gg* (Moscow, 1969), pp. 60–1; A.D. Kalmykov, *Memoirs of a Russian Diplomat: Outposts of the Empire, 1893–1917* (New Haven-London, 1971), pp. 14–15.
55. *Les Affaires Etrangères* . . ., ii, 152–9.

congratulation or condolence or to represent his sovereign at a coronation ceremony, were now becoming rare. Perhaps the last occasion on which they figured at all prominently was at the coronation of Alexander II of Russia in 1856. When they did take place they could still be very costly to those who undertook them: Earl Granville, who represented Britain in Moscow on that occasion seems to have paid £7,000 out of his own pocket for the privilege.[56] But by the middle of the nineteenth century they had lost most of even the symbolic importance they had had in earlier generations. The giving of often lavish presents to diplomats when they left a court to which they had been accredited, when a treaty was signed between two states or a special embassy of congratulation or condolence was sent, still a widespread practice in the first years of the nineteenth century,[57] fairly soon became unimportant. In 1834 British diplomats and consuls were forbidden to accept presents from any foreign government, an abandonment of one of the oldest of diplomatic traditions. The belief that lavish entertainment was an indispensable part of successful diplomacy was not quite dead by the mid-century: a generation earlier the vicomte de Chateaubriand on his appointment to London had been careful to take with him Montmirel, reputedly the best cook of the age. But this old-world assumption was clearly dying. When in 1850 Sir George Hamilton Seymour, then representing Britain in Lisbon and with thirty years of diplomatic experience behind him, told a parliamentary select committee that 'Certainly I consider that giving dinners is an essential part of diplomacy; I have no hesitation in saying so. I have no idea of a man being a good diplomatist who does not give good dinners', he provoked widespread ridicule.[58] An attitude which had for generations seemed common-sense now appeared archaic, part of a vanishing world.

More importantly, but in a not altogether dissimilar way, in the lower and middle ranks of diplomacy at least seniority gained ground as a reason for promotion at the expense of nepotism and favouritism. In 1856 French secretaries of embassy and legation were divided into three classes and it was ordered that no one was to reach the third and lowest class without having already served as an attaché for three years, while everyone must spend at least three more in each class before being promoted to a higher one. This put promotion by seniority on a more regular basis than ever before in any major European diplomatic service. In Britain Lord Clarendon in the 1860s seems to have been the first foreign secretary to apply systematically the principle of seniority in the appointment of

56. Sir H. Maxwell, *The Life and Letters of George William Frederick, Fourth Earl of Clarendon* (London, 1913), ii, 141–2.

57. *Les Affaires Etrangères . . .*, i, 545.

58. Jones, *The British Diplomatic Service*, p. 98.

attachés; and from that decade onwards heads of British missions abroad were expected to report each year on the conduct and abilites of those under their control.[59] Even at the highest level, where politics and family connections still so often determined appointments, there were signs that the claims of mere ability were beginning to be heard. Lord Lyons, who was given the Paris embassy in 1867, has been called 'the first major British diplomat who owed his appointment to professional rather than political considerations'.[60]

The scattered efforts made during the eighteenth century to develop some form of systematic training continued; but they were almost as desultory and short-lived as their predecessors, and little more effective. In France the later head of the foreign ministry archives, the comte d'Hauterive, set up in 1800 a school for this purpose which, like its predecessor almost a century earlier,[61] stressed heavily the study and analysis of diplomatic documents. It was clearly meant to provide serious training,[62] and d'Hauterive even cherished the vain hope of being able to admit students to it by competitive examination. In fact most of its pupils were young men seconded from the *conseil d'état* and admitted through family influence. By 1815 there were only four of them left and the school was moribund: by 1830 it had ceased to exist. Like the earlier effort by Torcy it left no real legacy.[63] D'Hauterive, nevertheless, was both persuasive and persistent. In 1825 he induced the then foreign minister, the comte de Damas, to experiment with an essay competition as a means of choosing the most able young attachés for promotion to secretary of embassy or legation; and in 1830 the Prince de Polignac, who had succeeded Damas, was persuaded to set up another training course. This was to last two years and to be focused on public law and, once more, the study and analysis of diplomatic documents: the pupils were also to have a knowledge of either English or German. But it remained a paper exercise. D'Hauterive died only three months after the new regulations were introduced. Other schemes for the training of diplomats were less ambitious and even less effective. In Russia a proposal of 1802 to set up an institute which would offer an elaborate course extending over eight years to prepare young men for a diplomatic career led

---

59. S.T. Bindoff, 'The Unreformed Diplomatic Service, 1812–60', *Transactions of the Royal Historical Society*, 4th series, xviii (1935), 146–7.

60. Jones, *The British Diplomatic Service*, p. 31.

61. See above, pp. 92–3.

62. See d'Hauterive's 'Conseils à un élève du Ministère des Rélations Extérieures', *Revue d'Histoire Diplomatique*, 1901, 161–224.

63. The best general account is A. Meininger, 'D'Hauterive et la formation des diplomates', *Revue d'Histoire Diplomatique* (1975).

nowhere. The same is true of a more modest suggestion put forward in 1820.[64] The training school in the Sardinian foreign ministry which was seriously considered at the end of the 1840s[65] never came into existence. Other efforts were too limited in scope to have much effect. In Britain there were occasional complaints about the complete absence of any sort of organised training for diplomats. In 1836 one pamphleteer urged the creation of a 'Diplomatic College' for this purpose (though significantly he assumed that it would produce only attachés, secretaries and consuls and that ambassadors and ministers would always be appointed on grounds of 'rank and property').[66] Palmerston tried to ensure that attachés in the missions to the German courts should at least be able to read German script; and in the 1840s and 1850s there were efforts to send students of oriental languages from Oxford and Cambridge to Constantinople, where they were to form a new class of oriental secretaries and replace the Greek and Levantine dragomans who had for decades acted as translators and interpreters there.[67] In France the now outmoded system of *jeunes de langue* created by Colbert was gradually replaced by the more up-to-date teaching provided by the *Ecole Spéciale des Langues Orientales Vivantes* set up in 1795.[68] But all this was very small-scale and ineffective. Efforts to train diplomats remained as unsuccessful, the real value of such training as open to question, as a hundred years earlier.

## NEW TASKS AND WIDENING SCOPE

International relations in Europe from the middle of the nineteenth century to the First World War were more and more influenced by several factors which, if not always new, were growing rapidly in importance. From the 1850s and more particularly the 1870s onwards military considerations – new weapons, the importance of rapid and effective mobilisation in case of war, the balance of military and to a lesser extent naval power in general – were more prominent and pervasive than in the past. The fostering of trade was preoccupying foreign ministries as never before. Cultural diplomacy, efforts to spread in other countries

64. *Arkhiv Knyazya Mikhaila Illarionovicha Vorontsova*, ed. P.I. Bartenev (Moscow, 1870–1897), xv, 433–40; Grimstead, *Foreign Ministers of Alexander I*, p. 241fn.

65. R. Moscati, *Il Ministero degli Affari Esteri, 1861–1870* (Milan, 1961), pp. 6–9, 39–50.

66. *A Few Remarks on our Foreign Policy*, pp. 54–6.

67. A. Cunningham, ' "Dragomania": The Dragomans of the British Embassy in Turkey', *St. Antony's Papers*, xi (Middle Eastern Affairs No.2) (London, 1961).

68. M. Degros, 'Les "Jeunes de Langue" de 1815 à nos jours', *Revue d'Histoire Diplomatique* (1985) 58.

knowledge of a particular national language and sympathy for an allegedly distinctive national culture, was beginning to show itself. And the indefinable element of public opinion, of the need of governments to present their policies in a form which gained popular support, was making itself felt.

## New dimensions: military and naval attachés, economic and cultural diplomacy

The first of these forces underlay the emergence of a new type of quasi-diplomatic post, the military and naval attaché. It is hardly surprising that the reign of Napoleon I, an era of warfare on an unprecedented scale, should have seen the first tentative moves in this direction. Armies of unheard-of size, fighting on a scale never before known, generated an unprecedented demand for military information. From at least 1805, therefore, there existed within the French foreign ministry a bureau which collected details of foreign armies and navies and their movements.[69] In 1806 a captain was attachéd to the French embassy in Vienna specifically to collect and send back to Paris information about the Austrian army, while other officers were sent to Berlin for similar work in anticipation of the war which broke out in that year. Indeed, under Napoleon I, French diplomats in general, and sometimes also consuls, were expected to provide information on foreign armed forces to an extent never seen before. In 1830 Prusssia posted a captain to her legation in Paris, her first true military attaché, while in the later 1830s four French army officers were seconded to the diplomatic service, working sometimes in Paris and sometimes abroad. Another was attachéd to the French embassy in Madrid in 1841; and there is some record of a corresponding Spanish appointment in Paris three years later.[70]

It was from the 1850s, however, that these tentative beginnings crystallised into a new post which rapidly became generally recognised. The French government began from 1851 regularly to appoint a military attaché to its Berlin legation, while the first British ones were sent to Paris, Turin and Constantinople in 1855 (though they were not officially described as military attachés until two years later). The transformation of the European balance of power by the wars of 1854–71, the revelation in 1866 and 1870 of what sheer military efficiency could achieve, ensured that the new institution spread rapidly. Sweden appointed her first military

69. E.A. Whitcomb, *Napoleon's Diplomatic Service* (Durham, N.C., 1979), p. 24; *Les Affaires Etrangères . . .*, i, 474–5.
70. A. Vagts, *The Military Attaché* (Princeton, 1967), pp. 9, 18–19; *Les Affaires Etrangères . . .*, i, 589–90.

attachés, to Paris and St Petersburg, in 1858.[71] By the early 1880s, if not earlier, Italy had hers in Vienna, Paris, St Petersburg and Berlin, as well as naval ones in Paris and London. The British government had naval attachés in Paris and Washington from 1860, while a French one arrived in London in the same year. The rapid progress of military and naval technology, organisational changes, the sheer growth in the size of armies and navies, meant that states scrutinised each other's progress in these respects with increasing care, while the few serious armed conflicts of 1871–1914 became laboratories in which new weapons and methods could be studied and their effectiveness tested. During the Russo–Japanese war of 1904–05, by far the most important of these struggles, there were twenty-seven foreign officers acting as official observers with the Russian armies in Manchuria, as well as a considerable number on the Japanese side. By 1914, it has been estimated, the world's diplomatic services included some 300 or so such attachés.[72]

These men were not diplomats. They were a new and foreign element which a changing international situation had superimposed on Europe's existing diplomatic machinery. Military and naval attachés usually regarded their appointments merely as interludes in their service careers and often had little sympathy with the outlook and preoccupations of professional diplomats. In the military monarchies of central and eastern Europe, however, soldiers in posts of this kind could play roles of great importance outside the normal diplomatic channels, uncontrolled by diplomats or foreign offices. From the later 1830s the rulers of Prussia and Russia maintained at each other's courts military plenipotentiaries, high-ranking officers whose role in relations between the two monarchs was often more important than that of any diplomat. They reported directly to the ruler they represented, often using their own cyphers: it was quite possible for neither the foreign nor the war minister ever to see their reports. Their importance, though difficult to evaluate exactly, could be very great. General von Schweinitz, the Prussian military plenipotentiary in St Petersburg, seems to have played in 1866 a crucial role in explaining and justifying to an at first hostile Alexander II Bismarck's policy in Germany. His successor, General von Werder, who served almost continuously as military plenipotentiary in 1869–87, and later as ambassador in St Petersburg in 1892–95, was a key figure in Russo-German relations. The rapid worsening of these relations after 1890 meant that no such Prussian representative was sent to the Russian capital after 1891 (though the post was later revived, ineffectively, in 1906) and that the last Russian one left Berlin in 1892. But the influence of military attachés in general on

---

71. S. Tunberg et al., *Histoire de l'administration* . . ., p. 468.
72. Vagts, *Military Attaché*, p. 34.

German policy was growing in the generation before 1914. From about 1883, when Field-Marshal von Waldersee, the chief of the general staff, developed an active interest in foreign policy, they began to report directly to the general staff and, encouraged by Waldersee, to the emperor himself. Bismarck, who saw in Waldersee a serious rival, disliked this development, but was powerless to reverse it. In 1900, on the initiative of William II, it was made clear that military attachés were subordinate not to the head of the mission of which they were formally members but only to the kaiser himself. Their reports could be commented on by the head of mission; but they might well not be seen at all by the imperial chancellor, who had formal responsibility for the conduct of German foreign policy. In no other state was the influence of military attachés so great and so formalised as in Germany; but in others it could on occasion be significant. The Russian attachés in Sofia and Belgrade, Colonels Romanovskii and Artamonov, a good case in point, did much by their belligerent attitude to give the Balkan alliance of 1912 against the Ottoman empire a more aggressive and expansionist slant than it might otherwise have had. Military and naval attachés were essentially a product of an increasingly tense and competitive international situation; but in some instances at least their activities helped to deepen tensions and intensify competition.

The growing international importance of economic and particularly commercial forces now influenced diplomacy in a number of ways. There was a growth, notably from the middle decades of the nineteenth century, in the collection and publication by governments of information about trade and trade opportunities. Economic information from French consuls about the countries in which they were stationed had begun to be published in various forms from about 1829 onwards, notably in the *Annales du commerce extérieur* from 1843, while the *Bulletin consulaire français* began publication in 1877 and the *Moniteur officiel du commerce* in 1883. In Italy a roughly similar consular bulletin on trade relations with foreign countries and means of developing them appeared from 1862, though irregularly and often in rather skimpy issues. Belgium produced a *Receuil consulaire*, intended for merchants and industrialists, from 1855 onwards. In Britain the founding of the *Board of Trade Journal* in 1886 did something to improve the hitherto often dilatory and irregular publication of consular reports, while the Russian government published such material regularly from the 1890s.[73] The same pressures – the sharpening of international trade competition, a growing fear of being left behind by more

73. Some of these details are taken from the series of brief descriptions of the consular reports to be found in the archives of a number of countries printed in *Business History*, xviii (1981), 265–308.

enterprising or better-organised rivals – underlay the efforts increasingly made by foreign offices to adapt their structures to a new situation. In Britain the scanty government services provided to the nation's merchants had come until the 1860s almost entirely from the board of trade. From 1865, however, the foreign office had for the first time a department concerned entirely with commercial affairs.[74] In France the *direction des consulats et des affaires commerciales* which had been set up some years earlier was reorganised in 1882. More importantly, the amalgamation of consular with diplomatic services, the ending of the inferior status to which the former (and therefore by implication all commercial considerations) had traditionally been relegated, had for long been a favourite panacea of reformers in several countries. As early as 1842 Disraeli had moved a House of Commons motion calling for union of British diplomats and consuls in a single service.[75] In France, where already in 1793 the revolutionaries had placed consuls, hitherto supervised by the ministry of marine, under the control of the foreign ministry, the questioning of the country's institutions which followed the catastrophe of 1870–71 produced a series of such suggestions.[76] But change of this kind proved difficult and aroused much resistance. The quality of consular services was improved in a number of cases, notably in Britain where a departmental committee of 1903 introduced for the first time recruitment of consuls by limited competition (instead of as hitherto purely by nomination of the secretary of state for foreign affairs) and a rationalised salary structure. But in every major state consular and diplomatic services remained separate entities. In all of them commercial and economic affairs continued to have an aura of inferiority, of boring drudgery; and this attitude was often reflected in the organisation of foreign offices. Of the correspondence received by the French foreign ministry in 1893, for example, over 70 per cent dealt with commercial and consular affairs: but this had to be coped with by a staff of only twenty-one against the twenty-nine who handled the much smaller number of political despatches and telegrams.[77] Everywhere interchange between the consular and diplomatic services, though possible, remained relatively rare (though, interestingly, probably less so in Russia than in any other of the great states).

Perhaps the most obvious illustration of the extent to which trade was

74. There is a very useful account of official efforts to foster British trade from the 1860s onwards in D.C.M. Platt, *Finance, Trade and Politics in British Foreign Policy, 1815–1914* (Oxford, 1968), Appendix I.

75. *Hansard*, 3rd series, 61, cols. 220–81.

76. Herbette, *Nos Diplomates . . .*, pp. 21ff.; E. de Lévis-Mirepoix, *Le Ministère des Affaires Etrangères: organization de l'administration centrale et des services extérieurs (1793–1933)* (Angers, 1934), pp. 187–93.

77. *Les Affaires Etrangères . . .*, ii, 80.

forcing itself upon the often unwilling attention of traditional diplomacy was the creation of a new type of diplomat most clearly typified by the commercial attaché. The first significant appointment of this kind was that of Joseph (later Sir Joseph) Crowe as British commercial attaché in Paris in 1880. He was expected, quite unrealistically, to foster British trade throughout Europe; but by the first years of the twentieth century the attaché in Paris had been supplemented by others in Berlin, Vienna, Constantinople, Madrid, Pekin and Yokohama. Germany also began during the first years of the twentieth century to make some patchy and sporadic provision of much the same kind for her trade interests abroad. In France intermittent discussion from 1879 onwards, in which the advocates of change often pointed to Britain and Germany as models, bore fruit at last in the sending in 1904 of a commercial attaché to London at the special request of the embassy there: by 1908 the French diplomatic service included six such appointments. Commercial attachés were not a complete answer to the problem of coping with the increasing volume and importance of economic diplomacy. In 1914 they were still few in number and often had impractically large geographical areas to deal with. The British attaché in Berlin was expected to cover Holland and the Scandinavian countries as well as Germany, while his French counterpart was responsible not only for the Reich but for Holland, Belgium and Switzerland, and another had the whole of the Far East as his sphere of activity. Moreover, the fact that they usually did not come from commercial backgrounds and were stationed in political capitals rather than commercial or industrial centres also tended to limit their effectiveness. Nevertheless, something had been achieved. Other new appointments made in response to the changing balance in international relations between economic and political considerations were less significant. A British experiment in the first years of the twentieth century with commercial secretaries, diplomats detailed for a few years to make a special study of the trade of the area in which they were stationed, had little effect. The appointment from 1899 onwards of a number of short-lived commercial agents intended, in ways which were never clearly defined, to supplement the work of the consuls, had even less. In 1913 France broke new ground with the appointment to some of its missions abroad of technical counsellors, officials seconded from the ministry of public works to help French industry gain orders in areas such as the Chinese and Ottoman empires in the building of railways and port facilities; but this initiative was immediately overtaken by the outbreak of war.

Well before the cataclysm of 1914, however, it was clear that the narrow boundaries of the 'old diplomacy' as Richelieu, Metternich or even Bismarck had known it, had been permanently expanded. This process accelerated during the struggle as economic warfare and blockade, and the complications they created in relations with neutral states, became increasingly important. The *Comité permanent international d'action économique* set up in 1916 by Britain, France, Italy and their smaller allies was one of the more obvious illustrations of this; and it was supplemented by a wide range of other inter-allied bodies, including executives for the control and distribution of individual products such as wheat, sugar and nitrates. In 1917 the British government set up a new department of overseas trade designed to bring commerce and foreign policy into more effective contact: its head was to be responsible to both the foreign secretary and the president of the board of trade. Two years later a new commercial diplomatic service was created. Neither of these innovations had much success; but they showed more clearly than ever how a changed international situation was now being reflected in institutional change. In Germany the most important aspect of the reorganisation of the foreign ministry after the war was the creation of a new department to foster and supervise foreign trade, the *Aussenhandelstelle*, so large that it occupied over 120 rooms.[78] In France the same consciousness that an increasing proportion of international relations now lay completely outside the scope of traditional diplomacy was reflected in the fact that of the country's entire delegation to the Versailles peace conference the ministry of foreign affairs provided only about a quarter.[79]

Cultural diplomacy was still only a very minor factor in the international picture of the later nineteenth and early twentieth centuries. Where it existed it was characteristic of states which, although they had long and proud cultural traditions, had suffered serious setbacks or for some reason lacked self-confidence. Of these France was much the most important example, though in many ways Italy fell into the same class. In both of these there can be seen by the 1880s and 1890s an anxious defensiveness, a feeling that the nation's value and importance must be asserted in the face of more successful rivals. This was to be done not merely by political means but also by fostering its cultural influence and emphasising its cultural achievements. Most important of all, its language, now more and more generally accepted as the ultimate badge of nationality, must be supported and a knowledge of it spread as widely as possible. These ends were to be achieved not by direct government action but rather by government support of unofficial or semi-official bodies such as societies and religious missions. In France the Third Republic inherited

78. P.G. Lauren, *Diplomats and Bureaucrats: The First Institutional Responses to Twentieth-Century Diplomacy in France and Germany* (Stanford, 1976), p. 169.

79. *Les Affaires Etrangères . . .*, ii, 359.

from the old monarchy and the Second Empire a long tradition of such support for Catholic missions in the Near East and China and showed itself as willing as its predecessors to shoulder what it felt to be its obligations in this respect. There was an obvious paradox here. The republican regime which had taken shape in France by the later 1870s was deeply disliked by many devout Catholics; and the increasingly acute conflicts between church and state culminated in 1902 in a brutal severing of the links between the two forged by Napoleon I's concordat with the papacy exactly a hundred years earlier. Yet even at the height of this bitter struggle the foreign ministry made a considerable effort to foster Catholic missions in the Near East as vehicles of French influence there. Government support of this kind in fact increased substantially during the generation or more before the First World War, when the foreign ministry trebled its spending on cultural relations in general.[80]

Nor was official support and encouragement limited to Catholic organisations. Others which were non-Catholic, non-Christian or indifferent to all forms of religious belief – the *Alliance française* (1883), the *Mission laique française* (1902), the *Alliance israelite universelle* (1860) benefited in this way.[81] Indeed the effectiveness of policies of this kind depended largely on their flexibility and willingness to use a wide variety of instruments. In particular considerable attention was paid to fostering French educational enterprises abroad, predominantly in the Near East. Here there was a powerful tradition of French interest and influence tracing back to the Crusades, and some history of earlier French educational effort. In 1842, for example, the government had provided twelve bursaries for the education in France of the sons of sheikhs or emirs of the Lebanon; and a Jesuit seminary had been founded in Beirut a year later. But in the first years of the twentieth century the scale of such efforts sharply increased. Lycées were established in Cairo and Beirut in 1909 and in Alexandria in the following year. On the other side of the Atlantic the consul in New Orleans even attempted in 1907, with some success, to secure government finance for the teaching of French in Louisiana. It was not until 1911 that all this activity received some formal expression within the foreign ministry, with the creation of a *bureau des écoles et des oeuvres françaises à l'étranger*, and this was on a very modest scale.[82] France, however, clearly led the world in the development of what was to become an increasingly important element in international relations.

80. *Les Affaires Etrangères . . .,* ii, 270.
81. M. Burrows, ' "Mission civilisatrice": French Cultural Policy in the Near East, 1860–1914', *Historical Journal*, 29 (1986), 109–34.
82. A. Outrey, 'Histoire et principes de l'administration française des affaires étrangères', *Revue française de science politique* (1953), 723–4.

Elsewhere activity of this kind was much less important. In Italy a touchy and often aggressive nationalism, a feeling, rather as in France, that a great cultural tradition was being undervalued and might be in danger, was coupled with vociferous territorial demands in the Trentino, the Adriatic and Africa. These forces combined to produce considerable pressures for a spreading of the national language and culture. The most important vehicle for this, the Dante Alighieri Society, founded in 1889, soon became a semi-official purveyor of cultural propaganda, notably in the Trentino, the most important focus of its activities in its first years. By 1911, when Italy's newly launched first Dreadnought battleship was significantly named the *Dante Alighieri*, it claimed 50,000 members; but although it enjoyed considerable official support it had little influence on government policy. Elsewhere cultural diplomacy scarcely existed before 1914 in any significant way. In Germany in 1906 a department was set up in the foreign ministry to administer the *Reichsschulfonds*, money destined for the support of German schools abroad: there, as in Italy, there was a strong feeling that the national language must be kept alive among the large emigrant communities now established overseas. But the states for which the nineteenth century had been a success story, Germany and still more Great Britain, showed little or nothing of the desire for officially-backed dissemination of their culture and advertisement of their intellectual achievements which was so noticeable in France.

## Newspapers, public opinion and pressures for more open diplomacy

Cultural diplomacy was a force which worked, if at all, slowly and in ways which were difficult to measure. Of more immediate concern to governments and, it seemed, likely to produce much quicker and more clearly identifiable results, were the growing efforts which many of them were now making to use for their own purposes the new or greatly strengthened force of the newspaper press. Cheap newsprint; new technology which made it possible to attract readers by printing illustrations relatively cheaply; growing mass literacy, at least in western Europe; mass newspaper readerships; a resulting growth of mass public feeling, often emotional and volatile, on international questions: all these were now adding another element to the changing picture of relations between the European states. 'Each day', asserted a French newspaper in 1900, 'the press becomes . . . more of a diplomatic force of the first order'.[83] This was a highly exaggerated estimate. Nevertheless, contemporaries were well aware that a potentially important new force

83. Quoted in Lauren, *Diplomats and Bureaucrats*, p. 184.

was at work and governments were anxious to use it to their own advantage. There were several ways in which this could be done. The first of these was essentially passive: the press, and particularly the foreign press, might be closely scrutinised, and clues thus obtained to the movement of public feeling in the different states on the international questions of the day. In France the *cabinet du ministre* in the foreign ministry included from 1886, under a number of slightly varying titles, a section which translated and analysed articles from the foreign press: by 1907 it was drawing on 175 newspapers for this purpose.[84] This sort of activity could be paralleled in many other states. By 1910 the equivalent unit in the Russian foreign ministry was scrutinising more than 150 Russian and foreign newspapers, while even the Ottoman empire had equipped its foreign ministry as early as 1869 with a rudimentary press office whose duties included monitoring the foreign-language papers published on Turkish soil.[85] More important, though their practical effects are debatable and difficult to measure, were the active efforts made by many governments to influence the content and tone of newspapers, both within their own territories and abroad. This had been first attempted in the early years of the nineteenth century. Under Napoleon I the French government published for several years, until its suppression in 1810, an English-language newspaper, the *Argus*, in an effort to undermine British influence in continental Europe. Simultaneously French diplomats, as part of a sustained propaganda offensive, distributed the bulletins of the *Grande Armée*, set up a newspaper in Poland, and in Germany influenced others in favour of France and struggled to suppress those considered hostile to the emperor.[86] Contemporaries were impressed, indeed overimpressed, by these efforts. 'The daily published bulletins of the French army with which Germany and all Europe are flooded', wrote Metternich in 1805, as Austrian minister in Berlin, 'are a new invention and deserve the most serious attention. The gazettes are worth an army of 300,000 men to Napoleon. Public opinion is the most powerful of weapons'.[87]

Such direct methods were hardly possible except with the backing of military power. But the possible advantages of influencing foreign public opinion, as that mysterious entity slowly evolved during the nineteenth century, were never lost to sight. In 1815, during the making of the Vienna settlement, both the Russian and the Habsburg ambassadors in

84. *Les Affaires Etrangères* . . ., ii, 51, 335.

85. Bolsover, 'Izvol'sky and Reform . . .', 26; Findlay, *Bureaucratic Reform* . . ., p. 188.

86. *Les Affaires Etrangères* . . ., i, 468–9; Whitcomb, *Napoleon's Diplomatic Service*, pp. 106–7.

87. Quoted in A. Fugier, *La Révolution française et l'empire napoléonien* (Histoire des rélations internationales, vol. iv) (Paris, 1954), p. 200.

London tried to use British newspapers to arouse opposition to Castlereagh's policies and weaken his position in the negotiations. In the following year the duc de Richelieu, the French chief minister, sent an agent to Switzerland, Germany and the Kingdom of the Netherlands to report on the press there and the possibility of France influencing it in her favour.[88] Under the Second Empire at least one French foreign minister, Drouyn de Lhuys, had at his disposal a bureau which sent to French embassies and legations abroad would-be opinion-forming articles translated into the main European languages and ready for publication in their areas.[89] In the later nineteenth and early twentieth centuries such methods were more difficult to use; but the press bureaux with which more and more of the foreign offices of Europe were now equipping themselves (the Habsburg empire in 1879, Russia in the first years of the twentieth century, Sweden in 1909) were used increasingly to channel information to foreign journalists and news agencies and thus, it was hoped, create a favourable climate of opinion. Even in Britain in the last years of the nineteenth century a high foreign office official had fairly frequent interviews, on the instructions of Lord Salisbury, the prime minister and foreign secretary, with Reuter's agent in London and gave him selected information considered helpful to British policy. A few years later William Tyrell, private secretary of the foreign secretary from 1908 onwards, 'went out of his way to cultivate relations with the Press'.[90]

Efforts to manipulate newspapers were often not very effective. Press bureaux, where they existed, were small; and the fact that they were usually headed by officials rather than experienced journalists did nothing to increase their efficiency. In 1910 the German one was a tiny organisation with a staff of only three; while in 1913 the head of its Italian equivalent pressed strongly for it to be run by journalists rather than diplomats, since the latter usually stayed too short a time in Rome to establish the necessary good relations with newspapers and correspondents.[91] Straightforward bribery seldom played a role in these efforts to manipulate public perceptions of international questions. There is, however, one well-known case of a major state attempting to influence attitudes in another by this means. This is the relatively lavish spending of the Russian government from about 1897 onwards on payments to French newspapers, editors and journalists. In 1904–06 particularly, and

88. *The History of The Times* (London, 1935–84), i, 216.

89. *Les Affaires Etrangères . . .*, ii, 334.

90. K.G. Robbins, 'Public opinion, press and pressure groups', in *British Foreign Policy under Sir Edward Grey,* ed. F.H. Hinsley (Cambridge, 1977), p. 81.

91. G. Valentine Williams, 'The German Press Bureau', *Contemporary Review*, xcvii (1910), 315–25; Ferraris, *L'amministrazione centrale . . .*, p. 51.

again after an interval in 1913, considerable sums were dispensed in this way, sometimes through distinctly shady intermediaries. In May–October 1905, when expenditure of this kind was at its height, 200,000 francs of Russian money was being paid each month to about fifty French newspapers, periodicals and press agencies, some of them important opinion-formers – *Le Figaro, Le Temps, Le Petit Parisien* and the Havas agency. The successful negotiation of a large French loan to Russia in April 1906, a matter of supreme importance to statesmen in St Petersburg hard-pressed by defeat and revolution, immediately reduced the need for such payments; and it is very doubtful whether in any case they made any real difference to the course of events. Both Nelidov, the Russian ambassador in Paris, and Kokovtsev, the minister of finance, thought they did not.[92] Control of the flow of official information to newspapers and agencies and the giving of carefully orchestrated interviews to foreign correspondents were now usually more likely to be effective in moulding opinion than the mere spending of money; and France, with its plethora of small, financially insecure and often venal newspapers, was something of a special case.

Moreover, the high estimates of press influence on international relations which were widespread by the beginning of the twentieth century, and which have been repeated by some historians, were much exaggerated. Certainly the attitude of newspapers could sometimes be significant. The bitter attacks on Germany by the fledgling but rapidly developing Russian press, after the Berlin settlement of 1878 had so disappointed Russian hopes in the Balkans, helped to push Bismarck towards the alliance with the Habsburg empire which took shape in 1879. Press campaigns on both sides did something, though just how much is still debated, to worsen Anglo-German relations in the two decades before 1914. Newspaper attacks brought down two French prime ministers, Ferry in 1885 and Caillaux in 1911, in both cases with considerable international repercussions. Yet on the other hand governments were quite willing to disregard clearly expressed public feeling when this seemed in the national interest. Serious negotiations were opened by the British government for an alliance with Germany in 1901, at a time when much opinion in both countries was markedly hostile to such an idea. Successive French governments maintained the alliance with Russia which had taken shape by 1894, in spite of the hostility to it of the powerful

92. Some discussion in English of these Russian activities can be found in J.W. Long, 'Russian Manipulation of the French Press, 1904–06', *Slavic Review*, xxxi (1972), 343–54; F.L. Schuman, *War and Diplomacy in the French Republic* (New York, 1931), pp. 203–05; and E.M. Carroll, *French Public Opinion and Foreign Affairs, 1870–1914* (New York, 1931), pp. 268–70.

socialist and radical parties and the great body of French opinion they represented.[93] Nevertheless, during these years many statesmen placed a higher value than ever before on public feeling as voiced by newspapers, and made unprecedented efforts to court and shape it. In Germany notably, where the government was a good deal less influenced by domestic opinion than in France and Britain, there was marked official sensitivity to the comments of foreign newspapers and an anxiety to present the best possible face to the outside world. Prince von Bülow during his tenure of the imperial chancellorship in 1900–09 took a higher view than any of his predecessors of the importance of the press and gave frequent newspaper interviews, while the German government, and William II himself, reacted strongly to the hostile attitude of the *Times* and its Berlin correspondent, George Saunders.[94]

The coming of war in 1914 quickly gave new impetus to the hitherto rather limited and amateurish propaganda efforts of governments. In Britain the foreign office acquired a news department almost at once; later two improvised bodies staffed largely by journalists and created for particular purposes, the Neutral Press Committee and the War Propaganda Bureau, were set up. This led to a good deal of overlapping and interdepartmental rivalry, notably between the foreign and war offices: propaganda in the neutral states which it was most important to influence was in fact carried on largely by the British diplomatic missions there, often supported by groups of expatriates and local anglophiles. Early in 1917 control was more efficiently centralised in a new department of information with its headquarters in the foreign office; and finally in February 1918 a fully-fledged ministry of information was created. Underlying these organisational changes, and more important, was an explosive growth of the whole official information-controlling and opinion-forming effort. Traditional propaganda techniques centred on the newspaper press were used on an unprecedented scale: by 1917 four chateaux were being used as hotels for journalists and influential visitors to the front in northern France. Simultaneously a dozen Greek newspapers were being financed by British money, which was also used in the same year to set up a pro-British magazine in Japan. Illustrated newspapers were produced in a variety of languages for distribution abroad; and from late in

93. The much-discussed question of the influence of newspapers on international relations in the two decades or more before 1914 can be no more than very lightly touched on here. For a summary discussion see B.E. Schmitt, 'The Relation of Public Opinion and Foreign Affairs before and during the First World War', in *Studies in Diplomatic History and Historiography in Honour of G.P. Gooch, C.H.* (London, 1961), pp. 322–30.
94. *The History of The Times*, iii, Appendix I: Sources, xi, 'Saunders at Berlin'.

1915 films began to be used as a propaganda medium.[95] All this reflected a recognition at the highest political level that the country's foreign relations must include, at least for the time being and probably permanently, an unprecedented effort to shape and direct opinion abroad. The fact that David Lloyd George, who became prime minister in December 1916, had a well-developed taste for publicity and a personal interest in the potentialities of propaganda strengthened this change of attitude. Lord Beaverbrook, who headed the new ministry of information in 1918, saw it as 'a second Foreign Office at home with a new set of representatives abroad' and thought and spoke of propaganda as 'the popular arm of diplomacy'.[96] The new aspect which foreign policy had been acquiring for two or three decades had suddenly grown to startling dimensions.

Elsewhere similar processes were also to be seen. In France a new press bureau for war purposes was set up in the first days of fighting. It was not, however, until the beginning of 1916 that any official French propaganda organisation on a large scale came into existence. This was the *Maison de la Presse*, the creation mainly of a very able foreign ministry official, Philippe Berthelot. This was reorganised and changed its title in the following year, and again in May 1918: like its British counterparts it drew its manpower from a variety of sources – the universities, the army and the professions – as well as from diplomacy. As in Britain, again, the French wartime propaganda effort was improvised and its full potentialities seen only slowly; but in France also the growth in the sheer amount of activity was striking. The money which the French government allocated for propaganda purposes at the outbreak of war had grown fivefold by 1917.[97] In Germany, too, a new situation brought forth new institutions and a vast expansion of what had been hitherto a limited and rather ineffective opinion-forming effort. Very early in the war a new body, the *Zentralstelle für Auslandsdienst*, was set up to influence neutral opinion, a vital propaganda target of all the major belligerents. Later the press bureau of the foreign ministry, so small before the war, was greatly enlarged and became the *Nachrichtenabteilung*. As in Britain and France, new methods and techniques were exploited with effect: Germany used films and the cinema as part of her war effort earlier than Britain.

---

95. M.L. Sanders, 'Wellington House and British Propaganda during the First World War', *Historical Journal*, xviii (1975), 132–6.

96. P.M. Taylor, 'The Foreign Office and British Propaganda during the First World War', *Historical Journal,* 23 (1980), 892; A.J.P. Taylor, *Beaverbrook* (London, 1972), p. 145.

97. *Les Affaires Etrangères . . .,* ii, 334ff.

## A democratic diplomacy?

These efforts by foreign offices to influence opinion in part reflected an increasing feeling among sections of the public, visible well before 1914, that diplomacy was now too important to be left to diplomats. More and more the assertion could be heard, long before the guns began to fire, that the 'cabinet diplomacy' of the eighteenth century, of Metternich or even of Bismarck, no longer met the needs of a changing world. This can be seen in the demands for some form of parliamentary control of the making and carrying-out of foreign policy which became more frequent in one or two European states from the end of the nineteenth century and which reached a peak during and just after the First World War.

Some opening of diplomacy to parliamentary and even public scrutiny had by the later nineteenth century a considerable history in Britain, though it was by no means one of steady or continuous growth. During his short tenure of the foreign office in 1807–09 George Canning had published official correspondence relating to foreign affairs on a markedly larger scale than any of his predecessors, though what appeared in print was still limited in scope and carefully edited. Nevertheless, contemporaries realised that the tradition which made foreign policy one of the most arcane aspects of government was being breached: a well-informed former diplomat noted that the laying of so much diplomatic correspondence before parliament was a 'sort of new habit'.[98] During his second and more important period as foreign secretary in 1822–27 Canning went considerably further in this direction. He hoped thus both to strengthen his hand in the cabinet, several of whose members were by no means convinced supporters of his policies, and to counteract the influence at court of the hostile Austrian and Russian ambassadors, who could usually count on the sympathy of George IV. Nevertheless, parliamentary influence over or even interest in foreign policy was still slight, and that of the general public even less. The Vienna settlement of 1814–15, the foundation of international relations for two generations to come, received strikingly little parliamentary discussion: only one or two aspects of it aroused any real public interest. In the 1830s and early 1840s Palmerston was able to handle both the Belgian question and the Near Eastern crises of 1832–33 and 1839–41 with little interference from parliament, so that in 1839 an acute observer of British politics could say with much justification that 'foreign affairs are never discussed except at the House of Lords'.[99] The 1850s and 1860s saw, however, a marked growth in parliamentary interest and influence. Parliamentary papers (Blue

98. Malmesbury, *Diaries and Correspondence*, iv, 404.
99. Maxwell, *Clarendon*, i, 173.

Books) relating to foreign policy were now published much more freely than ever before. Often they were detailed and informative; and many were published under pressure from the House of Commons rather than by the free decision of the government, though the fact that they normally related to negotiations which had been concluded rather than to any still in progress inevitably limited their usefulness as a weapon of parliamentary control. More fundamentally, this was a period when British political parties were fragmented and governments correspondingly unstable. This tended to increase the influence of parliament; and in 1858, for the first time in British history, a government was driven from office on a foreign policy question.

By the 1870s and 1880s, however, the pendulum was swinging in the opposite direction. Party structures were solidifying and governments more securely based and less at the mercy of House of Commons votes. By the 1880s Blue Books almost always originated from the government and not in response to parliamentary demands. The marked tightening-up of the hitherto very lax standing orders of the House of Commons from 1881 onwards (a response to organised obstruction by Irish members) tended to limit parliamentary control over foreign policy as over other aspects of government. Critics might complain of what one of them called 'the mysterious and irresponsible manner in which foreign politics are arranged';[100] but there was little they could do to change the situation. Finally, the rise of the new Labour party helped to ensure that the House of Commons from 1906 onwards had an increasing proportion of members whose interests lay primarily or exclusively in domestic issues and who knew little of those in the outside world.

None the less, the obvious and growing dangers of the international situation in the decade before 1914 brought increasing demands, at least from the left of the political spectrum, that foreign policy be brought under more effective parliamentary control. This, it was argued, could be achieved by the establishment of a parliamentary standing committee to supervise its conduct; the Foreign Relations Committee of the American Senate was often quoted as a possible model. The idea was not new. In 1858 Lord Clarendon, as foreign secretary, had feared that the vocal group of radical liberals in the House of Commons might be able to force the creation of such a body, and the idea surfaced occasionally in the decades which followed. But by the early years of the twentieth century such proposals were receiving more serious and widespread attention than ever before. In 1911, when the second Moroccan crisis had shown how easily

100. J. Lorimer, *Of the Denationalisation of Constantinople and its Devotion to International Purposes* (Edinburgh, 1876), p. 17.

Europe might now be engulfed by war, it was discussed by parliament for the first time. At the end of the same year an unofficial foreign affairs committee was formed within the ruling Liberal party to mobilise public opinion in favour of fuller discussion of foreign policy in parliament, though it never represented more than a minority of Liberal members. Pressures and activities of this kind were a facet of the increasingly active discussion of problems of international peace, and the ways in which it might be preserved, which were preoccupying many radicals and idealists in western Europe during the last decades before the war.[101]

Pressures for some 'democratisation' of foreign policy and for weakening the dangerous grip on international relations of allegedly cynical and reactionary foreign offices were not confined to Britain. In revolutionary France the Legislative Assembly set up in October 1791 a permanent diplomatic committee before which the foreign minister could be called to account; and this process was pushed to its logical conclusion when in April 1794 the Convention abolished the ministry of foreign affairs and replaced it with a Commission of Foreign Relations subject to the Committee of Public Safety. The vagaries of French history in the following decades meant that the principle of parliamentary control was ignored or rejected by successive regimes. But it was never totally forgotten. Napoleon III carried on an active personal diplomacy, not merely without the knowledge of the Chamber of Deputies and the Senate, but behind the backs of his own ministers. Republicans after 1871 therefore believed, with some justification, that the country's diplomatic service was dominated by royalist and Bonapartist influences and that it must be made more responsive to republican ideas. A writer in the 1880s described it as 'this old refuge of creatures from the former régimes'.[102] By the end of the nineteenth century there had been considerable changes. The French Yellow Books now performed some of the functions of Blue Books on the other side of the Channel. The Chamber of Deputies was now beginning to use its power of the purse to scrutinise the foreign ministry and its doings and to attack what it saw as inefficiency and conservatism there.[103] In France, as in Britain, the crisis of 1911 gave new strength to demands for more 'open' diplomacy and greater parliamentary control, though with as little practical result. In Germany, too, pressures for the Reichstag to be given a greater say in the conduct of foreign policy could be felt. The imperial constitution and the prevailing political temper of the country made them even less effective than in

101. See below, pp. 253ff.
102. Hippeau, *Histoire diplomatique. . .*, p. 310.
103. Lauren, *Diplomats and Bureaucrats. . .*, pp. 48ff.

144

Britain or France; but the *Daily Telegraph* incident of 1908[104] and its effect in undermining the authority of William II helped to intensify them. In Germany as in Britain and France they tended to focus on demands for a standing committee of the legislature with powers to enquire into, and supervise the conduct of, foreign policy; and here too there were radicals and peace campaigners who called for diplomacy to be made more open and its processes easier for the public in general to understand.[105]

It would be wrong, however, to imagine that the liberals, socialists and democrats of various colours who pressed for more open diplomacy and greater parliamentary control of foreign policy represented a powerful, still less a dominant, force. Even in Britain and France these pressures had no practical effect. Neither in Germany nor in the Habsburg empire did they make the slightest difference to the way in which foreign policy was decided and carried out. In all the major states of Europe it was still made not even by the government as a whole but by a small group within it – the chief minister and foreign minister, supplemented according to circumstances and personalities by those for war, colonies or other concerned departments – with the support or at least the acquiescence of the monarch. In the great continental monarchies the influence of the ruler over foreign affairs was still powerful and sometimes decisive. In Vienna, almost to the end of his long reign, Francis Joseph could have very real control. When in 1911 the fire-eating chief of staff, Marshal Conrad von Hötzendorff, complained that the attitude of the foreign minister, Baron Aehrenthal, was too pacific, the emperor replied firmly that 'I make policy; it is my policy. My policy is a policy of peace . . . my minister of foreign affairs carries on my policy in this sense'.[106] Nor was this an empty boast. Two years later Francis Joseph showed that his controlling influence was a reality when, during the Balkan crisis of 1913, he ignored the demand of the entire council of ministers for the presentation of an ultimatum to Montenegro. In Berlin William II interfered repeatedly with the conduct of German diplomacy in a way which helped to conceal the extent to which his effective authority in many areas was ebbing away. In 1912 he insisted, against opposition from

104. An article in the *Daily Telegraph* of 28 October 1908 reported the assertion of William II, during a visit to Britain of the previous year, that he had frustrated efforts during the Boer War to construct a Russo-Franco-German coalition against her. This produced sharp criticism in Germany of his irresponsibility and demands for legislation to curb his personal power.

105. For example, E. Schlief, *Der Friede in Europa; eine völkerrechtlich-politische Studie* (Leipzig, 1892), pp. 223ff., where traditional diplomacy is attacked for its secrecy and its confusing (*Umnebelung*) of public opinion; A.H. Fried, *Die Grundlagen des revolutionären Pacifismus* (Tübingen, 1908), pp. 65–6.

106. F. Engel-Janosi, 'Der Monarch und seine Ratgeber', in *Probleme der Franzisko-Josephinischen Zeit, 1848–1916* (Munich, 1967), p. 17.

the foreign ministry, that Prince Lichnowsky be appointed to the London embassy, saying 'I send only *my* ambassador to London, who has *my* confidence, obeys *my* will, fulfills *my* orders with *my* instructions'.[107] In Russia most of all the making of foreign policy had been, throughout the nineteenth century, the exclusive personal prerogative of the ruler, in practice as well as theory. An official report of 1837 on the work of the foreign ministry was uncompromising on this point. The ministry, it declared, had been for over a generation 'merely the faithful executor of the intentions' of Alexander I and Nicholas I, so that 'its every action was carried out under the orders and instructions of the tsars themselves'. Under Alexander II, Count (later Prince) Gorchakov, who headed the foreign ministry for a quarter of a century after 1856, wrote that 'in Russia there are only two people who know the policy of the Russian cabinet: the emperor who makes it and myself who prepares and executes it'.[108] This view of the foreign minister as a mere official, an instrument in the hands of his master, was fully shared by the tsars themselves. 'Who does not know', said Alexander III in 1886 of Gorchakov's successor, 'that the pitiful Giers (N.K. Giers, foreign minister 1881–94) is nothing more than an executor of my will?',[109] while almost two decades later an even more self-effacing foreign minister had no doubt that 'my duty consists in telling the emperor what I think about every question, and then when the Sovereign decides I must obey unconditionally and try to see that the Sovereign's decision is executed'.[110] The status of the foreign minister as merely a high-ranking bureaucrat meant that the diplomats whom he directed, and in particular the heads of the more important Russian missions abroad, often looked on him as more or less an equal and hardly as a superior at all. In the years just before 1914 Count A.K. Benckendorff, the ambassador in London, or A.P. Izvolskii, his counterpart in Paris, addressed the minister, S.D. Sazonov, in an offhand and sometimes directly critical tone which no British diplomat of the period would have used to Sir Edward Grey. Nor did the constitution of 1906 and the Duma which it created do anything to bring the foreign ministry and Russian diplomacy under any effective parliamentary control. The Duma discussed foreign policy only once a year, when the ministry's budget came under scrutiny: it has been estimated that it spent less than 1

107. Cecil, *German Diplomatic Service . . .*, pp. 217–18.

108. Quoted in G.H. Bolsover, 'Aspects of Russian Foreign Policy, 1815–1914', in *Essays Presented to Sir Lewis Namier*, ed. R. Pares and A.J.P. Taylor (London, 1956), pp. 322–3.

109. Margaret Maxwell, 'An Examination of the Role of N.K. Giers as Russian Foreign Minister under Alexander III', *European Studies Review*, i (1971), 367.

110. D.C.B. Lieven, *The Russian Establishment in the Reign of Nicholas II: The Appointed Members of the State Council* (PhD Thesis, University of London, 1978), p. 296.

per cent of its time on foreign affairs. In 1906–14 successive foreign ministers were authorised by the tsar to report to it on only five occasions.

In pre-1914 Europe, therefore, almost as much as at any time in the past, the making and, to a lesser extent, the conduct of foreign policy by the great states remained in the hands of a small, sometimes very small, number of individuals who were effectively uncontrolled by the peoples for whom they acted. Even in the most politically advanced parts of the continent foreign affairs still attracted, for the most part, much less attention than internal problems. There is no reason at all to suppose that the policies of these states would have been more intelligent or less influenced by fear and ambition if they had been decided by parliaments elected on the widest and fairest franchise possible and carried out by diplomatic services freed from social distinctions. But there was, in any case, no possibility of the ideals of radicals and democrats being put to the test.

The unheard-of losses and strains of the war years greatly strengthened, at least in Britain, the pressures for a new order in foreign policy and diplomacy, for policies more democratically decided and diplomacy more openly conducted by men more representative of society in general. 'Potentates, diplomatists and militarists made this war', claimed the most important and vocal British radical group of this kind only a few weeks after the outbreak of the conflict. 'They should not be allowed to arrange unchecked and uncontrolled the terms of peace and to decide alone the conditions which will follow it.' Other radicals demanded that foreign policy should no longer be at the mercy of 'the ideas, valuations and methods of a sporting aristo-plutocracy' or 'the obscure convolutions of diplomatic staffs', that 'there must be an end of the secret diplomacy which has plunged us into this catastrophe' and that the working classes should 'lay down our own terms, make our own proclamations, establish our own diplomacy'.[111] In this storm of righteous indignation few commentators made the important but disheartening point that, except in moments of obvious crisis, the man in the street was as a rule little interested in foreign policy questions.[112] In spite of so many hopes of a new order the old one proved tough enough to survive essentially

111. Union of Democratic Control, *The Morrow of the War* (London, 1914), p. 19; J.A. Hobson, *Towards International Government* (London, 1915), p. 68; G. Lowes Dickinson, *After the War* (London, 1915), p. 34; D. Marquand, *Ramsay MacDonald* (London, 1977), p. 209. Other examples of the large body of radical British writing on this issue are: A.P. Ponsonby, *Democracy and Diplomacy* (London, 1915); P. Snowden, 'Democracy and Publicity in Foreign Affairs', in *Towards a Lasting Settlement*, ed. C.R. Buxton (London, 1915); E.D. Morel, *Truth and the War* (London, 1916), Chapter xii; F. Neilson, *How Diplomats make War* (New York, 1916), especially pp. 371, 376.

112. G.G. Coulton, *The Main Illusions of Pacifism* (Cambridge, 1916), pp. 257–8, was one of the few.

unchanged. Even the Russian revolution of 1917 could not escape its clutches. The first efforts of the Bolsheviks were directed to overturning the traditional system of international relations, by the publication of the secret treaties signed during the war by the tsarist regime and by direct appeals, over the heads of their governments, to the peoples of the world for support. But the revolutionaries very soon found that they could not turn their backs completely on the methods of the past. Under G.V. Chicherin, who became head of the People's Commissariat for Foreign Affairs (*Narkomindel*) in March 1918, Soviet diplomacy rapidly readopted many of the methods of the old regime. Chicherin himself had roots in pre-revolutionary diplomacy. He had been employed before 1917 in the archives of the foreign ministry and one of his ancestors on his mother's side had been Russian ambassador in Vienna during the 1814–15 congress. He urged that Soviet diplomats should improve their understanding of the foreign policy problems of a communist Russia by studying the diplomatic history and traditions of the tsarist empire. For several years after 1918 the Bolsheviks maintained contact with the outside world through such channels as trade missions, the Red Cross, academic and scientific bodies and the Communist International founded in 1919, rather than through conventional diplomatic ones.[113] But this was because the outside world insisted on ostracising them at least as much as by any choice of their own.

The Versailles conference of 1918–19 took place against a background of intense public feeling and excited mass emotion in France, Britain and, to a lesser extent, the United States. The statesmen who made the settlement could not ignore the pressures this placed upon them: to that extent public opinion was a significant element in the process of peace-making. But in most of the specific decisions they took the Allied leaders wielded a personal power which the makers of the settlements of 1648, 1713 or 1814–15 had never tasted. Wilson, Lloyd George and Clemençeau, wrote an observer a year or two later, 'were in the conduct of public affairs more imperious than any Caesar had ever dared to be in any empire, pagan or Christian'.[114] The dream of a 'new diplomacy' remained, in spite of the outburst of hope generated by the creation of the League of Nations, no more than a dream. The diplomats of 1919, many of the methods they used and the ways in which they were instructed and controlled, even many of the policies they attempted to carry out, would have been clearly recognisable to their predecessors in the age of Metternich or even of Louis XIV.

113. T.J. Ulricks, *Diplomacy and Ideology: The Origins of Soviet Foreign Relations, 1917–1930* (London–Beverly Hills, 1979), Chapter 2 passim.
114. Anon., 'Is there a New Diplomacy?', *Fortnightly Review*, cxvii (1922), 707.

# CHAPTER FOUR
# The Balance of Power

## THE ORIGINS: TO THE AGE OF LOUIS XIV

The metaphor of balance, of an opposition of competing forces which counteract each other and hence leave unchanged the position or state of the body upon which they act, is a very ancient one. In the fifth century B.C. Hippocrates wrote of the need, for the health of the human body, of a balance between the four humours – blood, phlegm, and yellow and black bile – which determined its physical and mental condition; an idea which remained medical orthodoxy until the eighteenth century. Theologians sometimes spoke of a balance, in sinful fallen man, between vice and virtue. In modern Europe, however, the metaphor has been used increasingly in a political context. This has not been confined to international relations. In the seventeenth century it was possible to speak of a necessary balance between church and state or between religious and political considerations and forces within a state.[1] In early eighteenth-century England the phrase 'balance of power' was quite frequently used by writers when discussing the internal politics of states: to them it suggested theories of a 'mixed constitution' and the equilibrium of competing political forces which, it was claimed, made such a constitution viable.[2] A balanced political structure of this kind, one in which monarch,

1. For example, *The Ballance Adjusted: or, the Interest of Church and State weighed and considered upon this Revolution* (London, 1688?) and *Le Balance de la réligion et de la politique* (Philadelphia, = somewhere in the Dutch Republic, 1697).
2. See, for example, *A Discourse of the Contests and Dissensions between the Nobles and the Commons in Athens and Rome* (London, 1701), reprinted in *A Collection of State Tracts* (London, 1705–06), iii, 210–29, and *Two Essays on the Balance of Europe*, ibid., p. 774, where the author speaks of a 'balance of power between prince and people'.

aristocracy and people each had a role to play and in which none of these elements could predominate over the others, came to seem a clear proof of the superiority of English political life to that of the great continental states and of the survival in England of historic freedoms which had been lost elsewhere. Swift, for example, lamented in 1715 'the Destruction of the Gothick Balance in most Kingdoms of Europe'.[3] Rousseau in his *Social Contract* (1762) spoke (though without using the word 'balance') of the need for some effective countervailing force within a state to limit the autocracy of a despotic ruler; and only a year or two earlier the Abbé de Mably had written similarly of a *'balancement perpetuel'* in any monarchical government between the prince, who inevitably sought to increase his personal power, and the people who struggled to maintain their liberties.[4] It was, again, quite possible to speak of a changing balance between political parties and factions as they struggled for office.[5]

However, it was above all in discussion of the relations between states that the idea of a balance and questions as to its nature, its justification and its effectiveness generated, most notably in the century from the 1680s onwards, an extensive literature. This writing had considerable defects. It did not distinguish clearly between the widely varying shades of meaning which the elastic term 'balance of power' can easily assume.[6] Sometimes it took for granted that the supreme objective of any system of inter-state equilibrium was the maintenance of peace. At other times it justified great and devastating wars on the grounds that they were essential to defend a balance between the states of Europe. Its logical coherence and analytical acuteness were often far from impressive. Nevertheless, at its eighteenth-century best it showed considerable penetration and sophistication.

## Italian beginnings and the spread north of the Alps

It is hardly surprising that more or less explicit, though also usually brief and general, statements of the idea applied to inter-state relations should be found first, like the permanent ambassador and the professional

3. 'An Enquiry into the Behaviour of the Queen's last Ministry', in *Political Tracts, 1713–1719* ed. H. Davis and I. Ehrenpreis (Oxford, 1953), p. 180.

4. G. Bonnot de Mably, *Des Principes des négociations pour servir d'introduction au droit public de l'Europe* (Amsterdam, 1757), p. 42.

5. For example, *The Political Balance, in which the Principles and Conduct of the two Parties are weighed* (London, 1765). The earliest example I have found of the use of this sort of terminology in the context of factional struggles within a state is *La Balance d'estat; tragi-comédie allégorique* (n.p., n.d., ?early 1650s) which is a satire on events in France during the second Fronde upheaval.

6. For a discussion of these see M. Wight, 'The Balance of Power', in *Diplomatic Investigations: Essays in the Theory of International Politics* (London, 1966), pp. 151ff.

diplomat, in Italy. There by the fifteenth century the existence of a group of highly developed states, in constant contact with each other and constantly sensitive to a growth in the relative power of any one of them, was stimulating analysis of their relationships in a way as yet unknown elsewhere in Europe. The earliest clear reference to a balance of power within the Italian peninsula appears to come in 1439 from the Venetian Francesco Barbaro, who claimed that his own state was the main force working for the maintenance of such a balance.[7] A century later the historian Piero Guicciardini, in his *Storia d'Italia*, noted that Lorenzo di Medici as ruler of Florence had taken every care to ensure that the relations of the Italian states were kept in a state of balance (*'in modo bilanciate si mantenessero'*).[8] Venice, which during the fifteenth and much of the sixteenth centuries was, with the possible exception of Rome, the scene of more active diplomatic exchanges than any other European capital, liked to flatter its self-importance by claiming to hold the balance in Italy between the Habsburgs and their French rivals: claims of this kind were repeated, though without any sustained analysis of the workings of Europe's still embryonic international system, by a number of writers. The best-known of these, Paolo Paruta (who had served as Venetian ambassador in Rome in 1592–95), asserted in his *Discorsi Politici* (1599) that the political stability of Italy in the second half of the sixteenth century had been brought about by 'the counterpoising of greater forces (*il contrapeso di forze maggiori*)' than those of the Italian states themselves, while these outside forces, the French and imperial armies, 'counterbalancing each other (*dandosi di se stesse contrapeso*)' had been prevented from disturbing the peace of the peninsula or carrying out ambitious schemes of expansion there. The way to maintain this peace was to keep affairs in a state of balance (*tenere in modo bilanciate le cose*) and thus moderate the fears and ambitions which had, from the 1490s, so devastated Italy.[9]

The sixteenth century saw, as Valois–Habsburg and then Bourbon–Habsburg rivalries became rooted in European political life, a slow growth in the use of balance of power terminology in comments on international relations. Language of this kind was now spreading northwards from its Italian origins. In 1535 Mary of Hungary, the younger sister of Charles V whom he had installed as his regent in the Netherlands, said of the minor princes of Italy that 'their fear of the greatness of the two rivals (Charles V and Francis I) leads them to balance

7. C. Morandi, 'Il concetto della politica d'equilibrio nell'Europa moderna', *Archivio Storico Italiano*, lxxxvii (1940), 6.

8. Quoted in C. Curcio, *Europa: storia di un'idea* (Florence, 1958), i, 202.

9. *Opere politiche di Paolo Paruta*, ed. C. Monzani (Florence, 1852), ii, 312–13, 316.

their power'; and almost two decades later she spoke of the threat to the small states of Italy from Charles and Henry II of France and of the care taken by these states 'to balance their power'.[10] In 1554 the Venetian ambassador in France told his government that Henry II believed the Venetians were reluctant to ally with him because they feared that should Charles V die France might become too strong and believed that it was essential to 'keep matters in a state of equality (*tener le cose in equale stato*)' – the balance of power under a slightly different name.[11] A generation later there appeared what may be the first political pamphlet to use clear balance of power terminology, the *Discours au Roy Henri III, sur les moyens de diminuer l'Espagnol, du 24 Avril, 1584,* by the Huguenot leader Philippe Duplessis-Mornay. This spoke explicitly of '*la balance*' between France and Spain and envisaged an anti-Spanish alliance which would unite England, the Dutch, Denmark, Venice, the Swiss cantons and even the Turks with France in resistance to the power of Philip II – a foreshadowing of the main lines of French foreign policy down to the reign of Louis XIV.[12] A German pamphlet of the following year also urged union of the European states to bar any further growth of Spanish dominance, though apparently without any use of the term 'balance', while in the 1570s an English writer had already argued that 'France and Spain are as it were the Scales in the Balance of Europe, and England the Tongue or the Holder of the Balance'.[13] In awarding to his own country this decisive position he was merely restating in different and more forward-looking language a claim which had already flattered the vanity of Henry VIII earlier in the century.

There was thus, by the second half of the sixteenth century, beginning to be some treatment of international problems in more or less clear-cut balance of power terms. The extent and importance of this should not be exaggerated, however. It is very doubtful whether Machiavelli, for example, had any clear vision at all of the workings of a balance of power within the European state-system. Discussion of this sort was still very rare when compared with the great outpouring of it which marked the eighteenth century. The balance of power was now becoming established in practice, at least in a crude way, as a major guideline of international relations, perhaps the most important one of all. Probably any relatively close grouping of competitive independent states will give rise spontaneously to policies of this kind; and the closer and more continuous

10. G. Livet, *L'Equilibre européen de la fin du XVe à la fin du XVIIIe siècle* (Paris, 1976), p. 13; *Papiers d'état du Cardinal de Granvelle* (Paris, 1843), iv, 121.

11. E. Kaeber, *Die Idee des europäischen Gleichgewichts in der publizistischen Literatur vom 16. bis zur Mitte des 18. Jahrhunderts* (Berlin, 1907), p. 21.

12. Kaeber, *Die Idee . . .*, p. 24; Livet, *L'Equilibre . . .*, p. 14.

13. Kaeber, *Die Idee . . .*, pp. 26–8.

the relations between them the more closely each will scrutinise the activities of the others and the more conscious they will all be of the need to prevent the dominance of any one of them. Italy in the second half of the fifteenth century, until the irruption of French power in 1494, had seen a fairly effective balance of power regulating the relations between its component states. In the sixteenth century the monarchies of western Europe followed the Italian example in this respect rather as they did in the creation of a network of permanent diplomatic representatives. The efforts of many rulers to combine, however ineffectively, against Charles V after his apparently overwhelming victory over France at Pavia in 1525 was correctly seen by many later writers as a clear early example of an effort to create a workable balance of power on a European scale and thus avert the danger of 'universal monarchy'. But there was as yet no attempt to analyse the working of the balance or to ask serious questions about its nature and justification. As so often in politics of any kind, the reality existed long before theoretical discussion or intellectual analysis of it had got under way.

The first decades of the seventeenth century saw increasingly frequent references to a balance of power in Europe and a growing use of balance terminology. Words such as 'counterpoise' and 'equipoise', as well as 'balance', began to appear in political writings of all kinds, and particularly in the polemical pamphlet literature now being published in increasing quantities. Thus the Italian Traiano Boccalini could take for granted 'a general received opinion, That the Potentate, who in State and Forces is suffered to grow unto such greatness, that he find no other Prince able to counterpoyze him . . . cannot possibly be impeached from obtayning the Universall Monarchy'.[14] Almost simultaneously his countryman Tommaso Campanella spoke of the Austrian Habsburgs and the Ottoman Empire balancing each other's power in the Danube valley (*stanno quasi in bilancia*); while in 1617 a French pamphleteer could use such terms as '*le contrepoids des affaires*' and '*la balance du Monde*' with apparent confidence that they would be immediately intelligible to his readers.[15]

Moreover, there was now visible a tendency not merely to describe a balance of power between the states of Europe as a political and military fact but to justify it as inevitable and indeed as desirable, even essential. Giovanni Botero, perhaps the most penetrating thinker on political questions of the early seventeenth century, in his *Relazione della Repubblica di Venezia* spoke in 1605 of a system of balance between states as being

14. *The New-Found Politicke* (London, 1626), pp. 112–13. This is an English translation of Boccalini's very successful *Ragguali di Parnasso*, which first appeared in 1612–13.

15. T. Campanella, *Discorsi politici ai principi d'Italia* (Naples, 1848), p. 4; Kaeber, *Die Idee . . .*, p. 32.

founded in 'the order of nature and the light of reason'. Therefore although each ruler concerned might think only of his own advantage, none the less this individual selfishness worked to the benefit of the whole continent and 'from the plurality of Princes it follows that the balance (*contrappeso*) is useful and good, not from its own nature but by accident'.[16] Only a year or two later the international lawyer Alberto Gentili claimed that Europe must act to save herself from the dominance of a single over-mighty power. 'Do not all men', he wrote, 'with complete justice oppose on one side the Turks and on the other the Spaniards, who are planning and plotting universal dominion? . . . Is this not even today our problem, that one man may not have supreme power and that all Europe may not submit to the domination of a single man? Unless there is something which can resist Spain, Europe will surely fall'.[17] Though Gentili never uses the term 'balance', this is clearly a call for an effective balance of power. By the middle of the century there can be found the first references in treaties between European states to the need to preserve the balance as something which helps to make the continent more stable and peaceful than it otherwise would be. Thus in that signed by France and Denmark in 1645 both rulers agreed to maintain in the Baltic and North Sea 'that old and healthy balance (*ancien et salutaire équilibre*) which has until now served as the foundation of peace and public tranquillity'.[18] Political writers of all kinds for generations to come were to justify the balance of power by arguments, or rather assertions, of this sort.

## Habsburg or Bourbon the threat? England the arbiter?

Until at least the 1630s almost all writing of this kind had as its target the threatening power of Spain in close alliance with the Austrian Habsburgs. Any effective counterpoise to this menacing preponderance could be led only by France: therefore until well into the second half of the century Franco–Spanish rivalry was seen by every commentator as the centre around which international relations in western and much of central Europe turned. 'There be two Powers in Christendome', wrote one of the best-known, 'which are as the two Poles, from whence descend the influences of peace and warre upon the other States, to wit, the Houses of France and Spaine'.[19] For a generation or more there was a growing flow

16. Quoted in Curcio, *Europa* . . ., i, 202–3.
17. *De Jure Belli Libri Tres* (Oxford, 1933; first published 1612), ii, 64–5.
18. J. Dumont de Carlscroon, *Corps universel diplomatique* (Amsterdam, 1726–31), vi, Pt I, 329.
19. Henri, duc de Rohan, *A Treatise of the Interest of the Princes and States of Christendome* (London, 1641), Preface. The French original appeared in 1638.

of pamphlets by French authors stressing the vital necessity, for the continent as a whole, of resistance to Spanish power and the need for the smaller states of western Europe, in self-defence, to side with France in such resistance. Thus in the first years of the reign of Louis XIII a French pamphleteer urged the Protestant states of Germany to aid France against the threat of Spanish dominance. A Protestant Germany acting in this way, he claimed, 'holds the balance (*die Wage halt*)' between the two great Catholic rivals.[20] In the 1620s and 1630s the menace of overwhelming Habsburg power and the need to oppose and weaken it became a constant refrain in French writing on international events. Some of this anticipated policies which were later to become important. A pamphlet of 1621, for example, put forward, perhaps for the first time in an explicit form, the argument that to preserve the general balance in Europe as a whole it was essential to create a subsidiary one in Germany between the power of the Holy Roman Emperor and that of the German princes formally subordinate to him: this is an early statement of the idea of minor regional balances, in Germany, Italy or the Baltic, as necessary elements in the European one and in the stability which it alone could bring.[21] Another writer in 1629, arguing largely along the same lines, stressed the danger to France of a united Germany under Habsburg rule and urged that when next the imperial throne became vacant it should be filled by the elector of Bavaria, thus breaking the line of Habsburg emperors which had been uninterrupted since 1438.[22] This foreshadows the emergence later in the century of Bavaria as France's main ally in the German world and later still the establishment for a few years in 1742–45, with French help, of its ruler as emperor.

Until about 1640 there was unanimous agreement that it was Spanish power which threatened to overturn whatever precarious equilibrium might exist in Europe. As yet Richelieu had done no more than begin the process of making France the greatest European power. Even before the middle of the century, however, it was beginning to be clear that she in her turn would be the target of arguments derived from the balance of power and policies at least ostensibly based on it. Already in the 1640s German pamphleteers were alleging that France, not Spain, now threatened the freedom of the lesser European states.[23] By the 1660s, with

20. Kaeber, *Die Idee* . . ., pp. 30–1.
21. Kaeber, *Die Idee* . . ., p. 35. A still earlier English statement can be found in Sir Thomas Overbury, 'Observations on the State of France in 1609 under Henry IV', in *Stuart Tracts, 1603–1693* (London, 1903), ed. C.H. Firth, where the author talks in terms of a west-European balance between France, Spain and England, one composed of Muscovy, Poland, Sweden and Denmark in the east, and an intervening German one.
22. Kaeber, *Die Idee* . . ., p. 38.
23. Kaeber, *Die Idee* . . ., pp. 45–7.

Spanish power unmistakably in decline, Germany enfeebled by the losses of the Thirty Years War and the ambitions and self-confidence of Louis XIV only too clear, this had become the new orthodoxy. French victories in the 1660s, 1670s and 1680s stimulated pamphlet warfare on a scale not hitherto seen in international relations; and in this France's opponents stressed with increasing urgency the need for the formation of a large and effective anti-French coalition. Nothing less, it was claimed, could keep Louis' aggressions and French expansion within bounds. Such arguments were put forward in the most famous political polemic of the century, the *Bouclier d'Etat et de Justice contre le Dessin . . . de la Monarchie Universelle* of Baron François Paul de Lisola (1667), and were echoed repeatedly in the generation which followed. Without some combination of other states to act as a counterpoise to the menacing power of France, argued Lisola, aggression and disregard of treaties 'would destroy the whole Commerce of Mankind, and render humane Societies as dangerous as the company of Lions and Tigers', whereas a balance of power in Europe 'is very wholsome [*sic*] in itself'.[24]

Apart from having France as its target there were two other ways in which much of this pamphleteering of the 1660s–80s differed from that of the age of Richelieu. In so far as resistance to France had any single foundation or leader this was now to be found in the Austrian, not the Spanish, Habsburgs. Spanish power was clearly in eclipse; but that of Austria, bolstered by the reconquest from the Turks in the 1680s of much of the Danube valley, was more impressive than ever before. 'What has hitherto made for the safety of the princes of Europe', wrote a pamphleteer in the 1680s, 'has been the equality which has subsisted between the Houses of Bourbon and of Austria.' A year or two later an English commentator had no doubt that France and the Austrian Habsburgs were equal contenders for dominance in Europe. 'None but knows', he wrote, 'that in Europe there are two principal Houses that are at strife for Dominion, that of Austria, and that of France. All the World also knows, that the general Interest of other Princes is to hold these two Houses in equality, because that if the one swallowes up the other, it is certain, that its power would augment in such manner, that all the other States of Europe could not resist it'.[25] Moreover, and a more important signpost to future developments, England was now beginning to play a significant role in these controversies. Until late in the century her part in the affairs of Europe had been in general small and ineffective. Internal divisions, the pitiable weakness of her army for long periods, a general

24. *The Buckler of State and Justice* . . . (London, 1667), pp. 274, 278.
25. *Nouveaux Intérêts des Princes de l'Europe* (Cologne, 1685), p. 1; *The True Interests of the Princes of Europe in the Present State of Affairs* (London, 1689), p. 10.

lack of consistent and well-thought-out policies, had combined to keep her a second-rate force in international relations. By the 1660s, however, English political writing was tending more and more to appeal to the idea of a necessary balance of power as a weapon against the growing strength of France; and winning her over to the anti-French side was now becoming an important objective of the enemies of Louis XIV. In the early 1670s several pamphlets with this aim (one of them probably by Lisola himself) appeared in Germany; and the same years saw the beginnings of a considerable output of English ones, or at least of pamphlets published in English, urging cooperation with France's enemies, and particularly with the Dutch, as the only means of checking the advance of French power and guaranteeing England's own long-term security.[26] The revolution of 1688–89, which transformed her relationship with Europe and made her more and more the centre of resistance to France, raised hopes that she might be able to use the balance of power not merely to protect herself against threats from across the Channel but also to achieve a new level of international importance. If his fellow-countrymen held the balance between France and Austria, wrote an English pamphleteer in 1689, 'by this means they may become the Arbitrators of all Europe, and may always maintain Peace among the Christian Princes', while another in the same year urged that 'Did the King of Great Britain know the Strength of the Country he Rules in, and his own Interest, he might be not only the Mediator and Arbiter of the whole World, but give Peace when he pleas'd to all Christendom'.[27] The idea of England as relatively invulnerable to direct attack and in some sense above the European mêlée was now well established and was to live on to our own day.

## National character: one foundation of the balance?

All balance of power thinking was based on the assumption of rivalry and at least implicit hostility between the European states. It took for granted that the major ones had differing and irreconcilable objectives and that they were driven by an insatiable appetite for domination. Peace and stability depended on making it clear to them that this could not be achieved, or at least could be achieved only briefly and at ultimately ruinous cost. Rivalries, sharp distinctions between the outlooks and ambitions of different states, were of the essence of any balance. It seems likely, therefore, that the growing use of the imagery of balance and

26. Kaeber, *Die Idee . . . .*, pp. 50–1, 55–62.
27. *The True Interest of the Christian Princes* (London, 1689), p. 42; *The Spirit of France and the Politick Maxims of Lewis XIV laid open to the World* (London, 1689), pp. 37–8.

counterpoise drew strength from the universal assumption during the sixteenth and seventeenth centuries that each of the European peoples had its own distinctive character and aptitudes, its strong and weak points, which were rooted in nature and hence permanent and unchanging, and which distinguished it clearly from its neighbours and rivals. If Europe were a patchwork of states whose populations differed in this fundamental way it became easier to believe that these states could be controlled, and their rivalries kept within bounds, only by the discipline of some effective balance of power. That peoples were made fundamentally different by natural forces, above all by that of climate, hardly anyone doubted: indeed the general idea of distinctive national virtues and vices can be traced back at least as far as the very early middle ages, in the aftermath of the barbarian invasions.[28] 'Each Nation', wrote one seventeenth-century commentator, 'has its particular Character, and Specific Seal imprinted, as well upon the Bodies as Minds of its Inhabitants, which . . . is that Principle of Individuation, which distinguishes one from the other'.[29] In particular French and Spaniards were assumed by the later sixteenth century if not earlier to be divided by profound differences of character and temperament. The French, it was usually agreed, were quicker, more lively, more intellectually active, so that they produced and read many more books; but at the same time, at least in the eyes of unsympathetic observers, they were more superficial, quarrelsome and changeable. The Spaniards were more devout and better at keeping secrets, but also more lethargic and vindictive. Conventional judgements of this sweeping and completely unscientific kind were repeated, decade after decade, in dozens of political commentaries, pamphlets and travellers' accounts.[30] This was an age when the idea of the European states as forming parts of a single community, in some sense a political and judicial unity, was acquiring with the beginnings of modern international law a new precision and increased weight. Yet it was also, paradoxically, one which saw assumptions so divisive and so favourable to conflict flourishing luxuriantly.

28. J. Le Goff, *Medieval Civilization, 400–1500* (Oxford, 1988), p. 277.

29. Carlos Garcia, *France and Spain naturally Enemies, Or, Several Reasons to prove it impossible they should long be Friends* (London, 1704), p. 124.

30. Good examples are F. de la Mothe le Vayer, *Discours de la contrariété d'humeurs qui se trouve entre certains nations* (Paris, 1636); *The Frenchman and the Spaniard Display'd . . . showing the great Antipathy that is between 'em* (London, 1704); and Garcia, *France and Spain . . .* . The Spanish original of the last was written in the 1620s: its republication in English without essential change almost eighty years later is an indication of the tenacity with which this type of thinking held its ground.

*Challenges to the balance idea: religion and legalism*

The emergence of the balance of power as the dominant concept in international relations, a necessity to which, in the eyes of its advocates, almost all else must be sacrificed, was neither rapid nor easy. The growing tendency to judge the actions of rulers and states in terms of it was an important step in the secularisation of political life in general. The idea of such a balance was uncompromisingly materialist. It considered merely the strength of the states concerned, in so far as that could be measured. It completely ignored the morality of their policies and the justice of their claims. Its growing influence was thus a significant victory for 'that Ancient and all-commanding Idol call'd Reason of State'.[31] In an age of often bitter religious strife it inevitably conflicted with the claims made and the allegiances demanded by the competing churches. For at least a hundred years, therefore, from the mid-sixteenth to the mid-seventeenth century, there can be found, particularly in Catholic Europe, a continual undertow of criticism of an idea so unmistakably secular. The rivalries of Charles V and Francis I could not extinguish the widespread feeling that all Christian rulers had some obligation to unite for the defence of Europe against the Turkish threat in the east and to roll back the tide of Ottoman advance. Incidents such as the spectacular interview between the two monarchs at Aigues-Mortes in 1538, and the fact that every peace-treaty between them contained provisions for consolidating and perpetuating the newly made settlement by marriages between the Valois and Habsburg dynasties, helped to keep such hopes alive. There is no doubt, moreover, that Charles V at least sincerely shared them. The decades which saw the balance of power idea with its deeply secularist implications first take more or less explicit shape north of the Alps were thus also influenced by ideals, inherited unchanged from past centuries, of some politically effective Christian unity.

For generations to come these ideals were to retain at least some of their attractive power. In Italy during the later sixteenth and early seventeenth centuries a series of writers – notably the Neapolitans Campanella and Giovanni Ammirato – pushed them to the extent of dreaming of a single world-monarchy (usually to be headed by the Spanish Habsburgs) which, apart from repulsing the Turks, might also end religious divisions by restoring Catholicism throughout Europe.[32] Only a few mystics and enthusiasts went so far as this; but the idea of at least

---

31. Garcia, *France and Spain . . .*, Translator's Preface, unpaginated.
32. A. Pagden, 'Instruments of Empire: Tommaso Campanella and the Universal Monarchy of Spain', in his *Spanish Imperialism and the Political Imagination* (New Haven-London, 1990), pp. 49–50; F. Bosbach, *Monarchia universalis. Ein politischer Leitbegriff der frühen Neuzeit* (Göttingen, 1988), pp. 64–73.

some *de facto* unity against the Turk died only slowly. The reconquest of the middle Danube basin by the Austrian Habsburgs in the 1680s and 1690s thus assumed for many of those who took part in it, including many young noblemen from western Europe serving as volunteers in the Habsburg armies, something of the character of a crusade. Even well into the eighteenth century a great joint offensive of the European states against the infidel could still be seriously suggested,[33] though no government now contemplated for a moment such an idea. To those who thought in these traditional terms the balance of power was therefore for long at best an irrelevance and at worst, through the divisions between Christian states it created or sharpened, a serious impediment.

A more frequent target for the criticisms of religious idealists, however, was the way in which the search for a balance led states, in pursuit of purely secular ends, to ally with heretics against co-religionists. The first important example of this was the onslaught in the 1620s by the opponents of Richelieu on his anti-Spanish policies and their implications. The cardinal's efforts in 1624–26 to deny Spain the use of Alpine passes vital for the movement of her forces from northern Italy to the Netherlands meant the building of a far-reaching anti-Spanish coalition. This inevitably involved relatively close relations with Protestant states and leaders – a French subsidy paid to Spain's Dutch enemies, an English marriage for the French Princess Henrietta Maria, French aid to the opponents of Habsburg power in Germany. Such policies drew down on Richelieu severe criticism both from the papacy and from his opponents within France: this continued to some extent to the end of his life. He had to justify his eventual declaration of war against Spain in 1635 by arguing that she was using the ostensible defence of Catholicism merely as a cover for her own aggressive plans and that France, by resisting these, was therefore serving the cause of true religion. Three years later he forced Louis XIII to dismiss his confessor, Père Caussin, because of the latter's opposition to a war against Catholic Spain waged in concert with heretics such as the Dutch and Swedes. Conflict between the two points of view – religious and idealist on the one hand, secular and power-orientated on the other – appeared during these years in France with unprecedented sharpness. There were still many inconsistencies and ambiguities: the triumph of balance of power and reason of state was still incomplete. Richelieu had around him as advisers men whose attitude to foreign affairs was essentially pragmatic, free from strong religious feelings. It was possible for at least one French pamphleteer, in 1638, openly to

33. The best-known pamphlet example is *Cardinal Alberoni's Scheme for reducing the Turkish Empire to the Obedience of Christian Princes* (London, 1736).

justify alliance with the Protestant Dutch and Swedes on simple grounds of state interest.[34] But at the same time the cardinal in his negotiations with foreign powers consistently did all he could to defend Catholicism – for example in the provision in the treaty of 1630 signed with Gustavus Adolphus of Sweden that Catholics should have liberty of conscience in any territory conquered by the Swedes in their projected invasion of Germany. A sincere Catholic – he wrote religious tracts and supported monastic reform – Richelieu, like some of his advisers and Louis XIII himself, made no distinction between the cause of Catholicism and the political interests of France.

Another heritage from the past which was implicitly hostile to the materialist and calculating attitudes called for in balance of power thinking was the vein of unrealistic legalism inherited from the middle ages. This still appealed powerfully to many men of the sixteenth and seventeenth centuries. The tangle of legalistic and pseudo-historical claims put forward on behalf of many European rulers to the territories of others is the most obvious illustration of this point. France is again a striking case. There it was often argued that the king was entitled to dominion over the entire empire of Charlemagne, whose successors and heirs the rulers of France were. On this basis claims were put forward not merely to territories on France's borders which she might reasonably hope to gain, such as Spanish-controlled Flanders and the three bishoprics of Metz, Toul and Verdun (which had in any case been under French control since 1552) but also to Castile, Aragon, Navarre, Portugal, Sicily and Naples. For Richelieu quasi-legal rights and arguments based on them were important weapons in his efforts to extend French power. This emphasis on law, indeed, more than any other aspect of his policies gives him some claim to be considered a man of principle.[35] His own use of legal arguments was essentially realistic. He employed archivists and lawyers to collect documents which could be used to support French territorial claims; but these were to territories on France's frontiers which she might well one day acquire. However, side by side with rational policies of this kind went alluring and ludicrously ambitious pseudo-historical assertions of French claims to rule a high proportion of western Europe and of the right of the kings of France, as heirs of Charlemagne, also to be Holy Roman Emperors. The War of Devolution of 1667–68, fought by Louis XIV on the pretext of asserting the title of his wife, a Spanish princess, to territory in the Spanish Netherlands, both produced and was preceded by a burst of official propaganda in which claims of this kind were put forward by

34. W.F. Church, *Richelieu and Reason of State* (Princeton, 1972), pp. 351–2, 396.
35. Church, *Richelieu . . .*, p. 372.

French writers and rebutted by defenders of Habsburg rights.[36] Such assertion of far-reaching and often quite unrealisable historico-legal claims was in part an aspect of the intense preoccupation of early modern Europe with titles, precedence and all the paraphernalia and outward signs of distinction and superiority. It was also a result of the still widespread belief, nourished in part perhaps by the mediaeval romances which were the favourite reading of the European ruling classes until far into the sixteenth century, that to a powerful, brave, well-advised and lucky ruler very much was possible, that spectacular conquests, great and rapid territorial changes, the expulsion of the Turks from Europe, were not beyond the bounds of possibility. The effective role of this sort of romantic dreaming in the policies of rulers and governments was not often important. From the age of Charles V onwards it steadily declined. But so long as it continued to exist the victory of the sort of mental attitudes, calculating, self-interested, level-headed, which underlay the whole balance of power idea could not be complete.

There were other factors besides religious prejudice and legal antiquarianism which meant that even in the age of Louis XIV Europe was still only beginning to see the balance of power as the self-regulating and almost infallible mechanism which some of its advocates during the following century imagined it to be. Sometimes smaller or medium-sized states, instead of uniting to oppose a major one which theatened to dominate, were tempted to seek temporary security or easy territorial or other gains by allying with it. The most obvious examples of what has sometimes been called a 'reverse balance of power' policy of this kind can be seen in the later decades of the seventeenth century. In the 1670s and 1680s the power of Louis XIV seemed so great that other rulers often hesitated before committing themselves to opposition to him. French greatness might be an obvious threat to any balance of power in Europe; but for that very reason a small state might find safety, at least in the short term, by becoming an ally and protégé of France. Opposition to her, on the other hand, however necessary to preserve the balance, offered only a difficult and costly struggle against a very formidable opponent. Thus the 'Great Elector' Frederick William of Brandenburg was torn in the 1670s and 1680s between fear of French ambitions in Germany and a competing desire to replace Sweden in the now traditional pattern of French alliances and benefit territorially by clinging to the coat-tails of Louis XIV. In the same way, the English government, after joining Sweden and the Dutch in 1668 in a triple alliance to restrain France, soon deserted its Dutch allies

---

36. The best-known example on the French side is Antoine Bilain, *Traité des Droits de la Reyne très-Chrétienne sur divers Etats de la Monarchie d'Espagne* (Paris, 1667), a substantial work in two volumes, and on the Habsburg one Lisola's *Bouclier d'Estat et de Justice* (n.p., 1667).

and in 1672 embarked as a *de facto* ally of Louis on what it thought would be an easy and commercially profitable war with them. Sir William Temple, the English ambassador to The Hague, was one of the most intelligent diplomats of the age. He saw clearly that balance of power considerations were now an essential element in international relations. Yet such was his desire for England to take over as much as possible of the immense Dutch carrying trade that he argued in 1671 that she should encourage a French attack on the United Netherlands by promising neutrality or should even, as happened in the following year, herself join in such an attack.[37] Clearly the temptation to take the apparently winning side, which is a part of ordinary human nature, was given unusual strength during the 1670s and 1680s by the apparently almost irresistible power of France: to that extent an effective balance of power was made more difficult to construct. In the century which followed, the golden age of balance theorising, no ruler achieved such superiority over his fellows as Louis XIV and it became easier to think of the balance as a normal and natural state of affairs and therefore as one not difficult to achieve.

## THE GOLDEN AGE: THE EIGHTEENTH CENTURY

The century which separates the apogee of Louis XIV in the 1680s from the French Revolution was the most productive period of balance of power theorising. The idea that an equilibrium between the different states of Europe was the basis of the continent's political stability and a precondition of its political progress was never universally accepted. The concept of balance was always the target of criticism which was sometimes searching. Yet never before or since has it been the object of so much generally favourable discussion by so many different writers. Never before or since has a single idea been so clearly the organising principle in terms of which international relations in general were seen. Swift, one writer among many, could take it for granted that 'the Balance of Europe' was by the early eighteenth century an idea so well known and generally accepted as to need no explanation, and that 'watching the severall Motions of our Neighbours and Allyes and preserving a due Ballance among them' was the normal and inevitable task of any government.[38] The balance was also an orthodoxy whose acceptance was now more

37. 'A Survey of the Constitutions and Interests of the Empire, Sweden, Denmark, Spain, Holland, France and Flanders; with their Relation to England in the Year 1671', in *Works* (London, 1754), ii, 20, 27–8.
38. *Political Tracts, 1713–1719*, pp. 188, 78.

formal and explicit than ever before. The Anglo-Spanish treaty signed in July 1713, as part of the Utrecht peace settlement, identified in its preamble as one of its major objectives the securing and consolidating of peace in Europe through the working of a balance of power. This was the first such avowal in so important an international instrument; but a series of similar statements can be found in a number of treaties of the eighteenth and early nineteenth centuries. When, therefore, in 1720 an English pamphleteer wrote that 'There is not, I believe, any doctrine in the law of nations, of more certain truth, of greater and more general importance to the prosperity of civil society, or that mankind has learnt at a dearer rate, than this of the balance of power'[39] he was stating what to most of his contemporaries was now established truth. The obvious necessity of some equilibrium of this kind now seemed to most writers on current politics demonstrated by both common-sense and history.[40]

## The balance moralised

From the beginning balance of power thinking had been rooted in the assumption that states and rulers were inherently and inveterately jealous of each other's power. Rohan in the 1630s had made the point succinctly: 'it be a maxime common to all Princes to hinder the growth of their Neighbours'.[41] But this belief that fear and envy, institutionalised in the balance, were the necessary foundation of international relations, was more frequently voiced during the century from 1680 onwards than ever before. An English pamphleteer was speaking for many other writers when in 1689 he asserted that 'It is a Maxim of true Policy that whensoever any Prince is exalted too high . . . the other Princes ought to enter into League together, to pull him down, or at least to hinder him from growing greater'.[42]

Statements of this kind were not merely more numerous during the eighteenth century than before. They were also often different in tone. French condemnation of Spanish power in the first decades of the

---

39. *Two Essays on the Balance of Europe*, p. 770. The discussion in the following pages relies heavily on M.S. Anderson, 'Eighteenth-century Theories of the Balance of Power', in *Studies in Diplomatic History: Essays in Memory of David Bayne Horn*, ed. Ragnhild Hatton and M.S. Anderson (London, 1970), pp. 183–98.

40. This is repeatedly asserted in the most elaborate pseudo-scholarly treatment of the subject in the early eighteenth century, J.J. Lehmann, *Trutina vulgo bilanx Europae* . . . (Jena, 1716), for example at pp. 162–3. The victory of the balance of power as the dominant legitimating idea in international relations by the first years of the century is well brought out in H. Duchhardt, 'Westfälischer Friede und internationale Beziehungen im Ancien Regime', *Historische Zeitschrift*, 249 (1989), 539–40.

41. *A Treatise* . . ., p. 31.

42. *The True Interest of the Christian Princes*, p. 31.

seventeenth century, Dutch, Austrian or English calls for that of Louis XIV to be reduced, had almost always assumed that these threatening concentrations of strength were being used in a deliberately aggressive way, that Philip IV or Louis, Olivares or Louvois, were bullying and oppressing their neighbours with some deliberate evil intent. By the eighteenth century, however, it was more and more taken for granted that any great concentration of power in the hands of a single state was always inherently dangerous in itself and must be resisted, even though the rulers of that state might have no aggressive intentions. At the height of the struggle with Napoleon I the best-known German political commentator of that age, Friedrich von Gentz, made the point well. 'I consider any nation dangerous to the tranquillity of others', he wrote, 'when it wants nothing to injure them but the will; whether it be governed by virtuous or depraved characters, guided by true or false principles.' He went on to claim that 'It is a leading maxim in every rational system of practical politics, that every power is dangerous to the rest, which possesses the means of disturbing the general peace, and wants nothing but the will to use them'.[43] A balance of power thus appeared to many observers as something with moral justification of its own, almost independent of any practical value it might have. Fénelon, Archbishop of Cambrai and the greatest Catholic moralist of the early eighteenth century, could thus argue, in a memorandum written in its first years for the education of the grandson of Louis XIV, that rulers had a positive duty, not merely a *de facto* right, to resist excessive growth in the power of any one of them.[44] A little later a pontificating German academic gave as his first 'law of the balance' that all rulers and peoples 'so far as they can, ought with the utmost diligence to support so salutary an institution' and went on to declare flatly that 'no one is entitled to oppose the balance (*nemini licitum esse, aequilibrio se opponere*)'.[45]

From a slightly different direction, moreover, another current of thought also stressed its moral value. The greatest international lawyer of the age, the Swiss Eméric de Vattel (who was also a practising diplomat), based it on the absolute right of the smaller states to combine to protect their independence against the threat posed by a greater neighbour; and this view was later echoed by another very influential lawyer, Georg Friedrich von Martens.[46] The balance of power thus became an aspect of

43. F. von Gentz, *On the State of Europe before and after the French Revolution* (London, 1802), pp. 214, 255. The German original appeared in 1801.
44. *Oeuvres de Fénelon* (Paris, 1802–30), xxii, 307–8; Lehmann, *Trutina . . .*, pp. 173–4.
45. Lehmann, *Trutina . . .*, pp. 162–3.
46. E. de Vattel, *Le Droit des Gens, ou principes de la loi naturelle* (Leyden, 1758), ii, 296–7; G.F. de Martens, *Précis du Droit des Gens moderne de l'Europe*, 2nd edn. (Göttingen, 1801), p. 190.

the expanding current of eighteenth-century thought and feeling which centred around the idea of nature, seen as the ultimate source of true morality, and of natural rights. This probably strengthened a growing tendency to see as justified any war which, whatever its immediate origins, could be presented as one in defence of this essential equilibrium.

## The balance and the eighteenth-century mind

More importantly, balance of power thinking now won wider acceptance than ever before because it was in tune with much of the intellectual temper of the age. Religious passions were sometimes still able to influence powerfully feelings about international events. The anger and alarm aroused in Brandenburg-Prussia and even in Great Britain in 1719 by the execution of a number of Protestants in the Polish city of Thorn (Torun) – the 'blood-bath of Thorn' – or the admiration which Frederick II's quite undeserved status as a 'Protestant hero' won him during the Seven Years War are obvious illustrations of this. But in so far as religion had ever played any decisive role in the actions of governments it had now long ceased to do so. Nationalism, the coming secular religion of the nineteenth and twentieth centuries, was already a far from negligible factor in European life. Governments might find in it a powerful source of support for their foreign policies, as when in 1709 Louis XIV, faced by the very severe peace terms which his enemies were pressing upon him after a series of disastrous French defeats, was able to make an unprecedented direct appeal to the French people for their support in this moment of crisis. But national feeling was often still too embryonic to generate emotions as powerful as those it later produced. From the age of Marlborough to that of Metternich, or at least to that of Robespierre, therefore, Europe lived through a century or more during which the emotional temperature of international relations was probably lower than either before or after. Men still allowed themselves without hesitation the luxury of fearing and even hating their neighbours; but in general they did this less wholeheartedly than during the Counter-reformation or the nationalist rivalries of the later nineteenth and twentieth centuries. The limited and formal nature of eighteenth-century war when it did break out, the extent to which it spared non-combatants and was less destructive than in former generations, can easily be exaggerated. Yet there was a widespread belief that in western Europe at least states and their armies now showed far greater restraint in wartime than they had in the past. At the end of the century a British writer had no doubt that 'the refinement of modern ages has stripped war of half its horrors', while another believed that now 'war is made with little national animosity and battles are fought without any personal exasperation of those who are engaged; so that parties are, almost in the heat of a contest, ready to listen to the dictates of humanity or reason'.[47] In such an atmosphere an idea like that of the balance of power – rationalistic, stressing calculation, adjustment and manipulation, and implicitly hostile to any idea of overwhelming and permanent victory – was a congenial one.

Moreover, balance of power ideas did not appeal merely to these negative characteristics of the age, to its relative lack of powerful religious, national and military emotions. They also drew support from one of its most intellectually positive aspects, its faith in the physical sciences, in the fundamental truths of physics and astronomy which Newton most of all had now unveiled. The greatest ambition of the social sciences, as they slowly took shape during the eighteenth century, was to construct a science of humanity which would embrace and explain the workings of societies as Newtonian physics had done so much of the natural world. The methods which had yielded such wonderful results in the one sphere must, if correctly applied, be productive in the other. It must be possible, therefore, to reduce international relations to a set of rules and principles which would allow the statesman who understood them to achieve his aims.

There was, of course, much superficiality in all this. Many ministers liked to talk glibly of the 'system' they were pursuing in foreign policy: one of the most famous, Prince Kaunitz in Vienna, spoke of his 'geometrical methods' in diplomacy.[48] The vast political literature of the period contains many comparisons of relations between states with impersonal mechanisms both great and small. Kaunitz certainly believed that the balance of power functioned to some extent automatically, as a mechanism rooted in the nature of the world and independent of human control, while his great rival Frederick II compared the working of international relations to that of a watch.[49] The most popular of all these analogies, however, was that between the balance of power and the solar system as revealed by Newton. A British pamphleteer in mid-century asserted that 'What gravity or attraction, we are told, is to the system of the universe, that the ballance [*sic*] of power is to Europe: a thing we cannot just point out to ocular inspection, and see or handle; but which is as real in its existence, and as sensible in its effects, as the weight is in

47. Quoted in Anderson, *War and Society in Europe of the Old Regime, 1618–1789* (London, 1988), p. 188.

48. P.R. Rohden, *Die klassische Diplomatie von Kaunitz bis Metternich* (Leipzig, 1939), p. 4.

49. Rohden, *Die klassische Diplomatie*, p. 5; *Oeuvres de Frédéric le Grand* (Berlin, 1846–56), vii, 3; and Frederick's Political Testament of 1752 in *Politische Correspondenz Friedrichs des Grossen: Ergänzungsband*, ed. G.B. Volz (Berlin, 1920), p. 48.

scales'.[50] More than four decades later another drew the analogy even more explicitly, making a detailed comparison between gravitational forces in the planetary system and the balance of power

> which regulates the mutual actions of the European nations; subjects each to the influence of others, however remote; connects all together by a common principle; regulates the motions of the whole; and confining within narrow limits whatever deviations may occur in any direction, maintains the order and stability of the vast complicated system. As the newly-discovered planets are found to obey the same law that keeps the rest in their orbits; so the powers, which frequently arise in the European world, immediately fall into their places, and conform to the same principles that fix the positions and direct the movements of the ancient states.

He went on, logically enough, to argue that a genuine science of international relations must therefore be possible, since they could be reduced to general principles and the part played in them by personal and accidental factors was already small and would inevitably become still smaller.[51]

Between attitudes of this kind, which saw the balance as essentially part of the natural world and therefore morally neutral, and others which saw it as having some moral value of its own, as something which *ought* to exist and which the states of Europe must therefore consciously strive to uphold, there was an obvious conflict. No theorist succeeded in bridging this gap: most of the pamphleteers and publicists who wrote so copiously on the subject simply ignored it. Clearly, however, most of them assumed more or less without argument that the balance of power was in part man-made, or at least something which states and statesmen were obliged consciously to foster and safeguard. If it alone could give some degree of security to the lesser states and defend effectively their natural right to exist, then it was a supreme good in international relations, one which overrode lesser and competing goods. These, however desirable in themselves, must if necessary give way to the overwhelming need to maintain a workable balance of power. A ruler might thus be justified in breaking his word and disregarding a treaty if this were essential to safeguard the balance; in this way *raison d'état* would serve the interests of Europe in general rather than those of a single state.[52] Just as an individual, again, could be forced to sacrifice some of his personal wealth

---

50. *Occasional Reflections on the Importance of the War in America, and the Reasonableness of supporting the King of Prussia* (London, 1758), p. 58.

51. Henry, Lord Brougham, 'The Balance of Power', *Works* (London–Glasgow, 1855–61), viii, 11–12, 18–28. This essay was written in January 1803.

52. *Nouveaux Intérêts des Princes de l'Europe* (Cologne, 1685), pp. 2–3, is the earliest clear assertion of this kind I have found.

to the needs of the society to which he belonged, so a ruler might justifiably be asked to surrender territory, even territory to which he had good title, for the benefit of the state–system as a whole. As one writer following this line of argument claimed, 'the most legitimate owners must sometimes give up their rights to procure the maintenance of the balance'.[53] Another in 1743, at a moment when the Habsburg lands in central Europe and Italy were threatened by powerful enemies, argued that 'this is a matter of the PUBLIC INTEREST of all Europe to which, according to all the laws of man and nature the INDIVIDUAL INTEREST of any State or Potentate whatever should be sacrificed'; therefore even if the opponents of Maria Theresa had valid claims to parts of her territories these must be disregarded to safeguard the stability of the continent as a whole.[54]

There was complete agreement that it was legitimate to prevent any state from becoming by territorial expansion dangerously strong and a menace to others. But this was not the only way in which a state might achieve a threatening pre-eminence. It might gain it also by strengthening its armed forces, by developing its economic life and increasing its wealth, by improving its administration, or on a more fundamental level by changing its entire political and social structure and thus releasing hitherto untapped reserves of popular energy (as happened in France after 1792–93). If its fellow-states could legitimately resist its strengthening by territorial expansion, were they not logically justified in resisting also its becoming stronger by internal changes of this kind? Hardly any eighteenth-century writer was willing to confront squarely this very awkward question. Not many were willing even to consider it at all. One of the few who did was the German cameralist Justi, the author of the most penetrating criticism of the whole balance of power idea produced during this period. He pointed out that if the idea of the balance as an overriding necessity were pushed to its logical conclusion every state must live continuously in danger of interference from others which feared that internal change might make it unduly strong. All would thus exist in a kind of '*réciproque Sklaverei*'.[55] But no advocate of the balance was willing to go to this logical extreme. Those who considered the problem at all took refuge in the claim that a state which grew strong by internal growth somehow threatened the balance less than one which did so by territorial expansion, or at least in the rather feeble assertion that only very violent

53. L.M. Kahle, *La Balance de l'Europe considérée comme la règle de la paix et de la guerre* (Berlin–Göttingen, 1744), p. 147.
54. *Histoire de la grande crise de l'Europe* (London, 1743), pp. 1–3. For similar arguments see Fénelon, *Oeuvres*, xxii, 309 and *Two Essays on the Balance of Europe*, p. 773.
55. J.H.G. von Justi, *Die Chimäre des Gleichgewichts von Europa* (Altona, 1758), p. 60.

and sudden change within a state could justify interference by its neighbours.[56]

## Overseas empires and the balance of power

By the eighteenth century the balance had also acquired two new and very important facets which until at least the 1690s had scarcely existed. In the first place, it now increasingly embraced the colonial empires of the European states, or at least those in America. The wealth which these possessions brought to their owners was now a significant, indeed often an over-valued, element in estimates of their relative strength. Secondly, the rise of Russia to great-power status had now not merely widened the network of formal diplomacy[57] but also introduced into all balance of power calculations a new and very important element.

Until late in the seventeenth century discussions of the balance had seldom paid much attention to colonial or commercial considerations. A few references to them can be found. A German pamphlet of 1585 (though apparently without using precise balance of power terminology) had blamed the threat of a Spanish 'universal monarchy' for the decline of Germany's foreign trade.[58] From the middle of the seventeenth century onwards it had increasingly been argued that England ought to join in opposition to the growth of French power because of the threat this offered to her commercial future. But it was only with the consolidation of the new colonial empires of Holland, England and France, supplementing and partly replacing the older ones of Spain and Portugal, that trade, predominantly colonial trade, began to play an important role in discussion of the European balance. The Spanish–Dutch treaty of 1648 was the first to make any attempt to settle colonial conflicts; and there were similar efforts in the Anglo-Spanish treaty of 1667 and the Franco-Spanish treaty of 1684. As it became increasingly clear that several states, most of all Britain, based their economic strength in part on their overseas empires and oceanic trades, these inevitably began to appear as significant elements in the much-discussed European equilibrium. 'Can a nation be Safe without Strength?', asked the English mercantilist Charles Davenant in 1696, writing in an overseas trade context. 'And is Power to be compass'd and Secur'd but by Riches? And can a country become Rich any way, but by the Help of a well Managed and Extended

---

56. Kahle, *La balance de l'Europe* . . ., pp. 106–7; (J. Campbell), *Memoirs of the Duke de Ripperda* (London, 1740), Appendix, p. 358; Brougham, 'The Balance of Power', 36–7; Gentz, *On the State of Europe*, p. 112.

57. See pp. 69–71 above.

58. Kaeber, *Die Idee* . . . , p. 42.

Traffick?'.[59] Almost simultaneously the French soldier-economist Marshal Vauban, in two remarkable memoranda of 1699 and 1700, urged that the real future of France lay not in further difficult and expensive territorial growth in Europe but in colonial expansion. She must build up great colonies of settlement in Canada and the Mississippi basin; and this meant good relations with her European neighbours which would free her hands for the struggle for colonial mastery with England and the Dutch on which her long-term future really depended.[60] These memoranda were not concerned with the balance of power as such; but they were the clearest recognition hitherto by any statesman of the extent to which the power of some west-European states was now coming to rest on colonial and oceanic foundations. As Vauban wrote, English resistance to possible French domination of Spain and her overseas empire was being inspired by the commercial strengthening of France and weakening of England which, it was alleged, would inevitably result, and by the implications of this for the relative standing of the two states in Europe. Even in Germany, with little extra-European trade of her own, a pamphlet of 1701 accused Louis XIV of aiming at world domination not merely through political and military power but also by monopolising trade with the Spanish empire, the Baltic and North Sea, and the Levant. The position of '*Alleinkauf oder Monopolio*' which this would give him, the author claimed, meant overwhelming commercial as well as military power for France.[61]

By the early eighteenth century, therefore, the idea that power drawn from commercial profits and colonial possessions was an important ingredient in the European balance, at least so far as some states were concerned, was becoming well established. By the middle of the century it had become part of the conventional wisdom. One British writer even argued, quite unhistorically, that 'we may safely say, that the Ballance [*sic*] of Power . . . was created by Trade, and must continue to be the Object more especially of Trading Countries, as long as they preserve their Commerce and their Freedom'. This was because states combined against the dangerous strength of any one of them largely from 'the just

---

59. *An Essay on the East-India Trade* (London, 1696), pp. 7, 61; an anthology of quotations from later seventeenth and eighteenth-century writing stressing the essential connection between international and especially intercontinental trade and state power can be found in E. Silberner, *La Guerre dans la pensée économique du XVI au XVIII siècle* (Paris, 1939), pp. 105ff.

60. *Vauban, sa famille et ses écrits, ses oisivetés et sa correspondance*, ed. E.E.A. Rochas d'Aiglun (Paris, 1910), i, 413ff.; see also W. Gembruch, 'Zwei Denkschriften Vaubans zur Kolonial–und Aussenpolitik Frankreichs aus den Jahren 1699 und 1700', *Historische Zeitschrift*, cxcv (1962), 297–330.

61. *Die an der Licht gebrachte Wahrheit des österreichischen Rechts und frantzösischen Unrechts zur Spanischen Succession* (Cologne, 1701), summarised in Kaeber, *Die Idee . . .*, p. 74.

Apprehension that this may, and indeed must, prove extremely prejudicial to Commerce in general, and to that of several Nations in particular who, to prevent this, will not scruple to take up Arms'.[62]

There was universal agreement that Britain was the outstanding example of a state made great by trade. 'After all', wrote an anonymous pamphleteer in 1743, 'the three advantages, the first of being a maritime power, the second of having a flourishing trade and the third of holding the balance of power, are so interlinked, so far as Great Britain is concerned, that it would be a waste of time to amuse oneself by proving it'.[63] The idea that trade and the colonial possessions which increasingly nourished it were essential ingredients in the balance of power could thus easily become a propaganda weapon for use against allegedly threatening British commercial and colonial power. In France particularly it was now more and more argued that an indispensable counterpart to any territorial and military balance in Europe was a colonial and maritime one overseas, above all in America. Without the second, it was claimed, the first had little value or durability. Such ideas were voiced with particular sharpness and anxiety during the Seven Years War, under the impact of disastrous French losses in America, the Caribbean and India. 'The trade balance of the nations in America', wrote a French official pamphleteer in the later 1750s, 'is like the balance of power in Europe. One could even add that these two balances make up a single one'.[64] Almost simultaneously the greatest French minister of the mid-century, the duc de Choiseul-Stainville, wrote that 'the real balance now lies in trade and America. The war in Germany, even carried on better than it is, will not ward off the evils which are to be feared from the great superiority of the English at sea.' A year later, depressed by news of the fall of Quebec, he believed that the destruction of so much of France's overseas trade meant that she had ceased to be a first-class power at all.[65] Two years later again, in 1762, one of his advisers argued that 'The possession of America is today the most abundant and the most dependable source of political power; it is only by reason of the riches that commerce bears thence that

62. J. Campbell, *The Present State of Europe* (6th edn, London, 1761), pp. 24–5. The first edition was published in 1750.

63. *Le Système politique de la Grande-Bretagne dans la conjoncture présente* (The Hague, 1743), pp. 123–4.

64. *Mémoires pour servir à l'histoire de notre temps* (Frankfurt–Leipzig, 1757–60), i, 56, 58; cf. G. de Réal de Curban, *La Science du gouvernement* (Paris–Amsterdam–Aix-la-Chapelle, 1761–65), vi, 448–50.

65. G. de Raxis de Flassan, *Histoire générale et raisonnée de la diplomatie française* (Paris, 1811), vi, 160, 279.

the nations may be compared with each other'.[66] The same idea was
taken up by the most influential English pamphlet of the period, which
argued that if Britain could dominate the Caribbean and monopolise its
very profitable sugar production the French, 'the great source of their
wealth being cut off with their islands', would be unable to fight
effectively in Germany.[67] Almost forty years later the most important
eighteenth-century French discussion of the European balance was yet
again a plea for the states of the continent to combine to resist British
maritime and commercial dominance. It stressed that this resistance must
be led by France, 'the only counterweight capable of guaranteeing its
[Europe's] continental and maritime balance' and urged that every alliance
of the powers should aim, in both peace and war, to 'guarantee the
political interests of the continent against the exaggerated ascendancy of
maritime interests'.[68]

All this emphasis on the importance of colonies and oceanic trade was
in a sense merely a recognition of changing realities. It sometimes sprang
from a vague but growing realisation that in the long run Europe might
herself become merely an element in a world balance of power. Indeed,
the unprecedented integration of struggles within Europe with others
thousands of miles away, seen in the years 1755–62 as Britain and France
fought out the first approach to a world war, had already given rise to
some forebodings in parts of the continent less favoured by history and
geography. 'What a fate!', lamented a German pamphlet in 1760. 'Must it
be the way of the world that Germany atones for India's mistakes?'[69] By
the later years of the century it was possible to find pessimists who
believed that in the not too distant future Europe must fall under the
ascendancy of either the new American republic or the newly great
Russian empire, the enormous and partly non-European states with which
the future of the world lay. Yet the playing-down of the continent's own
potentialities and the stressing of her dependence on the outside world
which such attitudes involved was pushed much too far. It was absurd for
Choiseul in 1760 to lament that France had ceased to be a first-rate
power. By doing so he grossly undervalued her military strength and

66. M. Savelle, 'The American Balance of Power and European Diplomacy', in *The Era of the American Revolution: Studies Inscribed to Evarts Boutelle Greene*, ed. R.B. Morris (New York, 1939), p. 163.
67. I. Mauduit, *Considerations on the Present German War* (London, 1760), pp. 64, 137.
68. Comte A.-M. d'Hauterive, *De l'Etat de la France en l'an VIII* (Paris, 1800), pp. 44, 66.
69. 'Welch Schicksal! Muss die Welt so in Verhältnis stehen,
    Das Deutschland büsen muss, was Indien versehen?'
Quoted in G.A. Rein, 'Die Gegenwartsbedeutung der kolonialen Expansion für das europäische Gefüge', in his *Europa und Übersee: Gesammelte Aufsätze* (Gottingen–Berlin–Frankfurt, 1961), p. 107.

domestic economic resources. Almost as he wrote his despondent words, an English pamphleteer was justifiably pointing out that to France all her colonies combined were worth hardly half as much as control of the Austrian Netherlands would be.[70] Large territories and populations in Europe, the powerful armies which these territories and populations made possible – these were still the essential ingredients of the balance of power. This was shown unmistakably by the second major new element in it during the eighteenth century – the rise of Russia to great-power status.

## Russian power and the growing complexity of the balance

In the first years of the century there were still few observers who envisaged Russia playing a role of much importance in the politics of Europe. During the war of the Spanish Succession both Louis XIV and his opponents at times thought of using Russia for their own purposes. William III twice offered English mediation in the Great Northern War, the Russian struggle with Saxony and Sweden which had broken out in 1699–1700, in the hope that an end to it might free Swedish and Saxon forces for use against France in western Europe. The French government hoped, even more vainly, that an end to the war might open the way to Russian support for the Hungarian nationalist revolt against Habsburg rule which erupted in 1703. None of this had any result. But the crucial Russian victory over the Swedes at Poltava in 1709, the destruction of the Swedish Baltic empire, the immense personal prestige of Peter I in the last years of his reign, revolutionised the situation. West-European statesmen were now forced to think of Russia as at least a potential great power.[71] Yet though it was undeniable that a new and very important element had now been introduced into the European balance there remained a deep-seated feeling that Russia was still foreign, essentially un-European. In France particularly, which had seen her traditional allies, Sweden, Poland and the Ottoman empire, all suffer in varying degrees from the forward movement of Russia's frontiers and influence, there was great reluctance to recognise her as a permanent member of the European state-system. As late as the 1760s a French official propagandist denied that she was an integral member of the continent's political structure in even the way that so minor a power as Denmark was.[72] But the facts were

70. J. Perceval, *Things as they are. Part the Second* (London, 1761), p. 45.
71. M.S. Anderson, *Britain's Discovery of Russia, 1553–1815* (London, 1958), Chapter 4; H. Doerries, *Russlands Eindringen in Europa in der Epoche Peters des Grossen* (Berlin, 1939), Chapter 5.
72. J.N. Moreau, *Manloveriana, pour servir de supplément à l'Europe ridicule* (n.p., 1762), pp. 22–4.

undeniable. A long list of successes – Russia's role in the destruction of the Swedish empire and the partitions of Poland; her victories against Frederick II in the Seven Years War; her sweeping successes against the Turks in 1768–74 – made it impossible not to see that a great new political force had arisen.

From the 1760s onwards, as international relations centred increasingly around the problems of Poland and the Ottoman empire, Russian strength seemed to many observers threateningly complete, a menace to the security of the continent as a whole and to the balance of power. In 1787 the economist and statistician Sir John Sinclair, just returned from a visit to Russia, urged that 'all Europe must unite to check the ambition of a sovereign who makes one conquest only a step to the acquisition of another'.[73] Two years later, during a new war with the Ottoman empire which seemed to promise Russia great new gains, one of the most influential pamphlets of the period called in similar terms on the states of Europe to combine against the dangerous growth of her power.[74] In the spring of 1791 William Pitt tried unsuccessfully, in the 'Ochakov Crisis' of March–April, to rouse Britain to oppose the challenge to the balance of power allegedly offered by further Russian territorial advance in the Near East. A few years later an important French foreign ministry official even suggested that the problem of excessive Russian strength be solved by dividing the country into two separate states ruled respectively from Moscow and St Petersburg on the model of the Roman Empire ruled under Diocletian and his successors from Rome and Byzantium.[75]

Russia's spectacular rise, and to a lesser extent the marked growth of Prussian power from the 1740s onwards, meant that the European balance of power had become, by the second half of the eighteenth century, more complex than ever before. Until at least the 1690s it could still be seen as essentially a simple equilibrium between the two great dynasties of Bourbon and Habsburg in which all other states played ultimately no more than secondary roles. In spite of very important changes, habit and intellectual inertia ensured that this picture continued to be widely accepted down to the mid-eighteenth century. From the 1750s at latest, however, it was quite impossible to deny that the rising power of Britain, Russia and Prussia, together with the increasing importance of events in America and the growing weight of east and south-east European

73. *Observations regarding the Present State of the Russian Empire* (London, 1787), p. 17.

74. *Du Péril de la balance politique: ou exposé des causes qui l'ont altérée dans le Nord, depuis l'avènement de Catherine II au trône de Russie* (London, 1789). The pamphlet was probably written by Freiherr von Borcke, the Prussian minister in Stockholm but has been attributed to various authors, including Gustavus III of Sweden.

75. D'Hauterive, *De l'État de la France*, pp. 99–100.

problems, had created a new situation. More recent rivalries, between Britain and France at sea and overseas, between Prussia and the Habsburgs in the German world, were now acquiring the force of tradition, while that between Bourbons and Habsburgs by comparison almost faded into the background.[76] The relatively simple equilibrium of less than a century earlier had now been replaced by a much more complex one involving half a dozen great or semi-great powers and considerably influenced by events on the other side of the Atlantic. It may be that this more complex reality did something to encourage the development of more, and more searching, theorising about the balance.

## The balance idea challenged but triumphant

The eighteenth century, therefore, saw the balance of power more generally accepted as a guide to the conduct of states than ever before or since. Yet it was also an age during which the whole idea was subjected to often very hostile criticism. This took two forms; the one moral, the other essentially practical. On moral grounds both the theory and the practice of the balance were attacked as exacerbating international tensions and generating wars, as a destructive rather than a stabilising influence. 'What streams of blood the balance of Europe, this new idol, has caused to be shed', wrote a French critic. 'For long, to avoid evils which are distant and uncertain the princes have brought upon themselves immediate and genuine ones and, in trying to avoid war, have waged it'.[77] The same condemnation was voiced by many other writers, especially in the second half of the century, as humanitarianism and *bienfaisance* began to play a larger part in the intellectual and emotional life of Europe. At one ideological extreme a leading figure of the French Enlightenment, Lemercier de la Rivière, in his very influential *L'Ordre naturel et essentiel des sociétés politiques* (London–Paris, 1767) attacked the balance as dividing states and fostering conflict: it was thus a flagrant rejection of Europe's natural condition, that of unity as a single society. A generation later the English radical William Godwin dismissed it contemptuously with the remark that 'We shall be in little danger of error . . . if we pronounce wars undertaken to maintain the balance of power to be universally unjust'.[78] At the other extreme a leading German mercantilist criticised it

76. *Das entlarvte Frankreich, oder das entdeckte Projekt von der europäischen Universalmonarchie* (The Hague, 1745) summarised in Kaeber, *Die Idee* . . ., p. 91, appears to be the earliest pamphlet to recognise Austro-Prussian rivalry as a basic factor in German politics and a very important one in those of Europe as a whole.

77. Réal de Curban, *La Science du gouvernement*, vi, 446.

78. Curcio, *Europa* . . ., ii, 412; *An Enquiry concerning Political Justice*, ed. F.E.L. Priestley (Toronto, 1946), ii, 155.

savagely for essentially the same reason, while the young Edmund Burke, later the greatest of all English conservatives, had no doubt that 'that political torture by which powers are to be enlarged or abridged, according to a standard, perhaps not very accurately imagined, ever has been, and it is to be feared will always continue, a cause of infinite contention and bloodshed'.[79]

The whole idea of an international balance could also be dismissed as a mere fig-leaf used by unscrupulous and self-interested statesmen to cover their own selfish ambitions, or as camouflage for the designs of the greater powers at the expense of smaller and weaker states. In Britain, under a regime in which parliamentary debate had real significance, ridicule of the idea was a favourite ploy of opposition politicians attacking those in power. Lord Chesterfield in the 1740s, a typical example among many, spoke while in opposition of the entire conception of a balance of power as 'introduced among us by corrupt and designing ministers, to subject and fleece their deluded countrymen'.[80] On a less moralistic level the idea could be condemned out of hand as a meaningless shibboleth, as the elder marquis de Mirabeau, one of the most important of the Physiocrats in France, did in the 1760s, or as simply a delusion, 'a Phantom of the Creation of distemper'd Brains'.[81] It would not be difficult to multiply hostile comments of this kind.

But quite apart from all such objections, was an effective balance of power in any case really practicable? Could it work? Many critics thought not, for at least two reasons. In the first place, all thinking of this kind must be at least implicitly quantitative. It assumed that at any given moment the effective power of two competing states or groups of states, the weights in each pan of the scales, could be measured with some approach to accuracy. Was this possible? Could the power of a state be quantified in this way? Even those who believed strongly in the reality and value of the balance could not close their eyes to the difficulties. Every calculation of this kind was bound to include a large subjective element, especially in an age when reliable statistics of any kind hardly existed. At the beginning of the eighteenth century Charles Davenant, one of the most original of English mercantilists, gave this obvious truth one of its most sweeping statements. 'Opinion is the principal Support of Power', he wrote, 'and States are seldom any longer Strong or Wise, than while they are thought so by their Neighbours; for all great Things subsist more by Fame, than any real Strength'.[82] A French official with wide

79. Justi, *Die Chimäre* . . ., pp. 9ff., 26; *Annual Register* (1760), pp. 2–3.
80. *Natural Reflexions on the Conduct of His Prussian Majesty* (London, 1744), p. 33.
81. *Esprit de Mirabeau ou de l'Homme d'Etat* (Milan, 1798), iii, 33; *A General View of the Present Politics and Interests of the Principal Powers of Europe* (London, ?1747), p. 52.
82. 'An Essay upon the Balance of Power', in *Essays* (London, 1701), p. 31.

experience agreed a generation or more later that any balance of power 'resides largely in the opinion of men' and that it was 'a matter where everything, so to speak, is opinion, itself subject to variation'.[83]

The difficulty was a real one. Most pamphleteers and politicians met it, however, by pretending that it did not exist. There was, inevitably, a tendency for simple and visible criteria such as extent of territory, size of population or numbers of armed forces to be accepted as true indicators of the strength of a state; and if this were done in a mechanical and simple-minded way the problem could be sidestepped. One of the more interesting writers on economic problems of the second half of the century, for example, solved it by reducing it to a single military dimension. 'Those who are conversant in foreign affairs', he wrote, 'can estimate, in a minute, the force of Princes by the troops they are able to maintain; nothing is so easy as to lay down, on a sheet of paper, a state of all the armed men in Europe. . . . Hence the balance of power, formerly unknown, is now become familiar.' Even he could not altogether deny that there were some difficulties in estimating the relative strengths of different states; but he insisted that 'the strength of a nation lies chiefly in the valour and strength of the soldiery'.[84] As time went on commentators became more ready to give weight to such factors as wealth, efficient government and strategic position. There was some grasp of the fact that a state might be too large for any central government to be really effective, and that its resources might be more efficiently mobilised if its territories were a more manageable size. Brandenburg-Prussia was the most obvious illustration of the latter case; and count von Hertzberg, one of the chief ministers of Frederick II, provided shortly after the king's death the most sustained statement of it.[85] Another German, in one of the best-known discussions of the problem of measuring the relative power of states, divided those of Europe into four distinct classes in terms of their ability to wage war: in the first rank stood France and Britain, since they alone could make full-scale war by themselves, unassisted by any ally; in the second class came Austria, Russia, Prussia and Spain which, though formidable, needed allies and outside financial support in a long struggle; in the third could be found states such as Portugal, Sweden and the Dutch Republic, which could fight only as subordinate allies of greater ones; and finally came the negligible small states of Germany and Italy.[86] Such a classification would

83. A. Pecquet, *L'Esprit des maximes politiques* (Paris, 1757), pp. 107–8, 112.

84. Sir James Steuart, *An Inquiry into the Principles of Political Economy* (London, 1767), i, 447–8, 452.

85. 'Réflexions sur la force des états et sur leur puissance relative et proportionelle', in *Huit Dissertations* (Berlin, 1787–91), pp. 87–104.

86. Baron J.F. von Bielfeld, *Institutions politiques* (The Hague, 1760), ii, 84–5.

have been accepted by many of his contemporaries: certainly by the middle of the century if not earlier it was widely felt that the sheer wealth of Britain and France placed them in a class of their own. However no writer during the eighteenth century produced a really searching analysis of the problem of measuring state-power; this meant that efforts to erect the balance into a kind of pseudo-science were bound to ring somewhat hollow.

There was another intellectual problem, perhaps more profound, which the writers of the period also failed to face squarely. How far could any real balance, designed to provide stability in international relations, be reconciled with the incessant change which was the essence of these relations? Was it not a futile dream since, as a French historian put it over a hundred years later, 'for it to exist implies immobility, that is to say, an impossibility'?[87] Few eighteenth-century commentators were willing to go so far as this; but some were very conscious of the difficulty. A stable balance of power, contended one early in the century, was impossible since

> if all the Nations of the Earth were reduced to an equal Ballance even of a Grain Weight, then a Grain on any Side would cast the Ballance. And this Ten Thousand Accidents every Day would produce, a prosperous Voyage on one Side, and Unfortunate on another; a Wiser or a Weaker Administration in one Government than another, would turn the Ballance vastly, So that We must Ballance the Wisdom, the Industry and the Courage of Men, as well as their Honesty and Conscience; and likewise secure Providence not to favour one more than another, if we would fix the Peace of the World upon this Project of Ballancing.[88]

Other writers, though they were always in a minority, echoed these doubts; and at the end of the century a very well-informed French commentator could still argue that 'the general balance is from the outset somewhat of a chimera because of the virtual impossibility of establishing it with any hope of it lasting'.[89] Gentz, a few years later, tried to get round the difficulty by abandoning the traditional idea of a more or less rigid and stable balance. 'It perhaps', he wrote, 'would have been with more propriety called a system of *counterpoise*. For perhaps the highest of its results is not so much a perfect *equipoise* as a constant alternate vacillation in the scales of the balance, which, from the application of *counter-weights*, is prevented from ever passing certain limits'.[90] This was

---

87. A. Sorel, *L'Europe et la Révolution Française,* 3rd edn. (Paris, 1912), i, 34.

88. *Natural Reflections upon the Present Debates about Peace and War* (London, 1712), pp. 61–2. A similar argument, equally forcibly expressed, can be found in *A Project for Establishing the General Peace of Europe, by a more Equal Partition than has hitherto been proposed* (London, 1712), p. 5, and in Justi, *Die Chimäre . . .*, pp. 67–70.

89. D'Hauterive, *De l'Etat de la France,* p. 90.

90. *Fragments upon the Balance of Power in Europe* (London, 1806), p. 63n.

perhaps the most satisfactory answer yet given to a real problem which most commentators ignored almost completely.

It is not surprising that support for the idea of the balance of power should have reached its highest point during the eighteenth century. Much of the copious theorising about it reflected, as has been seen, the faith in science and in the ability of man to control the world and his own future which were the basis of the Enlightenment. Because of the emergence of a workable balance in early sixteenth-century Italy, wrote one of the most widely read historians of the age, 'Dangers were foreseen at a greater distance, and prevented with more ease. . . . Revenge and self-defence were no longer the only causes of hostility, it became common to take arms out of policy; and war, both in its commencement and in its operations, was more an exercise of the judgement, than of the passions of men'.[91] The popularity of the idea during the eighteenth century was at bottom an aspect of the growth of generally liberal and humanistic attitudes to politics and society during this period. An effective balance of power, it could be argued, showed man's control of one aspect of his world. It introduced greater certainty and predictability, a man-made certainty and predictability, into international affairs. Reliance upon it, wrote a critic at the end of the Spanish Succession war, shocked by the hubris which it seemed thus to express, 'is indeed no other than to take the Government of the World out of the hands of Providence, and Entrust it to our own Skill and Management. Instead of *Dieu et Mon Droit*, it is *Je Maintiendrai*'.[92] Nearly a century later a radical liberal, approaching the question from a very different starting-point, strongly defended the whole balance of power idea because 'by the modern system of foreign policy, the fate of nations has been rendered more certain; and the influence of chance, of the fortune of war, of the caprices of individuals upon the general affairs of men, has been exceedingly diminished'.[93] To control and regulate his own life, to escape the clutches of blind chance and the unforeseeable, is one of the desires most deeply rooted in man. Superficial as much of it was, the outpouring of eighteenth-century discussion of the balance of power both expressed and to some extent satisfied this desire.

91. A.W. Robertson, *The History of Scotland*, 14th edn (London, 1794), i, 89–90.
92. *Natural Reflections* . . ., pp. 62–4.
93. Brougham, *Works*, vii, 49.

# THE NINETEENTH CENTURY: CHALLENGE AND SURVIVAL

The nineteenth and early twentieth centuries saw much less of the sustained and quasi-scientific discussion of the balance of power which had marked the previous hundred years or more. The main reason for this is clear. The century which followed the Vienna settlement of 1814–15 was for Europe a period of unprecedented peace and of a hitherto unknown stability in international relations and most state frontiers. The eighteenth century had seen a long series of violent and dramatic changes. In its early years the Spanish and Swedish empires in Europe had been torn apart. In its later decades an independent Poland had been extinguished and the Ottoman empire had seemed marked out for a similar destiny in the near future. The power and prestige of Russia had grown enormously and the new quasi-great power of Brandenburg-Prussia had erupted suddenly in the German world while Spain, which until the 1640s had seemed to threaten 'universal monarchy', was by the time of the French Revolution clearly dropping out of the ranks of the major powers. Dreams of sweeping territorial changes quickly and fairly easily achieved had still allured eighteenth-century statesmen as they had done their predecessors in the age of Charles V and Philip II. At the time of their short-lived alliance of 1725 the Spanish and Austrian governments had envisaged the defeat and partition of France. During the Seven Years War there had been hopes in Vienna and St Petersburg of dividing the territories of Frederick II and destroying his upstart power. In the 1780s Joseph II and Catherine II had discussed the sharing between them of the still huge Ottoman territories in Europe. Most striking and alarming of all, the revolution in France had from 1793 onwards unleashed upon the continent for the first time the expansive energies which popular nationalism could now generate and to which ideas of balance and restraint were quite foreign. Burke in 1796 accused the Jacobins of creating 'a new description of empire, which is not grounded on any balance, but forms a sort of impious hierarchy, of which France is to be the head and guardian';[94] and this threat of French empire and of the permanent destruction of any viable equilibrium had been given an even more menacing form by Napoleon I.

The nineteenth century saw for most of its course no such spectacular upheavals. Certainly the stability which marked it was far from complete. The years 1859–71 saw a spasm of violent political and territorial change which created a national state in Italy, however imperfectly unified, and,

94. *Letters on a Regicide Peace* No.3, in *Works* (London, 1808–13), viii, 339.

much more important, a new politically united Germany which became at once the greatest power of continental Europe. Throughout the century upheaval in the Balkans continued to preoccupy statesmen; the 'Eastern Question' was the most continuous thread in the international relations of the period. But the dramas of 1859–71 separated two periods, each of over forty years, during which there was only one war between the major powers. That conflict, moreover, the Crimean War of 1853–56, was relatively short, fought far from western Europe and militarily disappointing to all the participants. Many minor states in Germany and Italy saw themselves in the 1860s merged into new and greater national ones; but the major international frontiers of Europe were unprecedentedly stable. That between Russia and her western neighbours, driven forward with such frightening success from the 1660s onwards, was still in 1914 where it had been in 1815 (apart from the relatively unimportant acquisition by Russia of part of Bessarabia). That between the Habsburg empire and the German states, so much a source of conflict in the decades after 1740, was completely unaffected by the decisive Prussian victory of 1866. That between France and the German world indeed altered dramatically with the annexation of Alsace-Lorraine in 1871 to the new German Reich; but this was a smaller change than those made under Napoleon I or even Louis XIV.

## The balance in the background: the Russian threat

Such stability meant that discussion and analysis of the balance of power lost much of the importance and urgency it had had in earlier generations. The balance had always been seen largely as a means of avoiding sudden and disruptive change in the European state-system: it had been advocated as a means to stability rather than as a guarantee of peace. That stability had now, apparently, been achieved. For those who believed in it the balance therefore was now, more than in the past, something which could be taken for granted. Specific allusions to it in political and diplomatic correspondence therefore became decidedly rarer than in the eighteenth century.[95] Moreover, Europe was never, for three generations or more after 1815, threatened seriously with domination by any single over-powerful state. Even among the major ones some were stronger than others. Britain emerged from the struggle against Napoleon as the only great modern industrial power, much the greatest naval power and, with the collapse of Spain's position in Latin America, by far the greatest

95. See the penetrating discussion in P.W. Schroeder, 'The nineteenth century system; balance of power or political equilibrium?', *Review of International Studies*, 15 (1989).

colonial power. No state had ever achieved such a position in the past. None, with the exception of the United States for some years after 1945, was ever to do so again. Yet Britain had neither the desire nor the ability to dominate the states of continental Europe. Her army was small and not very efficient. Dislike of European entanglements was strong among her people and became if anything stronger during much of the following century. Except in one or two strategically important areas – the Low Countries, the Straits, the Iberian peninsula – her interest in European complications was often tepid. Her successes and the sense of superiority to the rest of the world which they bred often irritated many observers across the Channel; but it was impossible for her to threaten the European balance of power or the independence of the European states as Louis XIV and still more Napoleon I had done. It is not difficult to find demands from continental observers, on the lines which had been so common in the eighteenth century, for the setting of limits to Britain's naval and imperial power by the establishment of a European maritime balance to parallel that which existed on land. Her ostentatious support of political and territorial equilibrium on the continent, it was often alleged, was no more than a means of keeping the other states of Europe divided and weak and thus consolidating her position as the pre-eminent world power. During much of the century criticism of this kind came most of all from her great traditional rival, France.[96] By the 1890s it was becoming most virulent and most freely expressed in the new and ambitious Germany. But until then anti-British feeling of this kind was peripheral to the main concerns of the major states of Europe. It was only as the German drive to world power gathered momentum that it took for a number of years the centre of the stage. Until then Britain might arouse envy and irritation; but it was difficult to see her as a direct threat to the vital interests of her neighbours, interests which were still for the most part confined within Europe's own geographical limits.

Nor was nineteenth-century France in a position to overthrow the European balance as she had done under Napoleon I or even to threaten it as she had done under Louis XIV. The Vienna settlement was largely an effort to make it impossible for her again to break out of her existing frontiers as she had done from 1793 onwards. The creation of a kingdom of the Netherlands, the strengthening of Prussia in the Rhineland, the establishment of the German Confederation, the guarantee of Swiss neutrality, the efforts to exclude French influence from Italy, were all directed to this end. The victories of the Napoleonic era had been so

96. Good pamphlet examples from a period when Anglo-French relations were under considerable strain are *L'Angleterre et la guerre* (Paris, 1858), p. 68; and *Jacques Bonnefoi et l'Angleterre* (Paris, 1858), pp. 43–6.

spectacular that fear of France's potentialities was slow to die. In 1832 a British pamphleteer had no doubt that any threat to the balance of power came from her: she was 'beyond all compare, the most powerful of the continental nations', and therefore Britain must never be her ally in any future conflict.[97] The upheaval of 1848 aroused fears that revolution in Paris might once more foreshadow an ideological war which would threaten the European balance, while the establishment of the Second Empire seemed even more menacing. The intervention of Napoleon III in Italy, his acquisition of Savoy and Nice, his apparent ambitions in the Near East, seemed to foreign observers to herald a threatening expansion of French power in Europe. The Anglo-French alliance against Russia during the Crimean War did little or nothing to lessen British fears of this kind. Russia, wrote one pamphleteer in 1855, 'should on no consideration be displaced from her position as one of the leading powers of Europe', for if she were completely defeated France, from whom the real threat to the balance came, would probably go on to seize the Rhine frontier and overrun Belgium.[98] Yet in retrospect it is clear that there was never during the century after the Vienna settlement any real chance of France becoming the dominant political and military force in Europe she had so often been in the past. Until after the Crimean War any effort by her to overturn the status quo was certain to meet concerted resistance by the other great powers; and after 1870–71 a relatively mild sense of grievance over the terms she had had to accept at Vienna was overtaken by a far deeper and more bitter resentment over the loss of Alsace-Lorraine. Though the economic progress she achieved was in many ways very respectable her population grew more slowly than that of any other European state; and at no time after 1815 did she recover the military superiority to her neighbours which had reached its peak in 1793–1814. In the seventeenth and eighteenth centuries discussion of the European balance of power had been, in a high proportion of cases, a reaction to her strength. As the nineteenth century went on this became less and less the case.

Most politically conscious Europeans, at most times during this century, would have agreed that by far the greatest challenge to the balance of power came from the east, from Russia. In the years after 1815 fears of this kind are easy to understand. Russia's military achievements in the struggles with the French revolution and Napoleon, in spite of many setbacks, had been remarkable, and had been crowned by the dramatic transformation of 1812. Even before the Vienna settlement she had already replaced France, in the eyes of many observers, as the obvious threat to

97. *The Balance of Power, Past and Prospective* (London, 1832), pp. 18–20.
98. *The War Unmasked. Its Causes, its Facts, its Consequences. By an ex-M.P.* (London, 1855), pp. 25–8.

the European balance and to the independence of the European states which that balance claimed to safeguard. For the next four decades at least she appeared a power whose size and military strength, and therefore whose potentialities for further growth, were on a quite different scale from anything to be seen in western Europe. Compared to 'this monster of an empire . . . the most monstrous empire, in extent, that ever spread over the face of the earth',[99] the western states seemed military and political pygmies. Nor was this apparent Russian threat merely a matter of brute strength. Not only the enormous Russian army but also skilful Russian diplomacy and the corrupting effects of Russian money were to be feared. An English writer in the 1830s spoke for many of his contemporaries when he explained past Russian successes by 'the astute system adopted by the Russian cabinet. They triumph by intrigue before they take the field; they bribe, cajole and overreach. They corrupt by gold more than they conquer by arms.' To meet this insidious threat a 'restitution of the balance of power' was needed; the major states of Europe must 'form a counterpoise' to hold their own against such strength and cunning.[100]

Even defeat in the Crimea did little to weaken the exaggerated fear and hostility with which Russia was widely regarded. The short Austro-French conflict of 1859 produced throughout much of central Europe a feeling that the German states should help the Habsburgs not merely against their immediate French opponent but, more importantly, against the still looming threat from the east.[101] A decade later, in the first days of the disastrous war of 1870, a great French intellectual argued that a fight to the finish between France and Prussia, by destroying the essential unity of western Europe, could help only Russia: if she united under her leadership the barbarian peoples of Central Asia, grouping them under 'a Muscovite Genghis Khan', she would become even more dangerous.[102] The last decades of the century nevertheless saw a marked decline in such fears. The creation of the Second Reich, with its impressive military

99. *Eclectic Review*, New Series, iv (1815), 375.

100. *The People of Russia and the People of England* (London, 1836), pp. 53, 70–2; for similar statements of British fears see *Remarks on the Conduct and Probable Designs of Russia* (London, 1832), pp. 9–10; *India, Great Britain and Russia* (London, 1838), pp. 34–5; S. Hibberd, *An Epitome of the War, from its Outbreak to its Close* (London, n.d.(1856)), pp. 50–1. The most detailed discussion of the growth of anti-Russian feeling in Britain during this period is H.-J. Krautheim, *Offentliche Meinung und imperiale Politik: das britische Russlandbild, 1815–1854* (Berlin, 1977).

101. For examples see E. Fischel, *Despots as Revolutionaries*, 2nd edn (London, 1860) (a translation of a German pamphlet) and *Untersuchungen über das Europäische Gleichgewicht* (Berlin, 1859), Chapter vii.

102. E. Renan, 'La guerre entre la France et l'Allemagne', *Revue des Deux Mondes*, 89 (1870), 265.

strength and growing industrial power, had now given Europe a strong centre more able than for centuries past to defend its eastern frontiers. The limits to Russia's military strength set by her technological backwardness and by the weaknesses of her essentially peasant army were now clearer than in the past: what one well-informed observer called 'the stolid ignorance of the Russian peasantry'[103] had in itself a significant reassuring influence in western Europe. But for two generations after the Vienna settlement it was Russia far more than any other state which seemed to threaten the European balance; and this threat, unlike those offered under Louis XIV or Napoleon, came from a power seen as still largely un-European and correspondingly more feared and resented.

## The great-power hegemony

Nineteenth-century discussions of the balance of power differed sharply from earlier ones in recognising explicitly that Europe's political destiny was now in the hands of a small number of clearly identified major states. Great disparities of strength had always existed between the different parts of the European state-system; but in the seventeenth and eighteenth centuries there was still a relatively smooth continuum of power between Spain, France and later Britain, the Habsburg empire and Russia at one end of the spectrum and the little principalities of Germany or Italy at the other. States which were not great powers – Bavaria, Saxony, Denmark–Norway, the kingdom of the Two Sicilies, Sweden, in the eighteenth century the Dutch republic – could still play on occasion significant roles in international affairs. The cataclysms of the revolutionary and Napoleonic era changed this situation. They made it finally and brutally clear that henceforth only a handful of states would take the decisions on which the continent's fate depended. From 1793 onwards the scale and cost of war grew spectacularly. This placed the ultimate exertion of international authority beyond the reach of all but a select group of powers with large territories and populations, or large revenues, or both. The Dutch republic, overrun by French armies in 1795; Sweden, now pushed increasingly towards the fringes of international relations; Bavaria and Saxony, which in 1807 became French satellites as members of the Confederation of the Rhine; Spain, treated at the Vienna congress (much to her chagrin) as a secondary power: all these were now less and less able to influence the mainstream of events. By the last stages of the struggle with Napoleon I the four states which finally brought him down, Britain,

103. Colonel J.F. Maurice, *The Balance of Military Power in Europe* (Edinburgh–London, 1888), p. 186.

Russia, Prussia and the Habsburg empire, were asserting clearly their right
to decide alone the main lines of the peace settlement. In the discussions
between them at Châtillon in February 1814 they explicitly claimed to
negotiate with Napoleon in the name of Europe as a whole; and though
the treaty of Paris which they signed with the newly restored Louis XVIII
at the end of May provided that the settlement of other outstanding
problems should be the work of an international congress, they agreed in
a secret article that final control of affairs should stay in their own hands.
Four months later, in a series of meetings in September, they agreed that
the congress when it met should be little more than the agent of what
Castlereagh, the British foreign secretary, called 'the powers of the first
order'. The use of this phrase has been described as 'the first expression of
the idea of the Great Powers, with rights as such, distinct from any
derived from treaties'.[104]

The 1814–15 settlement, and the efforts in the decade which followed
to sustain it against the forces of change, were the work of five major
states (the four anti-Napoleonic allies of 1813–14, supplemented by
France); and it was now being strongly urged that they had a right and
even a duty to control the activities and even the internal affairs of the
smaller ones. This right of surveillance and if necessary forcible
intervention, partly because of the opposition of Castlereagh, was not
pushed as far as Alexander I, its main advocate, desired. The system of
great-power congresses attended by foreign ministers and sometimes
monarchs (though neither Louis XVIII nor the Prince Regent ever
attended one and Frederick William III of Prussia did so only rarely) had
broken down by 1822. Henceforth the Concert of Europe, based on an
imprecise but widespread feeling that the major powers should act
together in any crisis and that major territorial changes should be made
only with the consent of them all, expressed itself in practice, apart from
the peace congresses of 1856 in Paris and 1878 in Berlin, merely in
conferences of ambassadors – most notably over the Belgian question in
London in 1830–39, and much later over African questions in Berlin in
1884–85 and Balkan ones in London again in 1912–13. But the
undisputed primacy of the great powers was to last until the First World
War. More and more they were felt to possess not only material strength
but also some quasi-moral authority as the ultimate guarantors of the
political and territorial stability of the continent. The '*Staatenaristokratie
oder Oligarchie*' which they constituted, wrote one German author in the
1850s, now wished to become a tribunal to which lesser states must come

104. C.K. Webster, *The Congress of Vienna* (London, 1945), p. 61.

for justice in their disputes and which would sanction all important international transactions and interpret international law.[105]

The conflicts of 1854–71 shook the unity of the great powers. The disappearance of the south-German states as independent political actors and their incorporation in a unified Reich probably helped to force Austria–Hungary into a close and ultimately dangerous dependence on the new Germany and certainly increased France's fears of the new power on her eastern border.[106] But these upheavals did not destroy, at least for the more optimistic and idealistic observers of the European scene, the belief in ultimate cooperation between them as the guardians of international stability. By the 1880s an English international lawyer could claim that their special position meant that belief in the legal equality of all sovereign states was now unsustainable. Europe, he argued, had for long 'been working round again to the old notion of a common superior, not indeed a Pope or an Emperor, but a Committee, a body of representatives of her leading states'. Their might, he contended, gave them rights, for 'it is not merely that the stronger states have influence proportionate to their strength; but that custom has given them what can hardly be distinguished from a legal right to settle disputed questions as they please, the smaller states being obliged to acquiesce in their decision'. In time, he concluded, this situation might be formalised and the great powers might develop into a 'Supreme Court of International Appeal'.[107] The nineteenth-century balance of power was thus in an important sense simpler than it had been in earlier ages. A loose but complex system, in which the distinction between first-class powers and second- and third-class ones was blurred had been replaced by an oligarchy of five (or six with the very questionable addition of Italy from the 1860s onwards) dominant and directing states. Large and unwieldy alliances whose members differed widely in size and importance, such as those against Louis XIV or the 1792–93 coalition against France, were followed, in those which developed from 1879 onwards, by groupings of two or, at the most, three great powers. On both sides of any balance there were now fewer elements than ever before whose weight needed to be assessed.

105. *Untersuchungen . . .*, p. 25.

106. See the interesting comments on this development in P.W. Schroeder, 'The Lost Intermediaries: the impact of 1870 on the European system', *International History Review*, 6 (1984), 1–27.

107. T.J. Lawrence, 'The Primacy of the Great Powers', in *Essays upon some Disputed Questions in Modern International Law* (Cambridge, 1884), pp. 192, 209, 213.

*Continuing criticism: challenge by the new ideologies*

There was no lack of nineteenth-century writers prepared to repeat many of the criticisms of the balance of power idea voiced by their predecessors. There were persisting accusations that it generated rather than averted conflict, that safeguarding the balance could all too easily serve as a convenient pretext for war. There were also allusions to the continuing problem of measuring and comparing with any accuracy the power of different states. It was now more clearly grasped than in the past that mere extent of territory and size of population were by themselves very unreliable guides in this, and that imponderables, such as the efficiency of an administrative system, the qualities of a ruler or the character and level of education of a people, had to figure prominently in any such calculation.[108] In particular the progress of industry and its power to transform the entire economic life of a state introduced very important new elements into the picture. A great but economically backward military–territorial empire, such as the Habsburg lands and still more Russia, it could be argued, was in reality far weaker than it appeared. Richard Cobden, the most vocal and influential of all British critics of the balance of power idea, asserted in the 1830s that 'The manufacturing districts alone – even the four counties of England, comprising Lancashire, Yorkshire, Cheshire and Staffordshire – could, at any moment, by means of the wealth drawn, by the skill and industry of its population, from the natural resources of this speck of territory, combat with success the whole Russian empire'.[109] This was a great overstatement: weapons technology was still primitive enough when Cobden wrote these words for an illiterate peasant army based on a backward agrarian society to be a formidable force, as the British and French were to find in the Crimea. But it underlined the new considerations which were now influencing the old problem of assessing the effective resources of different states and societies. It could also be argued, as in the past,[110] that the continual changes in the relative power of states as they gained or lost territory, fell under the control of more or less effective rulers, became richer or poorer by comparison with their neighbours, meant that no balance struck between them could be more than momentary or have much meaning. Thus at the end of the century the German nationalist Heinrich von Treitschke argued that the idea of such a balance 'is crude, and as thoroughly unpolitical as the notion of an eternal peace, for . . . the

---

108. *Betrachtungen über die Wiederherstellung des politischen Gleichgewichts in Europa* (Leipzig, 1814), pp. 138ff.; *Untersuchungen* . . ., pp. 25–6; *Das Europäische Gleichgewicht der Zukunft* (Berlin, 1859), p. 30.

109. *The Political Writings of Richard Cobden* (London–New York, 1867), i, 194.

110. See above pp. 179–80.

frontiers of states must be continually liable to fluctuation, and may not be thrust into narrow fetters'.[111]

As in the eighteenth century, again, there were commentators ready to claim that the balance of power, in spite of the frequent appeals to it by statesmen, diplomats and writers, was merely an illusion fostered by politicians too stupid, prejudiced or self-interested to see that it did not exist. In Britain, geographically separate from the European mainland and hostile by long tradition and deep-rooted popular feeling to involvement in European problems, this scepticism was at its strongest. Here again Cobden and his greatest ally in the cause of free-trade radicalism, John Bright, were scathing critics of the accepted wisdom. 'The balance of power', wrote Cobden, 'is a chimaera! It is not a fallacy, a mistake, an imposture — it is an undescribed, indescribable, incomprehensible nothing; mere words, conveying to the mind not ideas, but sounds like these equally barren syllables which our ancestors put together for the purpose of puzzling themselves about words, in the shape of *Prester John* or the *philosopher's stone*!' In very similar if less vehement terms Bright spoke of the balance as 'a phrase to which it is difficult to attach any definite meaning' and ridiculed it as 'like hunting for the philosopher's stone, or perpetual motion'.[112] This criticism was inconsistent and illogical. Cobden later attacked the balance of power because it had for many years successfully propped up the decaying Habsburg Empire and thus deprived many of the nationalities of central Europe of the liberty to which they were entitled,[113] surely a considerable achievement for an 'incomprehensible nothing'. Nor were his strictures always fair. He made much play with the fact that the states of Europe had never been bound together by any legal or constitutional links, and often implied that except within some formalised system of this kind no balance of power could possibly operate;[114] but this was to suggest something which no believer in the balance had ever asserted.

These criticisms, however, were merely a particular aspect, and not the most important one, of a fundamental and very far-reaching new line of attack. A growth of new aspirations was now threatening to make the whole balance of power concept meaningless. In the seventeenth and still more the eighteenth centuries there had been little ideological challenge to it. It might be attacked as hard to define and apply, or even as a complete sham; but there was no general idea which effectively competed

111. *Politics* (London, 1916), pp. 570–1. The German original appeared in 1897–1901.

112. Cobden, *Political Writings*, i, 258; *Hansard*, 3rd series, cxxxii, col. 254; D. Read, *Cobden and Bright: a Victorian Political Partnership* (London, 1967), p. 132.

113. J.A. Hobson, *Richard Cobden, the International Man* (London, 1918), pp. 189–90.

114. For example, *Political Writings*, i, 269.

with it as an organising principle of international relations. Religious traditions and prejudices could still in that age deeply affect public feeling; but they seldom had much influence on the policies of states or statesmen. They did not prevent Richelieu from allying with Lutheran Sweden to limit Habsburg power in Germany, or William III from combining with Catholic Spain against Louis XIV. The schemes of international organisation which proliferated in the eighteenth century[115] were certainly an implicit and sometimes explicit criticism of the balance and its effects; but almost all of them were put forward as practical expedients rather than as declarations of some overriding general principle.

By the nineteenth century, in contrast, the whole idea of the balance was being subjected to new forms of attack which previous generations had not seen. More and more it was now being challenged by new and more dynamic systems of belief, more emotionally appealing ideas about how the relations between states should be organised. Compared to these it now seemed to many observers merely a shabby and outworn expedient, a hangover from a discredited past. The balance was concerned with the relationships between states. These, their policies and the means available for their execution, were the only entities which it considered. But by the mid-nineteenth century it was being claimed more and more strenuously that the really important divisions of humanity in the mass were not between states but between peoples or social classes. 'Infallible signs', wrote the French historian Henri Martin in 1847, 'show that in a few years questions of nationality, combined with social questions, will dominate all others on the continent.'[116] Such a change, the intrusion of nationalism, and much less effectively liberalism and socialism, into international relations, must revolutionise the situation. If peoples, given self-consciousness by the ties of a common language and history, were the fundamental building-blocks of humanity, then the frontiers between states should and must become national ones. If, as many liberals increasingly argued, the effective links between different societies were provided not by foreign offices and diplomats but by a multitude of non-governmental contacts, by travel, intellectual exchanges, most of all trade, then nearly all the existing machinery of international relations was unnecessary and even dangerous. If, on the other hand, different social classes, capitalists and workers, those who owned property and those who did not, were the ultimate reality, and the divisions between them transcended national boundaries, then the future would be decided by class struggles in which all existing state institutions would inevitably be

115. See pp. 221–8 below.
116. Quoted in J.B. Duroselle, *L'Idée d'Europe dans l'histoire* (Paris, 1965), p. 209.

swept away. All these ideologies, in different ways, envisaged a future in which the balance of power would have little or no place.

Of the three, the nationalist one carried much the most effective emotional charge. Free-trading radicalism, for a few years in the 1860s, seemed a real political force over much of the continent. But it was always centred on a single country, Great Britain, and to a considerable extent on a single man, Richard Cobden. Except in Britain its effective influence on the policies of the major states was short-lived and sometimes non-existent. Rational and moderate, appealing largely to self-interest and making no call for heroism or self-sacrifice, hostile to all traditional ideas of what constituted the glory of a state or a nation, it could not tap the vague but very powerful emotions which gave the national idea such vitality and dynamism. The belief that the unrestricted movement of goods, people, capital and ideas would peacefully and inevitably bind the peoples of the world together, and thus expose the balance of power as dangerous nonsense, had already made a considerable impact in western Europe in the later eighteenth century.[117] But except in Britain it was never an ideology with widespread popular backing.

In retrospect it is easy to see that Cobden's belief in the unifying and pacifying effect of trade and other international contacts was very naive. His insistence on reducing relations between governments to the barest minimum and his rejection of the accumulated experience of the past in international relations narrowed and impoverished his outlook. Like Bentham and the Physiocrats before him he had little sense of history and was reluctant to admit that general principles might ever have to be modified to cope with a particular set of international circumstances. His ideas continued to find some support in continental Europe in the later nineteenth century and to form the basis of attacks on the whole traditional idea of equilibrium. 'The notion of preserving the balance of power in Europe has lost and, it is to be hoped, will continue to lose ground', wrote one of the most important of his continental disciples in 1872.[118] But it quickly became clear that the Europe in which economic interests would submerge political differences, to which so many radicals of different colours had looked forward so confidently in the 1850s and 1860s, was no more than a dream. In Germany, where the argument between free traders and protectionists was more lively and conducted at a higher intellectual level than anywhere else, the conversion of Bismarck to protectionism and the resulting tariff of 1879 were decisive and did much

117. See below, pp. 229–30.
118. E. de Lavelaye, *On the Causes of War and the Means of reducing their Number* (London, 1872), p. 8.

to push Europe as a whole in a protectionist direction. In France, where the free-trade tendencies of Napoleon III had always been unpopular, tariffs rose from 1881 onwards and the Méline tariff of 1892 made her a highly protectionist country. In Russia trade policy became more protectionist in the 1880s, and 1890–91 saw steep tariff increases. From the 1870s onwards Europe's political frontiers were becoming, for the first time, also well-defined economic ones. Long before the end of the century Britain was the only major state which still clung to free trade. If the balance of power were ever to be tossed into the dustbin of history it would not be by the sweeping away of economic barriers between states and a final triumph of *laissez-faire*.

The vision of a new world of peace and friendship between peoples based on revolutionary change, on the complete overthrow of existing political and economic structures, had by the middle of the nineteenth century deep historical roots. The French revolution in its more idealistic phase had claimed to be fighting the stultifying tyranny of rulers, aristocracies and priesthoods in the interests of peoples and of the harmony between them which would inevitably follow their liberation. In the English- speaking world Tom Paine's *Rights of Man* had provided in 1791 a forthright statement of the same general attitude. The welter of would-be revolutionary groups, often socially radical, which proliferated in western Europe down to the 1860s – Carbonarists, Mazzinian conspirators, various forms of utopian socialist – were all permeated, to varying extents, by ideas of a unity of the peoples of Europe. This, once achieved, would mean the end of conventional diplomatic machinery and balance of power calculations. The view of the world and of history which from mid-century onwards Marx began, slowly and to the accompaniment of bitter personal and factional struggles, to impose on this medley of different groups, embodied the same internationalist ideals and assumptions. This radical internationalism now seemed to be based, thanks to him, more securely than ever before on a 'scientific' vision of history and of the goal towards which it was irresistibly moving. Here, even more clearly than in the case of the free-trading radicals, was an ideology which shouldered aside the balance of power as a contemptible triviality for which the future had no place whatever. Yet socialist idealism had even less practical effect than that of the free traders. It failed to achieve victory in even a single country as Cobdenism had done; and its complete inability to avert the catastrophe of 1914 showed the hollowness of hopes which it had cherished for decades.

It is easy in retrospect to see that the crucial miscalculation of international socialism was its gross underestimate of the power and durability of national feeling, its belief that this was something superficial and transient, doomed soon to wither away. On the contrary, nationalism as the nineteenth century went on aroused popular passions in a way which neither radical liberalism nor socialism ever could. The emotions it called forth could easily become almost religious. 'Men make states', wrote Henri Martin, 'but God alone creates nations',[119] while Giuseppe Mazzini, the most vocal and influential of all nationalist ideologues, was deeply hostile to atheism and materialism, and even distrustful of human reason, since to him all fundamental truths were intuitive and essentially religious. Nationalism was in a number of ways deeply if implicitly hostile to the existing balance of power in Europe and, more fundamentally, to the very idea of any such balance. Its victory meant the radical transformation and probable dissolution of the Habsburg empire, a favourite target of very many believers in the nationalist ideal. It also involved the creation of some kind of unified German state whose position, size and resources were almost certain to make it, with the possible exception of Russia, the most powerful in continental Europe. Such changes would revolutionise the whole political balance of the continent. Moreover, what guarantee could there be that national states, whose existence expressed the idea of popular sovereignty and which embodied the emotions and ambitions of their citizens, would be more moderate in their foreign policies, less threatening to the stability which the balance was meant to promote, than the conservative monarchies which were still the norm in mid-nineteenth century Europe? 'In making the transition from royal families to plebeian masses', wrote an intelligent French conservative, 'has ambition become a more legitimate feeling, or one which has less need to be kept in check?'[120] A German pamphleteer, using stronger language, described nationalist propaganda as 'rockets with which the whole building of the old state-system can be set on fire'.[121]

Those advocates of nationalism who attached any value to the maintenance of a balance of power between the European states sometimes replied to these doubts by asserting that a new, more broadly based and therefore more stable balance would follow the reorganisation of the continent along national lines. A resurrected Poland, a united Germany, a Habsburg empire restructured as a federation of autonomous nationalities, it could be claimed, would have this effect. A continent of nation-states would evolve a new equilibrium more natural than, and therefore more effective and lasting than, any which had hitherto

119. *De la France, de son génie et de ses destinées* (Paris, 1847), p. 40.
120. A. de Broglie, 'La Diplomatie et les principes de la Révolution Française', *Revue des deux Mondes*, lxxiii (1868), 625.
121. *Das europäische Gleichgewicht der Zukunft*, p. 146.

existed.[122] But none of this could conceal the fact that the balance of power, as an organising principle of international relations, was now confronted by a highly dynamic and potentially disruptive idea whose challenge, at least so far as the man in the street was concerned, it could not meet.

There was another aspect of mid–nineteenth century nationalism which was impossible to reconcile with traditional balance of power assumptions. The whole idea of balance assumed that states were essentially similar in their nature and their foreign policy objectives. Some of them might be more aggressive than others, even dangerously so. But it was generally assumed (except in the more extreme hostile comment on Russia) that they did not differ in essence. All sought to safeguard their position within the existing European state-system and, in so far as was prudent, to strengthen and improve it. To these assumptions many theorists of nationalism now opposed the competing idea of national mission, of each nation being endowed by Providence with the right and duty to fulfill an identifiable historical function, even though one which was usually very loosely defined. Like much in nineteenth-century nationalism this idea was of German origin: foreshadowings of it can be found in the eighteenth century, and later notably in some of the writings of Hegel. By the mid–nineteenth century it had been taken up by a host of publicists of whom Mazzini was the most influential. For him 'Every nation has a mission, a special office in the collective work, a special aptitude with which to fullfil it: this is its sign, its baptism, its legitimacy.' Thus the mission of Britain was to develop trade and colonies; of Russia to civilise Asia (and thus direct her energies away from Europe, where she seemed so dangerous); of a resurrected Poland to assume leadership of the Slav peoples (and thus again help to exclude Russia from Europe); of the Germans, thought; of the French, action (the extreme vagueness of the wording brings out the cloudy mysticism which underlay this sort of thinking).[123] Clearly the traditional concept of a balance of power, pragmatic, often cynical, stubbornly anchored in the here and now, inhabited a different intellectual world from this. The two views of international relations were irreconcilable.

But nationalist idealists did not see the future as one of conflict. On the contrary, they very often assumed that once the new Europe had been remodelled as a group of national states this would usher in an era of lasting peace and harmony in which ideas of balance would be completely

---

122. For statements of this line of argument by two Italian nationalists see G. Romagnosi, *La scienza delle costituzioni* (Bastia, 1848), p. 386; and the anonymous *Le nazionalità e l'equilibrio europeo* (Bologna, 1870), pp. 17, 26.
123. G. Salvemini, *Mazzini* (London, 1966), pp. 51, 76.

irrelevant. Already in the 1780s J.-G. Herder, who more than anyone created nationalism as an ideology, had been sure that 'Cabinets may deceive each other; political machines may exert pressure on each other until one is shattered. *Fatherlands* do not march against each other in this way; they live quietly side by side and help each other like families'.[124] All humanity, in Mazzini's nebulous but, to many, inspiring vision, must form an association of national groups, and 'in this progress, this God-directed pilgrimage of the peoples, there will be neither conquest nor threat of conquest, because there will be neither man-king nor people-king, but only an association of brothers whose interests and aim are identical'. His last significant published work, the *Politica internazionale*, published in 1871, was a vision of a continent of free nations associated in this way.[125] The enormous achievements of Europe during the nineteenth century helped to consolidate the belief that she was the culmination of all human history, the summit of all intellectual and cultural endeavour: the growth of nationalism was thus combined with a growing feeling for the importance and unity of the continent as a whole, for the things which united the European states as well as for those which divided them. But in tone and feeling all this nationalist rhetoric was dismissive of, and often deeply hostile to, conventional balance of power thinking. To those who accepted it such thinking was at best an irrelevant hangover from the past, if not a positive obstacle to the inevitable triumph of the national principle.

## Continuing influence of the balance idea

Yet until the First World War, however much it might be challenged or scorned by nationalists, free traders or socialists, the balance of power continued to hold a significant place in discussion of international relations. It remained the basic assumption of many commentators on European politics and the most important guideline of foreign offices. On neither of these levels, however, was much that was new added to the stock of ideas on the subject produced by the eighteenth century. For some time after 1815 comparisons between the world of international relations and that of physics and astronomy, of the kind made so strikingly under the influence of the Enlightenment, continued to appear. The balance, wrote a Prussian foreign minister in the 1830s, allowed the states of Europe to 'maintain order, harmony and repose in the world of

---

124. F. Meinecke, *Cosmopolitanism and the National State* (Princeton, 1970), p. 29.
125. Mazzini, *Selected Writings*, ed. N. Gangulee (London, 1945), p. 140; L. Salvatorelli, 'Mazzini i gli stati uniti d'Europa', in his *Miti i Storia* (Turin, 1966), pp. 339–47.

political bodies, by the same means which produce order, harmony and repose in the physical world'. This now traditional analogy continued to be used until at least the 1850s.[126] But in general the nineteenth century was inclined to see the balance of power as something to be deliberately fostered and protected, rather than in these mechanistic terms. By the end of the great struggle with Napoleon I its maintenance had been recognised more formally and explicitly than ever before as a major common objective of the great powers. The treaties of alliance signed at Töplitz in September–October 1813 by the Habsburg empire, Prussia, Russia and Britain proclaimed as one of their objectives the restoration of such a balance, as did the Austro–Neapolitan one of January 1814; while in the preamble to the treaty of Chaumont of March 1814 the anti-French allies defined their essential war aim as the safeguarding of peace by the re-establishment of 'a just balance between the Powers'.[127] By the middle decades of the century it was sometimes being argued that the balance was more than a mere idea, however realistic, or an expedient, however useful. Time, it could be claimed, had given it quasi-legal status: it was now a kind of constitutional principle governing Europe's political life. A British international lawyer claimed in 1854 that it had been more than once 'most formally and distinctly recognised as an essential part of the system of International Law'; and a French writer a few years later described it as 'the federative charter of European society'.[128] The balance, it could be argued, had positive moral value, for to reject it was, in effect, to place the weaker members of any state-system at the mercy of the stronger ones.[129]

Moreover, the criticisms, implicit and explicit, to which by mid-century the idea was being subjected from a number of different directions may have forced statesmen, in Britain at least, to defend it as they might not otherwise have felt the need to do. Palmerston in 1864, for example, claimed that it was 'founded on the nature of man' and, as the only real defence of the independence of the smaller states, 'a doctrine worthy of being acted upon'.[130] The idea that the great powers, acting in concert, had some general obligation to see that the balance was not disturbed by the unilateral action of any one of them and to ensure that

---

126. F. Ancillon, *Tableau des révolutions du système politique de l'Europe depuis la fin du quinzième siècle* (Brussels, 1839), i, 22; C.Holbraad, *The Concert of Europe* (London, 1970), pp. 36 fn., 87.

127. G.F. de Martens, *Nouveau Receuil de Traités*, i (Göttingen, 1817), 596, 600, 660, 684.

128. R. Phillimore, *Commentaries upon International Law* (London, 1854–61), i, 456; De Broglie, 'La Diplomatie . . .', 619.

129. For example, *Russia. In Answer to a Manchester Manufacturer*, 2nd edn (London, 1837), col. 25b.

130. Quoted in Holbraad, *The Concert of Europe*, p. 138.

significant territorial changes were made only with the agreement of them all, grew weaker as time went on and never recovered the element of formality it had had during the congress period of 1815–22. But it never altogether disappeared. The Crimean War was fought essentially to vindicate such ideas against an apparent Russian attempt to ride roughshod over them: Gladstone, who seldom spoke explicitly of the balance of power, defended it in these terms.[131] Though the Franco–Prussian war and the treaty of Frankfurt meant that a great change in the contours of European politics had been made by the unilateral action of a single great power, both the Berlin congress of 1878 and the London conference of 1912–13 on Balkan affairs showed that the old concert attitudes still retained a good deal of vitality and that the idea of a balance of power was an important element in them.

Even the competing alliance and entente systems as they existed before 1914, soon to be so bitterly criticised, seemed to many contemporaries to support and strengthen the balance and thus to make war less rather than more likely. 'It is . . . certain', said *The Times* in December 1912, 'that were any unfortunate attempt made to humiliate or override any country which is a member of either group she would find her associates ready to support her. It is this fact, and the general knowledge of this fact, which indeed makes the group system the guarantee of "equilibrium and peace" which it is, and which we pray that it may long continue to be.' A few months earlier William II and Tsar Nicholas II, after meeting at Baltiiskii Port, had claimed that the value of the Triple Alliance and Triple Entente for the maintenance of peace was a proved fact.[132] Statesmen were now less ready than in the past to speak explicitly of a balance of power; but its importance was almost as much in their minds as at any time in the previous three centuries. Sir Edward Grey, writing after the First World War and in a completely different psychological climate of his years as foreign secretary from 1906 onwards, could claim that 'I have never, so far as I recollect, used the phrase "Balance of Power". I have often deliberately avoided the use of it, and I have never consciously set it before me as something to be pursued, attained and preserved.' Yet it is clear that the policies he pursued in 1906–14 were essentially traditional balance of power ones and that he and the foreign office saw them as such.[133]

131. Holbraad, *The Concert of Europe*, p. 144.
132. *The History of The Times*, iv, Pt. I (London, 1952), 87, 168.
133. Viscount Grey of Fallodon, *Twenty-Five Years, 1892–1916* (London, 1925), i, 5; K. Wilson, 'British Power in the European Balance', in *Retreat from Power: Studies in Britain's Foreign Policy of the Twentieth Century*, ed. D. Dilks, i (London, 1981), 21–3.

## A world balance?

Throughout the nineteenth century the balance remained in practice one confined to Europe. Many observers, however, had no doubt that this situation must soon change completely. From the 1830s onwards, as the economic growth of the United States became more and more impressive, prophecies could be heard of approaching American entrance into and dominance of it. Cobden and his supporters, deeply admiring the individualism, material success and isolation from international complications which they saw across the Atlantic, were among the most vocal of these prophets. Cobden himself in 1836 argued that no balance of power which excluded the Americas, and particularly the United States, could have any reality. Twenty years later, at the end of the Crimean War, he urged Britain and France to reduce their navies, since failure to do this might provoke the United States to become a significant naval power and she could then easily, within a year or two, make herself the greatest one in the world. Simultaneously Bright admonished British statesmen that if they could only 'get beyond those old nations which belong to the traditions of Europe, and cast their eyes as far westward as they are now looking eastward, they might there see a power growing up in its gigantic proportions, which will teach us before very long where the true "balance of power" is to be found'.[134] Such anticipations of predominant American influence, like fears of Russian domination, were at their height in the middle years of the nineteenth century. Between the 1830s and the 1850s the United States was visited by several of the most important political analysts of the period – the liberal Alexis de Tocqueville, the economic nationalist Friedrich List, the influential German publicist Julius Fröbel. Their books spread the idea, already far from new, that Europe's world leadership, and perhaps even her political autonomy, were now threatened by the growth of the two gigantic non-European powers, the United States and Russia. Such were their potentialities that leadership must soon inevitably pass to them: they were the only true world powers. 'There are only two peoples', wrote the great French critic Sainte-Beuve in 1847. 'Russia is still barbarous, but she is great. . . . The other youthful people is America . . . the future of the world is there, between these two great worlds'.[135]

In fact any American influence on the European balance was then still at least two generations in the future. Just as the myth of overwhelming

134. Cobden, *Political Writings*, i, 274–5, 278–80, and his pamphlet *What Next – and Next?* (London, 1856), pp. 49–50; Read, *Cobden and Bright*, p. 127.
135. Duroselle, *L'Idée d'Europe*, p. 231; D. Groh, *Russland und das Selbstverständnis Europas* (Neuwied, 1961), p. 270. The first use of the term *Weltmacht* appears to occur in 1853 in discussion of these issues.

Russian power was shaken by defeat in the Crimea, by the populist terrorism of the 1870s and 1880s and by the poor performance of the Russian army in the Turkish war of 1877–78, so that of approaching American leadership was greatly weakened by the civil war of 1861–65 and the isolationism which continued for the rest of the century to dominate the relations of the United States with the outside world. An American future seemed to most Europeans less likely, and probably less desirable, in the 1870s than it had in the 1840s or 1850s. Nevertheless, by the 1890s there were increasing signs that the United States and, much more unexpectedly, Japan might soon have at least some indirect influence on the European equilibrium. There was American participation in the Berlin African conference of 1884–85 and, more importantly, in the negotiations at Algeciras which ended the Moroccan crisis of 1905–06. Japan, by her spectacular defeat of Russia in 1904–05, sharply weakened for several years the ability of the tsarist empire to play an active or confident role in international affairs. It was beginning to be clear that the balance of power would soon cease to be merely European and become one covering the world. This was a fundamental change, tellingly illustrated when in December 1914 Britain, France and Russia jointly asked the Japanese government to give them military help in Europe. The request was refused; but the mere fact that it was made at all illustrates how the world was changing.

Yet in so far as discussion of the balance of power in the period 1870–1914 had an extra-European dimension it was one which recalled many of the claims and fears of the eighteenth century. Rather as Choiseul and his contemporaries had exaggerated the contribution which colonial empire and seapower made to the effective strength of a state in Europe, so in the later nineteenth century it seemed that colonies and bases overseas were now essential to any true great power. As the pace of imperial expansion quickened, Africa and Asia seemed to play a growing role in the European balance. Very often imperial rivalries there ended in agreements meant to create a stable equilibrium over a wide area, either by mutual concessions and compensations (as notably in the Anglo-Russian agreement of 1907) or by leaving a buffer-state to separate the territories or spheres of influence of two rival powers (as Siam separated those of Britain and France in south-east Asia, or Afghanistan Russian Turkestan from British India). More significant, this renewed emphasis on the importance of colonial empires, which sometimes threatened to become almost a new mercantilism, led to demands that the extra-European world should be shared more equally between the European empires. As in the eighteenth century, Britain was inevitably the main target of such demands; but whereas then they had come predominantly from France now it was above all the new expansionist Germany which voiced them. In 1899 the historian Hans Delbrück warned his countrymen that 'If all territories outside Europe go to only one or two nations, then one day these will crush all others with this preponderance of power.' A few years later, in 1907, an even more eminent scholar, Otto Hintze, argued that the objective of German *Weltpolitik* must be to avert such dangers by establishing a number of major colonial empires between which there would be a balance of power similar to what had hitherto existed only in Europe: this was essentially what Choiseul had urged a century and a half earlier.[136] Like some Frenchmen of the old regime, moreover, many Germans of the Second Reich felt that an effective balance of power in Europe, which restricted Germany's freedom of action and impeded her natural development, was merely a weapon in the hands of her rivals, most of all the British. Paul Rohrbach, one of the most active propagandists for German imperial expansion, is a good example of this attitude. A more extreme one is the ultra-nationalist General von Bernhardi, who demanded that 'the principle of the balance of power in Europe, which has, since the Congress of Vienna, led an almost sacrosanct but entirely unjustifiable existence, must be entirely disregarded'. Such a balance merely hindered the freedom of action of the European powers, most of all Germany, and made their forces 'mutually ineffective'. It was no more than a means by which Britain could stir up enmity between them and nullify their strength for her own advantage. A state-system and a balance of power were worth having therefore only if they covered the whole world.[137]

## 1914: The balance discredited

In many ways, then, the balance of power and discussion of it had changed surprisingly little between the French revolution and the First World War. It was still in 1914 an essentially European phenomenon though, as in the eighteenth century, there were urgings that it be completed by an equilibrium covering the colonial empires of the great European states. It was now more than ever before a balance between a small number of clearly identifiable great powers; but apart from the expansion of Prussia into the leader and controller of a united Germany and the much less important creation of a united Italy, these powers were still those which had played leading roles in the age of Frederick the

136. Holbraad, *The Concert of Europe*, p. 102; O. Hintze, *Staat und Verfassung; Gesammelte Abhandlungen zur allgemeinen Verfassungsgeschichte* (Leipzig, 1941), p. 459.
137. Holbraad, *The Concert of Europe*, p. 103; General F. von Bernhardi, *Germany and the Next War* (London, 1912), pp. 107–9.

Great. The balance was still the target of the same criticisms – that it provoked rather than prevented wars, that it was too vague and imprecise to be of practical use, or that it was no more than meaningless verbiage. On a deeper level, like all other mechanisms and concepts of international relations, it had to meet the condemnation offered by the new ideologies of radical liberalism, international socialism and most of all nationalism. But in many ways it is the absence of change that is most striking.

The outbreak of war in 1914 rapidly focused and vastly intensified criticism, most of all in Britain but to varying extents in almost every belligerent state. An incident in a remote corner of Europe had grown within little more than a month into the most devastating conflict in history. This seemed finally and for ever to explode the claim that the balance was any sort of stabilising influence. Had its workings not rather magnified enormously the destructive effects of what was, in itself, quite a minor event? The Union of Democratic Control, the newly formed British radical group which was now demanding an end to secretive and irresponsible foreign policies carried on by traditional methods, claimed in the first of the many pamphlets it published that 'But for the policy of the "Balance of Power" the results of the quarrel (between Austria–Hungary and Serbia) would almost certainly have been confined to the parties immediately affected, and an early mediation by the Neutral Powers would have been possible.' Did the balance idea in fact have any meaning at all? In the very same pamphlet the Union, quite inconsistently, fell back on the old accusation that it was merely a phrase used by selfish or inept politicians for their own purposes, 'little more than a diplomatic formula made use of by the mouthpieces of the interests from whose operations war comes'.[138] A few months later, as visions of a new world of peace, even perhaps of effective international government, gathered force,[139] it had become at best 'that old puzzle "the balance of power" ' and to less lenient judges 'the supreme engine of international mischief . . . the core of diplomatic falsehood . . . this inhuman theory'.[140] By the last days of the struggle the condemnation, at least in Britain, had become even sharper. In particular it had now become the conventional wisdom, at least among radicals and idealists of all kinds, that the pursuit of balance between competing alliance-systems of a rigid and durable sort must inevitably have fatal consequences. 'We remain in bondage to the Balance of Power', wrote an eminent historian in 1918, 'after it has lost its meaning and usefulness to the world . . . for while a just distribution of

138. Union of Democratic Control, *The Morrow of the War* (London, 1914), pp. 7–8.
139. See below, pp. 280–7.
140. F.N. Keen, *The World in Alliance: A Plan for preventing Future Wars* (London, 1915), p. 60; J.A. Hobson, *Towards International Government* (London, 1915), pp. 181–2, 186.

power among a number of States is a guarantee against aggression by one, nothing is more unstable than an equipoise between two opposing alliances'.[141] The intellectual and emotional pendulum, in these years of loss and suffering, had swung swiftly and violently. For the time being the assumptions of generations had been totally rejected by public opinion and even by many politicians. After a long gestation period and an active and successful maturity the balance of power idea now seemed decrepit, moribund, a tattered and unconvincing ghost. Yet many of those who so vociferously condemned it during and after the First World War were to see it, within little more than a decade, rise from the grave and show that it had a significant future as well as a long and chequered past.

141. A.F. Pollard, *The League of Nations: An Historical Argument* (Oxford, 1918), pp. 19–20.

# CHAPTER FIVE

# The Quest for International Peace

## THE FIRST ASPIRATIONS: TO THE END OF THE SEVENTEENTH CENTURY

War was endemic in early mediæval Europe. Efforts of rulers to enforce their authority over their subjects, struggles of rival noble families and factions, enmities between competing cities and communes, all made up a picture of incessant conflict. But for almost everyone the loss and suffering this entailed were an inescapable part of normal life. Like bad weather, famine or epidemics they might have their effects mitigated by prayer and even to some extent by human forethought; but they were ultimately inescapable. As recognisable states with increasingly effective central governments slowly took shape and war between them became by far the most important and destructive form of conflict, pressures to avert such wars became stronger. If Europe were truly a Christian commonwealth, united at the deepest level by community of religious belief and observance, then all conflicts between Christian princes were in a sense civil wars. It was therefore the duty of all Christians to avert them and thus strengthen Christendom for the great struggle which alone was completely legitimate, that with the threatening infidel world of Islam.

### Arbitration and universal empire

By the thirteenth century, the Catholic church, the creator and supreme guardian of the Christian world, the *custos morum* of its flock, was putting forward these arguments with growing insistence. The pontificate of Innocent III (1198–1215), when papal power in many ways reached its highest point, saw the pope assert more effectively than any of his predecessors the right to act as an arbiter in the quarrels of secular rulers, both between themselves and with their subjects. In 1200 he claimed to be supreme judge in the struggle then in progress between the rulers of France and England; and a few years later he intervened in England between John and his rebellious barons. A century later, in 1298, another ambitious and assertive pope, Boniface VIII, acted (though only in a private capacity) as arbiter between Philip IV of France and Edward I of England. In the fourteenth century Benedict XII and Gregory IX were to put forward similar claims in the long spasmodic struggle of the Hundred Years War. The famous division in 1493–94 by Alexander VI of the new world of America and the Indies between Spain and Portugal can be seen as another assertion of the right and duty of international pacification inherent in the papal office, while in the first years of the sixteenth century Leo X arbitrated in the disputes of the Emperor Maximilian I with the Venetian republic.

In so far as there was any generally recognised method of settling peacefully such conflicts in mediaeval Europe, then, that method was by arbitration. Nor was the pope by any means the only possible arbiter. Indeed there was often considerable reluctance to call upon either pope or emperor to act as such. Underlying the arbitration process was the deeply rooted idea of judgement by peers, of decision by a judge who was in some sense the equal of the contending parties and thus fitted to decide between them, a concept central to feudal justice. The claims to superiority over all other rulers put forward in different ways on behalf of both papal and imperial power made the men who embodied such pretensions difficult to fit into a picture of this kind. Kings and other secular princes, corporate bodies, occasionally even private individuals, therefore all acted on occasion as arbiters. Several rulers of France were called on in this way. Louis IX, who came closer than any other ruler of the middle ages to realising the mediæval ideal of kingship, arbitrated between Henry III of England and his barons in 1263. Philip IV performed the same function between a number of German princes and the king of Bohemia in 1334, while Louis XI acted in this way at least twice – between the rulers of Castile and Aragon in 1463 and between an Austrian archduke and the Swiss cantons in 1475. In Germany and Italy cities often acted as arbiters in disputes between other cities. The *parlements* in France, the powerful legal corporations which developed from the thirteenth century onwards, were also involved in such processes, though as mediators rather than arbiters. In 1244 that of Paris, by far the most important, attempted with little success to mediate in the bitter struggle between the Emperor Frederick II and Pope Innocent IV, while as late as 1613–14 that of Grenoble was involved in the same way in the rivalries between the Austrian Habsburgs and the duke of Württemberg. In 1570 a mere individual councillor of the *parlement* of Dijon, Jean Begat, acted as arbiter between Philip II of Spain and some of the Swiss cantons in a dispute (admittedly a minor one) over the frontiers of the Spanish-ruled Franche-Comté.[1]

By the seventeenth century, however, arbitration had very much receded into the background as a means of settling disputes between states and rulers. Even before the Reformation the declining prestige of the papacy and the evolution of quasi-national churches in several parts of Catholic Europe, notably Spain and France, had made the claims of Innocent III and Boniface VIII increasingly hollow. The chasms which opened in the religious life of Europe from the 1520s onwards completed this process. Simultaneously the slow but steady growth of national consciousness in the great western monarchies made their rulers less willing to submit to arbitration claims which often involved a large element of dynastic and national prestige. This did not mean that arbitration ceased altogether to figure in international relations. In 1655 England and France agreed to submit to the decision of the States-General of the Dutch republic any dispute between them over claims for losses caused by the privateering at sea in which both had indulged freely during the last fifteen years; and this agreement therefore marked an important advance. For probably the first time in modern history two major states had undertaken to submit future differences to arbitration instead of merely resorting to it *ad hoc* after a dispute had arisen. In 1678, again, the States-General was chosen to settle conflicting French and Spanish frontier claims in the southern Netherlands, while in 1697 Louis XIV and the Emperor Leopold I arbitrated in a succession dispute in the west-German state of the Palatinate. All these cases, however, involved conflicts of secondary importance. Arbitration as a means of settling international issues of genuine weight had now lost all real significance.

As this happened, other ideas and expedients acquired relatively greater prominence. One of the more obvious of these was the concept of some state or monarch as inherently superior to all others and thus charged by providence with the task of controlling and protecting them, a divinely appointed leader of Christendom imposing peace and harmony upon it. Claims of this kind on behalf of different rulers had already by the sixteenth century a considerable history. Dante was only the greatest of a number of mediæval writers who had made such assertions with the Holy

---

1. Many of the details in this and the preceding paragraph are taken from F. Dreyfus, *L'Arbitrage international* (Paris, 1892), pp. 24–7. M. Novacovitch, *Les Compromis et les arbitrages internationaux du XIIe au XVe siècle* (Paris, 1905), pp. 100–59, prints a long list of mediæval arbitrations.

Roman Emperor filling this dominant position. Moreover, the frightening progress of the Ottomans in the fifteenth and early sixteenth centuries helped to make Europeans more ready to accept as leader any ruler with the will and the means to defend them against the threat from the east. An assumption of his own inherent superiority to his fellow-monarchs certainly coloured the ideas of the Emperor Charles V; and this mode of thinking was slow to die completely. Much later, and in rather different ways, Louis XIV and even Napoleon I were tempted to see the world along the same lines.[2] So great a scholar as Leibniz, in the last years of the seventeenth century, wished the Holy Roman Emperor and the pope, as the temporal and spiritual heads of Christendom, to have authority over all other European monarchs and to keep the peace between them.[3] Throughout much of early modern history attitudes of this kind opened the way for propagandists to claim pre-eminence for the rulers they served, often on what now seem ludicrously flimsy grounds. Thus the great French scholar Guillaume Postel, in his *Les Raisons de la Monarchie, et quels moyens sont necessaires pour y parvenir* (1551) argued for a temporal primacy for the kings of France comparable to the spiritual one wielded by the pope. This he justified mainly by the alleged descent of the French from Japhet, the eldest of the three sons of Noah.[4] Half a century later, an even more visionary writer, the Italian Tommaso Campanella, in his *Monarchia Hispanica* (written 1599–1600 but not published until 1620) saw Spain as playing a leading role of this kind, especially as the head of a great anti-Turkish alliance which might even include non-European states such as Persia, Russia and the Georgian kingdoms. Later still, in his *Monarchia Messiae* (1633) he urged that supreme temporal as well as spiritual power be placed in the hands of the pope, who was to become head of an association of all states and rulers based on the religious reunification of Europe.[5]

Flights of fancy of this kind need not be taken too seriously and were not by contemporaries. The often pedantic and backward-looking scholarship of the age encouraged them: it provided an inexhaustible reservoir of precedents and pseudo-historical arguments which could be used to support claims to pre-eminence by several of the great European monarchies. The sixteenth and seventeenth centuries were an age of realism and hard-headedness in much of the detailed practical working-out of foreign policies, yet also one of frequent and irresponsible wishful

---

2. F.H. Hinsley, 'The Development of the European States System since the Eighteenth Century', *Transactions of the Royal Historical Society*, 5th series, xi (1961), 70–1.

3. G.W. *Leibnitii Opera Omnia* (Geneva, 1768), iv, 330–1.

4. C.L. Lange, *Histoire de l'internationalisme*, i (Christiania, 1919), 377–8.

5. E. Nys, *Thomas Campanella: sa vie et ses théories politiques* (Brussels–Leipzig, 1889), pp. 16–22, 28–32.

thinking in their formulation.[6] Nevertheless, the tenacity with which the claims of different states and rulers to some inherent superiority were maintained, and the slowness with which they disappeared, is in at least one respect instructive. It shows clearly, like the endless disputes over ceremonial and precedence,[7] how far Europe still was from the modern conception of the juridical equality of states and from a state-system based on such equality. Something of this kind was coming into existence; but it was only slowly that it overcame the deeply rooted idea of qualitative differences between states and the rulers who personified them, the belief that some were natural leaders of the others and must remain so.

## The humanists and the problem of peace

Christian teaching had always maintained not merely the fundamental distinction between a just and an unjust war but also the inherent superiority of peace to war. Conflict – between individuals, between peoples, between rulers – was the badge of man's imperfection. It was the outcome of his fallen state, the expression of his baser self, of his pride, anger and greed. The practical effect of such admonitions is difficult to measure with any accuracy. At the international level they were powerfully challenged by the tradition which saw successful war as the essential mark of the great ruler destined to leave his imprint on history. Every ruler, moreover, stood at the apex of a society deeply permeated by aristocratic values. He must therefore be quick to resent any slight (hence the obsessive interest in details of ceremonial and precedence) and assiduous in protecting and extending his possessions. Since no supranational judicial institutions existed and arbitration, always of limited effect, was now of very little practical importance, war or the threat of it was normally the only means by which this could be done. None the less, the Christian ideal of peace, however slight its effect, could never be totally forgotten or too flagrantly disregarded. The first decades of the sixteenth century, when so many aspects of spiritual and intellectual life were still very much as they had been for centuries past, saw it being powerfully urged by a number of Christian humanists. Simultaneously there was even some temporary and limited effort to translate it into practice.

The humanist condemnation of war had two main characteristics. In the first place, it was almost entirely moral and religious and hardly at all political. Secondly, it was addressed in the main to rulers and hoped to be

6. See above, pp. 161–2.
7. See above, pp. 15–20, 56–68.

successful by appealing to their better feelings and changing their hearts. Both aspects emerge clearly in its most famous and influential exponent: Desiderius Erasmus. Like the other writers who, in various ways, typified Christian humanism – Colet and More in England, Vives in Spain – he fully accepted the distinction, now deeply engrained in the church's teaching, between a just and an unjust war. Unlike many of them, however, he was willing to argue that even an obviously just war might be difficult to defend. 'I would boldly declare', he wrote in 1504 in his *Panegyric for Archduke Philip of Austria* (the first of his many works to attack the question of the proper use by a ruler of his powers), 'that it would be far better policy for the conscientious prince to maintain peace, however unjust, than to start on the justest of wars'.[8] Repeatedly he stressed the maintenance of peace as a Christian duty and bitterly contrasted the lip-service paid to it with the frivolity with which rulers rushed into conflict. 'Every Christian word, whether you read the Old Testament or the New, reiterates one thing: peace with unanimity; while every Christian life is occupied with one thing, war', he complained in his *Querela Pacis* (1516); while in the same pamphlet he dismissed the princes of Europe as 'beasts, not men, princes only in the tyranny they wield, using their wits only to do harm, never united except to damage the public interest'.[9] The suffering caused by war, the irrationality of rulers who by resorting to it inflicted on their subjects material losses for which no possible gain could compensate, he felt deeply. A quintessential civilian, moderate in temperament and deeply attached to political and social stability, he particularly feared and disliked the way in which wars were now fought largely by armies of mercenaries, badly disciplined, destructive and often uncontrollable. 'At the first mention and whiff, as it were, of a campaign', he wrote, with a mixture of fear and contempt, 'the dregs of humanity are roused to come out of their hiding-places, and collect like bilge-water from all over the world. . . . Wars have to be carried on with these sweepings of humanity; such dregs have to be received into cities and homes, although a whole generation will hardly be enough to clean the stink from your citizens' morals'.[10]

Yet all these pleas and denunciations led to hardly any precise or concrete proposals. Everything for Erasmus depended on a change of heart on the part of monarchs. For him as for all the remarkable humanist efflorescence of his generation, hopes of international peace were 'focused on an aristocracy of rulers bound to each other in a code of courtesy and

8. *Collected Works*, xxvii (Toronto–Buffalo–London, 1986), 55.
9. *Collected Works*, xxvii, 303, 306.
10. *Collected Works*, xxvii, 54–5; cf. 282–3.

humanity'.[11] Very occasionally he alludes to the possibility of using arbitration to settle peacefully disputes between princes.[12] In his later years he had some personal contact with the world of high politics: by 1520 he was in touch with Mercurio da Gattinara, the chancellor and main adviser of Charles V, while in the following year he was in Bruges during the peace negotiations there between the emperor, Francis I and Henry VIII. But almost all his specific suggestions were entirely negative. They were directed to minimising the risk of war rather than to any strengthening of peace. Thus he argued that members of ruling families should marry only within their own territories and in this way avert the danger of wars of succession (a suggestion to which the events of the next two centuries or more were to give much weight). At a deeper level, he was attracted by the idea of fixing the frontiers of the European states finally and irrevocably, and thus eliminating territorial conflict between them. This was an aspiration which many later authors of schemes to foster international peace, until well into the nineteenth century, were to find hard to resist. But in the warlike and rapidly changing Europe of the early sixteenth century this sort of enforced stability was a dream. It was totally unrealistic for Erasmus to argue that rulers should be forbidden [by whom?] to sell or transfer any part of their realms or that 'There should be agreement [how achieved?] between princes, once and for all, on what each of them should rule, and once territories have been assigned them, no alliance should extend or diminish these and no treaty tear them apart'.[13]

Nor were his contemporaries any more successful in suggesting institutional changes which might reduce the risk of war. Sir Thomas More agreed with him in attacking and satirising traditional ideas of military glory (and, more fancifully, in attributing man's readiness to go to war to his acceptance of the slaughter of animals for food). He also shared to the full Erasmus's fear and dislike of mercenaries and their destructive potentialities: the inhabitants of his Utopia pay to fight for them an entirely separate and inferior people 'hideous, savage and fierce . . . of a hard nature'. But no more than Erasmus did he put forward positive suggestions for the safeguarding of peace. Juan Luis Vives, the greatest Spanish humanist, appealed in 1522 to Pope Adrian VI to bring about a general pacification in Europe, and three years later urged Henry VIII to mediate between Francis I and Charles V, whose rivalry threatened to

11. R.H. Bainton, *Christian Attitudes toward War and Peace* (London, 1961), p. 127; cf. J.M. Headley, 'Gattinara, Erasmus and the Imperial Configuration of Humanism', *Archiv für Reformationsgeschichte*, Jahrgang 71 (1980), 80.
12. For example, *Collected Works*, xxvii, 284.
13. *Collected Works*, xxvii, 312.

generate a long series of conflicts. But for him, as for Erasmus and More, war grew out of the moral defects of individuals. It could therefore be ended only by a change in men's hearts and attitudes.[14] Union between princes based on their whole-hearted acceptance of Christian morality was, however, an impossible dream. Only a few years before Vives made his appeals events had shown very clearly its flimsiness as a defence against international conflict. The Anglo-French treaty signed in London in October 1518 has been called 'the last public expression of the unity of Catholic Christendom'.[15] Other secular princes, as well as the pope, were invited to adhere to it. When they had done so, if any of them were attacked, the other signatories would protest jointly to the aggressor, and if this had no result would themselves declare war on him. Both the way in which the protest should be made and the military obligations involved if it were ineffective were specified in detail. Henry VIII and Francis I proclaimed themselves 'desirous of spreading universal peace (*pacis universalis propagationem cupientes*)',[16] and the treaty was very favourably received by what embryonic public opinion as yet existed in Europe. Yet it did nothing to make the continent more peaceful. Its main practical result was to help involve England, in 1522, in the war between Charles V and Francis I which had broken out a few months earlier: since the emperor was at least technically the victim of aggression he threatened to call for help under the terms of the treaty and thus increased the pressures on Henry VIII and Wolsey to enter the conflict.

## *The first schemes of international organisation: Podiebrad, Sully, Crucé*

The great weakness, then, of the Christian humanists' approach to the problem of war was its almost exclusively moralising and religious character. The same criticism applies equally to most of their sixteenth-century successors. The reformed churches (with the unimportant exception of the Anabaptists) subscribed to the theory of the just war as completely as the Catholic one, and were as ready to see conflict simply as the result of moral defects and the inevitable outcome of human frailty. Yet the generations which separated the age of Lorenzo the Magnificent from that of Richelieu also saw serious proposals for new forms of international organisation designed to reduce or even eliminate war between the European states. These proposals were few, widely scattered in time, often imprecise and completely without practical effect. Nevertheless they have interest, and even a certain importance, as the first

14. Lange, *Histoire de l'internationalisme*, i, 184–7.
15. G. Mattingly, 'An early non-aggression pact', *Journal of Modern History*, x (1938), 28.
16. T. Rymer, *Foedera* (London, 1704–35), xiii, 624.

examples of an aspiration which was to recur repeatedly over four centuries or more with increasing force. Though they achieved nothing in their own day they were the first serious suggestions for bringing order to the international anarchy, the unbridled interplay of monarchical ambitions, which was so dominant a characteristic of early modern Europe. They were the first of a series of schemes of international organisation, even of international government, which were to reach a kind of climax in the eighteenth century and then, after something of a lull, multiply spectacularly from the later nineteenth century onwards.

The first of these proposals, surprisingly early and, for its own day, logically organised, was that put forward in the name of George Podiebrad, king of Bohemia, in 1462.[17] This suggested the formation, to resist the tide of Turkish conquest, of a league of European princes which would be divided into four regional sections, French, German, Italian and, as a later addition, Spanish. (The position of England was not specified; but it seems likely that the Scandinavian kingdoms were to have formed part of the German group.) The essential central institution of the league was to be a general assembly, a congress of ambassadors representing the member-princes. In this each of the regional groupings was to have a single vote; and considerable care was taken to specify the procedure by which the members of the group should decide how that vote was to be cast. The general assembly was to maintain peace between the members of the league and protect them against attack by non-members. To do this it was to have its own army, paid from the yield of taxes levied on the member-states. It was to have other important rights, notably that of issuing its own currency, as well as its own seal, archives and officials – an approach to an international civil service. Side by side with it was to be established an international court whose members the assembly would appoint. The general assembly was to meet for the first time in February 1464 in the Swiss city of Basel. Five years later it was to move to a city in France, and five years after that to one in Italy. It seems likely that Podiebrad saw himself as the first head of the league, possibly to be succeeded after a few years by Louis XI of France. This plan for the organisation of lasting peace between the Christian princes and perhaps even, after the defeat of the Turks, throughout the known world, had no practical result. Yet it was a remarkable one. It not only enunciated the

17. Some part in drawing up the plan was almost certainly played by a Frenchman, Antoine Marini, who was one of Podiebrad's advisers, and perhaps also by Martin Mair, the chief counsellor of the duke of Bavaria (F.G. Heymann, *George of Bohemia: King of Heretics* (Princeton, 1965), pp. 299–301); cf. T. Ruyssen, 'Un projet français de confédération chrétienne: Antoine Marini', in *Gegenwartsprobleme des internationalen Rechtes und der Rechtsphilosophie*, ed. D.S. Constantopolous and H. Wehberg (Hamburg, 1953).

ideal of lasting peace but suggested in unprecedented detail a means by which it might be achieved.[18]

The century and a half which followed the Podiebrad scheme saw no other of the kind so systematic and detailed. Lip-service continued to be paid to the idea of a union of Christian states against the Turkish menace. Popes still urged the secular rulers of the continent in that direction. Occasionally one of these, like Charles V, took the idea seriously. Fear of further Turkish advances was sometimes strong enough to overcome the new antagonisms released by the Reformation: when in 1565 the whole Christian position in the Mediterranean was threatened by the great Turkish attack on Malta, prayers were offered in the churches of Protestant England for its Catholic defenders. But territorial and dynastic rivalries were now far too deeply rooted for any union of the European states to be a possibility. Occasional proposals for something of the kind appeared, but usually in very vague and general forms. That of the French soldier François de la Noue, in his *Discours politiques et militaires* (Basel, 1587), for example, suggested a league of princes to drive the Turks from Europe, which would be regulated by an international assembly meeting in Augsburg under the presidency of the Holy Roman Emperor; but it failed to develop this idea in any detail.[19] Moreover, quite apart from the insuperable obstacle presented by the antagonisms between states there was a second and even more difficult one. If war were an inevitable result of the inherent sinfulness of man, as was so widely taken for granted, then no amount of organisational change or creation of new institutions would end it. For that there must be a transformation of the minds, even the souls, of individuals, most of all of rulers, of the kind Erasmus had despairingly called for; and this was hardly to be expected. The pessimism and fatalism bred by this attitude were for generations to make any plan for the safeguarding of international peace by human action seem childishly optimistic.

The early seventeenth century produced two far-reaching schemes of international organisation, those attributed to the duc de Sully, the chief minister of Henry IV of France, and to the mysterious figure of Eméric Crucé. The fact that both authors were French may reflect a relatively widespread interest in France during these decades in the idea of an organised and lasting peace in Europe;[20] but both contained large elements of the visionary and even the fantastic. That associated with Sully

18. The best summary of the plan in English is that in Heymann, *George of Bohemia*, pp. 304–15.

19. Lange, *Histoire de l'internationalisme*, i, 336–42.

20. Ch. Pfister, 'Les "Economies Royales" de Sully et le Grand Dessein de Henry IV', *Revue Historique*, lvi (1894), 329–30.

presents particular problems. It is contained in his *Sages et Royales Oeconomies d'Estat*, a partly autobiographical collection of letters and political and economic schemes. Most of it he probably wrote in 1617, after he had ceased to play any active political role: it was published only in 1638, near the end of his life. Even how far it was written by Sully himself has been questioned, though it seems likely that it was essentially his own work.[21] Moreover, the parts of the book which contain his scheme of international organisation appear to be additions made when, in old age, he decided on its publication; and whether they should be taken as serious proposals has been considerably debated. The author of the first detailed discussion of them dismissed them as mere rhetorical exercises or fantasies, whereas a more recent commentator has argued that the plan was a good deal more than the utopian dreaming of an old man.[22] It is clear that Sully's main objective was to continue and strengthen the now traditional French policy of opposition to the Austrian and Spanish Habsburgs. At various points in the *Oeconomies Royales* he urges the need for France to maintain good relations with England, Sweden, Denmark and the Dutch, and to strengthen its links with the smaller German princes and with anti-Habsburg forces in Hungary and Bohemia,[23] a general line of French policy already well established and to be adhered to for years to come. To this the proposals for a European union were probably no more than an afterthought.

In their final form they envisaged a redrawing of frontiers to create a Europe made up of states of very roughly similar size and strength. Of these some would be hereditary monarchies – France, Spain, England, Sweden, Denmark–Norway and Lombardy (a new creation to include Piedmont and the duchy of Milan). Others would be elective monarchies – the papacy (strengthened by being given the kingdom of Naples in addition to its existing territories), the Holy Roman Empire (leadership of which was to become genuinely elective and cease to be a preserve of the Habsburg family), Hungary, Poland and Bohemia. A Helvetic republic (including the Tyrol, Alsace, Franche-Comté and Istria), an Italian republic which would unite most of the small states of the peninsula, and a Belgian one made up the total. A permanent general council of representatives of these states, whose membership was to be renewed at three-year intervals, would deliberate on the political and religious affairs of the continent and settle disputes between the members of the union.

21. Pfister, 'Les "Economies Royales" ', *Revue Historique*, liv (1894), 307.
22. Pfister, 'Les "Economies Royales" ', *Revue Historique*, lvi (1894), 318; A. Puharré, *Les Projets d'organization européenne d'après le grand dessein d'Henri IV et de Sully* (Paris, 1954), pp. 51ff.
23. J.F. Michaud and J.J.F. Poujoulat (eds), *Nouvelle Collection de Mémoires pour servir à l'histoire de France*, 2nd series, ii (Paris, 1837), 219–21.

This would meet for a year at a time in a city selected from a list of fifteen, most of them in central Europe, every member-state in turn choosing its location. Under it there were to be six regional councils dealing with matters of local or secondary importance and if necessary referring issues to the general council, which could also intervene if necessary in the internal affairs of individual states. The general council would decide the composition of an international court, which would arbitrate in cases of dispute between the member-states; refusal to accept its decision would mean coercion of the recalcitrant state by an international armed force to which each member of the union would contribute in proportion to its resources. However, this force, whose size and composition was specified in some detail – 117 warships, 220,000 infantry, 53,800 cavalry, 217 cannon – would have as its principal task once more that of driving the Turks from Europe.[24]

In many respects this famous plan, which was to be constantly referred to by later authors, was backward-looking. Its main ostensible purpose was the traditional one of waging 'continual war' with the Turks, reconquering from them the Balkan territories they had overrun and perhaps even seizing some of their Asiatic possessions. In this way it reflected the crusading impulses which were still strong in France during the early seventeenth century and which were powerfully represented among the advisers who surrounded Richelieu.[25] Also, the Christendom which the union was to protect and if possible expand was that of west and central Europe only. Russia was explicitly excluded, since she was essentially non-European, too backward to cooperate easily with the more advanced European states, and with a population deeply sunk in idolatry. In any case it would be very difficult to help her, if she did join the union, in her conflicts with the Turks, Tatars and Persians.[26] But apart from these limitations the scheme, even if it were seriously intended, was weakened by its close association with French policies and ambitions. The desire to undermine Habsburg power was central to it. More than any other of the projects of this kind which were to appear over the following two centuries it was designed to serve the interests of a single state. It has even been argued that 'this peace project is so completely saturated with

24. There are convenient summaries of the plan in Puharré, *Projets d'organization . . .*, pp. 28–31 and Elizabeth V. Souleyman, *The Vision of World Peace in Seventeenth and Eighteenth-Century France* (New York, 1941), pp. 21–9. See also *Sully's Grand Design of Henry IV*, with introduction by D. Ogg (London, 1921) and H. Prutz, *Die Friedensidee. Ihr Ursprung, anfänglicher Sinn und allmähliche Wandel* (Munich–Leipzig, 1917), Chapter III.

25. G. Fagniez, *Le Père Joseph et Richelieu* (Paris, 1894), i, Chapter III; K. von Raumer, 'Sully, Crucé und das Problem des allgemeinen Friedens', *Historische Zeitschrift*, 175 (1953), 7–9; Th. Kukelhaus, *Der Ursprung des Planes vom ewigen Frieden in den Memoiren des Hertzogs von Sully* (Berlin, 1893), pp. 56–8.

26. Puharré, *Projets d'organization . . .*, pp. 13–14.

motives of power-seeking and state egoism that it would be inadmissible to count it as a real peace plan'.[27]

This cannot be said of the scheme of international organisation put forward by Eméric Crucé in his *Le Nouveau Cynée, ou Discours d'Estat représentant les Occasions et Moyens d'establir une Paix générale et la Liberté du Commerce par tout le Monde* (Paris, 1623). Crucé as an individual remains a mystery.[28] But his proposals, though they contain a large element of fantasy, are in some ways strikingly original. He begins by denying at length (on the lines of Erasmus, who was probably a source of inspiration here) that military glory is true glory at all, and by warning rulers of the dangers inherent in an unsuccessful war which may easily reduce them from prosperity to complete defeat and subjection.[29] Moreover, hostility between peoples is 'only political, and cannot take away the connection which is and must be between men'. Humanity is united at the deepest level by 'the similarity of natures, true base of amity and human society'; and war 'diminishes true religion instead of advancing it'.[30] Peace should therefore be consolidated by the meeting, probably in Venice, of a congress of ambassadors representing the princes of Europe and also the more important republics, Venice and the Swiss cantons. Differences between them could then be settled 'by the judgement of the whole assembly'; and 'if anyone rebelled against the decrees of so notable a company he would receive the disgrace of all other Princes, who would find means to bring him to reason'. This in itself is merely another of the vague and hopelessly optimistic proposals for some body of this kind which were now beginning to appear in western Europe. But in one respect the break with the past is striking. The assembly was to include representatives not merely of European rulers but of a wide range of non-European and often non-Christian ones – the sultan in Constantinople, the rulers of Persia and China, Prester John (the legendary ruler of Ethiopia), the 'Precop of Tartary' (i.e. the khan of the Crimea) and the grand duke of Muscovy. Moreover, these exotic potentates were not merely to be represented. Many of them were to be granted a higher status than most of the European princes. The sultan was to take precedence over the Holy Roman Emperor and rank second only to the pope. The rulers of Persia, Ethiopia, the Tatars, China and Muscovy were to rank higher than those of England, the Scandinavian countries or

27. Von Raumer, 'Sully, Crucé . . .', 19.
28. A. Saitta, 'Un Riformatore pacifista contemporaneo del Richelieu: E. Crucé', *Rivista Storica Italiana*, lxiii (1951), 183–92, brings together what little is known of his biography. It is possible that he may have been influenced by Grotius (Von Raumer, 'Sully, Crucé . . ., 26).
29. *The New Cyneas of Emeric Crucé*, ed. T.W. Balch (Philadelphia, 1909), pp. 22–42.
30. *The New Cyneas . . .*, pp. 84, 96.

Poland, though after those of France and Spain. If any disputes over precedence should arise (the attention Crucé gives to such issues is yet another symptom of the preoccupation of the age with rank and its outward manifestations) 'the Kings and Emperors will judge the difference between the . . . princes of lesser rank, and will assign to each his place, which they will accept, as is to be presumed, with good will'. A gathering of this kind could easily produce a general peace, for 'all the said princes will swear to hold as inviolable law what could be ordained by the majority of votes in the said assembly, and to pursue with arms those who would wish to oppose it'.[31]

All this of course was totally impracticable. The idea that the great rulers of Asia and Africa (Crucé included Japan, India and Morocco in his plan) could ever be induced to send ambassadors to a congress of this kind in Europe, or that there could be meaningful negotiations with most of them if they did, was the wildest fantasy. Even the assumption that the European rulers would all accept without demur any scheme of precedence was ludicrously optimistic. Yet the book is something of a landmark. For the first time a European writer had thought in terms of something which might be called a system of world politics, one in which non-European states and societies were as important as, sometimes more important than, European ones. In particular the degree of attention which Crucé gives to the Turks, and his balanced and even favourable estimate of them, are a striking break with the still prevalent view which saw them as the irreconcilable enemies of Christianity and Europe. In another respect also, though less strikingly, he showed himself forward-looking. He had a high opinion of the importance of trade as a force uniting different states and societies and wished to foster economic development generally, in part at least because of the pacifying influences it represented. Like many seventeenth and early eighteenth-century figures – Sully, Colbert and Peter I of Russia are obvious examples – he was particularly attracted by ambitious canal-building schemes and suggested several – a canal through southern France to join the Atlantic to the Mediterranean, and others to join the Rhine and Danube and the Volga and Don.[32] This emphasis on trade and technological achievement as stepping-stones to international harmony, though it sits strangely with the grandiose visions elsewhere in his book, seems almost a foreshadowing, though a faint and undeveloped one, of many of the liberal and radical assumptions of two centuries later.[33]

No other seventeenth-century writer put forward a scheme of

31. *The New Cyneas* . . ., pp. 120, 122.
32. *The New Cyneas* . . ., pp. 64, 66.
33. See below, pp. 241–2, 251.

international organisation comparable in scope to those of Sully and
Crucé. There were still those who hoped that some form of political
cooperation might be based on the restoration of religious unity, or at
least the establishment of religious toleration, in Europe. It has been
argued that the French writer Jean Bodin, because of his advocacy in the
later sixteenth century of the subordination of religious antagonisms to
political needs, deserves recognition as one of the pioneers of modern
strivings for international peace;[34] while almost a century later the great
Czech educational pioneer Jan Amos Comenius hoped for a unification of
Europe, and eventually of the whole world, to be based on tolerance and
a religious federation which would unite all churches in following Christ.
This in turn would emerge from the proper education of the young. Such
fundamental changes Comenius envisaged as being carried out by regional
assemblies, each reforming its own area, which would report to a general
one representing all the peoples of Europe; but these arrangements were
left very vague. In one respect he broke new ground. Since the unity he
sought was largely an intellectual one he suggested that it be supported by
the teaching of a universal 'philosophical' language developed specifically
as a medium of international communication. The suggestion, one of
many signs of the widespread seventeenth-century interest in new and
logically structured synthetic languages, had no effect whatever; but it is
perhaps the first recognition that any form of internationalism which
involved peoples as well as governments would have linguistic
implications and present linguistic problems.[35] At the other extreme from
this sweeping idealism was the cautious and limited approach of a number
of international lawyers. This still centred on the well-worn concept of
arbitration. Grotius himself spoke of the need to 'hold certain conferences
of Christian powers, where those who have no interest at stake may settle
the disputes of others, and where, in fact, steps may be taken to compel
parties to accept peace on fair terms'.[36] A generation or more later the
German jurist Samuel Rachel suggested that the European states should

> erect, of their own motion, by common agreement, a College of Fecials [the
> *fetiales* were the Roman priest-heralds concerned with the rites involved in the
> declaration of war and conclusion of peace] wherein, as a necessary first step,
> controversies which have arisen between States should be cognized and argued

34. Prutz, *Die Friedensidee* . . ., pp. 86–107.
35. These ideas of Comenius are summarised in Anna Heyberger, *Jean Amos Comenius
(Komensky): Sa vie et son oeuvre d'éducation* (Paris, 1928), pp. 193–5, on which this paragraph is
based. His best-known plea for international harmony, *The Angel of Peace* (New York, 1944;
the book was first published in Latin in 1667) is essentially a demand, buttressed by many
biblical quotations, for religious toleration and the reconciliation of the different Christian
churches.
36. *De Jure Belli et Pacis* (Oxford, 1925), ii, 563.

and decided, in sort that nothing save necessity would open the way to war, it being undertaken only against those who have declined to obey a judgement rendered, or who in other ways have shown contumacy towards the authority and decrees of this College.[37]

All these hopes and aspirations had to be set, nevertheless, against a political background hopelessly unfavourable to their realisation. Any scheme meant to bring order into relations between the European states still depended totally for its success on the support of a small number of major rulers. Yet the dynastic and territorial ambitions of these rulers, who saw war as a natural and inescapable aspect of political life and as usually the most obvious road to personal fame and success, were the most important of the engines which drove international relations. No earlier age had been so deeply affected as this by a dense network of dynastic claims and conflicts. Schemes for perpetual peace or proposals for compulsory arbitration of disputes had no influence whatever on these rulers or their ministers, the handful of men whose decisions determined events. Moreover, the prevalent belief that their policies ought to be determined by 'reason of state', that geography, tradition, most fundamentally of all the innate characteristics of different peoples, dictated to each government particular lines of policy from which any departure was dangerous, was profoundly hostile to any radical new departure in international affairs. 'Reason of state' was founded on deeply backward-looking assumptions. It assumed that these correct policies had been evolved over time by a process of trial and error. More particularly, it took for granted the existence of a set of traditional hostilities, rooted in nature and consecrated by time (most clearly between French and Spaniards, less clearly but still importantly between French and English, Swedes and Danes, Spaniards and Portuguese, Russians and Poles)[38] which no statesman could overcome or safely ignore. An outlook of this kind, pseudo-historical and pessimistic, was implicitly hostile to any sort of international idealism.

## THE EIGHTEENTH CENTURY: ESCAPE FROM THE STATE OF NATURE?

Just as the generations between Louis XIV and the French revolution saw old-regime diplomacy and theorising about the balance of power at their

37. *De Jure Naturae et Gentium Dissertationes* (Washington, 1916; first published Kiel, 1676), ii, 223–4. For a summary of these proposals by Grotius and others see P. Foriers, 'L'Organization de la paix chez Grotius et l'école de droit naturel', *Receuils de la Société Jean Bodin*, xv, *La Paix* (Brussels, 1961), 351–6.

38. See above, pp. 157–8.

height, so also they saw the apogee of ambitious schemes of international organisation. The nineteenth century, or at least its second half, was to see more widespread and effective public interest in the problems of peace and war. But the hopes and schemes then put forward, simply because they were usually more realistic and took more account of difficulties, have not held the attention of posterity as some of those produced during the last generations of pre-revolutionary Europe managed to do.

It is not surprising that ambitious programmes of this kind should appear more frequently in the eighteenth century than ever before. A consciousness of some genuine underlying unity of Europe, a belief that the states which made it up were all in some sense members of a single family, was now more powerful than in the past. The pervasive influence, though with great variations between different parts of the continent, of a high culture based on French models and the French language[39] did much to strengthen such attitudes. The weakening of religious antagonisms and still incomplete development of national ones which fostered discussion of the balance of power[40] also encouraged a feeling that this essential unity could, given goodwill on the part of rulers and governments, take some effective institutional form. Balance of power thinking and ambitious schemes of international organisation were at bottom irreconcilable. Logically each excluded the other. Yet both were the product of an age in which an appeal to reason, rising above religious or national hatreds, seemed the obvious way to discuss international problems. The reasoning of the advocate of the balance of power was based largely on history and experience. These showed, it could be claimed, that some form of balance alone could restrain the powerful and protect the weak. The protagonist of international organisation denied this: for him the balance was at best ineffective and at worst no more than a fig-leaf covering the destructive ambitions of rulers and their ministers. His arguments, most often, were based on the cruelty and destructiveness of war, on an essential humanitarianism in face of the loss and suffering it caused. This might be accompanied by a restatement of the venerable argument that conflict between Christians was sinful, by a humanistic claim that war was a betrayal of man's highest nature, or by more utilitarian efforts to show that no gain which could be reasonably expected from it could compensate for the inescapable losses it caused. But on both sides the appeal was essentially to reason, though to a reason which took different and conflicting forms.

39. See amongst much other writing on this L. Réau, *L'Europe française au siècle des lumières* (Paris, 1933; new edn, 1971). A series of quotations illustrating this intensified sense of cultural identity can be found in F.S. Ruddy, *International Law in the Enlightenment: The Background of Emmeric de Vattel's Le Droit des Gens* (Dobbs Ferry, 1975), pp. 51–3.
40. See above, pp. 166–7.

## Escape from the state of nature: Saint-Pierre, Bentham, Kant

Most eighteenth-century schemes of international organisation (like most of any age) started from the assumption, explicit or not, that the states of Europe were still in a 'state of nature' with respect to each other. Their policies were thus the product of selfish ambitions and of the fear and distrust which these ambitions inevitably bred. While this situation lasted they would continue to injure one another and ruin their subjects. An escape from this dismal situation must be found. It could take the form, as the schemes attributed to Sully and Crucé had already argued, only of some authority superior to these states and with the ability to control their behaviour. The balance of power had not led to peace and never would. For this some kind of international government or at least international institutions, in particular a court of law, were essential. Just as individual men had escaped from the dangers and miseries of their first natural condition by surrendering some of their rights to a higher authority and thus creating societies, so states must also enter into some form of social contract which would make possible the peaceful settlement of disputes between them. Peace, wrote the Quaker William Penn in his *Essay towards the Present and Future Peace of Europe*, one of the first schemes of this period which appeared in 1693, depended on justice, which in turn depended on government. But government in its turn 'was the result of society, which first came of a reasonable design in men of peace'. States must therefore combine to form a society with its own government and surrender to it some of their powers, as in the remote past individuals had done.[41]

This was not a new idea. Earlier writers, notably Grotius, had already urged the need for some such arrangement. But the concept of a social contract binding states and monarchs was now more attractive than ever before; and the claim that the existing inter-state anarchy in Europe marked the continent as still in some respects shamefully primitive was now being more freely made than in the past. To the Abbé de Saint-Pierre, for example, who produced at the end of the Spanish Succession war the best-known and most influential of all eighteenth-century peace projects, the European states were in the position of 'Heads of Families among Savages, who live without law', or of 'the petty Kings of Africa' or 'the miserable Caciques, or petty Sovereigns of America'.[42] From the last years of the seventeenth century, therefore, Europe saw a steady stream of proposals for the restructuring of

41. *The Peace of Europe, the Fruits of Solitude, and other Writings*, Everyman edn, pp. 7–8.
42. C. de Saint-Pierre, *A Project for settling an Everlasting Peace in Europe* (London, 1739), p. 3. Of this famous project, which went through a number of somewhat varying editions, the first two volumes appeared in 1713 at Utrecht and the third was printed at Lyons in 1717 but published under the false imprint of Utrecht.

international relations; and the typical form this endeavour took was that of a scheme for the creation of some authority superior to and controlling the individual states.[43]

As a rule these schemes harked back to the essential idea underlying the projects of Podiebrad, Sully and Crucé – that of some kind of European federation controlled by a central council made up of representatives of all its component states. It was possible, after all, to argue that there had for long existed in Europe viable federal structures – the cumbersome Dutch republic, the very loose grouping of the Swiss cantons, even the more and more ineffective Holy Roman Empire – and that this showed that some similar association covering the entire continent was a practical possibility. Saint-Pierre made such a claim: Jeremy Bentham was to echo it three-quarters of a century later.[44] Inevitably, however, the numerous schemes put forward during the 'long' eighteenth century between the 1690s and Waterloo differed very much, not merely in the details of the new structures they suggested but in the standpoints from which they were written. Some were very brief and vague, little more than generalities or pious hopes. The sketchiest of all was the suggestion thrown out early in the century by Fénelon for some unspecified kind of assembly of states meeting at three-year intervals so that rulers could renew any alliances they might have made and discuss matters of common interest.[45] Rather similarly, in 1776 the English radical Richard Price suggested in very general terms the creation of a senate in which all the states of Europe would be represented: this would have power to act in all their common concerns and arbitrate in disputes between them. But this proposal also, made in passing in a discussion of quite different issues, put no flesh on these very bare bones. In particular Price did not elaborate at all on his suggestion that the senate, to make good in practice its decisions, should have at its disposal 'the common force of the states'.[46] A generation later in France another writer was even more unspecific, ending a vague and rhetorical pamphlet with a call merely for a 'confédération défensive' of the powers to maintain an international order based on natural law and the law of nations.[47]

43. P. Schrecker, 'Leibniz, ses idées sur l'organization des relations internationales', *Proceedings of the British Academy*, xxiii (1937), 218–19.

44. Saint-Pierre, *Project*, Preface, p. iv. He argued particularly that the fact that 'all the Sovereignties of Germany' had formed 'a permanent Society' showed that the same was possible for the European states in general (pp. 23–45). J. Bentham, *A Plan for an Universal and Perpetual Peace* (London, 1927), p. 27. This scheme, not published until a decade after Bentham's death in 1832, was drawn up in 1786–89.

45. *Les Aventures de Télémaque* (Paris, 1920 edn), Bk. xi, p. 48.

46. R. Price, *Observations on the Nature of Civil Liberty* (London, 1776), pp. 8–9.

47. Baron J. Enchasseriaux, *Tableau politique de l'Europe au commencement du XIXe siècle, et moyens d'assurer la durée de la paix générale* (Paris, 1802), pp. 59–60.

Some proposals were even more visionary, clearly the work of
moralists or enthusiasts with no grasp of political realities. Such was the
suggestion of a convict, Gargaz, for a congress at Lyons to which each
European sovereign was to send one 'mediator'. As soon as ten of these
had assembled, provided that at least five of them represented hereditary
sovereigns (this condition reflects the continuing assumption of the
inferiority of any mere elected ruler) they were to 'pass judgement, by a
plurality of votes, upon all the differences of their Masters', with the
president, the agent of the oldest hereditary sovereign represented, having
a casting vote.[48] But a project of this kind, again, had no more than
curiosity value. The same is true of the scheme of another French writer,
Ange Goudar, who in 1757, in his *La Paix de l'Europe ne peut s'établir qu'à
la suite d'une longue trêve*, proposed that the states of Europe simply agree
not to go to war on any pretext for the next twenty years. If any broke
this agreement all the others would unite against the delinquent; and
during this twenty-year truce peace would take root and become a habit
which states were unlikely to break.[49] The confusion of means and ends
here is too glaring to need comment.

The summit of visionary unreality was reached during the French
revolution in the dream of the German revolutionary Anacharsis Cloots of
a coming integral unity of all humanity, irrespective of race, religion or
language, to be achieved spontaneously without political action or
organisation. 'Everyone', he wrote, 'will hasten to mingle in the great
society, to share its benefits, to taste its pleasures and to avoid being
influenced unfavourably by it. The economies will be immense, the costs
light, and the happiness unlimited.' He went on to claim that 'this happy
tendency of men of all climes to find, by different means, the common
level given by nature, tells us of the approaching final levelling, the single
nation, the HUMAN PEOPLE'.[50] Even at the height of the revolution this
messianic enthusiasm seemed ridiculous. But it shows that under the
pressure of unprecedented events the drive towards the union of nations
and the ending of war could take forms very different from the moderate
and rationalistic plans of Saint-Pierre and still more Bentham.

Even between the more practical and thoroughly worked-out schemes
the contrasts were still considerable. If some assembly of representatives of

48. P.-A. Gargaz, *A Project of Universal and Perpetual Peace* (New York, 1973), pp. 11–12.
The pamphlet was first published in 1782, by Benjamin Franklin on his private press at Passy.
Gargaz had been condemned in 1761 to serve twenty years in the galleys for murder; he
apparently drew up the project towards the end of his sentence.

49. The proposal is summarised in Souleyman, *The Vision of World Peace* . . ., pp. 95–9.

50. *La République universelle, ou Addresse aux Tyrannicides* (Paris, An IV de la Rédemption,
1792), pp. 18, 189. The same ideas can be found in his *Bases constitutionelles de la république du
genre humain* (Paris, 1793). For the ridicule they aroused see, for example, J.B. Girot,
*représentant de la nation française à Anacharsis Cloots, représentant de l'univers* (Paris, 1792).

all the European states were to be created, should the great non-European or partly-European ones on the continent's eastern periphery, Russia and the Ottoman empire, be included? Penn thought it 'but fit and just' that they should be; and his fellow-Quaker John Bellers some years later agreed, since 'the Muscovites are Christians and the Mahometans Men'.[51] Yet Saint-Pierre, though he included Russia among the eighteen European states which he hoped would form a federal union to preserve peace by arbitration, envisaged the Ottoman empire as merely one of the 'Associates of the Union', together with Morocco and Algiers, and not as a full member.[52] Indeed the 1730s saw some last flickers of the idea, which had underlain many peace proposals from Podiebrad onwards, that the Christian states should compose their own differences by uniting to conquer and divide the Turkish dominions. The author of *Cardinal Alberoni's Scheme for reducing the Turkish Empire to the Obedience of Christian Princes* (London, 1736) envisaged the raising by Christian Europe, under the leadership of the Holy Roman Emperor, of huge forces (an army of 370,000 men, a navy of a hundred ships of the line, forty frigates and a hundred galleys) with which the Turks could be overwhelmed. The conquest of their territories would be followed by a complex partition in which all the European states would share, with the duke of Holstein-Gottorp being established as 'Emperor of Constantinople'. This in turn would lead on to the setting-up in Ratisbon (Regensburg) of a 'Perpetual Dyet' of representatives of the different states. This would settle by majority decision international disputes brought before it and coerce by military action any ruler who refused to accept its decisions. But the discussion of this body and its work is very cursory. Clearly what interested the author was the anti-Turkish war and the ensuing partition: that this might pave the way to ending conflict between the Christian states was to him no more than an afterthought. Almost simultaneously a French statesman, the marquis d'Argenson, was also envisaging the destruction of Turkish power. In a memorandum of 1738 he foresaw the imminent collapse of the Ottoman empire and its conquest by the Christian states of Europe. These, he hoped, would divide it peacefully between themselves and re-establish Christian rule in Greece and parts of Asia Minor. If the peace could be kept in Europe (he seems here to assume, though the wording is vague, that Saint-Pierre's scheme or something like it would be put into effect) its major states could then turn their attention to gaining colonies for themselves in the Near East,

---

51. A. Ruth Fry, *John Bellers, 1654–1725, Quaker, Economist and Social Reformer* (London, 1935), p. 103. This reprints at pp. 89–103 a large part of Bellers' *Some Reasons for an European State* (1710).

52. *Project . . .*, p. 159.

probably first of all in Egypt, like those they already possessed in America and the East Indies. This would help forward the europeanisation and Christianisation of the world, a process in which the building of a Suez canal under international control would clearly be crucial.[53] Schemes of international organisation which were unmistakably pacifist, such as those of Penn and Bellers, can thus, at least until well into the eighteenth century, be found side by side with others based on ambitious programmes of conquest and territorial expansion.

Many of the peace projects produced during this period therefore contained large elements of the grossly optimistic, the bombastic and the visionary. Even the philosopher Immanuel Kant, by far the most intellectually distinguished of their authors, does not escape this criticism. His *Vom ewige Friede* (Königsberg, 1795) was not a programme for action by the European states and their rulers but rather a statement of Kant's own beliefs about human nature and the possibility of constructing a political framework within which its higher aspects could develop and have free play. Kant was an admirer of both the American and French revolutions and his pamphlet was particularly influenced by the hopes aroused by the latter; but he did not expect his ideas to have any practical effect, at least in the short term. In the end peace must triumph, since it was part of the natural order of things; but this would happen only in the long, perhaps very long, run.[54] War he saw as inevitable within a system of independent sovereign states; yet at the same time it could not be reconciled with the essential moral nature of man. The solution to this dilemma, for him, was to be found not so much in any scheme of international organisation, any creation of supranational structures or international armed forces, as in the growth within states of 'republican' institutions. By this he meant those which were free and representative rather than republican in any strict constitutional sense, and in particular a separation of executive from legislative power. Greater freedom of this kind for the peoples of Europe, which would give them greater control of their own destinies and allow their higher moral aspirations to assert themselves, would make them less likely to be drawn into conflict and more resistant to calls to war of any kind. This peaceful and moral world, moreover, was most likely to emerge in small political units: in them man's moral nature could develop and flourish much more easily than in great states with extensive territories. The essential, in other words, was not so much to organise or regulate the relations between states but rather to moralise them. This was a powerful statement of a particular point of

---

53. *Journal et mémoires du Marquis d'Argenson*, ed. J.B. Rathery (Paris, 1859–67), i, 361–7.

54. J.T. Johnson, *The Quest for Peace: Three Moral Traditions in Western Cultural History* (Princeton, 1987), pp. 193–8.

view; and its linking of peace between states to political freedom within them, and to the full realisation of the moral potentialities of the individual, was a theme which was to recur frequently in various forms in later writing.

Not all propounders of schemes for the consolidation of international peace were vague or visionary, however. A good many were fairly specific about the sort of international institutions they hoped to create. Penn, for example, proposed a central supranational body on which states would be represented in proportion to their wealth (though with no suggestion as to how this might be measured). It would have ninety members in all, ranging from the twelve representatives of the states of the Holy Roman Empire (with no indication of how these were to be chosen) down to the single ones sent by the duchies of Holstein and Courland. It was to take decisions only by at least a three-quarters majority and to use either Latin or French as the language of its deliberations.[55] To constitute the 'Annual Congress, Senate, Dyet, or Parliament' which he proposed, Bellers suggested dividing Europe into a hundred cantons (or some other number if this seemed more effective) each returning one member, so that every existing state sent at least a single representative. Each canton was to raise 'upon any Public Occasion' a contingent of 1,000 soldiers or an equivalent in money or ships. This, he claimed, would ensure 'that the Strong may not refuse to associate with the Weak, to preserve the Public Peace'.[56] The complexities of reconciling this superficially neat division into cantons with existing state boundaries, however, he did not attempt to disentangle. Saint-Pierre envisaged a smaller central body, a senate with twenty-four members, each with a single vote, and that states would contribute to its expenses in proportion to their wealth (again with no indication of how this principle could be applied in practice). The senate would settle disputes between the member-states 'by Arbitral Judgement by Plurality of voices provisionally, and by three-fourths of the Voices definitively'; but the crucial question of how such judgements were to be enforced he left completely open.[57] A rather similar but much less well-known French scheme published anonymously in 1745, *Projet d'un nouveau Système de l'Europe*, made it clear that the congress of representatives of European sovereigns which it envisaged would have at its disposal armed forces paid for by the contributions of the member-states. It would therefore be able to compel reluctant rulers to join the union as well as to enforce, if necessary by coercion, its decisions (taken by a three-fourths majority) on disputes submitted to it.

55. Penn, *The Peace of Europe* . . ., pp. 10–12.
56. Fry, *John Bellers* . . ., pp. 92–3.
57. *A Project* . . ., pp. 106–33 gives the Fundamental Articles of his scheme.

There was a broad similarity between these schemes. All called for an association of states united by some kind of central representative body able to control or coerce recalcitrant members. This was by no means the only possible model: the messianism of Cloots and the moralising of Kant clearly departed from it. So in a quite different way did the much more limited and pragmatic scheme produced by Jeremy Bentham in the later 1780s. This centred around two fundamental demands: for the reduction of armed forces to a low and fixed level, and for the abandonment by the European states of all their overseas colonies. His proposals had thus a much narrower focus than many earlier plans; an international assembly of the kind thought essential by Penn, Bellers, Saint-Pierre and many others had no part in them. Bentham sought peace by limiting the foreign commitments of states rather than by imbuing them with moral principles as Kant was to urge a few years later. In so far as any state was to be subject to formal control this would be exercised by a 'Common Court of Judicature' which could hear and settle disputes. But it was to have no coercive power: on this Bentham was uncompromising. Any international armed force of the kind so often suggested by his predecessors was quite foreign to his thinking. Instead the court would be able, if freedom of the press were established everywhere, to mobilise with great effect the new force of public opinion in support of its decisions. Merely by giving publicity to its judgements it would gain the backing of ordinary intelligent men, no longer blinded by ignorance, prejudice and false ideas of state interests and national honour. A free flow of information, combined with man's natural reasonableness, would defeat the forces which produced destructive and futile conflict. Colonial empires Bentham saw as a particularly clear illustration of the irrationality of existing international relations. They were a fruitful cause of war (here he is thinking of the Anglo-French imperial struggles which had reached their climax in the 1750s and early 1760s). They were seldom, if ever, really profitable to the mother-country. Possession of them complicated its government, and appointments in them, made for personal or party reasons, generated corruption. Most serious of all, they confused and misled peoples, blinding them to their true interests. In a state with a great overseas empire 'the stock of national intelligence is deteriorated by the false notions which must be kept up, in order to prevent the nation from opening its eyes and insisting upon the enfranchisement of the colonies'.[58]

This was, as might be expected from an author so opinionated and suspicious of received beliefs of any kind, one of the most idiosyncratic of the peace plans of the period. Its demand for substantial disarmament by

58. *A Plan for an Universal and Perpetual Peace*, p. 17.

the European states was not without parallels. Bellers, three-quarters of a
century before, had called for limitation of armed forces; and Kant a few
years later was to propose the progressive abolition over a period of all
standing armies.[59] But in the peace proposals of the eighteenth century in
general disarmament played no role comparable to that it was to achieve
from the 1870s or even the 1860s onwards.[60] The idea of controlling the
aggressive ambitions of the states solely or mainly by judicial means, by
the authority of some kind of international court, can also be paralleled in
other schemes, now totally forgotten, of the eighteenth century.[61]
Bentham's hostility to colonial empires, again, was to be echoed by Kant;
while Saint-Pierre, though he did not ask for their abandonment, had
argued that they were usually valueless or even a source of loss to the
states which possessed them.[62] Indeed Bentham's attitude on this issue can
be seen as merely one of many illustrations of the growing radical dislike
during the later eighteenth century, on both moral and material grounds,
of colonial possessions. This dislike found its most persuasive literary
expression in the Abbé Raynal's *Histoire . . . des Etablissements et du
Commerce des Européens dans les deux Indes* (1770) and was strengthened by
the successful assertion of independence by Britain's American colonies.
The clearest echo of Bentham's ideas came in the early nineteenth
century, when his most important direct disciple, the Scotsman James
Mill, in an article published in the *Encyclopaedia Britannica*, repeated his call
for the drawing up of a code of international law and the creation of an
international tribunal to interpret it and judge disputes between states.
Here can be seen once more a naively confident reliance on the ability of
mass opinion, mobilised by all the available engines of publicity, to give
effect to the decisions of such a tribunal. Like Bentham, Mill set his face
firmly against any coercion of a recalcitrant government. But each verdict
of the tribunal he proposed, he had no doubt, would 'fix and concentrate
the disapprobation of mankind'; and in making these verdicts widely
known 'publicity should be carried to the highest practicable perfection'.
All this would be enough to ensure that most of them at least were

59. Fry, *John Bellers . . .*, p. 94; I. Kant, *Perpetual Peace, a Philosophical Essay* (London, 1903), pp. 110–11.
60. See below, pp. 260–1.
61. For those put forward in Germany by Johann von Palthen in his *Projekt, einen immerwährenden Frieden zu erhalten* (1758) and K.G. Gunther in his *Europäischer Völkerrecht zu Friedenszeiten* (1787) – though the latter, unlike Bentham, wanted his court of arbitration to enforce by coercion obedience to its verdicts – see V. Valentin, *Geschichte des Völkerbundgedankens in Deutschland* (Berlin, 1920), p. 93.
62. Kant, *Perpetual Peace*, pp. 139–42; Saint-Pierre, *Project*, pp. 142–3.

obeyed. He even proposed that the code of international law applied by the tribunal and select cases brought before it be studied in all schools.[63]

## Late eighteenth-century radicalism: the Physiocrats

Bentham stands somewhat apart from the main current of eighteenth-century thinking on the problem of international peace. None the less, his insistence that disputes between states should be settled by judicial decision and not by political action, combined with his rather narrow utilitarian and materialist view of the subject (for example in his indifference, unlike many earlier writers, to religion as a significant bond between the European states) mark him out as a leading representative of an attitude now being more and more widely expressed in the Atlantic world. It is no accident that his pamphlet supports its argument with many illustrations drawn from Anglo-French relations but completely ignores the great problems of eastern Europe, those of Poland and the Ottoman Empire, which bulked so large when he was writing. The growing radical tradition in international relations, of which Bentham and Mill were a somewhat idiosyncratic part, had one of its roots in the isolationist feeling which had always been strong in Britain, and which was to become still more powerful in the new American republic.[64] British dislike of European commitments and of spending money on foreign alliances, a widespread feeling that clearly identifiable commercial interests were alone worth fighting for, provide the background to Bentham's desire to keep foreign policy within narrow utilitarian limits. Side by side with these traditional and almost instinctive British attitudes there emerged among French intellectuals from the 1760s onwards the belief, articulated in a more sophisticated but no less dogmatic way, that commercial ties between states and the material benefits they brought were the only effective means of ending international conflict. 'The natural effect of commerce', wrote Montesquieu in mid-century, 'is to promote peace. Two nations which do business together make themselves dependent on one another'.[65] A few years later the Physiocrats (the school of writers on economics and indirectly on politics so prominent in France from the later years of Louis XV) gave this attitude a more sharply defined and intellectualised form. Central to their thinking was the belief in an

---

63. 'The Article Law of Nations, reprinted from the Supplement to the *Encyclopaedia Britannica*', in *Essays* . . . .. (London, 1828), pp. 31–2.

64. The best general discussion of these developing late eighteenth-century attitudes to international relations is F. Gilbert, *To the Farewell Address* (Princeton, 1961), on which the following paragraphs are largely based. Its conclusions are summarised in the same author's 'The "New Diplomacy" of the Eighteenth Century', *World Politics*, iv (1951–52).

65. *Oeuvres*, ed. A. Masson (Paris, 1950–55), i, 445–6.

underlying harmony, not merely between individuals or groups within a state but between states themselves, a harmony rooted in the nature of the world which would quickly show itself once the artificial obstacles which opposed and impeded it had been removed. This led them logically to advocate free trade as the most effective means of overcoming the antagonisms which had for so long divided Europe. Such an attitude had some affinities with the simpler Anglo-Saxon belief that commercial success and growing national wealth were the only worthwhile objectives of foreign policy, at least as commercial success began slowly to be identified with freer international trade. By the later eighteenth century, therefore, the still largely embryonic free trade movement had become, in the eyes of some of its adherents, also a movement for international peace. Indeed to them it seemed the only effective such movement. Free trade, accompanied by free movement of men and ideas, would bind states and societies together as paper plans and artificial supranational institutions never could. In the generation before the French revolution a body of essential ideas can be seen to have been taking shape which were to inspire radicals of many differing shades, from Cobden and Proudhon downwards, in the century which followed.[66]

This exaltation of the economic factors in international relations and downgrading of political ones meant that Physiocrats in France and utilitarians and radicals in England united in a very hostile view of the practices and institutions of diplomacy as these had now developed. To them the diplomatic system which Europe had evolved over the last three centuries seemed at best an unnecessary nuisance and at worst a positive threat to peace. If trade and the exchange of material advantages were the real links between states what need was there for diplomacy? After all, claimed (very inaccurately) many of the Physiocrats, Venice and the Dutch republic had flourished over long periods by avoiding political alliances and basing their international position on trade alone. In the future states might be able to do without any political agreements at all; in a reformed world, simpler and more natural, trade treaties alone would be needed.

To men who thought in this way there were many features of the international scene which were unattractive in themselves and dangerous in their possible consequences. The balance of power, they agreed, was a delusion and potentially a very destructive one. Aggressive and expansionist ambitions of any kind they completely rejected. More particularly, martial glory and territorial conquest seemed to them merely the selfish ambitions of rulers and their ministers and generals. A systematic playing-down and ridiculing of the military virtues had been

66. See pp. 192–3, 243, 273ff.

characteristic of much of the Enlightenment in France; and this attitude was still strong in the years before the revolution. Already Voltaire in his *Dictionnaire Philosophique* of 1764 had dismissed war as the outcome of nothing more than 'the imagination of three or four hundred persons spread over the surface of the globe under the name of princes or ministers'.[67] A generation later this attitude was if anything more widespread. Monarchs and their hangers-on made wars: the people were naturally peace-loving and, once given the power to do so, would render them a thing of the past.

There was also considerable hostility among radical reformers to the secrecy which traditionally shrouded so much diplomacy. Bentham demanded that it be opened to public scrutiny, while the revolution in France released vociferous demands for much more effective control of it by some elected body such as the diplomatic committee set up by the Legislative Assembly which ruled for a year from the autumn of 1791 onwards.[68] Many radicals, again, were deeply hostile to the aristocratic privilege and exclusiveness which still enveloped traditional diplomatic practice. To them the foreign policy of a state was at bottom merely an expression of its social structure and forms of government; here Kant was in essence following their lead. It was wrong to regard it as of primary importance and having a life and validity of its own independent of the society which produced it. 'Flatterers', wrote in 1765 a French statesman strongly influenced by the philosophes, 'persuade princes that internal affairs should merely serve external ones; but duty tells them the opposite'.[69] This insistence on the essentially secondary and dependent nature of foreign policy was a sharp break with the past. It challenged the assumption, generally accepted in the seventeenth and most of the eighteenth centuries, that the foreign policy of a state, though it might be powerfully influenced by its geographical position or the inherent characteristics of its inhabitants, had little to do with the structure of its government or society. Yet in the nineteenth century it was to become a commonplace of many forms of political and social radicalism. To those who thought in this way it seemed that a more rational and equal society of the sort which the French revolution sought to achieve could not be represented abroad by a diplomatic service rooted in a monarchical and aristocratic past. In the extreme case this feeling could become a demand

67. *Oeuvres*, xix (Paris, 1879), 318.
68. Bentham, *A Plan* . . ., pp. 31ff.; for France see for example *Opinion de F. Lobjoy, ancien maire de Colligis, député de l'Aisne, sur la nécessité d'organiser le département des affaires étrangères dans le sens de la Constitution* (Paris, 1792), pp. 12–13. This little-known pamphlet illustrates well many aspects of the 'enlightened' criticism of conventional diplomacy.
69. Quoted in Gilbert, 'The "New Diplomacy" . . . ', 7.

for the abolition of what one radical called 'this feudal mish-mash (*cette bigarrure féodale*), of diplomatic ranks and its replacement by a service in which all diplomats ranked equally.[70]

All this, in other words, came close to the assertion that the best of all foreign policies was to have no foreign policy at all. Few writers made such a claim explicitly; but even as early as the 1750s one, himself a deposed monarch, in one of the imaginary voyages which were so popular a vehicle for radical criticism of European societies and institutions, clearly expressed such a feeling through the Brahmin he used as a mouthpiece. 'In my opinion', said this critic, 'the best policy in the government of states as in the conduct of life is to have none, and to make use in all one does only of the means which common sense provides and reason authorises'.[71] Many of the ideologues of the French revolution would have been in complete agreement.

The second half of the eighteenth century thus saw the emergence of an important, in some ways fundamental, split in the forces which strove to end or reduce conflict between states. On the one hand were those who, in the tradition of Podiebrad, Sully, Crucé or Saint-Pierre, believed that progress was to be achieved through organisation, through the deliberate and conscious application of human ingenuity to the problem of building a lasting peace. To them the creation of at least some minimum of international institutions seemed essential. Opposed to this attitude stood those to whom harmony between different states and societies was not in any fundamental way difficult to achieve. In their eyes it was not something which needed to be organised or planned for. Rather it was immanent in the nature of men and the world, something which would show itself as soon as the artificial obstacles which had so far stultified it, the monarchical, aristocratic and military influences which had hitherto deformed the life of mankind, were removed. This feeling, strongest of all in the new American republic, was now influential in western Europe also. In a variety of forms and with differing shades of emphasis it was to remain strong for a century to come. These two aspirations towards a peaceful future were not, of course, irreconcilable. Indeed they could well be mutually supportive. A coming together of peoples united by the natural and unforced bonds of trade and intellectual intercourse might be a very powerful support for deliberately created international institutions. But the aspirations were different; and it was in the later eighteenth century that the deep difference between them first revealed itself.

70. *Opinion de F. Lobjoy* . . ., pp. 13–16.
71. (Stanislaus I, former King of Poland), *Entretien d'un européen avec un insulaire du royaume de Dumocala* (n.p. , 1752), pp. 50–1.

*Confronting the real world*

Eighteenth-century comment on the problem of international peace, for all its unprecedented copiousness and variety, had little influence on the rulers and ministers who directed relations between the states of Europe. The dismissive remark of Frederick II to Voltaire in 1742 that to become effective Saint-Pierre's proposals needed only 'the agreement of Europe and a few other trifles'[72] was merely a typically acerbic statement of the attitude of them all. Nor were most intellectuals much better disposed. Though Saint-Pierre continued to press his scheme on statesmen and to write about the problem of international peace until his death in 1743, not merely a habitually destructive critic such as Voltaire but so great and potentially sympathetic a figure as Leibniz criticised and ridiculed his ideas.[73] Moreover, any idea of lasting peace as a practical possibility seemed finally to be exposed as naive by the unprecedented scale and destructiveness of the great cycle of wars unleashed after 1792. Friedrich von Gentz, a disillusioned former believer in many of the revolutionary ideals, could thus argue with much apparent justification, in a pamphlet of 1800, that the entire concept was impractical and even nonsensical. Individual states, he contended, would never allow any supranational authority to have powers or forces superior to their own; and in any case war was necessary and natural, since 'the state of nature is the state of war'[74] and conflict, by providing an outlet for the hatred and aggression inherent in man, made possible at least some intervals of peace. Pessimism of this kind, which was widely shared, shows how far internationalist idealism, shaken by the cataclysms of the 1790s, had still to go even after a hundred years of well-intentioned schemes and optimistic dreams. A few signs of its influence on policy-making can be found. The efforts in the 1770s and 1780s of the Grand Duke Leopold of Tuscany to make his territories a permanent and guaranteed neutral in international affairs can be seen as a practical expression of the isolationism and rejection of all unnecessary involvement in diplomatic complications which was an important component of much radical thought. In Denmark the Bernstorffs, uncle and nephew, who conducted the country's foreign policy during most of the period from the 1750s to the 1790s, showed an impressive degree of internationalism and markedly pacific tendencies which perhaps owed something to the intellectual climate of the Enlightenment. But these were small states to some extent above the battle in which greater powers could not avoid engaging; and in the case

---

72. Voltaire, *Oeuvres*, xxxvi (Paris, 1880), 124.

73. J. Drouet, *L'Abbé de Saint-Pierre: l'homme et l'œuvre* (Paris, 1912), pp. 133–4, 137–9.

74. H. Lamm, 'Friedrich Gentz et la paix (De la paix perpetuelle – 1800)', *Revue d'Histoire Diplomatique* (1971), 135.

of Tuscany Leopold could draw upon, and was perhaps influenced by, an already long tradition of neutrality in great-power conflicts. As early as 1691 the completely unenlightened Medici Grand Duke Cosimo III, a Catholic bigot, had signed an agreement with Louis XIV and his major opponents which provided for the neutralisation of Tuscany in the war then in progress between them; and similar conventions were arranged on several occasions during the struggles of the eighteenth century.[75] Moreover, the pacific attitudes of at least the elder Bernstorff were the product of religious feeling more than of enlightened intellectual attitudes.

At a deeper intellectual level the eighteenth century failed to solve or even seriously to confront a fundamental problem. This was an age of change in frontiers and political geography on a scale never seen before. Yet virtually all those who hoped for a peaceful future, most explicitly those who thought in terms of a system of international relations controlled by supranational institutions, assumed that such instability could be more or less completely banished from a future Europe. Saint-Pierre had laid down as the fourth of the Fundamental Articles of his proposed union of states that once it had been formed existing frontiers were not to be changed in any way: even peaceful exchanges of territory were to be made only with the consent of the union. This concern for stability as an ultimate value extended also to the internal government of the states. The union he envisaged was not to intervene in the domestic affairs of any member 'unless it be to preserve the Fundamental Form of it' – that is, hereditary or elective forms of government were to be rigidly safeguarded as they stood without possibility of change: moreover, another article provided for the powers of any monarch to be protected by the union during minorities and regencies. One of the most acute of nineteenth-century commentators on the peace problem expressed well a fundamental though obvious criticism when he complained that Saint-Pierre 'aimed at finality, the realisation of which was an impossible object, and would not have been a just object had it been possible'.[76] The criticism applies equally to a wide range of other schemes of this kind. The anonymous *Projet d'un nouveau Système de l'Europe* of 1745, for example, insisted that the federal union of states which it envisaged must guarantee to all rulers their existing territories. Some small ones which had been recently seized without justification by a stronger neighbour might be returned to their former owners; but in future no frontier changes were to be recognised under any pretext and no future treaty between

75. H. Holldack, 'Die Reformpolitik Leopolds von Toscana', *Historische Zeitschrift*, clxv (1941–42), 39–41.

76. J. Lorimer, *The Institutes of the Law of Nations* (Edinburgh–London, 1883–84), ii, 222–3.

members of the federation was to be valid without the consent of three-quarters of the whole membership. As with Saint-Pierre, resolute opposition to all change extended also to purely domestic affairs: rebellion within any member-state was to be repressed by forces sent for the purpose by the senate of the federal union.[77] The ideas which underlay the Holy Alliance of 1815, though stripped of the religious veneer then given them by Alexander I, were thus already clearly to be seen many decades earlier. The best-known twentieth-century commentator on Saint-Pierre correctly pointed out that he had 'dreamed of a Holy Alliance'.[78] The same concern to avoid change in the political map stands out in the 1757 proposals of Ange Goudar, which insisted that none of the existing European states should ever be allowed to merge with another; while a quarter of a century later Gargaz was equally insistent that once his congress of 'mediators' had met no ruler should be allowed to enlarge his territories or should have them diminished for any reason whatever.[79] Later still Kant himself sounded the same note. The second of his Preliminary Articles of Perpetual Peace between States provided that 'No state having an independent existence – whether it be great or small – shall be acquired by another through inheritance, exchange, purchase or donation'. He, it is true, justified this attitude in higher terms than those of mere expediency. Every state, in his eyes, was a moral person; and to destroy its separate existence, on whatever pretext, and make it merely part of another was to deprive it of this status and reduce it to a mere object.[80] But the effect was the same: to make the existing international order sacrosanct and immutable.

The deep conservatism of these attitudes was not new. It underlies many of the comments and criticisms of Erasmus and is at least implicit in the proposals of Sully and Crucé. It was also inevitable. The easiest and most obvious way of preserving peace and maintaining stability, after all, is usually to leave things so far as possible as they are: change must always imply at least the possibility of conflict. But as schemes of international organisation multiplied, the difficulty (which had also become clear in at least some discussions of the balance of power)[81] of reconciling much-desired stability with unavoidable change, of creating any lasting peace which allowed the continent to adapt to the play of new forces, became clearer. To this fundamental problem the nineteenth century, almost as much as the eighteenth, provided no satisfactory answer.

77. Souleyman, *The Vision of World Peace* . . ., pp. 92–5.
78. Drouet, *L'Abbé de Saint-Pierre*, p. 125.
79. Souleyman, *The Vision of World Peace*, pp. 97–9; Gargaz, *A Project* . . ., p. 15.
80. *Perpetual Peace*, pp. 108–10.
81. See above, p. 179.

## THE NINETEENTH CENTURY: HOPES AND REALITIES

### (1) Vienna to Sedan: peace societies and utopias

The peace plans of the eighteenth century, or at least the better-known among them, those of Saint-Pierre, Bentham and Kant, have been generously treated by posterity. Historians have given them considerable attention, more perhaps than their intrinsic importance and their effect in their own day justify. Yet the great age of the quest for lasting international peace was then still far in the future. It was the nineteenth century which saw the emergence for the first time, at least in one or two countries, of a peace movement with significant popular support. It also saw in its later decades a more systematic and conscious use than ever before of international law and quasi-legal methods to support the search for peace. From the 1870s onwards pressures of this kind gained a dynamism and width of appeal hitherto unseen and began even to have some practical importance and to play some role in the thinking of a few statesmen. Until the mid-nineteenth century the peace idea remained no more than an aspiration and an ideal. It was only one strand, often a tenuous one, in the continent's intellectual and emotional life. By the later decades of that century, however, it had acquired new dimensions and become more diverse, more organised and more solidly based. It was now generating demands which, focused and greatly intensified by the unprecedented struggle which began in 1914, were to culminate in the creation of the League of Nations.

*The Vienna settlement and the Congress System* The conflicts of 1792–1815 were equally unprecedented in their own day and it is not surprising that when they ended they left a Europe in which the demand for peace and stability was strong and clearly visible on several different levels. On that of rulers and governments the rivalries seen at the Vienna congress, which at the beginning of 1815 momentarily brought the great powers to the verge of a new war, showed that this desire for peace had very definite limits. Yet hostility to the disruptive revolutionary movements of which France was taken to be the natural centre, fear of 'Jacobins' or 'liberals', and most of all of the new international struggle which it was assumed a major revolution anywhere in Europe must inevitably unleash, were powerful enough to force some cooperation and compromise on the powers. The Holy Alliance, the agreement drawn up and sponsored by Alexander I of Russia and signed in September 1815 by him and the rulers of Prussia and the Habsburg empire, was little more than a paper declaration. The promise of the signatories to make themselves 'a true and indissoluble fraternity' based on the precepts of Christianity meant virtually nothing in practice. Though almost every European government, with that of Britain the only major exception, soon adhered to it, its impact on international relations was negligible. The driving force behind it was little more than the tsar's growing messianism and his desire to increase Russian influence in Europe. The periodic meetings of sovereigns and chief ministers which developed after 1815 promised more. In 1818, when this 'Congress System' was at its height, the British foreign secretary, Lord Castlereagh, was optimistic enough to speak of it as 'extinguishing the cobwebs with which diplomacy obscures the horizon . . . and giving to the counsels of the Great Powers the efficiency and almost the simplicity of a single State'.[82] Yet it lasted for only a few years before inevitable conflicts of interest brought it to an end.

On a less exalted level, however, a willingness of the powers to cooperate effectively sometimes survived considerably longer and achieved some significant, even important, results. Standing conferences of their ambassadors in one of the major capitals set up to handle particular problems were until the end of the 1830s the most constructive practical innovation of the period in international affairs. One such on the abolition of the slave trade was set up in London after the end of the Vienna congress and survived, producing annual reports, until 1820. Another, made up of the ambassadors of Russia, Prussia, the Habsburg Empire and Britain, the powers which had defeated Napoleon, was established in Paris at the beginning of 1816 to observe and supervise the activities of the still not wholly trusted French government: this lasted until the end of 1818. Another met in Paris at the end of 1822 to consider the problems posed by revolution and instability in Spain and continued to function until 1826. Late in 1823 Alexander I tried to create a similar one in St Petersburg to deal with the complications stemming from the Greek revolt of 1821, though Austrian foot-dragging undermined this from the beginning. Yet another met in Rome in 1831 to draw up, with little practical result, a programme of reform for the misgoverned papal state. Much the most important and productive was the ambassadorial conference which, meeting at intervals in London throughout the 1830s, had by 1839 acted successfully as midwife to the new independent kingdom of Belgium. The achievements of these conferences were thus very variable. But that they could go on meeting, often over considerable periods, and sometimes achieve constructive results, shows how the temper of international relations in the age of Metternich differed from what it had been in the era of Louis XIV or Frederick II.

82. C.K. Webster, *The Foreign Policy of Castlereagh, 1815–1822* (London, 1925), p. 153.

The rulers and statesmen of the post-Vienna generation aimed at regulating these relations, not at transforming them. They hoped to make conflicts of interest between the powers less acute and overt, and therefore less dangerous. But they did not dream of ending such conflicts or of creating any supranational authority which could unite the powers effectively or permanently. Underlying their policies, even in the relatively liberal great states of western Europe, Britain and, after 1830, France, was a lurking fear of another devastating cycle of war. Such a conflict might, as in the past, be the result of the rivalries of the powers. But it was at least equally likely to be set off by a serious revolutionary upheaval almost anywhere in Europe. Here can be seen, intensified by the catastrophes of 1792–1815, the instinctive feeling already visible in the eighteenth century, that peace was in some ultimate sense conservative, or at least that it could be safeguarded most easily by unyieldingly conservative policies. This groundswell of belief that political and still more social revolution must threaten international peace survived throughout the nineteenth century. The 1870s, marked spectacularly by the Commune in Paris in 1871 and the populist terrorism in Russia which culminated in the murder of Alexander II a decade later, saw it gain for a time new strength. Not merely a conservative statesman such as Bismarck but writers by no means illiberal were sometimes powerfully influenced by it. One such in Germany, for example, could argue in the 1880s that since in the past every important revolution had led to international conflict it was the duty of those working for peace to destroy or undermine revolutionary forces everywhere in Europe.[83] This was an exact echo, half a century or more later, of the fears which inspired Metternich in the 1820s and 1830s.

*Idealism and the peace societies* The declarations, congresses and ambassadorial conferences of the post-Vienna generation were (apart from the exceptional case of Alexander I) the work of practical men facing more or less immediate problems. All these expedients were therefore directed to essentially short-term purposes. Side by side with them, however, can be found a new outpouring, stronger and more widespread than anything seen in the seventeenth or eighteenth centuries, of idealism and demands for a radical attack on the problem of war. Some of this was essentially legal in temper and hence in a sense traditional. Thus in Germany K.C.F. Krause, in his *Entwurf eines europäischen Staatenbundes* of 1814 called for a union of states, disputes between whom were to be settled by a system of

83. F. von Holtzendorff-Vietmannsdsorff, *Die Idee des ewigen Völkerfriedens* (Berlin, 1882), p. 49.

international law recognised and accepted by all. No individual state was to have the right to wage war; and any which refused to accept a legal verdict given against it was to be expelled from the union. Almost simultaneously another German writer, Arnold Mallinckrodt, in his *Was thun bey Deutschlands, bey Europas Wiedergeburt?* (Dortmund, 1813), urged the creation of a pemanent congress of representatives of the European states and a permanent arbitration tribunal which would apply an agreed code of international law: he hoped also, even more ambitiously, for a code of municipal law common to all states and a common religious organisation for them. A quarter of a century later J.B. Sartorius in his *Organon des volkommenden Friedens* (Zürich, 1837) made rather similar proposals for a union of the European states equipped with a tribunal made up of representatives from all of them, and again applying a recognised international law-code. As a liberal he insisted that their internal political structures' must be democratic, and took the United States as one of the models for the union he desired.[84] The fact that the German world had suffered very badly during the revolutionary and Napoleonic period, combined with the heritage of the Holy Roman Empire and its at least quasi-federal structure, and the genuine cosmopolitanism and width of intellectual vision which were the most attractive features of much German life before the Bismarckian unification, help to explain the production of these and other schemes of international organisation during these years. In essentials, however, they carried on a tradition already fairly well established during the eighteenth century; and none of them attracted any significant popular interest or support.

Two quite different lines of criticism of the existing structure of international relations which began to take root during the same years were more dynamic and, in widely differing ways, emotionally attractive. Both aimed at more than mere patching-up of specific difficulties or temporary smoothing-over of frictions. One, limited in the main to Britain and the United States (in the latter in effect to New England), was the religious pacifism which became extremely vocal during the first half of the century. The other, centred on France, was a utopian and often revolutionary radicalism with dreams of a rationally reordered world. This was the most visionary intellectual current of the age.

The first Peace Society was founded in New York in 1815 and the first British one in June of the following year. By 1819 there were branches in ten towns in England and the movement there had become an active and vocal propaganda force. It began to publish a periodical, *The Herald of*

---

84. These German-language proposals are summarised in Valentin, *Geschichte des Völkerbundgedankens*, pp. 50, 122, 96–105.

*Peace*, in the same year and was already distributing tracts on a large scale. In 1842 it petitioned parliament for the first time, protesting against the wars then being waged by Britain in China and Afghanistan, and by extension against war in general. Elsewhere in Europe organised religious pacifism of this kind had much less appeal. By 1830 peace societies existed in France and Switzerland; but to the French *Société de la Morale Chrétienne* founded in 1821 international peace was only a secondary issue, and no more such groups were created in any continental state until 1867. That pacifism should have been so much more active and appealing in the English-speaking countries is easy to understand. Britain, and still more the United States, enjoyed a very high degree of security against outside attack. In neither was there any feeling that the national interest demanded changes in the international situation of the kind which could be achieved only by war. Both occupied in these respects a highly privileged position. Both therefore could afford the luxury of active pacifist movements.

Also, this religious pacifism clearly provided, in England at least, an outlet for unsatisfied emotions and ambitions. Its most active adherents were inspired by a mystical and messianic faith in the coming of a millenium destined to be crowned by the triumph of Christianity throughout the world. Many of them were deeply conscious of living in an era of change, swift, exciting and with virtually unlimited potentialities. Railways and telegraphs on the technological level, the 1848 revolutions on the political one, gave weight to this feeling, while free trade, with its power to unite the nations by unbreakable ties based on material progress, was sometimes endowed with quasi-millenial properties.[85] At the same time the peace movement, like many of the pressures for change in early Victorian Britain, expressed the resentment of middle-class groups (though in this case commercial, administrative and professional rather than industrial ones) who felt themselves unjustly excluded from political power and social influence. Its adherents thus could easily see it as one aspect of a struggle to wrest greater civil liberty from an unreformed aristocratic ruling class.[86] By the 1840s, therefore, the activity and vociferousness of the movement in Britain contrasted sharply with the relative quiescence of the continental states. The first general Peace Convention, which met in London in 1843, included among its 324 delegates only six from continental Europe; and in the series of even larger meetings which followed – at Brussels in 1848, Paris in 1849,

---

85. A. Tyrrell, 'Making the Millenium: The Mid-Nineteenth Century Peace Movement', *Historical Journal*, 20 (1978), especially pp. 89, 91.
86. E.W. Sager, 'The Social Origins of Victorian Pacifism', *Victorian Studies*, 23 (1980), passim.

Frankfurt in 1850 and London once more in 1851 – the same disparity was to be seen, though in a rather less marked form. The *Times* correspondent described the Frankfurt congress, not very unfairly, as 'Englishmen and Americans . . . talking to each other, diversified by a little sprinkling of Frenchmen and Germans'.[87]

The 1851 London congress was the climax of the Anglo-American peace movement with its radical Protestant (very largely Quaker) roots and its millenial overtones. Its decline thereafter was rapid. The 1850s and 1860s brought a series of crippling setbacks – popular panics in Britain over possible French invasion in 1852 and 1860; the Crimean War and the outbreak of bellicose anti-Russian feeling it aroused; across the Atlantic the civil war of 1861–65. A movement founded on emotion rather than on any structure of ideas was not well placed to withstand such shocks; and by the later 1850s pacifism in Britain had lost much of the self-confidence so apparent only a few years before.

*The utopian radical solution*    French utopian radicalism, the other major form taken by internationalist idealism in the Europe of Metternich, Palmerston and Nicholas I, showed greater staying-power. It was a curious mixture. It combined sometimes striking vision and realism as regarded the longer-term future of international relations with an often childish optimism about the ease and speed with which great changes in society and government could be made. Like the idealists of free trade, those of utopian socialism had no doubt that history was on their side. Economic and technological progress was driving the states of Europe irresistibly towards closer cooperation on all kinds of practical issues. On this material level international contacts could not be left to the mercies of chance or of worn-out myths such as that of the balance of power: they must now be directed and controlled. 'The philosophy of the last century', wrote Saint-Simon, the most original and important of all these thinkers, 'was revolutionary; that of the nineteenth century must be organisational'.[88] A generation later one of his most important disciples was confident that the peace and unity of Europe would inevitably be fostered by a wide variety of indirect means – the spread of representative government; the parallel spread of education; the growth of newspapers, of peace societies, of international congresses and meetings of all kinds.[89] Underpinning all this, however, was the irrestible forward march of modern industry, symbolised

87. Quoted in Tyrrell, 'Making the Millenium', p. 91.

88. C.-H. de Saint-Simon and A. Thierry, *De la réorganisation de la société européenne* (Paris, n.d., 1925; first published 1814), p. 4.

89. C. Pecqueur, *De la paix. De son principe et de sa réalisation* (Paris, 1842), pp. 155–256 passim.

by great public works such as canals and railways whose benefits would be diffused far beyond the frontiers of any single state. The Saint-Simonians from the beginning pinned many of their hopes to such undertakings and the impact both psychological and material which they must have. Mankind, seen from this perspective, was advancing towards an inescapable new order in which the needs and values of industry and science would be paramount. This meant necessarily a close association of the peoples of Europe and an end to war between them. 'The Europe of industry thirsts for peace, for accord and for liberty', claimed another of their most industrious propagandists.[90]

Some of this vision was, at least in the longer term, realistic. The last decades of the century were indeed to see an unprecedented flowering of practical cooperation between states on a very wide range of important bread-and-butter issues.[91] In grasping the inevitability of such a change the radical idealists of the 1820s, 1830s and 1840s showed themselves more aware of the essential drift of European history than statesmen such as Metternich or Palmerston. Yet when they came to discuss the new institutions needed by the union of European peoples which they so eagerly anticipated they slipped at once into wishful thinking and fantasy; and as to how these institutions might be brought into being they were silent or at least extremely vague. Saint-Simon envisaged a union between France and Britain, with the latter, as the more developed of the two, as the senior partner, which would form the nucleus of a wider European whole. (Though he also saw that Germany, once given political unity, would soon be the leader of the continent.) He also called for the creation of a European parliament, though this was to be a markedly élitist body with strict and high property qualifications for membership of both the houses which made it up. The best way of maintaining peace was for this parliament to be continually active in undertaking great public works – for example a canal joining the Rhine and Danube – in encouraging European colonisation and development of other continents, and in supervising public education and enforcing throughout Europe a '*code de morale*' which inculcated the principles on which the unity of the continent must rest.[92] But as to how this union and parliament were to be brought into existence he had nothing to say. In much the same way his follower Constantin Pecqueur envisaged a federal Europe modelled to some extent on the United States with a supranational parliament, armed forces and system of taxation, and with provision for arbitration of disputes between its component states and, if necessary, settlement of them

90. V. Considérant, *La dernière guerre et la paix définitive en Europe* (Paris, 1850), p. 7a.
91. See below, pp. 251–3.
92. Saint-Simon and Thierry, *De la réorganisation* . . ., pp. 47–52.

by an international judicial tribunal; but again how the transition to this ideal future would or could be made was left entirely unclear. Victor-Prosper Considérant, one of the vaguest and most messianic of this vague and messianic school, looked forward to perpetual peace on the basis of a European confederation of free nations, bound together by a great network of railways, roads and canals which 'will form from Cadiz to Petersburg the structure of veins and arteries of the great European body';[93] but he too put this forward as an aspiration, not as a programme.

Like Christian pacifists buoyed up by religious faith, Marxists sustained by a vision of social apocalypse, nationalists fired by trust in popular virtue, or liberals who relied on the more prosaic potentialities of free trade, these utopian socialists, inspired by belief in science and their own kind of rationality, were deeply optimistic. History imposed its own necessities: men could not escape them. Its forward march demanded the unity of Europe and permanent peace between its peoples. Already by the 1830s there can be heard from the Saint-Simonians the argument, destined to acquire considerable influence by the end of the century, that irresistible change was making war impossible. In a Europe more and more bound together by economic and technological progress, it was contended, large-scale conflict would produce so much economic disruption and create so much unemployment and poverty, with the attendant dangers of social upheaval, that no government would resort to it. This idea was by no means new. It had roots in the eighteenth-century Enlightenment; and already a leading French liberal had proclaimed that 'we have arrived at the age of trade, an age which must necessarily replace that of war, as that of war had necessarily to precede it'.[94] But the Saint-Simonians made the point more dogmatically than ever before. In 1832, for example, Michel Chevalier, of them all the one destined to play the most important role in practical politics, argued that among the European powers only Russia, since she alone had not yet reached the industrial stage of economic growth, could want war.[95] By mid-century the belief that peace between nations was indissolubly bound up with social progress and the general advance of civilisation was more than ever before a commonplace among radicals of every shade.[96] Even the realities

93. *La dernière guerre* . . ., p. 11a.

94. *Benjamin Constant et la paix* (Published by *Conciliation Internationale*, 1910), p. 13. This is a reprint of the third (1814) edition of Constant's *L'Esprit de conquête*, a short book which put forward more forcibly than any of its predecessors the argument that a modern state could not gain by even a successful war.

95. G.G. Iggers, *The Cult of Authority: The Political Philosophy of the Saint-Simonians* (The Hague, 1970), pp. 131–2.

96. For a typical example see E. Morhange, *Mémoire sur la paix universelle*, (Brussels, 1850), Pt II, Chapter i, especially pp. 56–8.

of national and ethnic rivalry, soon to show themselves so intractable, seemed unable to resist history's march towards international peace. Many of the Saint-Simonians (though not Saint-Simon himself) believed, along the lines later copied by Mazzini, in the primary importance of national groups and in the possession by each of its own distinctive spirit and historical mission. Nor did they doubt the right of developed nations to control less developed ones, or of Europe to conquer and colonise other parts of the world. Pecqueur even hoped that participation by all the European peoples in overseas expansion of this kind might be a means of binding them together and maintaining some rough equality of power between them.[97] But to idealists of this stamp national rivalries seemed of essentially secondary importance. No more than Mazzinian idealists could utopian socialist ones see national antagonisms for what they were – the most deep-rooted of all obstacles to European peace and unity. 'In a word', wrote Considérant offhandedly in 1850, 'the political map of Europe forms itself of its own accord, in accordance with ethnographic affinities'.[98]

*The 1850s and 1860s: the situation becomes more complex* The four decades between Waterloo and the Crimean War were therefore, in spite of the tensions which divided the European states, an age of innocence in much discussion of the future of international relations. This attitude went deeper than organisational schemes. It can also be seen in a feeling that the case for peace was so strong that it needed only to be clearly stated to win widespread support among men of good will. Faith in the power of public opinion, once aroused, to produce fundamental change was generally shared by radicals of all kinds. British and still more American religious pacifists, who could point to such achievements as the victory of the anti-slavery movement in Britain and the strength of the temperance one in the United States,[99] were particularly prone to this kind of optimism. To them it seemed that educated public opinion was everywhere becoming the ultimate ruler of states and maker of policies. 'The pen is soon to take the place of the sword', wrote one of their most tireless propagandists, 'and reason is soon to be substituted for brute force, in settling all international controversies. Already there is no civilized nation that can withstand the frown of public opinion. It is therefore necessary, only to enlighten public opinion still further, to insure the success of our plan.' Simultaneously one of his compatriots was confident

97. C. Pecqueur, *De la paix* . . ., p. 239.
98. *La dernière guerre* . . ., p. 6a.
99. For example, W. Jay, *War and Peace: The Evils of the First, and a Plan for Preserving the Last* (New York, 1842), pp. 1, 4–5.

that 'the exhibition of truth, and . . . bold and persevering appeals to the conscience and the understanding' must make the cause of peace victorious, since 'At the present day all governments are more or less controlled by public opinion; and the progress of education and the power of the press enables every individual to sit in judgement on the conduct of his rulers.'[100] The same noble and pathetic faith in words, in the power of rhetoric, can be seen equally clearly among French radicals.[101] The breakdown in 1853 of any remnants of great-power concert, and the forcible frontier changes and transformation of the European balance in 1859–71, inevitably shook some assumptions and showed the hollowness of some hopes. Yet they did not destroy the idealism without which aspirations towards permanent peace could not exist.

Indeed even in these years of conflict there were developments upon which supporters of the peace movement in its differing forms could found new hopes. Christian pacifism in the English-speaking world might lose much of its impetus. Radical idealism in France might be shaken by the failure of the 1848 revolution and the coming of the Second Empire. Yet there were still in the 1850s and 1860s grounds for optimism about the future of international relations. The Declaration of Paris, which in 1856 abolished privateering as an auxiliary arm of naval warfare, seemed to mark an important step in the progress of international law. The creation a few years later of the first Red Cross societies did something to strengthen humanitarian restraints on conflict between states (though the international aspect of the movement can be easily exaggerated; it took shape as a group of national societies each of which became to a considerable extent an aspect of the military machinery of its own state).[102] International cooperation on practical and technical issues, still in its infancy, began to gain some impetus. The international commission created in 1856 to supervise navigation on the Danube was a rather limited example of this. Another was the creation in 1851 of a small section in the French ministry of foreign affairs concerned with the protection of literary and artistic property and with the making of international copyright and other agreements for this purpose.[103] This was the first such institutional recognition of the new dimensions which were

100. W. Ladd, *An Essay on a Congress of Nations for the Adjustment of International Disputes without Recourse to Arms* (New York, 1916; first published, 1840), p. 77; Jay, *War and Peace*, pp. 2, 63.

101. See for example, E. Potonie-Pierre, *Historique du mouvement pacifique* (Berne, 1899), pp. 17–65, a long description of the 1849 Paris congress which he had witnessed as a boy.

102. G. Best, *Humanity in Warfare: The Modern History of the International Law of Armed Conflict* (London, 1980), pp. 142–3.

103. *Les Affaires Étrangères* . . ., i, 682.

now being added to international relations. On a different level the International Workingmen's Association, the First International, which began its short and troubled life in 1864, showed the same realisation that there were more and more international issues in the new age of large-scale industry and science which simply could not be handled adequately by the use of traditional diplomatic mechanisms.

Schemes and pleas for lasting international peace continued to appear during the 1850s and 1860s; but their character was changing. As the Christian pacifism of earlier decades lost ground, even in its Anglo-American homelands, the peace movement as a whole became much more directly political and its main European focus moved decisively across the Channel. It was among radical democrats, liberals and republicans in France that significant discussion of this kind had, by the 1860s, become largely concentrated. To them international peace, reduction of armaments and the creation of some kind of European federation seemed inseparable from political and economic reform within individual states. Democracy, in the form of representative government and manhood suffrage; a free press which would give the ordinary man access to new ideas and undermine the baleful influence of tradition and customary authority; free trade with its inevitable pacifying influences: these were the bases on which, once established, some wider union could be built. The purely material advantages of such changes figured prominently in liberal and radical republican propaganda; and though it very often appealed to general moral principles its specifically religious content was extremely small. Many French liberal economists – Frédéric Bastiat, Michel Chevalier, Horace Say and Gustave de Molinari – had attended the 1849 peace congress in Paris; and during the 1850s and 1860s much internationalist and anti-war writing in France took the form simply of detailing the huge human and material cost of large-scale conflict and the morally corrupting effect of preparations for war, and sometimes of appeals for the replacement of standing armies by citizen militias which were cheaper and militarily effective only in a defensive role.[104] The *Ligue de la Paix* set up in Paris in 1867 was dominated by this kind of high-minded but also materialist rationalism, and had economic liberals such as Chevalier, Frédéric Passy and Paul Leroy-Beaulieu among its leading members. In the same year a peace congress held at Geneva, with Garibaldi as its chairman and attended by a wide variety of political and

104. P. Leroy-Beaulieu, *Les guerres contemporaines (1853–1856)* (Paris,n.d.); F. Passy, *Conférence sur la paix et la guerre faite à l'École de Médecine de Paris le 21 Mai 1867* (Paris, 1867); Comte L. de Dreuille, *Comment on pourrait reduire l'armée tout en assurant la défense nationale* (Paris,n.d.); L.A. Beaudemoulin, *La guerre s'en va*, 3rd edn (Paris,n.d.; first published 1867), pp. 75–8; A. Umilta, *Histoire d'une utopie: l'idée de la paix à travers les siècles* (Neuchâtel, 1911, but written in the early 1880s), pp. 129–96.

social radicals, decided that although Europe must be reorganised as a federation this could be made up only of free peoples among whom universal suffrage and a free press had taken root. It attempted to give effect to these ambitions by setting up the *Ligue Internationale de la Paix et de la Liberté*, a more radically political body than its Parisian rival. The replacement everywhere of monarchies by republics, the separation of church and state and the abolition of standing armies were among its demands, and it became at once a focus of republican opposition to the regime of Napoleon III.

The radicals who supported the peace movement, however, were in agreement on little more than a small number of very general principles and their desire to end international conflict. Some were interested primarily in peace for its own sake, others rather in various forms of sweeping political or social change. Some were convinced supporters of the national idea, while others saw the threatened disruption by nationalism of large political units such as the Habsburg Empire as increasing the danger of war and obstructing the complete triumph of free trade. The *Ligue Internationale de la Paix et de la Liberté*, for example, drew support from the Englishman John Stuart Mill, a liberal, the Frenchmen Edgar Quinet, a radical republican, Louis Blanc, a socialist, and Charles Longuet, who was Marx's son-in-law, as well as the Russian anarchist Mikhail Bakunin. Such heterogeneous backing was from one point of view impressive; but it was unlikely to make for unity or effectiveness.

By 1870, then, there had emerged in addition to the surviving strain of Christian pacifism in the English-speaking world at least three other types of peace activity. Side by side with one, typified by Passy in France, which concentrated on improving the conduct and tone of international relations and tended to rely heavily on the virtues and effectiveness of liberal economics as a way of doing this, could be found another, more radical, which argued that better relations between states must depend on far-reaching political and even social reform within them, while a third, socialist, one was beginning to claim that war could never be ended while the capitalist system survived.[105] There were still even a few dying flickers of ideas widespread generations earlier but now no more than historical curiosities. One French writer, for example, proposed to ensure disarmament and peace between the nations by the unsurprising means of setting up an international tribunal to arbitrate in disputes between them; but this tribunal was to have as its most pressing task the centuries-old one

105. See the summary in S.E.Cooper, 'The origins and development of European peace movements: from Vienna to Frankfurt', in *Friedensbewegungen: Bedingungen und Wirkungen*, ed. G. Heiss and H. Lutz (Munich, 1984), p. 94.

of driving the Turks from Europe.[106] Much more important, the most original of all French radicals of the period, P.-J. Proudhon, was in this as in other respects a law unto himself. Impervious to the claims of nationalism, rejecting ideas of linguistic unity and natural frontiers, deeply distrustful of great concentrations of power of any kind and of the dominance of international relations by a few great states, he called for a Europe made up of a large number of small republics combined in a federation but retaining much autonomy. Each would be bound to exchange freely its products with the others; but there was to be no central authority which might force a greater degree of unity upon them. A minimal political structure of this kind for the continent, he consistently argued, could alone safeguard political freedom: he pointed repeatedly to the Swiss federation and the American republic as models in this respect. In the first flush of optimism at the outbreak of the 1848 revolutions he had believed that Europe was about to transform itself in this way,[107] and until his death in 1865 he never ceased to argue for a loose and voluntary association rather than any more rigid and potentially coercive federalism. Like so many nineteenth-century ideologues he vastly exaggerated the power of economic change to override the forces of political conflict and national rivalry. For him the age of politics was at an end in Europe. One dominated by economics was beginning. 'There is no more nationality, no more fatherland, in the political sense of the word', he wrote in 1851. 'Political economy . . . is the queen and ruler of the age.'[108] He was in some ways the most genuine radical of the mid-century decades; and his ideas on European union won some support in his own day.[109] But he had little in common with the central current of thinking during these years on the problems of peace and European unity.

## (2) Sedan to Sarajevo: law and institutions, disarmament and international government

*Hopes and weaknesses* The two generations between the triumph of Bismarckian Germany in 1870–71 and the disaster of 1914 saw discussion

106. N. Villaume, *L'Esprit de la guerre* (Paris, 1864), pp. 35–7. He also suggested (pp. 34–5), in an even more striking effort to resurrect the past, that quarrels between states might be settled by single combat between their rulers.

107. *Correspondance de P.J. Proudhon* (Paris, 1875), ii, 285, 297.

108. *Idée générale de la révolution au XIXe siècle* (Paris, 1851), pp. 328, 245.

109. For example, G. de Boom, *Une Solution politique et sociale. Confédération–Décentralisation–Emigration* (Paris, 1864), which suggested (pp. 147–54) the reorganisation of Europe as a federation of fifty-eight small units with no internal tariff barriers and its capital at Frankfurt, Geneva or Brussels. Proudhon's ideas on international relations are conveniently summarised in J.-L. Puech, *La Tradition socialiste en France et la Société des Nations* (Paris, 1921), Chapter vi, and N. Bourgeois, *Les Théories de droit international chez Proudhon* (Paris, 1927), pp. 42ff.

of the problem of international peace become more widespread than ever before. This was for believers in the peace idea an age of optimism, one in which Christian pacifists, political ideologues of widely differing colours and international lawyers could all believe, sometimes with much apparent justification, that their dreams were on the way to realisation. Peace societies proliferated outside the English- and French-speaking worlds as never before. They appeared in the Netherlands in 1870, in Belgium in 1871, in Italy in 1878, in Denmark in 1882, in Norway and Sweden in 1883. An international congress of such societies met in Paris in 1878; and from 1889 onwards there were annual Universal Peace Congresses (the tenth of these, in Glasgow in 1901, officially adopted the new term 'pacifist'). An International Peace Bureau was established in Berne in 1892, the first effort to federate these different societies and thus give them greater effect. By 1903 it could be claimed that there were 111 of them in existence in Europe and America.[110] So much activity, so many speeches and pamphlets, such an outpouring of high-minded and well-intentioned words, generated a quite baseless optimism. Thus in 1895 the most vocal member of the tiny group of German pacifists claimed that the annexation of Alsace-Lorraine in 1871 had in fact served the cause of peace by making clear the folly of another war. Divisions within states – between socialists and conservatives, liberals and anti-semites – he argued, were now more difficult to appease than those which separated nations.[111]

To people like this it was easy to overlook the persisting weaknesses of the whole movement. In some parts of Europe it made some appeal, though always a limited one, to the ordinary man. In Britain notably the Workmen's Peace Association founded in 1870 was a body of some significance. Until 1883 its income was larger than that of the increasingly important Trades Union Congress created in 1868, while of the twelve working-class men elected to parliament in 1885 nine were its members or supporters.[112] It had deep roots in the nonconformist and evangelical Protestantism which had been the breeding-ground of the peace societies of the first half of the century, as well as in memories of the Chartist movement.

But over much of the continent the situation was very different. In the Habsburg Empire the peace movement which developed during the 1870s and 1880s was confined to a well-to-do upper middle class and a liberal-minded minority of the aristocracy. It had no mass appeal, gained the support of no significant political grouping and had no native roots (it

110. E. Duplessix, *Vers la paix* (Paris, 1903), p. 21.

111. A.H. Fried, *Elsass-Lothringen und der Krieg* (Leipzig–Paris, 1895), pp. 76–7, 112–13.

112. Its activities are discussed in E.W. Sager, 'The Working-Class Peace Movement in Victorian England', *Histoire Sociale/Social History*, 12 (1978), 122–44.

was inspired in the main by ideas imported from Great Britain).[113] More important, agitation for international peace could make much headway neither in Russia nor, most significant of all, in the new German Reich. No national peace society was founded in Germany until 1892. A number of local ones had come into existence a little earlier; but of the five mentioned in a list of 1888 two were inactive or defunct and the others very small.[114] German support for the movement remained both slight and with a tellingly uneven geographical distribution. In 1913 more than a quarter of its members were concentrated in the small state of Württemberg in south-west Germany, where the liberal and democratic tradition was unusually strong: in Prussia by contrast, and especially in Prussia east of the Elbe, its membership was tiny. Such support as it had came everywhere in the empire largely from the lower middle-class, small businessmen or school teachers with little political weight. It was almost totally without backing from the German churches. In 1913 of over 35,000 clergy in the empire, both Protestant and Catholic, only 117 were members. The best study of it concludes that 'there were probably no more than two to three hundred men and women in Germany willing to sacrifice any significant amount of time or money for the peace movement'. Relying entirely on persuasion and the assertion of moral principles, unwilling as well as unable to take any kind of political action, it displayed a pathetic gulf between aspiration and reality; and in what was now increasingly the greatest of the European powers this gulf was important.[115] Even the *Verband für internationale Verständigung*, founded with the support of some leading German intellectuals in 1911, though it was not a pacifist organisation and was careful to keep the peace societies at arm's length, was no more than a tiny and almost impotent élite group.[116] Outside Germany it was possible for workers for international peace, ever optimistic and impressed by words, to be blind to the real weakness of their counterparts in the Wilhelmine Reich; but events were to show how complete that weakness was.

*Working together: the growth of practical cooperation between states* There were, however, much more solid reasons than the activities of the societies for believing, in the long period of general stability which followed the treaty

---

113. R.R. Laurence, 'The Peace Movement in Austria, 1867–1914', in *Doves and Diplomats: Foreign Offices and Peace Movements in Europe and America*, ed. S.Wank (Westport, Conn.–London, 1978), pp. 24–7.

114. *Entstehung und Entwicklung der Friedensgesellschaften* (Leipzig, 1888).

115. R. Chickering, *Imperial Germany and a World without War* (Princeton, 1975), pp. 47, 59–60, 197, 66–7.

116. R. Chickering, 'A Voice of Moderation in Imperial Germany', *Journal of Contemporary History*, 8 (1973).

of Frankfurt, that the continent might be moving towards an age of international peace. War, even if it occurred, seemed likely to be considerably more humane than ever in the past. In 1864 the representatives of twenty-five states, meeting in Geneva, had produced the Convention for Bettering the Condition of Wounded Soldiers. This Geneva Convention, which was revised and extended in 1906, was followed by other such meetings in St Petersburg in 1868 and Brussels in 1874 (both proposed originally by the Russian government) which attempted to regulate the conduct of war more effectively than had ever before been contemplated. Neither of the conventions they drew up was formally ratified by the powers; but that of 1874, much the more important, was in practice accepted by them as a part of international law. Achievements of this kind helped to strengthen the hope that eventually tighter restrictions on warfare, combined with the inevitable civilising tendency of material progress, might mean the withering away of physical conflict between states. The 'technical regularity of warfare' fostered by the agreements of 1868 and 1874, wrote an English lawyer in 1880, 'may be silently nurturing the very moral sentiments which, in time, will become the direct agency for the abolition of war itself'.[117]

The most substantial justification for optimism, however, the most concrete and visible, was the striking growth in cooperation between states on a widening range of practical issues. This seemed to justify the belief that the whole drift of history, propelled by technological change and economic growth, was inevitably towards greater interdependence and away from conflict. International communication by letter and telegraph was the first and most important area in which such a development became clear. The need for states to work closely together in this respect was undeniable. An American pacifist of the first half of the century had hoped for the creation of 'an international post-office, to extend all over the world',[118] while the Paris peace congress of 1849 passed a resolution demanding that contacts between peoples be broadened by postal reform. Government action did not lag very far behind. Bilateral treaties regulating the sending of international telegrams were signed from that year onwards and an International Telegraphic Union was formed in 1865. The Universal Postal Union set up in Berne nine years later was an efficient body and the most successful of all efforts at practical international cooperation. The spectacular growth in the scale of international contacts of this kind (rather more than five million international telegrams were

117. S. Amos, *Political and Legal Remedies for War* (London, 1880), p. 336. For a somewhat similar attitude in Germany see H.Hetzel, *Die Humanisierung des Krieges in den letzten hundert Jahren* (Frankfurt, 1891).

118. Ladd, *An Essay on a Congress of Nations*, p. 31.

sent in 1868 and eighty-two million in 1905)[119] seemed to many observers to foreshadow a peaceful and progressive future. 'The great ideal of international freedom and union', wrote one at the end of the nineteenth century, 'is to be found in the post-office. Wherever you see the red pillar-box, there you see a dumb prophet of the Millenium. . . . The International Postal Union is the avant-courrier, or John the Baptist, of the Kingdom of Heaven, in which all frontiers would disappear and all mankind would be made free of the planet in which they dwell.' Another had no doubt that 'The victories of Alexander and Napoleon are cast into the shade by the triumphal procession of the tiny postage stamp around the world.'[120] From the letter and the telegram such cooperation broadened out into a wide spectrum of other areas. Efforts at international action to improve public health had begun in 1851, when the French government summoned an international conference in Paris to discuss steps to combat the spread of cholera. This was ineffective: but a series of similar meetings in the early 1890s had more result; and by 1903 there was an international code of rules for the control of epidemic diseases. In intellectual life success came earlier. The 1850s and 1860s saw a remarkable growth in the number of international scientific meetings and congresses; and this process accelerated throughout the decades down to 1914.[121] Later in the nineteenth century there was a significant development of national institutes established in foreign countries for academic purposes: the partial opening to scholars of the Vatican archives in 1883, in particular, led to the creation in Rome of a number of historical foundations of this kind. International exchanges and visiting appointments of academics began between Germany and the United States in 1905–06, though as yet on a very small scale.[122]

Not all the hopes during these decades of more effective internationalism of this practical kind were completely realised. Some were hardly realised at all. The dream of a unified world system of weights and measures was given greater substance by the setting-up in 1875 of the *Bureau International des Poids et Mesures* to control the metric system, and by the triumph of that system in the physical sciences; but the English-speaking countries continued, so far as the ordinary man was concerned, to be a separate world in this respect. Efforts to give trade unionism an effective international dimension, from the founding of the

119. F.S.L. Lyons, *Internationalism in Europe, 1815–1914* (Leyden, 1963), p. 41.

120. W.T. Stead, *The United States of Europe on the Eve of the Parliament of Peace* (London, 1899), p. 14; K.P. Arnoldson, *Pax Mundi* (London, 1892), p. 139.

121. Lyons, *Internationalism* . . ., pp. 223–4.

122. Brigitte Schroder, 'Characteristiques des relations scientifiques internationales, 1870–1914', *Journal of World History*, x (1966–67), 162, 168.

International Miners' Federation in 1890 onwards, had very little effect. The very debatable belief that direct communication between different nations, unhampered by differences of language, must contribute greatly to international peace stimulated many fruitless initiatives. In 1869 Michel Chevalier had proposed that English, French and German be taught for this purpose in 'all respectable education'. A generation later another Frenchman suggested that French be taught throughout the English-speaking world while all French students should be made to learn English; this, he argued, would give the two languages a dominant international position.[123] But such ideas remained no more than paper proposals. The synthetic international languages which appeared towards the end of the century (Volapuk in 1880, Esperanto a decade later, Ido a few years later still), and which were the most radical of all efforts to break down linguistic barriers between nations, never won the support of more than small groups of enthusiasts.

Nevertheless, the scale and momentum of the movement towards practical cooperation of all kinds between states deeply impressed many contemporaries. From these workaday beginnings, it seemed, political union and an end to war might well emerge. Even at the highest political level the eye of faith could detect occasional developments (the international agreement of 1887 for the neutralisation of the Suez Canal in time of war was the most obvious) which seemed to give substance to this hope.

*International arbitration and its difficulties* Until at least the 1860s it had been widely believed by radicals of all shades that lasting international peace was possible only if it were underpinned by far-reaching political, and perhaps also social, changes within the major European states. From the 1870s onwards this situation changed. It was now increasingly felt that peace might well be achieved without such a revolutionary breach with the past. New legal or quasi-legal expedients might by themselves be sufficient. In particular international arbitration might bring peace even though many of the states involved in it remained monarchies, and sometimes highly autocratic ones. After the almost complete neglect of such arbitration during the eighteenth century the Anglo-American Jay treaty of 1794, which provided for its use to settle a range of outstanding conflicts – on frontier questions, American debts and British maritime seizures – began its revival, at least in the English-speaking world. The first half of the nineteenth century saw a slow growth in its popularity even in continental

---

123. London Peace Society, *Facts and Illustrations in Reference to War, Peace and International Arbitration* (London, 1872), p. 55; A. Guérard, *A Short History of the International Language Movement* (London, 1922), p. 47.

Europe. The Congress of Vienna used it to decide one minor issue, that of the disputed duchy of Bouillon on the north-east frontier of France; and by the 1820s it was possible for an experienced diplomat to hope for the emergence of some form of arbitration acceptable to all governments.[124] The treaty of Paris of 1856, which ended the Crimean War, provided for its use in any future dispute between any of the European powers and the Ottoman empire and also expressed a somewhat pious hope that all states would henceforth have recourse to the good offices of a friendly power before going to war. In 1864 an encyclical of Pius IX asserted the inherent superiority of church to state and therefore the position of the papacy as the supreme international arbiter, though the claim was now a very empty one.[125] A year or two later a well-informed commentator could feel that 'The practice of referring to arbitration disputes of secondary importance . . . has made just so much progress as to warrant the hope that it will make more'.[126] The claim was justified: the mere eight international arbitations recorded during the two decades 1821–40, according to one calculation, had been followed by twenty in 1841–60.[127]

The greatest single impetus to the increased use of international arbitration, however, was the settlement in 1871 by an arbitral commission (the first important one to have a majority of neutral members) of the American claims against Great Britain in the *Alabama* case. This was a serious dispute. American claims for compensation arising from the successes during the Civil War of the famous Confederate commerce-raider fitted out in a British port had produced a great deal of ill-feeling. The peaceful settlement of the issue in this way therefore generated much optimism about the future potentialities of arbitration in international relations. The *Alabama* judgement, wrote a Belgian liberal, 'will probably be one of the finest moments of our century', and those who made it 'have deserved well of all humanity', for the movement in favour of arbitration was now gaining ground and must soon become irresistible.[128]

Many contemporaries echoed these hopes. The early 1870s saw the introduction in several European parliaments of resolutions calling for a greatly increased use of this means of settling international disputes. In

124. A. de Stourdza, 'Avis aux jeunes diplomates', *Oeuvres posthumes religieuses, historiques, philosophiques et littéraires* (Paris, 1858–61), iii, 443–4.

125. Dreyfus, *L'Arbitrage international*, p. 329.

126. M. Bernard, *Four Lectures on Subjects connected with Diplomacy* (London, 1868), p. 101.

127. J.B. Scott, *The Hague Peace Conferences of 1899 and 1907* (Baltimore, 1909), p. 226.

128. E. de Lavelaye, *Des Causes actuelles de guerre en Europe et de l'arbitrage* (Brussels–Paris, 1873), pp. 191–2; cf. M. Revon, *L'Arbitrage international; son passé – son présent – son avenir* (Paris, 1892), pp. 327–9.

1873 the House of Commons passed one in favour of a permanent system
of international arbitration (something Cobden had never achieved) and
this example was immediately followed by the Italian Chamber of
Deputies. In the following year very similar motions were adopted in
Sweden, the Netherlands and Belgium. Clearly in some states at least
there had been a recognisable change in the political climate; and many
commentators later in the century also had no doubt that the *Alabama*
judgement marked an important and hopeful turning-point.[129] The
impetus of the 1870s was maintained and indeed increased throughout the
years down to 1914: of a little over 300 arbitral settlements agreed to by
states in dispute during the whole period 1794–1914 almost exactly half
date from after 1890.[130] The Inter-Parliamentary Union formed in 1889
did more than any other body to foster the idea of international
arbitration and in particular pressed for a general arbitration treaty which
all the powers might sign. This was not achieved; but a number of
bilateral arrangements between major states (notably an Anglo–French one
of 1903, which had considerable psychological significance though its
practical scope was very limited) gave more encouragement to the belief
that the tide of history was flowing irresistibly in this direction. After all,
from a series of merely bilateral arrangements some more wide-ranging
structure might soon emerge. The hopes of the peace movement, always
too easily aroused, were now increasingly pinned to such methods and by
the end of the century running high. In the 1890s Passy, now nearing the
end of a long career, rejoiced that 'upon the slightest disturbance, appeal is
made to arbitration as an unfailing resource'. Simultaneously an American
enthusiast had no doubt that 'it is the resistless logic of modern humane
progress which is bringing arbitration into such esteem'; and another
French one claimed that 'the idea of a Tribunal of International
Arbitration has become universal'.[131] All this produced a crop of schemes
for the setting-up of some kind of permanent international machinery to
replace merely *ad hoc* arbitral arrangements. Some of these suggestions
showed much of the impractical idealism which marked so many
internationalist aspirations.[132] One eccentric even suggested that recourse

129. Comte L. Kamarowsky, *Le Tribunal international* (Paris, 1887), pp. 264–5; Dreyfus, *L'Arbitrage international*, p. 205.
130. A.M. Stuyt, *Survey of International Arbitrations, 1794–1970* (Leyden–Dobbs Ferry, 1972), passim.
131. F. Passy, 'Peace Movement in Europe', *American Journal of Sociology*, ii (1896), 6; B.F. Trueblood, *The Federation of the World* (Boston–New York, 1899), p. 103; C. Richet, *Peace and War* (London, 1906; French original 1899), p. 70.
132. Larroque, *De la création d'un code de droit* . . ., pp. 128ff.; P. Lacombe, 'Mémoire sur l'établissement d'un tribunal international ' in A. de Marcoartù, *Internationalism* (London, 1876), pp. 143ff.; Lavelaye, *Des Causes actuelles* . . ., Pt iii; N. Notovich, *La Pacification de l'Europe et Nicholas II* (2nd edn, Paris, 1899), pp. 178–83.

to arbitration be enforced upon states by what amounted to a system of fines, though typically he said nothing on the crucial question of how these were to be enforced.[133] A few, the work of international lawyers, were more detailed and professional.[134] Almost all expressed a deep-rooted optimism about the future of international relations.

This optimism was not universal. Other observers saw clearly how difficult any complete victory for the principle of arbitration would be. In spite of the considerable volume of continental European, notably French, writing on it, it was most of all the English-speaking powers which in practice made use of this method of settling disputes. In Britain both the religious and the free-trading forms of international idealism were exceptionally strong. This was coupled with a powerful legal tradition which influenced every aspect of political life and favoured the use in foreign policy of a legal or quasi-legal expedient such as arbitration. All this bred a notable tendency among her European neighbours to regard Britain, in the 1870s and even later, as the leader in many aspects of the peace movement. 'We, at the present day', wrote a Spanish idealist, 'resort to Great Britain as to the Temple of Peace, from all the distant corners of the world, to solicit the favour of her divinities and carry back the new religion to our lares'.[135] So far as arbitration was concerned this attitude had a good deal of justification. Of all the successful international arbitrations of the years 1870–1914 Great Britain was a party to about half and the United States to about a third. But in Germany, Russia, Italy, even France, where history and geography had produced different attitudes, readiness to welcome arbitration was inevitably less. German official dislike of it was particularly marked. Arbitration contradicted, at least by implication, the idea now deeply embedded in German political philosophy and legal theory of the state as an end in itself. If used in a really serious dispute it would delay the outbreak of hostilities and thus weaken the position of a government which might benefit from rapid mobilisation of its army, as Prussia had done in 1870. It assumed the juridical equality of states and thus tended to have an internationally levelling effect and to mitigate inequalities of power. Moreover, it could

---

133. E.P. Frost, *Safeguards for Peace: A Scheme of State Insurance against War* (Cambridge, 1905), pp. 22–8. A group of states were to contribute fixed sums to a Common Fund to be invested in 'sound securities' all over the world. Dividends in proportion to their contributions would be paid to the contributing states; but any of them which refused to submit to arbitration a dispute with another, or which was declared by an international court to be the guilty party in case of the outbreak of war, was to forfeit all its contributions which would then be divided among the other, law-abiding, members of the group.

134. The most obvious example is Kamarowsky, *Le Tribunal international*, Bk IV, Chapter iii.

135. Marcoartù, *Internationalism*, p. 52.

be argued that it was likely to strengthen democratic forces and parliamentary control of foreign policy in any state which made use of it. For all these reasons it was looked on with deep suspicion by the government of the Reich:[136] in this way again the attitude of so great a power could only weaken and undermine the peace movement. Moreover, there were obvious caveats which even writers generally favourable to the idea of arbitration felt compelled to make. Would it always be possible to find arbiters in any quarrel acceptable to both sides? Would states ever be willing to accept a judgement of this kind on matters touching their physical safety or what they chose to regard as their honour? If one side in a dispute refused to accept an arbitral decision, how was that decision to be enforced?[137]

*An international court and an international code?* Arbitration, then, was not a complete solution to the problem of lasting international peace. It was rather, in the eyes of many observers, a step towards a more fundamental solution – the creation of a permanent supranational court of law whose decision in international disputes would be obeyed and which would bring an essential element of legality into the relationships of states as nothing else could. But such a court would be of little use unless it could apply an agreed code of international law, just as national courts did the municipal law of their own states. Arbitration could never be an adequate substitute for law, for it could not *prevent* disputes as an effective law-code would.[138] Indeed such a code would have value even if no court to apply it were established. In that case it could still guide those called upon to arbitrate *ad hoc* between states in dispute, for mere equity, it could be argued, was by itself an inadequate guide in such cases.[139] Court and code went hand in hand; but the latter tended to attract more attention from publicists and academics and to inspire more specific and detailed proposals.

The idea of a codification of international law, of rescuing it from its existing status as a mere amalgam of historical precedents and general moral principles, was far from new. The peace congresses at Frankfurt and London in 1850 and 1851, to go no further back in time, had stressed the need for action of this kind. But the later nineteenth century, and

136. Chickering, *Imperial Germany* . . ., pp. 220–3.

137. For doubts of this kind see E. Rouard de Card, *L'Arbitrage international dans le passé, le présent et l'avenir* (Paris, 1877), pp. 111–18; and the same author's *Les Destinées de l'arbitrage international depuis la sentence rendue par le tribunal de Genève* (Paris, 1892), pp. 206–08; Holtzendorff-Vietmannsdorff, *Die Idee des ewigen Völkerfriedens*, pp. 41–3.

138. E. Goblet, Comte d'Alviella, *Désarmer ou déchoir. Essai sur les relations internationales* (Brussels–Paris, 1872), pp. 163–9; F. Seebohm, *On International Reform* (London, 1871), pp. 104–6; P. Fiore, *Un Appel à la presse et à la diplomatie* (Paris, 1890), pp. 20–1.

139. L.-A.-J. Bara, *La Science de la paix* (Brussels–Paris, 1872), pp. 154–5.

particularly the 1870s, saw it attract a hitherto unknown amount of attention. Many of the proposals put forward were, perhaps inevitably, vague and imprecise. The most important of the British peace societies called for a 'Permanent Court of Nations' to fix and declare such a code, though without any indication at all of how this might be achieved.[140] Some French republican radicals urged that the peace societies, or jurists, publicists and philosophers nominated by them, be entrusted with the task of codification.[141] Another visionary of a more politically conservative but equally impractical kind suggested that each of the European nations send to an international assembly an ambassador appointed by its government, two electors chosen by 'the two chambers of the nation' and a magistrate appointed by 'the supreme tribunal' and the universities: this body would first of all formulate principles of international law which were already generally agreed and go on from this to 'the scientific preparation of the bases of the Code of Nations'.[142] Other suggestions were more specific and professional. The National Association for the Promotion of Social Science set up in 1866 a commission to codify international law; and this bore fruit in the publication six years later of an elaborate document of over 700 articles.[143] An Association for the Reform and Codification of the Law of Nations and an Institute of International Law both came into existence in 1873. An American lawyer, in one of the most realistic and clear-headed discussions of the problems involved, emphasised that such a code must not try to achieve too much too quickly. It should not, in particular, interfere with the internal politics of states. Nor should it attempt to change existing frontiers or call for immediate or compulsory disarmament. Moreover, it was unlikely to end entirely conflict between the states which subscribed to it; and it would be impracticable to enforce it by sanctions.[144] Such realism, however, was very much the exception.

As to the international court which would apply this code once it had been agreed, attitudes were also divided. There was a fairly widespread feeling among writers on the problem of international peace that some permanent judicial machinery was essential for this purpose; merely *ad hoc* arrangements for arbitration were not enough.[145] But as to the form this

---

140. London Peace Society, *Facts and Illustrations* . . ., pp. 51–3.

141. Bara, *La Science de la paix*, pp. 158–9; Larroque, *De la création* . . ., pp. 124–5.

142. Marcoartù, *Internationalism*, pp. 14–15; a somewhat similar proposal was made by Fiore, *Un Appel* . . ., pp. 30–1.

143. Dudley Field, *Draft Outlines of an International Code* (New York, 1872).

144. A.P. Sprague, *The Codification of Public International Law* (printed as an appendix to Marcoartù, *Internationalism*), pp. 89. 104–5, 111, 121. The difficulties of successful codification were also stressed by Rouard de Card, *L'Arbitrage international*, pp. 86–8.

145. For example, Seebohm, *On International Reform*, pp. 121–5; T., *World Politics* (New York-London, 1898), Chapter xiv; L. Appleton, *The Foreign Policy of Europe* (London, n.d.), pp. 368–70.

machinery might take, ideas differed widely. Quite often suggestions were couched in very vague terms, such as the English one which called simply, without further explanation, for 'A Court, consisting of Judges, deputed by the various Governments of Europe'.[146] A slightly more specific proposal was for a tribunal, sitting perhaps in Geneva or Lausanne, to which each European state should send a single member designated by its parliament (as a good radical the author assumed that all these states would soon have some form of parliamentary and probably republican government).[147] Another envisaged a much larger panel of judges appointed for life (by whom was left unclear) though only a small proportion of these would act in any particular case.[148] Another, on rather similar lines, aimed simply at formalising arbitration procedures by the setting-up of a permanent body of fifty or sixty eminent jurists, historians and retired statesmen from which states in dispute would agree on a number to decide each case.[149] Yet another, at the end of the century, envisaged some kind of unspecified permanent arbitral tribunal sitting at The Hague with the pope as its permanent president.[150] A few years later, obviously inspired by the Hague conference of 1899 and the hopes it aroused, still another proposed an international council whose membership would be decided by a rather rough system of proportional representation.[151] On how the decisions of any body of this kind, however constituted, were to be enforced, there was considerably more agreement. Physical coercion, at least in any gross form, was almost always ruled out. Instead reliance was placed on public opinion and non-violent sanctions. If the states, argued one of the most idealistic of the writers of the 1870s, merely severed normal relations with any of their number which refused to accept the decision of a duly established tribunal, the moral and intellectual effect of this would be so irresistible that it would almost invariably bring the offender to heel. With slightly differing degrees of confidence this optimistic argument was echoed by the other theorists who could bring themselves to face so thorny a problem.[152]

146. J. Noble, *Arbitration and a Congress of Nations as a Substitute for War in the Settlement of International Disputes* (London, 1862), p. 18.

147. Larroque, *De la création* . . ., pp. 128, 135: cf. the roughly similar scheme of a British free-trading radical, L. Levi, *War and its Consequences* (London, 1881), Chapter viii.

148. Sprague, *The Codification* . . ., pp. 114–15.

149. Lacombe, *Mémoire sur l'établissement* . . ., pp. 145–6, 148.

150. Notovich, *La Pacification* . . ., pp. 178–83.

151. Duplessix, *Vers la paix*, pp. 71–2.

152. Larroque, *De la création* . . ., pp. 138–9; cf. Sprague, *The Codification* . . ., pp. 125–6; Lacombe, *Mémoire sur l'établissement* . . ., pp. 185–6; Noble, *Arbitration* . . ., p. 27. There were exceptions, however, e.g. Duplessix, *Vers la paix*, pp. 139–40 and Fiore, *Un Appel*, pp. 33–4, who envisaged the coercion of recalcitrant states by an international armed force.

*Disarmament and the Hague conferences* Side by side with a codified international law and some supranational judicial body to interpret and apply it went a third obvious objective of internationalist idealism: disarmament. Until the 1860s this had attracted only limited and rather intermittent attention. At the governmental level interest in it had been rare and, when shown, ineffective. In 1816 Alexander I had suggested in very general terms a reduction of armaments by the European states, while in Britain the Prince Regent had tentatively proposed that an international conference of military men might decide the size of the forces to be retained by each of them. But none of this was more than words. Metternich in particular was very suspicious of the tsar's proposals, arguing that the situations and needs of different states differed so much that it was impossible to set fair limits to the size of the forces to be maintained by any one of them; he also feared that the huge and remote Russian empire was better able than its western neighbours to conceal the true strength of its army. Almost half a century later Napoleon III proposed, late in 1863, that an international disarmament congress should meet in Paris. But he suggested that it should also consider revision of the territorial settlement of 1814–15; and this was enough to damn the idea in the eyes of the other powers, notably in those of Great Britain. Early in 1870, again, the French government tried, through the British foreign secretary, Lord Clarendon, to sound that of Prussia on a possible reduction of armaments; but Bismarck dismissed such an idea out of hand. At the popular and unofficial level also interest, though not totally lacking, was usually tepid until the 1860s or 1870s. The peace societies in Britain and the United States certainly favoured mutual reduction of armaments by the powers; but in their propaganda this usually took second place to arbitration as the main and most effective road to peace.

By the mid-century, however, large and costly armed forces were coming under increasing attack, and the direction of the attack was changing. Hitherto big armies and navies had been condemned largely on moral and religious grounds, as both the tools and the stimulants of greed and aggression. Now they were being more and more challenged also for material and pragmatic reasons, as devouring resources which could otherwise be used more constructively. If the world, as industry and technology expanded, were inevitably to be bound together by free exchanges from which all its peoples benefited, then great armed forces were merely irrational obstructions in the path towards this inescapable future. The high taxes and conscription which they demanded were wasteful, burdensome and stupid. In 1851 Cobden had moved in the House of Commons the first resolution in favour of reduction of armaments to be debated in any European parliament. A French radical a few years later, after suggesting that the powers might agree to limit their armies to a fixed proportion (perhaps 1 per cent) of their male population or, better still, to abolish all armed forces apart from small gendarmeries needed as police forces, summed up this attitude in the claim that 'European disarmament would be the triumph of the economic idea; and in future outside the economic idea there will be no politics'.[153] From at least the 1860s onwards, therefore, there were three relatively distinct sources of pressure for a reduction of armaments in Europe. The old condemnation of them on religious grounds was still being voiced in the English-speaking world. Side by side with this went the utilitarian criticism with its very strong overtones of free-trading determinism, sometimes backed by the argument that the growing economic power of new countries such as the United States and perhaps Australia made it imperative to stop wasting Europe's resources in this way and thus fit her better to meet such competition.[154] Finally there were the political and social radicals, most vocal in France, who saw standing armies as the tools of autocratic monarchies and oppressive aristocracies and therefore as very dangerous in terms of domestic politics as well as international relations.[155]

Not all those who pleaded for arbitration or a code of international law were also advocates of disarmament. Some thought it desirable only if every state involved were more or less equal in strength. One at least, writing under the immediate impact of the 1848 revolutions, made the obvious point that war had sometimes served the cause of political freedom.[156] Others questioned how far disarmament was practicable without the previous creation of some kind of European federation to enforce it: one such at the end of the century placed his hope in the formation of a league of neutrals (Britain, Holland, Belgium, Denmark and Switzerland) which would throw its weight against any state threatening aggressive war, and thus make such war impossible and promote general disarmament.[157] Others again hoped for new constitutional provisions within states which would deprive monarchs of the right to declare war and reserve it to elected assemblies.[158] Yet in spite of doubts and disagreements, interest in disarmament was in the later nineteenth century at a higher level than ever before. The 1878 congress of peace societies in Paris called on the powers to reduce their armed

153. E. de Girardin, *Le Désarmement européen* . . .(Paris, 1859), pp. 16–19, 28.

154. For example, Alviella, *Désarmer ou déchoir*, Chapter iv; Noble, *Arbitration*, pp. 36–9; H. Dumesnil, *La Guerre. Étude philosophique* (Paris, 1873), pp. 210–11.

155. For example, Larroque, *De la création* . . ., pp. 73, 77–9.

156. Bara, *La Science de la paix*, pp. 198–202.

157. G. de Molinari, *Grandeur et décadence de la guerre* (Paris, 1898), pp. 263ff.

158. Sprague, *The Codification* . . ., pp. 106–07; Marcoartù, *Internationalism*, Chapter ii; Rouard de Card, *L'Arbitrage* . . ., pp. 145–6.

forces. Resolutions on the subject proliferated in the parliaments of Europe. In the early 1890s there were rumours that the new ruler in Berlin, William II, intended to call an international peace conference on whose agenda the subject would appear; while in 1894 the British prime minister, Lord Roseberry, had tentative discussions with the Russian ambassador in London about a possible agreement between the two powers to limit their armed forces. It is easy to exaggerate the importance of all this. Nowhere had the cause of disarmament really touched the common man on the one hand, or rulers, ministers, diplomats and generals on the other. Like arbitration, an international judicial tribunal, or codification of international law it remained the preserve of enthusiasts whose optimism and loquacity can easily give an exaggerated impression of their real significance. Nevertheless, something had been achieved. Problems of this kind were playing some role, if still a minor one, in the political and intellectual life of Europe, in a way which had not been seen in the past.

Much of the internationalist optimism of the later nineteenth century was focused and summed up by the Hague peace conferences of 1899 and 1907. Their aspirations were modest and their achievements limited. To the more uncompromising internationalists, the advocates of some form of supranational government,[159] they were no more than a step on the road. Yet to many contemporaries they seemed to confirm that disarmament and the substitution of law for force in international affairs were now the wave of the future.

The limited result of the two meetings was clear to realistic observers. The 1899 conference achieved something by setting up a Permanent Court of Arbitration. But this was a minor step. A British proposal to make appeal to the court compulsory in certain types of dispute was abandoned in face of determined German opposition; and even the British prime minister, Lord Salisbury, envisaged it as handling only minor disagreements and not dangerously sensitive quarrels. 'The substantive provisions contained in the Arbitration Convention', noted a leading British international lawyer immediately after the conference ended, 'amount really to nothing'.[160] In 1907 there was further discussion of making arbitration compulsory in some circumstances: once more this had no result. Disarmament occupied rather more time at both meetings; but here too the results were slight. The 1899 conference stemmed from a rescript of Nicholas II calling for a halt to the arms race between the great powers which now seemed to be reaching dangerous proportions; but this

---

159. See below, pp. 265–9.
160. T.E. Holland, 'Some Lessons of the Peace Conference', *Fortnightly Review*, 72 (1899), 957.

appeal aroused very little governmental response. From the moment the delegates met 'the reasons against its adoption were all too well understood to be overwhelming'.[161] The conference prohibited the use of dum-dum bullets and poison gas and the launching of projectiles 'from balloons or by similar methods'. The 1907 meeting limited the use of floating mines and torpedoes and declared itself once more against poison gas and the dropping of explosives from the air, as well as the bombardment of undefended cities.

But at both conferences there was a failure to come to grips with any of the really difficult questions. The fundamental problem was that any proposal to freeze armed forces at the level prevailing at some particular moment, or to prevent the development of new weapons, had like most proposals designed to safeguard peace a built-in conservative bias. Such suggestions implied an acceptance of the military and naval status quo; and there were always powers to whom this was unacceptable. Thus in 1899 Britain, with the most powerful fleet in the world, was willing in principle to discuss setting limits to the size of navies. Russia, however, felt she had to maintain her now threatened lead over Germany and Japan; while the Japanese government was unwilling to agree to any limitations until it had achieved great power status at sea, and the rapid growth of the American fleet was a further complication. Similarly France and Austria–Hungary, supported by some of the smaller states, were unwilling to contemplate any ban on the new and untried weapon of the submarine which they felt might be useful to them in any future naval conflict.[162] In 1907 the prospects for disarmament were even worse. The German government was strongly opposed to its being discussed at all: Prince Bülow, the Reichschancellor, declared at the end of May, before the conference opened, that Germany would have nothing to do with the issue. The opposition from Paris and Vienna, though less explicit, was almost as strong.

Nor had the delegates at either meeting the slightest faith in their ability to overcome these obstacles or, in most cases, any desire to do so. On both occasions the proceedings were enveloped from the beginning in a blanket of cynicism. The head of the American delegation in 1899 felt that 'probably, since the world began, never has so large a body come together in a spirit of more hopeless scepticism as to any good result',

---

161. Holland, 'Some Lessons . . .', 947.
162. Sir J. Headlam-Morley, 'Proposals for the Reduction of Armaments', in his *Studies in Diplomatic History* (London, 1930), pp. 271–2; C.D. Davis, *The United States and the First Hague Peace Conference* (Ithaca, 1962), p. 120. For criticism by an international lawyer of the failure of the conference to limit effectively warfare at sea see T.J. Lawrence, *International Problems and Hague Conferences* (London, 1908), Chapter viii.

while the chief German delegate, anxious to do something to save the tsar's face, wrote that 'we can . . . not allow the conference to end with an entire fiasco and must try to cover it with a peaceful-looking cloak'.[163] Another of the German representatives was the author of a pamphlet which vigorously denounced aspirations towards lasting international peace as neither practicable nor desirable.[164] In 1907 a French observer with much experience of high politics dismissed the conference of that year as a meeting where 'words fall like a fine rain and veil the distant contours of reality'.[165] Between this world-weary realism and the enthusiasm which the conferences aroused among so many members of the peace movement the contrast was sharp indeed. Nicholas II himself may not have been immune to such generous feelings. The circular of 24 August 1898, in which he suggested to the powers the calling of the first of these conferences, was undoubtedly inspired largely by considerations of Russia's own interests. It stemmed from a suggestion by Kuropatkin, his war minister, for a moratorium on the introduction of new quick-firing artillery into the Russian and Habsburg armies, a development which Russia could at that moment ill afford. Moreover, the foreign minister, Muraviev, hoped to use the conference to improve relations with Britain and perhaps delay or even prevent the strengthening of the German army. Yet it seems that Nicholas was also driven by 'a fuzzily defined sense of mission' and that 'uppermost in the czar's mind were feelings of genuine idealism'.[166]

Whatever the motives behind it, the tsar's initiative aroused great enthusiasm among the vocal minorities in western Europe and the United States which had taken up the cause of international peace. The circular immediately set off agitation by the peace societies to mobilise support for the tsar's proposals: few of them seem to have attached much importance to the humiliating fact that the most serious high-level peace initiative for decades had come from an autocratic monarchy in which the peace movement was almost non-existent. W.T. Stead, the radical British newspaper editor who had taken up the peace cause with the headlong wholeheartedness characteristic of him, made the most spectacular of such efforts when, in the autumn of 1898, he travelled around much of Europe

---

163. C. de A. Davis, *The United States and the Second Hague Peace Conference* (Durham, N.C., 1975), p. 25, and the same author's *The United States and the First Hague Peace Conference*, p. 88.

164. K. von Stengel, *Der ewige Friede* (Munich, 1899).

165. G. Hanotaux, *La Politique de l'équilibre* (Paris, 1912), p. 22.

166. D.L. Morrill, 'Nicholas II and the Call for the First Hague Conference', *Journal of Modern History*, xlvi (1974), 304–05, 311–13, 299–300. See also J. Dulffer, *Regeln gegen den Krieg? Die Haager Friedenskonferenzen von 1899 und 1907 in der internationalen Politik* (Berlin, 1981), pp. 19–38.

in an effort to organise a 'Pilgrimage of Peace' in defence of Nicholas's initiative.[167] Even in Germany the first of the two Hague conferences at least stimulated an unaccustomed, indeed unique, spasm of popular interest in the settlement of international disputes without recourse to war. The spring of 1899 was the only moment during the Second Reich when the peace movement there managed to hold public meetings in several large cities. The meagre practical results of the conferences did little to check this enthusiasm. Submission of international disputes to the new Hague court would gradually become compulsory, and its decisions would be accepted merely through the force of opinion and habit, with no need for coercion. Europe was now launched on a course which would make her first of all a loose union of states and then a genuine federation on the model of the United States or Switzerland.[168] The conference of 1899 had the same historical significance, it was even claimed, as the discovery of America or the first use of gunpowder.[169] The two Hague conferences were 'the two greatest and most important meetings of an international character the world has ever seen' and formed 'something not altogether unlike a legislature for the Society of Nations'.[170] It is understandable that statesmen and diplomats, faced with such exaggerated views of what had been achieved, felt that the whole peace movement was irritatingly unrealistic. The head of the American delegation to the 1907 meeting spoke for the conference as a whole when he complained that 'the merely eloquent pacifists write us as though it were only necessary for the conference to decree that there should be eternal peace and that then eternal peace would be'.[171]

*Schemes of international government* Arbitration; a codified international law and some international tribunal to apply it; disarmament: all these were frequently advocated for their own sake. But all of them could also be seen in a different and more ambitious perspective as steps towards some form of positive international government. The flow of schemes for something of this kind became almost a torrent in the two generations before 1914. They took widely differing forms. Most called, often again in general and unspecific terms, for some kind of European federation: very often the United States was here once more put forward as an example to

---

167. See his *The United States of Europe* . . ., especially pp. 205–8.

168. J. Novicow (Novikov), *La Fédération de l'Europe* (Paris, 1901), pp. 761–7, 771–2.

169. A.H. Fried, *Die Haager Conferenz, ihre Bedeutung und ihre Ergebnisse* (Berlin, 1900), Introduction, p. viii.

170. W. Evans Darby, *The Political Machinery of Peace during the Past Year* (London, 1908), pp. 6, 10; cf. L. Bourgeois, *Pour la Société des Nations* (Paris, 1910), pp. 287, 302; W. Schücking, *Der Bund der Völker* (Leipzig, 1918), pp. 113–14, reprinting an article published in 1913.

171. Quoted in Davis, *The United States and the Second Hague Peace Conference,* p.194.

be followed. As in the past, thinking of this kind was usually utilitarian and pragmatic and often politically radical, sometimes markedly so. It stressed heavily the wastefulness of a multiplicity of expensive national armed forces and its proponents, virtually without exception, were strong partisans of free trade.[172] Some of those who wrote in this strain were realistic in their expectations and understood that so great a change must be the work of time. The federation they envisaged might well begin, therefore, merely as a combination of one or two of the more advanced European states which others would join as time went on.[173] Sometimes they showed a prudent reluctance to make excessive claims as to what such a federation might accomplish, at least in the short term.[174]

Other schemes, however, were more ambitious and less liberal in spirit. A French one of 1859, whose author looked to Napoleon III for its realisation, demanded that the legislature of each of the European nations should choose members of a diet to make laws for the entire continent, and also a European high court of justice. These two bodies together would then elect from the reigning sovereigns of Europe a president of the federation. He would command a federal army able to enforce obedience to any decision of the European court, while the individual states would be compelled to reduce their own forces on a scale to be decided by the diet. Moreover, the court was to judge not merely disputes between states but also those between rulers and their subjects: this scheme was strongly monarchical and conservative and thus very different from most of those which multiplied from the 1870s onwards.[175] A rather similar German plan, a few years later, also called for a central tribunal with a powerful army of its own which would intervene in conflicts

172. At the beginning of these decades C. Lemonnier, *Les États-Unis d'Europe* (Paris, 1872), pp. 128–32, is a good example of a politically radical proposal of this sort. Its author, a Saint-Simonian, demanded that all the member-states of the federation he proposed should be republics and denounced monarchical and clerical traditions as the greatest of all obstacles to peace. C.D. Farquharson, *The Federation of the Powers* (London, 1897), especially pp. 38–9, illustrates well the heavy emphasis often placed on the economic gains to be made by reducing military burdens and ending conscription. Sir M. Waechter, 'England, Germany and the Peace of Europe', *Fortnightly Review*, 99 (1913), 829–41, and the same author's 'The Federation of Europe. Is it possible?', *Contemporary Review*, 102 (1912), 624, show the rather more restrained attitudes of a free-trading liberal. From a strongly Catholic point of view P. Defourny, *Le Militarisme et les impôts modernes* (Grenoble, 1890), especially pp. 10–12, made some of the same points.

173. For example, d'Alviella, *Désarmer ou déchoir*, p. 210.

174. For example, the moderate proposal put forward by the English liberal peer Lord Amberley in an article in the *Fortnightly Review* of May 1871 and summarised in B. Russell and Patricia Russell (eds), *The Amberley Papers: The Letters and Diaries of Lord and Lady Amberley* (London, 1937), ii, 428–37.

175. P. Sigaud, *Confédération européenne, principalement pour l'abolition de la guerre* (Paris, 1859), pp. 16–17.

within as well as between states. It would have the duty of suppressing revolutions as well as wars, and the right to fix the size of the armies of its member-states and coerce any which disregarded its decisions. It would also help forward the Europeanisation of the world, by setting up *Culturstationen* in Africa and Asia which would become bases for religious missions and scientific expeditions and for the control of indigenous savage tribes.[176] This highly centralised, militaristic and expansionist structure was a long way from the dream of liberal idealists. A little later an anonymous and highly idiosyncratic writer proposed a European government made up of three distinct organs: a council of communes (in effect merely of capital cities) to be concerned with international economic relations; a council of states whose members would be elected by the different national parliaments and which would handle matters of international law and diplomacy; and a council of churches (including also schools, universities, learned societies and bodies such as the Freemasons) which would have as its sphere European colonial empires and religious missions outside Europe. This cranky scheme, embedded in much rhetoric and verbiage, was also markedly unsympathetic to many of the classical liberal attitudes. Its author was openly hostile to any far-reaching political or social change within the European states and anxious that, once united, they should have complete control of Africa and Asia.[177] A little later still a French writer called for the creation of an international army more powerful than the forces of any one state or group of states and the abolition of all navies other than an international one. These forces would be at the disposal of an international government and an international tribunal which would have very wide powers of supervision and inspection to ensure that no state could covertly increase its capacity to make war.[178]

Republican or monarchical in their presuppositions, liberal or conservative in tone, these schemes made little impression in their own day and are now almost completely forgotten. Rather more significant were the proposals published in the 1880s by the Scottish international lawyer, James Lorimer. These attracted greater attention and stimulated considerable discussion, at least in academic circles. Lorimer had no hesitation in rejecting the balance of power as a guarantee of peace and stability. It was 'an empty diplomatic fiction' and 'a mere proclamation of international anarchy'. The real problem was to 'project into international

---

176. (M. Adler), *Der Krieg, die Congressidee und die allgemeine Wehrpflicht* (Prague, 1868), summarised in Kamarovsky, *Le Tribunal international*, pp. 381–3.

177. *Mission actuelle des souverains. Par l'un d'eux* (Paris, 1882), Chapter xii.

178. R. de la Grasserie, *Des Moyens pratiques pour parvenir à la suppression de la paix armée et de la guerre* (Paris, 1894), pp. 57–64, 88–99.

life the institutions of which we have had experience in national life'.[179] This was to be done by the creation of an international legislature of two houses. The upper, the senate, was to consist of representatives chosen by the monarch in each of the European states, acting together with the upper house of the state legislature if there were one. The lower, the chamber of deputies, was to be chosen by the lower house of each state legislature or, if none existed, by the monarch. A rough system of proportional representation was to apply. Each of the six major powers (Germany, France, the Habsburg Empire, Russia, Italy and Great Britain) was to send five senators and fifteen deputies to the European parliament; but smaller states were to be represented only in accordance with their international importance as this was determined by the great powers. There was to be an international ministry of fifteen members (five senators elected by the senate and ten deputies chosen by the lower house) which must always include at least one representative of each of the great powers, and which would choose the president who controlled this international machinery. The legislation passed by the two chambers and assented to by the president would constitute new international law; in this respect the scheme was essentially one of constitutional monarchy expanded to an international scale. There was to be an international court (fourteen judges and a president to be chosen by the international ministry) and, an original touch, an international bar made up of members of the bars of the individual states or those who had taken the highest law degrees in the universities of Europe. Decisions of the court and enactments of the legislature would be enforced by an international army to which each state contributed men or a money equivalent, again in proportion to its international importance. All its officers above the rank of colonel must be commissioned by and responsible solely to the international ministry. In the same way the expenses of the new structure were to be met by an international tax, with states again contributing in proportion to their importance.[180]

This was the most workmanlike and detailed plan of international government hitherto produced anywhere. It was realistic in its recognition that the future of Europe was in the hands of a small number of great powers and that any scheme of this kind must safeguard their position if it were to have any chance of success. It understood that any workable plan of international organisation must make provision for political and

179. *The Institutes of the Law of Nations* (Edinburgh–London, 1883–84), ii, 205–6, 239. The essentials of his scheme had been published more than a decade earlier in his 'Proposition d'un congrès national, basé sur le principe de facto', *Revue de Droit International et de Législation Comparée*, iii (1871), 8–11.

180. The scheme is given in full in *Institutes* . . ., ii, Chapter xiv.

economic change. Nevertheless, it drew the fire of critics who despaired of the possibility of international government or dismissed it out of hand as an objective unworthy in itself. Of these the German lawyer and political writer J.G. Bluntschli was the most prominent. Writing even before Lorimer's proposals had taken their final form, he agreed with him that the status quo could not be permanently fixed, but accused him of aiming at a republicanising of Europe to which the continent's whole historical development was opposed. His proposals for an international legislature in particular Bluntschli denounced as 'completely republican'.[181] Such a European parliament was unworkable: it would contain no coherent political parties and would have no political tradition of its own to draw upon. In the same way the international governing committee which Lorimer had suggested would be divided by conflicting national interests and unable to act effectively, while the states would refuse to reduce their armed forces and entrust their security merely to the new international machinery. The plan, in fact, was no more than 'a fantasy which can never be realised (*lebensunfähiges Phantasiegebilde*)'.[182] Bluntschli went on to put forward a competing scheme of his own, but one much more limited and cautious than that of Lorimer. This provided for an international legislature of two houses in each of which every great power was to have twice as many representatives as any of the smaller states. This, he agreed, could create new international law. However, the lower house, the only democratic element in the structure, was to meet only every two or three years, except in emergencies; and the representatives of any state were to be able to demand its exemption from the effects of any new legislation. Moreover, the confederation was to have no army or finances of its own. If any member-state must be coerced this could be done only by the great powers; and Bluntschli stressed the difficulty of any effective action when the essential interests or independence of any state appeared to be in question. Real power, he had no doubt, must remain with the individual states. It was futile to subject them to either a monarch or a president, or to any kind of European parliament, while a single European state was a contradiction in terms so long as there was no single European people. He therefore made no high claims for his proposals. They did not mean disarmament or an end to war: they would merely help to slow or halt the growth of armaments and reduce the likelihood of conflict. They harked back, he contended, to the ideas of Sully and were quite distinct from the utopian fantasies of Saint-Pierre and Lorimer.[183]

181. *Gesammelte kleine Schriften* (Nordlingen, 1879–81), ii, 293–5.
182. *Gesammelte kleine Schriften*, ii, 296–8.
183. *Gesammelte kleine Schriften*, ii, 303–12.

*But is peace possible?* Bluntschli's tepid view of his own proposals reflected, in diluted form, a cynicism about the possibility or even the desirability of lasting peace which still ran deep all over Europe. The hopes and idealism of the peace movement were still voiced, however loudly, by only a small minority. Everywhere the dominant if often unspoken assumption was still that conflict between states and nations was inevitable. The belief, centuries-old, that war was part of the natural order and beyond the power of man to end, was still acquiesced in almost without question by the great majority of Europeans. The stress which the advocates of peace placed on the disruptive and destructive effects of war was met partly by claims that these had been exaggerated, that modern arms and military methods had in fact made international conflicts shorter and less bloody;[184] and the brief wars of 1859, 1864, 1866 and even 1870–71 and 1877–78 gave some plausibility to such claims. Sometimes it was argued that military service had important educative effects and that armies focused and strengthened feelings of national unity.[185] At a deeper level the peace movement now found itself challenged more than ever in the past by the assertion that conflict was not merely inescapable but beneficial, an essential engine of progress. In one form this found expression in claims, put forward mainly in the German world, that war could help or force a state to develop its industrial capacity and thus increase its economic power and wealth: temporary sacrifices might thus produce fundamental and lasting benefits. Friedrich List, the greatest single figure in the history of economic nationalism, had argued along these lines in the 1840s; and he was followed by an entire school of German economists, often very able ones – Schmoller, Roscher, Knies and others – who stressed the possible constructive effects of conflict between states.[186] More far-reaching, however, was the repeated assertion that struggle underlay all human advance, that through it alone could higher forms of society triumph, as progress demanded, over lower ones. By concentrating and focusing human energies, by putting humanity to the greatest of all tests, war fostered the noblest aspects of human nature – courage, discipline, comradeship, self-sacrifice – and allowed, even compelled, men to rise above the selfish materialism which would otherwise corrupt them. The permeation of so much intellectual life in the last decades of the nineteenth century by attitudes derived from Darwinian evolutionary theory provided an apparent scientific foundation

184. For example, Holtzendorff-Vietmannsdorff, *Die Idee des ewigen Völkerfriedens*, p. 44; M. Jähns, *Ueber Krieg, Frieden und Kultur: Eine Umschau* (Berlin, 1893), p. 361.
185. A good example is S. Stella, *La pace perpetua e l'esercito* (Turin, 1891), pp. 25–8.
186. E. Silberner, *The Problem of War in Nineteenth-Century Economic Thought* (Princeton, 1946), pp. 149–50 and Chapter x. For a similar attitude see Jähns, *Ueber Krieg*, pp. 60–80.

for such attitudes. But this insistence on the creative nature of international conflict went further; it had powerful emotional overtones as well as pseudo-scientific ones. General attitudes of this kind were far from new. The idea of a cyclical process governing human affairs which meant that peace inevitably led to self-indulgence and materialism, which could be remedied only by the stresses and sacrifices of war, was many centuries old. In its late-nineteenth-century variant, however, it was put forward with an insistence hitherto unknown. Assertions of this kind came from many sources. Radicals often showed as much faith in them as conservatives. Proudhon, for example, though he believed firmly that war was destined to give way to the economic forces making irresistibly for international peace, had none the less seen it as creative through its ability to evoke courage and self-sacrifice.[187]

But it was from the 1870s onwards that this moralising of conflict reached its highest point. War could be presented as a divinely ordained force for the improvement of humanity, as when an English pamphleteer claimed that it was 'appointed by a Higher Power as one of the means of education and discipline for the human race' and that nations deprived of its vivifying influence were doomed to stagnation.[188] The best-known statement of this attitude came in a letter from Helmuth von Moltke, the great Prussian chief-of-staff, to Bluntschli in 1880: 'Perpetual peace is a dream, and not even a beautiful dream. War is an element of the divine order of the world. In it are developed the noblest virtues of man: courage and self-denial, fidelity to duty and the spirit of sacrifice; soldiers give their lives. Without war the world would stagnate and lose itself in materialism'.[189] Compulsory arbitration of international disputes, it could therefore be argued, was highly undesirable, for it undermined the basic obligation of all states to follow their own consciences and be guided by their own conceptions of right and wrong. An arbitral tribunal could apply only law; but 'there is unquestionably a higher Law than law', and war was far preferable to 'acquiescence in recognized wrong'.[190] Other observers, though they discarded this quasi-religious phraseology, had no less confidence in the rightness of the underlying attitudes. 'The day when humanity became a great pacified Roman empire and had no more external enemies', wrote Ernest Renan, one of the greatest French intellectuals of the century, 'would be the day when morality and

187. J.-L. Puech, 'Proudhon et la guerre', in *Proudhon et notre temps* (Paris, 1920), pp. 208–12.
188. *War, its Causes and Consequences and how it may be averted* (London, 1871), pp. 6–7.
189. Quoted in Best, *Humanity in Warfare*, p. 145.
190. A.T. Mahan, 'The Peace Conference and the Moral Aspect of War', *North American Review*, 169 (1899), 442, 446.

intelligence would be in the greatest danger'.[191] Almost two decades later the novelist Emile Zola, like Renan far from a militarist in any normal sense of that term, asked in 1891: 'Would not the end of war be the end of humanity? Is not war life itself? Nothing exists in nature, is born, grows, multiplies, except by struggle. We must eat and be eaten so that the world goes on. Only the warlike nations have prospered; a nation dies as soon as it disarms. War is the school of discipline, of sacrifice, of courage.'[192] Such assertions were most frequent and forthright in Germany, where even active supporters of the peace movement had sometimes to admit that a cosmopolitan outlook and internationalist feeling were much weaker than in Britain, France, Belgium or the Netherlands.[193] But they could be found everywhere; and the attitude which underlay them was the most potent intellectual and still more emotional barrier to the growth of effective internationalism. Lasting peace, in this scheme of things, would preserve artificially weak and declining states and prolong their lives undeservedly. It would thus prevent the growth at their expense of stronger and more efficient ones which were better adapted to survive and therefore more deserving of survival. Competition in armaments was healthy, a less destructive substitute for outright war. In an arms race the stronger and more enduring would triumph for, as a leading American exponent of these attitudes succinctly put it, 'armament represents the aggregate of the natural forces inherent in any community'.[194]

Even for some time after 1914 thinking of this type survived, so that in 1916 an English historian could still argue that 'the living nation . . . has generally been the warlike nation'.[195] In the United States particularly, able to watch the cataclysm in Europe from a safe distance and draw vicarious excitement from it, such attitudes remained strong. There many radicals, anxious for far-reaching internal reforms, felt until the country's entry into the conflict in April 1917 that its neutrality denied it the purifying and character-building effects of belligerence. One complained in the summer of 1916 that 'the American nation needs the tonic of a serious moral adventure' and another had no doubt that 'if this war had not come, we should all have been rotten'. Near the end of the struggle

191. *La Réforme morale et intellectuelle* (Paris, 1874), p. 111.

192. Quoted in K. Hildebrand, 'Europäisches Zentrum, überseeische Peripherie und neue Welt', *Historische Zeitschrift*, 249 (1989–90), 67. Zola also wrote a good deal attacking war and its effects, however.

193. K. Lamprecht, *Die Nation und die Friedensbewegung* (Berlin–Leipzig, 1914), pp. 8–9; K. von Stengel, *Weltstaat und Friedensproblem* (Berlin, 1909), Preface, p. x.

194. A.T. Mahan, *Armaments and Arbitration, or, The Place of Force in the International Relations of States* (New York–London, 1912), p. 11.

195. G.G. Coulton, *The Main Illusions of Pacifism* (Cambridge, 1916), pp. 79–80.

the same writer consoled himself for the losses it had brought by the thought that 'this war, terrible as it seems, may do us much good. . . . It caught us just soon enough: before swelling luxury ruined us: while the spirit of sacrifice was strong upon us.'[196]

*Norman Angell and his critics: the utilitarian tradition restated* The social Darwinists and those who praised the moral effects of war did not have the argument all their own way. Their opponents could easily claim that even if there were a Darwinian struggle for survival in the natural world this proved no need for such a struggle between nations. Moreover, must not war inevitably eliminate the best rather than the weakest individuals in any society and thus retard rather than forward its improvement?[197] In the years before 1914, however, the most successful and widely read attack on the idea of war as either inevitable or constructive came from a different direction. It took the form of a kind of reconstituted Cobdenism, a restatement of the idea of war as essentially silly, the result of the smothering of intelligence by feeling, an emotional indulgence that sensible men rationally pursuing their own material interests could never succumb to. This reiteration of many of the essential attitudes of mid-nineteenth century free-trading liberalism (and also of the eighteenth-century Enlightenment) was the work of the Anglo-American publicist Norman Angell.

In a series of books published just before 1914, of which much the most widely read was *The Great Illusion* which first appeared in 1909, Angell argued that war was now more than ever irrational and that it must inevitably defeat its own ends. Morality and self-interest coincided; and their coincidence could be seen by anyone with intelligence and the will to use it. His whole attitude was flat-footedly rationalistic. Common sense in the service of material self-interest must draw the nations towards peace and cooperation: the only real obstacle to this was 'wild nature and human error, ignorance and passion'. The more modern and developed a society, the more completely involved in the increasingly dense network of international communications and economic contacts, the more it must be driven towards cooperation with its neighbours. There was war in the Balkans in 1912 only because its peoples 'have been geographically outside the influence of European industrial and commercial life'.[198] In *The Great*

---

196. Quoted in J.A. Thompson, *Reformers and War: American Progressive Publicists and the First World War* (Cambridge, 1987), pp. 173–4, 230.

197. The Russian sociologist J. Novikow (Novikov), among many others, made these points in his diffuse and emotional *War and its Alleged Benefits* (London, 1912), Chapters iv and xii.

198. *Peace Theories and the Balkan War* (London, 1912), pp. 32, 59.

*Illusion* he argued that there was no necessary connection whatever between military strength and territorial expansion on the one hand and economic growth and well-being on the other. 'The factors which really constitute prosperity have not the remotest connection with military or naval power, all our political jargon notwithstanding.'[199] Victory in war could confer no material benefit on the victor. Nor could he for any length of time damage the prosperity of the vanquished. If he attempted to do so the collapse of credit in the defeated state would inevitably mean, because of the rapid internationalisation of the credit mechanism which had been in progress for a generation or more, a similar collapse, to a large extent at least, in the victorious one. The imposition of a war indemnity could not enrich the victor who imposed it. Wealth could not be transferred between states as it could between individuals: the recipient one must either accept goods, which would damage its own industry, or gold, which would raise its domestic price-level and reduce its industrial competitiveness.[200] A country's trade could not be destroyed by military conquest, while the possession of a colonial empire, however large, added nothing to the wealth of the imperial power. It was, however, above all on the financial interdependence of the major states and the international credit structure that Angell relied to avert war. Any major conflict must destroy this fragile but essential mechanism and necessarily lead to general impoverishment. Therefore such a war would not take place. Elementary self-interest, a kind of salutary selfishness, would make it impossible. Men needed only to be clear-headed enough to see where the obvious balance of material advantage lay.

Morality was irrelevant. 'The difference between the Pacifist and Militarist is not, at bottom, a moral one at all . . . but an intellectual one.'[201] At the end of *The Great Illusion* he put the point even more unequivocally. 'What is morality', he asked, 'but the codification of the laws of general interest?'[202] Bentham never put the utilitarian point of view more brutally; and it is not surprising that Angell's copious writings on international questions in the pre-1914 years contain no mention of arbitration or any form of international government. Nor did he advocate any form of peace crusade or pacifism in the normal sense of these terms. His hopes were pinned firmly on a rational self-interest so obvious that no sensible man could or would ignore it. In this he was much narrower and more uncompromising than Cobden. The great apostle of free trade had

---

199. *The Great Illusion* (New York, 1911), p. 66. All references are to this American edition of the book.

200. *The Great Illusion*, Pt I, Chapter vi.

201. Introduction by Angell to Novikow, *War and its Alleged Benefits*, p. ix.

202. p. 371.

based his faith in the effects of free and unhindered contacts between peoples on a belief, though one never very clearly formulated, that these were in some way inherent in nature and rooted, though he did not use the term, in a kind of natural law. Angell, by contrast, justified his arguments in essentially historical terms, and short-range ones at that. From the 1870s onwards the growth of communications had laid the foundations of an immense structure of international credit. Large–scale war would bring down this structure, with disastrous consequences for the whole world. Mankind must adjust to this situation; and the only rational response was the abandonment of war. This combination of superficial clarity and essential narrow-mindedness runs through all his work.[203]

*The Great Illusion* was a very successful book. It was translated into at least seventeen languages; and by 1914 there were in Britain alone about a hundred societies and organisations devoted, to varying extents, to the propagation of its ideas. A monthly periodical, *War and Peace*, was set up in 1913 for the same purpose. Angell was so successful because he put forward very forcibly ideas which had long been widespread and were now diffused more widely than ever before. The belief that even the victor was likely to lose by war had by now a considerable history; and the rapid growth of a world economy from the 1870s onwards gave it greater plausibility. Already in the early 1870s it had been argued that international flows of capital before the Franco–Prussian war meant that 'it became impossible to ruin others without imperilling one's own investments, or to strike an enemy without killing a debtor'; while a few years later it could be confidently predicted that the states of Europe would be brought together by a growing realisation of 'their inability to do harm' to each other.[204] There was now a fairly widespread feeling that capitalists, especially financiers of all kinds, were the group most likely to be damaged by war and most conscious of the risks they ran.[205] In the years just before 1914 beliefs of this kind were stronger than ever and were being voiced across the whole political spectrum. On the Left the German Social Democrat leader August Bebel told the party congress in 1911 that 'German industry and German commerce have expanded enormously. Great amounts of French, English and American capital have been invested in Germany, whereas German capital goes abroad to be

203. On the contrast between Angell and Cobden see C. Novari, 'The Great Illusion revisited; the international theory of Norman Angell', *Review of International Studies*, 15 (1989), 342. For a contemporary attack on the essential amorality of Angell's ideas see W.L. Grane, *The Passing of War: A Study in Things that make for Peace* (London, 1912), pp. 7–14.

204. Lavelaye, *On the Causes of War*, p. 3; J. Novicow (Novikov), *La Politique internationale* (Paris, 1886), p. 355; cf. L. Levi, *Peace the Handmaid of Commerce* (London, n.d.), pp. 7–8, and de la Grasserie, *Moyens pratiques . . .*, p. 22.

205. For example, Molinari, *Grandeur et décadence de la guerre*, pp. 166–7.

invested there. I openly admit that perhaps the greatest guarantee of world peace lies in this international export of capital.' At the following year's congress another of the party's leaders, Hugo Haase, acclaimed the trend towards economic interdependence of the major states as 'a factor working against the warmongers'.[206] Many capitalists were equally sure that the whole drift of economic change was in favour of peace. In 1911 there were suggestions in the United States (though these never went further than private discussion among a few individuals) that a grandiloquently named International Society to Control the Finances of the World in the Interests of Peace might be created. This in turn might establish a neutral bank or some comparable agency which would build up a huge reservoir of funds to be used in some unspecified way for the preservation of peace.[207] Two years later another American put Angell's case at least as forcibly as he himself had ever done:

> 'great wars ending perhaps – whoever is victorious – in the total destruction of European credit, present appalling risks unknown to any earlier generation. The bankers will not find the money for such a fight, the industries of Europe will not maintain it, the statesmen cannot. There will be no general war until the masters direct the fighters to fight. The masters have much to gain, but vastly more to lose, and their signal will not be given.'[208]

Even at the highest political levels Angell-type assumptions sometimes came to carry much weight. In the final crisis of July 1914 Sir Edward Grey assured the Austrian ambassador in London that a great conflict 'must involve the expenditure of so vast a sum of money and such an interference with trade, that a war would be accompanied or followed by a complete collapse of European credit and industry'.[209]

Angell thus struck a note to which the response was widespread and immediate. He brought together in a persuasive mixture many of the elements which had over generations contributed to mainstream liberal thinking about war and the world economy. The emphasis on rationality of the philosophes of eighteenth-century France; the stress on material benefits of the British utilitarians; the faith of Cobden and his followers in the unifying force of economic ties: all these came together in his work. He was in many ways the culmination of a long tradition; and some of his

206. Both are quoted in R.A. Fletcher, 'Cobden as educator: the free-trade internationalism of Eduard Bernstein, 1899– 1914', *American Historical Review*, 88 (1988), 576.

207. W. Kuehl, *Seeking World Order: The United States and International Organisation to 1920* (Nashville, 1969), p. 153.

208. D.S. Jordan, *What shall we say? Being comments on current matters of War and Waste* (Boston, 1913), pp. 20–1.

209. Quoted in K.M. Wilson, *The Policy of the Entente. Essays on the Determinants of British Foreign Policy, 1904–1914* (Cambridge, 1985), p. 13.

assertions were indeed to be borne out by events. His insistence that a victor could not in practice exact large indemnities from a defeated state was justified in the years after 1918. On a longer time-scale his claim that the European states would eventually realise that their colonial empires were not worth having was also borne out. Yet it is not difficult to see how superficial many of his arguments were. Like internationalists of so many different kinds, not least Marx and his followers, he grossly underestimated the importance of national feeling. To him exclusive nationalism was irrational and backward-looking, and therefore unimportant. This was a crucial limitation of his thinking. For him the significant divisions were not between nations and states but between occupational and professional groups: the common interests which bound together trade-unionists or business men of different countries were more real than any division between nations. He even suggested a system of pairing across national frontiers between members of such groups. Thus for every member of a disarmament pressure group enrolled in Britain one might be recruited by a similar body in Germany. A member of parliament might oppose any increase in British armaments if a member of the Reichstag undertook to do the same in Germany. This principle might be applied equally to academics, students, trade-unionists, churchmen and other groups.[210]

The unreality of many of Angell's assumptions came under immediate attack from some at least of his contemporaries. Their criticisms focused not so much on his insistence that war could never pay (though even here there were complaints that he had pushed his arguments much further than historical experience and contemporary facts justified),[211] but rather on his ignoring of popular emotions, of which national feeling was by far the most important. 'I hold', wrote his most trenchant American critic, 'that the interest of the nation is indeed the business of the government, but that the danger of war proceeds mainly from the temper of the people, which, when aroused, disregards self-interest'; and he concluded that 'the entire conception of the work (i.e. *The Great Illusion*) is itself an illusion based upon a profound misreading of human action'.[212] A British journalist with decades of experience of international relations made essentially the same comment. 'The steadying influence of *la haute finance*, of finance in general', he wrote, 'is certainly all that it is represented to be;

210. *The Great Illusion*, pp. 359–60.
211. See in particular J.H. Jones, *The Economics of War and Conquest: an Examination of Mr. Norman Angell's Economic Doctrines* (London, 1915). Jones made the telling point that in all his writings Angell never quoted in support of any of his claims a professional economist of real standing.
212. Mahan, *Armaments and Arbitration*, pp. 124, 153.

but such peaceful influence as it exerts is exercised, in our time, almost solely upon Governments. In presence of the rise of a sudden gust of chauvinistic passion, Governments will be forced into line at the head of the self-maddened mob, and the philosophers in the van will have to advance with the rest.'[213]

Angell's utilitarian rationalism brought him very close to saying that war was now impossible: though he never made this claim explicitly it was implied in much of what he wrote.[214] It meant that he also grossly underestimated the willingness of the ordinary man, once war had broken out, to shoulder burdens and accept losses of a kind unknown for generations. In this underestimate he was joined by every liberal, every commentator influenced, often more or less unconsciously, by utilitarianism, of the pre-war years. If men naturally sought pleasure (which in terms of international relations meant primarily the free flow of goods and capital between states) and avoided pain (in the form not merely of casualties and material destruction but also of economic disruption) then war, even if it came, would be relatively short. No normal man would be willing to face the enormous cost of a long conflict. Even almost a year after the great struggle had begun, in May 1915, one leading British radical could confidently assure another that 'Germany can't suffer complete defeat, short of a four or five years war, and . . . none of the allied peoples will stand that'.[215] This complete failure to grasp the energising effects of mass struggle was particularly clear in the gross underestimate, in the immediate pre-war years, of the financial resources which could be mobilised by a great nation in case of conflict. One well-informed author in 1912, for example, had no doubt that Britain 'must be rapidly approaching the limit of its taxable capacity' and that 'Thirty to forty millions sterling a-year is the extreme limit of war taxation available to us, and that could only be levied at the risk of curtailing consumption, and thus obtaining less instead of more revenue'.[216] Yet only a few years later the last wartime budget, presented

213. W.M. Fullerton, *Problems of Power. A Study of International Politics from Sadowa to Kirk-Kilissé* (London, 1913), p. 228; for a more detailed attack on Angell's assumption that states would act rationally in international affairs see pp. 161–3.

214. After 1914 he attempted on several occasions, not altogether successfully, to defend himself against allegations of this kind: the most important of these apologias is the long Addendum to his *The Fruits of Victory* (London, 1921).

215. M. Swartz, *The Union of Democratic Control in British Politics during the First World War* (Oxford, 1971), p. 68.

216. W.H. Lawson, *Modern Wars and War Taxes* (Edinburgh–London, 1912), pp. 117, 339. The same author, however, made the important point, which had quite escaped Angell, that a highly developed world financial and credit network might greatly strengthen any country with access to it in case of war (p. 436).

by Bonar Law in 1918, provided for the raising of total revenue of £842 million and expenditure of £2550 million – virtually £7 million a day.

The central weakness of the tradition of which Angell was an extreme example was that it neglected, indeed was hardly aware of, the huge possibilities for both good and evil of the unified mass societies which now existed in the great states of western Europe. Mass emotions, mass sacrifices, mass triumphs, played little or no part in its thinking. Born in the eighteenth century among a small intellectual élite, it had been shaken by the cataclysms of 1792–1815; but then a century of general peace and rapidly growing physical comfort and security, especially from the 1870s onwards, had fostered its renewed growth. Nothing in its history had prepared it for the new situation it faced after 1914. Its essential failure was one of imagination; and such a failure could hardly have been avoided.

## (3) Armageddon and after: international organisation and a new world

The war dealt a devastating blow to the hopes of the pre-1914 years. The realisation in all the belligerent states that they had embarked on an unprecedentedly costly and difficult struggle meant that in many of them, and above all in the English-speaking world, demands and proposals rapidly multiplied for a radical remodelling of the international system which would make impossible future catastrophes of this kind. Outright pacifism, where it was allowed to express itself, became more vocal. In Britain it centred largely around resistance to the threat of conscription: a small group of radical pacifists began as early as November 1914 to plan organised resistance to any proposal for compulsory military service,[217] and by early in the following year the No-Conscription Fellowship was in existence. In Germany the tiny peace movement at the end of 1914 condemned all territorial annexations which might result from the war (but only within Europe and if they ran counter to the desires of the population concerned), while in the summer of 1916 a small group of pacifist intellectuals formed the *Zentralstelle Völkerrecht* to agitate for the restoration of Belgium, an end to competing power alliances, and international disarmament.[218] In France a *Comité pour la reprise des relations internationales* was founded at the beginning of 1916 by a radical trade-unionist to work for a peace without annexations, while the government late in the same year felt that pacifist tendencies in the

---

217. T.C. Kennedy, *The Hound of Conscience: A History of the No-Conscription Fellowship, 1914–1919* (Fayetteville, 1981), p. 46.

218. F.L. Carsten, *War against War: British and German Radical Movements in the First World War* (London, 1982), p. 90.

country were strong enough to justify a long official report on them.[219] Some effort was made to bring these forces together across national frontiers: for example the International Congress of Women which met at The Hague in April 1915 set up an International Committee of Women for Permanent Peace. Simultaneously the Central Organisation for a Lasting Peace, which had been formed under Dutch and Swiss leadership with its headquarters in The Hague, included in its Minimum Programme the whole range of classical internationalist demands: self-determination for all peoples, reduction of armaments, freedom of the seas, parliamentary control of foreign policy, the creation of an effective international court and united international action against any state disturbing the peace. But none of this had the slightest effect on government policies or mass emotions. In Britain, where it was most vocal, pacifism was weakened by its lack of unity. It was divided, as in the past, between adherents who rejected all wars without exception and those who were willing to accept wars of self-defence. It was also split between groups whose refusal to fight was based on religious belief and radicals who rejected war as an inevitable outcome of the capitalism they wished to overthrow. It was an amalgam of different groups – the old nineteenth-century peace society movement, now a mere ghost of its former self; the Quakers (though in fact about a third of all British Quakers of military age joined the armed forces);[220] the new Union of Democratic Control created to change completely the conduct and organisation of British foreign policy; the religiously-inspired Fellowship of Reconciliation formed in 1914; and the No-Conscription Fellowship – which never made up a united movement.[221] In Germany the *Zentralstelle Völkerrecht* was allowed to carry on some very modest activities precisely because it was a tiny and ineffective body which posed no threat to the war effort. In France the anarchist and syndicalist opposition to the war which developed in 1915–16 had very little influence; the strikes and mutinies there which appeared for a time in 1917 so menacing were the outcome of privations and losses, not of widespread rejection of war on principle.

*A league of nations: limited and legalistic approaches* Far more important than outright pacifism was the demand for a radical remodelling of international relations which would make future wars impossible.

219. P. Renouvin, 'L'opinion publique en France pendant la guerre, 1914–1918', *Revue d'Histoire Diplomatique* (1970), 305–6, 311.

220. Kennedy, *The Hound of Conscience*, p. 41.

221. These divisions are brought out in Kennedy, *The Hound of Conscience*, and K. Robbins, *The Abolition of War: The 'Peace Movement' in Britain, 1914–1919* (Cardiff, 1976).

Agitation and proposals of this kind began to appear in Britain and to a lesser extent in France very early in the conflict. The old system, it was argued, based on crude power politics, controlled by aristocratic and military influences, cynical and secretive, had totally failed. It must be replaced by something quite different and indisputably better. The popularity of such attitudes was reflected in a very sharp growth in the membership of the newly formed Union of Democratic Control, notably in 1915. Sir Edward Grey himself was from the beginning of the war strongly attracted by the idea of far-reaching change in the international order. In August 1915 he told Colonel House, the personal envoy of President Wilson, that 'the pearl of great price . . . would be some League of Nations that could be relied on to insist that disputes between any two nations must be settled'.[222] A few months earlier the League of Nations Society, an outgrowth of a group of scholars and politicians formed in the autumn of 1914 with Lord Bryce as chairman to study the problems of international organisation, had begun to propagandise, while across the Atlantic the League to Enforce Peace embarked on similar work. By 1917 it could be claimed that in Britain 'this phrase "A League of Nations", which was unknown two years ago . . . is in everybody's mouth today'.[223] In France, with German armies established deep in her territory, a deep sense of vulnerability coupled with a long tradition of territorial expansion in Europe meant that such idealism was never as strong as in Britain. Many Frenchmen could still think of the war as a struggle for the recovery of Alsace-Lorraine and a permanent weakening of Germany, rather than for any international order.[224] But here too the demand for some fundamental remodelling of the international system could be clearly heard. In 1915 the *La Paix par le Droit* group put forward a scheme for compulsory arbitration of all future disputes between states; while at the end of that year the main French socialist party committed itself to disarmament, democratic control of foreign policy and the compulsory arbitration of international disputes backed by military and economic sanctions. In July 1917 the Chamber of Deputies set up a commission to produce a scheme for a league of nations. The report it published almost a year later envisaged a stronger league with greater coercive powers than most British and American plans were willing to

222. E.H. Buehrig, *Woodrow Wilson and the Balance of Power* (Bloomington, Ind., 1955), pp. 206–7. A series of public declarations by British and French statesmen from 1914 onwards in favour of some form of league can be found in M. Leroy, *La Société des nations: but suprême de la guerre* (Paris, 1917), pp. 13–17.

223 A. Williams, *A League of Nations: How To Begin It* (London, 1917), p. 22.

224. For example, A. Aulard, *La Paix future d'après la Révolution francaise et Kant* (Paris, 1915), a pamphlet by a leading French historian, which demanded (p. 29) the permanent division of Germany into its former component states, the strict limitation of their armies, and the creation in the Rhineland of a buffer-state to protect France from future attack.

envisage. By the last stages of the war a French League of Nations Society presided over by a former foreign minister, Léon Bourgeois, was working to influence public opinion.

But how far was this reshaping of the international system to go? Should membership of the new league be open to all nations? Or should it, at least in its first years, be essentially a continuation of the wartime cooperation of the Entente powers from which the defeated Central ones should be excluded? British and American projects tended, often without discussing the point, to assume the former, though some envisaged little more, at least in the first place, than a regrouping of the traditional great powers.[225] The schemes proposed from continental Europe, of which there were considerably fewer, were much more likely to take the less generous view.[226] Even more important, what should be the powers of such a league? Some suggestions went no further than an alliance whose members would undertake not to go to war with one another and to resist any breach of the peace by non-members. At the end of the war a British historian urged that anything more than this would be unrealistic and called for 'a League of Nations formed simply for security rather than for the more ambitious idea of justice'.[227] Many proposals went a step further and urged the safeguarding of peace by essentially legal means, by a strengthening and extension of international arbitration and conciliation. Such schemes provided for disputes which had a large legal or quasi-legal element and were obviously justiciable to be submitted to arbitration. More serious ones which could be held to involve the security, vital interests or honour of a state should be decided by some form of council of conciliation (the title differed in different schemes) which would be a political rather than a strictly legal body. Any power which refused to accept a decision of the council, it was generally agreed, must be forced to do so by economic sanctions (there was a general though usually implicit assumption that these would be rapidly effective and not too difficult to apply). In extreme cases physical coercion to the point of war might be used. Schemes of this kind appeared in Britain throughout the war;[228] and

225. For example, Williams, *A League of Nations*, pp. 16–17. He saw Germany and Austria-Hungary, however, as founder-members, as well as the United States and Japan.

226. For example, A. Mater, *La Société des Nations* (Paris, 1918); A. Sacerdoti, *Progetto Americano di una lega internazionale per il rafforzamento della pace* (Florence, 1918).

227. A.F. Pollard, *The League of Nations: An Historical Argument* (Oxford, 1918), pp. 51, 66.

228. A. Williams, *Proposals for a League of Peace and Material Protection among Nations* (London, 1915), pp. 9, 11; G. Lowes Dickinson, *After the War* (London, 1915), pp. 24ff.; M.D. Dubin, 'Toward the Concept of Collective Security: the Bryce Group's "Proposals for the Avoidance of War", 1914–1917', *International Organization*, xxiv (1970), 288–318; Viscount Bryce and others, *Proposals for the Prevention of Future Wars* (London, 1917); R. Unwin, *Functions of a League of Nations* (London, 1917), pp. 15–20; G. Murray, *The League of Nations and the Democratic Idea* (Oxford, 1918), pp. 21–3.

though in continental Europe they were notably fewer they could be found there also.[229]

This approach was relatively cautious and limited in scope. One leading British liberal saw the formation of such a league as 'merely an adding together of the present arbitration treaties'.[230] Others felt that anything more far-reaching, such as an international body with quasi-legislative powers, was impractical.[231] An Italian commentator feared that a league with extensive authority would be dominated by a small number of great states and that the smaller ones might find they had 'sacrificed the integrity of their sovereign powers on the altar of a divinity which cannot protect the independent development of their existence'.[232] To such observers any move towards world government seemed both likely to fail and, in so far as it was successful, probably dangerous.

*A league of nations: more far-reaching schemes* Other schemes, however, were more optimistic and more ambitious. Broadly speaking, the more politically and socially radical a writer, the more likely he was to favour some form of international organisation able to take positive action, to initiate and control events, and not confined merely to responding to them. Very early in the war there appeared in Belgium the most far-reaching of all such schemes. This envisaged a full-scale international government – a legislature of two houses, of which the upper was to be composed of representatives nominated by international associations, corporations and other bodies of all kinds to speak for great economic, social and intellectual interests; an international council, with one member from each component state of the league, which would choose a supreme executive of twelve members; an international court to which states must submit all disputes; and disarmament (so that the peacetime strength of any state's armed forces would never exceed one man for each 300 of its population). There was to be an international bank which would issue an international currency. All tariffs must be abolished. Postal charges must be equalised throughout the world, while landlocked states were to be guaranteed access to the sea through the territory of others. The whole of Africa was to become a *domaine international* in which free trade and the open door reigned supreme (a first approach to the League of Nations mandate idea as it took shape after 1919). There were also to be

229. E. Rigono, 'Les Facteurs de la guerre et le problème de la paix', *Scientia*, xviii (1915), 43–5; E. Catellani, *La Lega delle Nazioni* (Padua, 1919), p. 19.
230. Murray, *The League of Nations*, p. 21.
231. Bryce et al, *Proposals . . ..*, p. 28.
232. Catellani, *La Lega delle Nazioni*, p. 18.

international measures for the conservation of natural resources (a remarkably prescient suggestion not paralleled in any other of the many proposals put forward in the years which followed) and greatly increased international support for education and cultural activities of all kinds. The author even specified the official emblem of the new league (an orange sun on a white ground). These proposals were the most sweeping made during the war in any scheme of this kind; and in spite of its utopian elements this little-known proposal was an impressive one, penetrating and imaginative.[233]

The best-known and perhaps the most influential proposals of this interventionist kind, however, were those put forward by three leading British radicals, J.A. Hobson, L.S. Woolf and H.N. Brailsford. Hobson's significantly-titled *Towards International Government*, which appeared in 1915, called not merely, like so many other schemes, for arbitration and conciliation as means of settling international disputes, but also for an international executive elected by the member-nations of the league he proposed to create. This would have 'full powers to make and interpret international law'. The tasks of this supranational government, he emphasised, would not be merely negative, confined to preventing war and limiting armaments: they must be 'progressive'. In particular it must have full authority to cope with the changing situations which the future was sure to bring as world economic and social development unfolded.[234] Woolf too called for active international institutions: a high court whose decisions were to be binding on individual states, an international council which should decide the most important and dangerous inter-state disputes which were non-justiciable, and an international secretariat which the council would appoint.[235] Brailsford in his turn assumed that the league must have an executive, and a powerful one, though his discussion of the details was rather summary.[236] Even more than Hobson, he attached great importance to finding some means of accommodating peacefully within the international system evolving economic and social conditions and the changes, for example in frontiers, which the future would demand. He grasped very well the underlying conservative bias of almost all the peace schemes which had hitherto appeared over the centuries, the fact that 'the historic conception of a League of Peace took no account whatever of the world's need of change, growth and readjustment'. Peace, he insisted, must not be thought of merely in defensive and negative terms, for 'Life is

233. (P. Otlet), *Traité de paix générale basé sur une charte mondiale déclarant les droits de l'humanité et organisant la confédération des états* (Brussels, 1914), especially pp. 12–17.
234. See pp. 109, 147.
235. *International Government* (London, 1916), Chapters v–vii.
236. *A League of Nations* (London, 1917), pp. 307–10.

change, and a League of Peace that aimed at preserving peace by forbidding change would be a tyranny as oppressive as any Napoleonic dictatorship'.[237] More than the advocates of relatively cautious and legalistic schemes, Hobson and Brailsford were deeply aware of the economic component in state power and of the way in which economic change could undermine any given international status quo. To such change the political framework of international relations must adjust; and for such adjustment some effective supranational authority was needed. Moreover, Hobson claimed, 'Capital and labour alike are coming to realise that few of their deeper problems are any longer susceptible of merely national solutions'.[238] The irresistible force of economic advance therefore demanded at least a first step towards a world government which would be both strong and flexible. Since both he and Brailsford firmly believed that economic rivalry, and particularly competition for colonies and the markets and raw materials they could supply, had been a major cause of the war, they were both insistent that the league they hoped to create should foster international economic cooperation. It must break down exclusive national spheres of economic interest and control in colonial areas, foster the 'Open Door' everywhere, and be able to supervise trade routes, commercial practices, perhaps even labour standards and international migration. Brailsford in particular insisted that 'raw materials, including the staple foods, have become the pivot of world-politics' and by the end of the war looked forward to 'the rationing of the world's raw materials by a super-national authority'.[239]

Other British writers put forward roughly similar proposals. Lowes Dickinson, another radical idealist, envisaged the emergence of some form of international legislature to 'lay down rules for the peaceful intercourse of nations, in order to prevent the growth of the friction which leads to war': this to him meant in particular free trade and the universal application of the 'Open Door' principle.[240] Another, now less well known, urged the creation of an international council on which states would be represented roughly in proportion to their population (both Hobson and Brailsford had also seen the need for some form of proportional representation in this context). This would act as a parliament of nations and be able to draw up 'a complete written code of international law'. States would be forced to observe this by a system of

237. *A League of Nations*, pp. 81, 83.

238. J.A. Hobson, *Towards International Government*, (London, 1915) p. 196.

239. *The Covenant of Peace* (London, 1918), pp. 21, 31.

240. G. Lowes Dickinson, *The Crisis before Us* (London, 1917), pp. 220–3. For another scheme which stressed the need for flexibility and adaptation to change see F.N. Keen, *A League of Nations with Large Powers* (London, 1918), pp. 11–12.

fines and if this proved ineffective by military and naval coercion, preferably by an international force made up of contingents supplied by individual states.[241] As the war went on some schemes of this kind tended to become more and more far-reaching. One particularly ambitious British plan of 1917 demanded not merely an international parliament made up of representatives of all nations, an international court whose judges this parliament would nominate and an 'International Armament' strong enough to enforce any decision it might reach, but also international control of the arms industry everywhere. The parliament would ration strictly supplies of arms to individual states, allowing each of them only 'sufficient munitions of war to guard against reasonable contingencies'. To make this possible every arms factory throughout the world was to be fortified and guarded by units of the international army.[242] Another notably vague British proposal demanded a 'Supernational Court backed by Power under its own direct control' which must have 'Power incomparably greater than any State or group of States'. This would have at its disposal a great international army, an integrated force independently recruited and not made up merely of contingents from different states. It would also decide questions relating to colonial expansion and the availability of colonial raw materials (here there are distinct echoes of Hobson and Brailsford). Its work might be consolidated by the introduction of an international language: the author favoured a revival of Latin for this purpose.[243] Such schemes approached, and sometimes crossed, the borders of fantasy. Nevertheless, by the later stages of the war all the most important publicists and pressure-groups on the allied side and in neutral countries had come to accept the need for some form of permanent international body with substantial powers. The League of Nations Society in Britain; the League to Enforce Peace in the United States; the Central Organisation for a Lasting Peace, were in agreement on this. The British society, for example, supported an American proposal for an International Council, meeting at The Hague, which 'shall have power to propose measures which shall be the law as between the States of the League', and for a rudimentary international government which would superintend the use of force if necessary against any recalcitrant member-state.[244] A French proposal asked for the creation of an

241. F.N. Keen, *The World in Alliance: A Plan for Preventing Future Wars* (London, 1915), pp. 32–47, 53–7. The same essential ideas are repeated in his *Hammering out the Details* (London, 1917).

242. H.E. Hyde, *The International Solution: Will Great Britain lead the Way?* (London, 1917), pp. 14, 19–21.

243. Sir Charles Walston, *The Next War: Wilsonism and Anti-Wilsonism* (Cambridge, 1918), pp. 18–19, 49–50, 55.

244. *Tentative Draft Convention by an American Committee* (League of Nations Society, Publication No. 30; London, 1918), pp. 4, 6.

'executive directory' (the nomenclature significantly recalls the 1790s) whose members were to be nominated by the individual states. Its president would command an international police force made up of contingents supplied by these states and it would have complete control of all arms and munitions in state ownership. The author went in one respect further than any of the Anglo-American suggestions in calling also for the setting up of a *Banque des Nations* to which each belligerent country would subscribe in proportion to the war expenses it had incurred since 1914.[245] The very last days of the struggle saw the leader of one of the most important German political parties put forward proposals – a league of nations based on obligatory recourse to arbitration by an international court in case of dispute between states; disarmament; free trade and the ending of all economic monopolies in colonial areas; in extreme necessity coercion of recalcitrant states by an international army – which would have been perfectly acceptable to Hobson, Brailsford or Woolf.[246] Unprecedented strains and losses had thus by 1918 generated an unprecedented stream of far-reaching and even utopian schemes.

## The creation of the League

The differences of approach which had marked so much wartime discussion were carried over into the setting-up of the League of Nations as it emerged in 1919. On the one hand President Wilson, inspired by genuine idealism and driven by the need to reply to the peace propaganda of the new Bolshevik regime in Russia[247] wanted a 'peace without victory' and a league designed on generous lines which could embrace all democratic states. Even as late as November 1918 he hoped for an armistice which would leave Germany a significant military power able to counterbalance to some extent the British and French armies. On the other hand the French government, more than any other of the European Allies, saw the league simply as one of victors, a continuation of the wartime alliance. The international army and general staff with wide powers for which it hoped would thus be a guarantee of future French security against a resurgent Germany, indeed of French military

245. Mater, *La Société des Nations*, especially pp. 55–9; Leroy, *La Société des Nations*, was a more moderate proposal for a union which should be economic and administrative rather than political: it stressed the need to build on what international institutions already existed in such areas as communications and public health.

246. M. Erzberger, *Der Völkerbund: Der Weg zum Weltfrieden* (Berlin, 1918); a draft constitution for such a league can be found at pp. 184–94.

247. A.S. Link, *Wilson the Diplomatist: A Look at his Major Foreign Policies* (Baltimore, 1957), p. 104; but see the different view in A.J. Mayer, *Political Origins of the New Diplomacy, 1917–1918* (New Haven, 1959), pp. 370–1.

dominance of the continent. The crushing terms forced on Russia by Germany at Brest-Litovsk in March 1918, and on Romania at Bucharest two months later, made peace without victory impossible. After this there was no doubt, if there ever had been any, that the fight was one to a finish. Nevertheless, so far as the league was concerned, Wilson was able to ensure that his own conception, that of an association of all nations, was in the main realised, though he was forced to give way to French insistence that Germany be refused membership. However, the league which eventually came into existence in 1919 did so in a surprisingly unplanned and haphazard way. The interest in overhauling the entire structure of international relations which had been shown by so many individuals and unofficial pressure-groups during the war had been only faintly echoed at governmental level. In Italy, by 1918–19 the most disappointed and discontented of the Allied powers, interest in the creation of new international institutions had always been tepid. In Britain neither Lloyd George as prime minister nor Arthur Balfour as foreign secretary attached great importance to the league of nations issue, though some members of the cabinet took much more interest in it. Lord Hugh Cecil, the most consistent advocate among British statesmen of some form of league, had to admit in October 1918 that even then the government had 'no policy' on the question.[248] Wilson himself had few specific ideas about the form the league should take and felt that a successful one would grow over time and in the light of experience rather than be created at a stroke. Moreover, he consistently refused to discuss with his allies what ideas he had. In January 1918 he turned down the suggestion of a conference in Washington to consider its possible structure; and for the next year his attitude to the question remained unclear and unpredictable. He even pressed the British government to discourage public discussion of the sort of league which should be established.

Given such lack of planning by governments, and the atmosphere of haste and disorganisation, sometimes amounting almost to chaos, in which the work of the Versailles conference was done, it can be argued that the covenant of the League of Nations as it eventually took shape was a creditable achievement. Yet it fell in many ways far short of the hopes and demands so often voiced during the war. It was dominated by a handful of great powers in a way which most internationalists before 1919 had opposed and wished to avoid. It did not escape the conservative bias which had marked the majority of peace schemes for generations: Article 10 of the covenant, by which each member of the league undertook to

---

248. P. Yerwood, ' "On the safe and right lines"; the Lloyd George government and the origins of the League of Nations, 1916–1918', *Historical Journal*, 32 (1989), 131–55; V.H. Rothwell, *British War Aims and Peace Diplomacy, 1914–1918* (Oxford, 1971), p. 212.

defend against attack the territorial integrity and political independence of all other members, in effect attempted to guarantee a status quo which was unlikely to be lasting. It set up no machinery of the kind on which so many wartime hopes had been pinned to create or at least interpret international law. This meant that from the beginning the league could be seen as rooted simply in considerations of political power and advantage: a leading American academic lawyer claimed that 'from the standpoint of International Law it may be claimed that no modern treaty of peace has done this system such violence' and the failure to give the league any legislative or quasi-legislative powers became at once a target for criticism by disappointed idealists.[249] The international military force able to restrain powerful would-be aggressors, another object of many wartime hopes, was not created, though the French government fought hard for something of the kind. Wilson relied heavily on public opinion, working through democratically elected governments, as the effective sanction behind the league's decisions and actions: in this he stood squarely in a tradition which went back at least as far as Bentham. Radical critics, their pens sharpened by the mingling of hope and uncertainty which marked the immediate post-war years, could easily find a series of further charges to bring – the failure of the covenant to abolish the privately owned capitalist arms industry; the fact that it had not extended the 'Open Door' system to all the colonies of the European powers; its failure directly to further general disarmament.

It is easy to see in retrospect that the League of Nations laboured from birth under important defects and disadvantages. It was an experiment which, though by no means destined to fail, would have found success difficult even in the most favourable circumstances. Yet it was also an experiment which had to be made. The dream of secure and lasting world peace, of a new age in international relations, indeed of the end of international relations in their traditional form, had shown remarkable durability. The relatively sparse and often completely visionary schemes of earlier generations had become from the mid-nineteenth century onwards much more numerous. They had also begun, in their growing reliance on international law and arbitration and even in their increasing exploration of some of the possibilities of supranational government, often to be significantly more in touch with the real world. Without the enormous impetus given by the First World War in at least one or two major states the impact of the peace movement in all its aspects would have been very much less and very much slower to take effect. Yet in all its varied forms,

249. Kuehl, *Seeking World Order*, p. 341; F.N. Keen, *Revision of the League of Nations Covenant* (London, 1919), pp. 6–7.

its mixture of moral exhortation, appeal to material advantage and stubborn idealism, it had remained for generations, in spite of so many self-deceptions and disappointments, a significant element in the life and aspirations of Europe.

# Conclusion

After the peace settlement of 1919 many of the aspects of international relations which have been discussed in this book were still clearly visible. The political interests and energies of most of the major European states continued for two decades to be focused mainly and in some cases almost entirely on their own continent. Diplomatic services, though growing more rapidly than ever in the past, still showed many of the characteristics which had marked them before 1914. Yet much was also changing, and with unprecedented speed. The international world of the 1920s and 1930s was in many ways a different place from that of William II or Sir Edward Grey; and after 1945 it was almost unrecognisably different. The lesson which was being slowly learnt during the half-century before the First World War, that international relations now embraced much more than diplomacy in any conventional sense of the term, was after 1919 becoming more and more insistent and impossible to ignore. Inescapable practical necessities now meant that international cooperation on a vast range of economic, technological, scientific, medical and cultural issues, clearly visible before the collapse of 1914, was now growing at an unprecedented rate. Diplomacy was now concerned as never in the past with problems of a kind which Richelieu, Kaunitz or even Bismarck would have thought none of their business. The public opinion which statesmen before 1914 had sometimes feared and often tried to influence has never become a dominant factor in the relations of the great states; but since 1919 it has spoken more and more loudly and been listened to with more and more respect. The demand that lasting international peace be safeguarded by some formal scheme of international organisation which would outlaw war or at least make its outbreak more difficult has become

291

more insistent than ever in the past, voiced by immensely more people and accepted and even acted upon by governments as never before. Raised to a quite new pitch of intensity by the losses and suffering of 1914–18, frustrated and humiliated in the 1930s, it reasserted itself in a more sober and realistic form after 1945. The generations since the Versailles conference have thus been a period of change, change which has been rapid by the standards of any previous age, but none the less change many of whose roots can be traced to the decades before the First World War.

It is easy in retrospect to see that by 1914 'classical' diplomacy, cabinet diplomacy, a diplomacy merely of statesmen and diplomats, was slowly coming to an end. Even without the war and the criticisms and demands which it sharpened, the days of the old diplomacy were numbered. Yet in its day it made a real and valuable contribution to the life of Europe. Too often it was a tool in the hands of ambitious rulers and ministers; but in itself it was morally neutral, like any other tool. It was the defects of individuals in positions of great power, the desire for conquest and the taste for victory and reputation of a Louis XIV or a Napoleon, which made it an engine of expansion and conquest, rather than any inherent shortcomings of its own. There is not the slightest reason to suppose that if no such formalised and permanent system of interstate contacts had developed the history of Europe would have been more peaceful. On the contrary, the growth of a generally accepted body of diplomatic practice and tradition and its gradual extension to cover the whole of Europe clearly had a stabilising and unifying effect. In ages when no international political institutions existed, this set of diplomatic norms and the men who embodied and applied them were one of the few visible expressions of some underlying unity of Europe on more than a very limited cultural level. In a roughly similar way the idea of the balance of power provided a kind of intellectual focus or organising principle for theoretical discussion of relations between the states. Most of the writing it stimulated was mediocre and repetitive. By the eighteenth century it was under fire from often severe critics. Yet it too was in its way an expression, and an important one, of European unity. Even condemnation of it had its own significance through the contribution it made to the schemes of international organisation and lasting peace which, in all their differing forms, increasingly expressed a demand, in the end partially successful, that relations between the states be moralised. During the more than four centuries which this book has attempted to cover, both the working of diplomatic machinery and theorising about the relations between states were expressions of the outlook and assumptions of their own day, from the fiercely competitive states of Renaissance Italy to the alliance-systems of the years before 1914. Societies ruled by often autocratic monarchs and permeated by aristocratic values, an intense preoccupation with personal and state prestige, an acceptance as normal of power-politics often in their most naked form: all these left a deep mark on interstate relations in practice and almost as much in theory. Both theory and practice were the product of their own age and could not have been anything else. They changed only as the European society which had given rise to them itself slowly changed. None the less, within their own limits they were a civilising influence as well as an expression of slowly growing civilisation. Without them Europe would have been a more unstable, more anarchic, more dangerous place in whose history violence and destruction would have bulked larger.

# Suggestions for Further Reading

The list which follows, given the complexity of the subjects discussed in this book and the fact that different aspects of them have attracted widely differing amounts of attention from historians, is inevitably somewhat summary and arbitrary. An effort has been made to give prominence to relatively recent and accessible works wherever possible; but this has sometimes been difficult to achieve.

The most comprehensive single book on the European diplomatic system during the whole modern period is probably *The Times Survey of Foreign Ministries of the World*, ed. Zara Steiner (London, 1982): the entries for different states differ considerably in scope but within its own limits the book is an important work of reference. Of the individual states France is the best served in terms of both general surveys and monographs. Among the former *Les Affaires Étrangères et le corps diplomatique français*, ed. J. Baillou (2 vols; Paris, 1984) is outstanding. It is comprehensive, detailed, lavishly produced and certainly the best book of its kind. The first volume covers the period before 1870, the second the last century or more. Also important, though more summary, are three articles by A. Outrey, 'Histoire et principes de l'administration française des affaires étrangères', which appeared in the *Revue Française de Science Politique* in 1953. Much briefer still, but a useful bird's-eye view, is C. Laroche, *La Diplomatie française* (Paris, 1946). Comparable surveys for the other states of Europe are few; but S. Tunberg, C.-F. Palmstierna and others, *Histoire de l'administration des affaires étrangères de la Suède* (Uppsala, 1940) is a thorough study, and R.A. Graham, *Vatican Diplomacy: A Study of Church and State on the International Plane* (Princeton, 1959) is also useful. The origins of modern diplomacy from the later middle ages onwards have attracted a good deal of attention and inspired some excellent work. On the mediæval origins D.E. Queller, *The Office of Ambassador in the Middle Ages* (Princeton, 1967) is outstanding, while G. Mattingly, *Renaissance Diplomacy* (London, 1955) is the best-known book on its subject and one which deserves its reputation; it is both learned and well-written. M.A.R. de Maulde-la-Clavière, *La Diplomatie au temps de Machiavel* (3 vols; Paris, 1892–93) is a remarkable piece of scholarship based on very wide-ranging knowledge of sources and full of interesting information. Two other works of the later nineteenth century are also still very useful: O. Krauske, *Die Entwicklung der ständigen Diplomatie vom fünfzehnten Jahrhundert bis zu den Beschlussen von 1815 und 1818* (Leipzig, 1885) and A. Schaube, 'Zur Entstehungsgeschichte der ständigen Gesandtschaften', *Mitteilungen des Instituts für oesterreichischen Geschichtsforschung*, x (1889). On the subject of the latter the more recent L. Weckmann, 'Les origines des missions diplomatiques permanentes' *Revue Générale de Droit International Publique*, 3rd series, xxiii (1952) is a short but useful study. Central and eastern Europe, often relatively neglected by comparison with the western states, are well covered by B. Picard, *Das Gesandtschaftswesen Ostmitteleuropas in der frühen Neuzeit* (Graz–Vienna–Cologne, 1967) as is an important branch of western diplomacy in H. Biaudet, *Les Nonciatures apostoliques permanentes jusqu'en 1648* (Helsinki, 1910), while E.R. Adair, *The Exterritoriality of Ambassadors in the Sixteenth and Seventeenth Centuries* (London, 1929) remains the standard work on an important topic.

On the seventeenth century the most comprehensive recent study is W.J. Roosen, *The Age of Louis XIV: The Rise of Modern Diplomacy* (Cambridge, Mass., 1976) which brings together much earlier work by the author. France continues to bulk large, perhaps excessively so, in the literature. Two studies which retain their value are C. Picavet, *La Diplomatie française au temps de Louis XIV* (Paris, 1930) and C. Piccioni, *Les Premiers Commis des affaires étrangères au xviie et au xviiie siècles* (Paris, 1928), while a more recent one is J.-P. Samoyault, *Les Bureaux du secrétariat d'état des affaires étrangères sous Louis XV* (Paris, 1971). F. Masson, *Le Département des affaires étrangères pendant la révolution* (Paris, 1877) has still some value. England, and later Britain, are covered by M. Lee, Jr, 'The Jacobean Diplomatic Service', *American Historical Review*, 72 (1966–67) and Phyllis S. Lachs, *The Diplomatic Corps under Charles II and James II* (New Brunswick, N.J., 1965), and most effectively of all by the comprehensive and well-informed D.B. Horn, *The British Diplomatic Service, 1689–1789* (Oxford, 1961).

For the period 1789–1919 Britain continues to be well-served. C.R. Middleton, *The Administration of British Foreign Policy, 1782–1846*

(Durham, N.C., 1977) and with a wider time-scale R. Jones, *The Nineteenth-Century Foreign Office: An Administrative History* (London, 1971) are informative on the central mechanisms for the execution of policy, while Zara S. Steiner, *The Foreign Office and Foreign Policy, 1898–1914* (Cambridge, 1969) takes a wider and less purely administrative view. S.T. Bindoff, 'The Unreformed Diplomatic Service, 1812–60', *Transactions of the Royal Historical Society*, 4th series, xviii (1935) is informative. For France there is the useful E.A. Whitcomb, *Napoleon's Diplomatic Service* (Durham, N.C., 1979) and for Italy L.V. Ferraris, *L'amministrazione centrale del Ministero degli Esteri italiano nel suo sviluppo storico* (1848–1954) (Florence, 1955) and, on a smaller scale, R. Moscati, *Il Ministero degli Affari Esteri, 1861–1870* (Milan, 1961). The new Germany is covered in L. Cecil, *The German Diplomatic Service, 1871–1914* (Princeton, 1976) and P.G. Lauren, *Diplomats and Bureaucrats: The First Institutional Responses to Twentieth-Century Diplomacy in France and Germany* (Stanford, 1976). The efforts to respond to changing conditions of a state in some ways still peripheral to Europe are well treated in C.V. Findley, *Bureaucratic Reform in the Ottoman Empire: The Sublime Porte, 1789–1922* (Princeton, 1980). A. Vagts, *The Military Attaché* (Princeton, 1967) is a somewhat disappointing and opinionated book but the only effort at a comprehensive study of a significant subject.

The balance of power and the questions associated with it generated throughout much of the history of modern Europe a very large controversial and polemical literature on which what is said in this book is largely based. More general and balanced discussions have been considerably rarer. The intellectual problems of extracting from a vague and sometimes emotive phrase a relatively clear-cut meaning, and of distinguishing between different types of balance, have attracted a certain amount of attention. Two short essays by British writers, H. Butterfield, 'The Balance of Power', and M. Wight, 'The Balance of Power', both in *Diplomatic Investigations*, ed. H. Butterfield and M. Wight (London, 1966) are perhaps the most useful relatively recent efforts of this kind: I.L. Claude, Jr, 'The Balance of Power Revisited', *Review of International Studies*, 15 (1989) also makes some suggestive points. The early modern period, when the balance emerged as an at least ostensible preoccupation of statesmen, has attracted a good deal of attention. G. Livet, *L'Equilibre européen de la fin du XVe à la fin du XVIIIe siècle* (Paris, 1976) is brief and to the point though in some ways a little superficial, while G. Zeller, 'Le principe d'équilibre dans la politique internationale avant 1789', *Revue Historique*, ccxv (1956) is a mere sketch, as is C. Morandi, 'Il concetto della politica d'equilibrio nell'Europa moderna', *Archivio Storico Italiano*, lxxxvii (1940). E.Kaeber, *Die Idee des europäischen Gleichgewichts in der publizistischen Literatur vom 16. bis zur Mitte des 18. Jahrhunderts* (Berlin, 1907), however, is a very thorough survey of the pamphlet literature for the period it covers; it is particularly valuable for its summaries of relatively inaccessible German writing of this kind. G. Curcio, *Europa: storia di un'idea* (2 vols; Florence, 1958) performs a somewhat similar function, but on a larger scale and over a longer period. The emergence during the eighteenth century of overseas empires as an important element in the European balance is well covered in an article by A. Rein, 'Über die Bedeutung des überseeischen Ausdehnung für das europäische Staatensystem', *Historische Zeitschrift*, cxxxvii (1928).

For the nineteenth and early twentieth centuries there is less writing of a wide-ranging kind; but C. Holbraad, *The Concert of Europe; A Study in German and British International Theory* (London, 1970) discusses competently much of the still considerable contemporary literature on the balance and its problems. Ideas of the status of Russia in the European state-system from the sixteenth century onwards are surveyed very thoroughly in D. Groh, *Russland und das Selbstverständnis Europas* (Neuwied, 1961), and more briefly from the mid-nineteenth century onwards in G. Barraclough, 'Europa, Amerika und Russland im Vorstellung und Denken des 19. Jahrhunderts', *Historische Zeitschrift*, cciii (1966). P.W. Schroeder, 'The Nineteenth-Century System: Balance of Power or Political Equilibrium?', *Review of International Studies*, 15 (1989) is a careful and interesting analytical study.

Schemes of international organisation and efforts to secure international peace have attracted a good deal of attention from historians. C.L. Lange and A. Schou, *Histoire de l'internationalisme* (3 vols.; Christiania, 1919–63) is a somewhat mechanical survey of writing on the subject from the end of the middle ages onwards. More illuminating in many ways for the early modern period is E. Silberner, *La Guerre dans la pensée économique du xvie au xviiie siècle* (Paris, 1939). Some of the best-known proposals of these generations are discussed in A. Puharré, *Les Projets d'organization européenne d'après le Grand Dessin de Henri IV et de Sully* (Paris, 1954), K. von Raumer, 'Sully, Crucé und das Problem des allgemeinen Friedens', *Historische Zeitschrift*, 175 (1953) and, more generally though less analytically, Elizabeth V. Souleyman, *The Vision of World Peace in Seventeenth and Eighteenth-Century France* (New York, 1941). The radical idealism of the later eighteenth century, as applied to international relations, is best treated in the elegant book of F. Gilbert, *To the Farewell Address: Ideas of Early American Foreign Policy* (Princeton, 1961) which tells the reader as much about Europe as about the new United States.

On the nineteenth century there is again much of interest in E. Silberner, *The Problem of War in Nineteenth Century Economic Thought*

(Princeton, 1946), while the peace movement has proved an attractive subject to many writers. D.A. Martin, *Pacifism: An Historical and Sociological Study*, (London, 1965) is, as its title suggests, a work of sociology as much as of history; but P. Brock, *Pacifism in Europe to 1914* (Princeton, 1972) is solid and detailed, and A.C.F. Beales, *The History of Peace* (London, 1931) still has value. Recent articles of interest are S.E. Cooper, 'The Origins and Development of European Peace Movements: From Vienna to Frankfurt', in *Friedensbewegungen: Bedingungen und Wirkungen*, ed. G. Heiss and H. Lutz (Munich, 1984) and A. Tyrrell, 'Making the Millenium: The Mid-Nineteenth Century Peace Movement', *Historical Journal*, 20 (1978), while there are several useful essays in *Doves and Diplomats: Foreign Offices and Peace Movements in Europe and America*, ed. S. Wank (Westport, Conn.–London, 1978). Internationalism and peace plans in Germany from the sixteenth century onwards are covered competently though a little mechanically in V. Valentin, *Geschichte des Völkerbundgedankens in Deutschland* (Berlin, 1920); their weakness in the Bismarckian Reich is well brought out in R. Chickering, *Imperial Germany and a World without War* (Princeton, 1975). Of the large literature on pacifism and internationalism during the First World War it may be enough here to mention, very arbitrarily, K. Robbins, *The Abolition of War: The 'Peace Movement' in Britain, 1914–1919* (Cardiff, 1976) and F.L. Carsten, *War against War: British and German Radical Movements in the First World War* (London, 1982).

On disarmament there is the informative, but somewhat wooden, Merze Tate, *The Disarmament Illusion: The Movement for a Limitation of Armaments to 1907* (New York, 1942) and the short but pointed Sir J. Headlam-Morley, 'Proposals for the Reduction of Armaments', in his *Studies in Diplomatic History* (London, 1930). On the bread-and-butter internationalism of posts, telegraphs, health precautions, etc., F.S.L. Lyons, *Internationalism in Europe, 1815–1914* (Leyden, 1963) remains the most complete source of information. P. Renouvin, *L'idée de fédération européenne dans la pensée politique du XIXe siècle* (Oxford, 1949) is a short but workmanlike account of its subject. The great currents of thought and feeling – nationalist, liberal, socialist – which influenced nineteenth-century attitudes to international relations have of course produced immense literatures. Here it may be sufficient to mention only one well-known work on each: G. Salvemini, *Mazzini* (London, 1956); W.H. Dawson, *Richard Cobden and Foreign Policy* (London, 1926); and G. Haupt, *Socialism and the Great War: The Collapse of the Second International* (Oxford, 1972). Finally there are important books which, though not specifically on international relations in any narrow sense, provide indispensable background knowledge. Such are H. Gollwitzer, *Europabild und*

*Europagedanke: Beiträge zur deutschen Geistesgeschichte des 18. und 19. Jahrhunderts* (Munich, 1964); J.-B. Duroselle, *L'Idée d'Europe dans l'histoire* (Paris, 1965); and F. Meinecke, *Cosmopolitanism and the National State* (Princeton, 1970).

# Index

Incidental references to individual towns or countries have not normally been indexed

300

d', French foreign office official, 127

Hegel, G.W.F., German philosopher, 195

Heinsius, Anthonie, Dutch statesman, 75

Hennin, Pierre-Michel, French foreign office official, 93

Henrietta Maria, queen of England, 50

Henry II, king of France, 15, 73, 152

Henry III, king of France, 33

Henry IV, king of France, 23

Henry III, king of England, 205

Henry VII, king of England, 13, 47

Henry VIII, king of England, 6, 10, 11, 17, 24, 34, 39, 210, 211

Herberstein, Sigismund von, Austrian diplomat, 11, 37

Herder, Johann Gottfried von, German writer, on nationalism, 196

Hertslet, family of, 120

Hertzberg, Ewald Friedrich, count, Prussian statesman, 178

Hintze, Otto, German historian, on balance of power, 201

Hobson, John Atkinson, British political writer, scheme for international government, 284, 285

Holdermann, J.B., Jesuit, 91

Holland, kingdom of, smallness of diplomatic service and foreign office, 104, 110

Holles, Denzil, baron, English diplomat, 50

Holy Alliance (1815), has little impact on international relations, 236–7

Holy League (1495), 3

Hötzendorff, Conrad von, Austrian soldier, 145

House, Colonel E.M., American agent, 281

humanists, condemn war on moral grounds, 208–9

Ido, synthetic language, 253

Innocent III, pope, 204, 206

Innocent IV, pope, 205

Innocent VIII, pope, 73

Innocent XI, pope, 55

interception of letters, 21–2, 43–4, 115–16

Institute of International Law (1873), 258

International Committee of Women for Permanent Peace (1915), 280

International Congress of Women (1915), 280

international cooperation, growth of in later nineteenth century, 251–2

international court, proposals for, 257–9

international law, proposals to codify, 258

international languages, 253

International Miners Federation (1890), 253

international organization, treaty of London (1518) and, 211

Podiebrad proposal for, 212–13

Sully proposal for, 214–16

Crucé proposal for, 216–17

factors hostile to, 219

atmosphere favourable to schemes of in eighteenth century, 220

Saint-Pierre proposal for, 221–2

minor eighteenth-century proposals for, 222–3

Bentham proposal for, 227–8

differing eighteenth-century attitudes to, 232

stability an essential element in, 234–5

included by Crucé in scheme of
international organisation, 217
schemes to partition, 224–5

Paine, Tom, English radical, 193
Palmerston, Henry John Temple,
viscount, 115, 128
defends balance of power, 197
papacy, payment of diplomats by,
34
diplomatic organisation of, 73
papal state, government of, 237
Paris, *parlement* of, 205
declaration of (1856), 245
Paruta, Paulo, Venetian writer, on
balance of power in Italy, 151
Paschal, Charles, French writer, 82
Passy, Frédéric, French peace
campaigner, 246, 247, 255
Paul, tsar of Russia, 90
Pavia, battle of (1525), 9, 153
peace between nations, arbitration
and, 204–6
humanists and, 208–11
Kant and, 225–6, 228
ideas about in later eighteenth
century, 232
seen by Gentz as impractical, 233
schemes for increase in nineteenth
century, 236
seen as conservative force, 238
utopian radical hopes for, 241–4
doubts about possibility of, 270
agitation for after 1914, 279–80
peace conventions (1843–51), 240–1
peace societies, most active in
English-speaking countries, 239–41
provide outlet for emotions and
ambitions, 240
decline of in 1850s and 1860s, 241
revival of from 1870s, 249–50
weakness of in Germany, 250

Pecquet, Antoine, French foreign
office official, 87, 93
Pecqueur, Constantin, French utopian
socialist, and European union,
242–3, 244
Pélissier, A. J.-J., French soldier, 122
Pellicier, Guillaume, French diplomat,
15
Penn, William, Quaker, and
international peace, 221, 224, 226
Perez, Gonzalo, Spanish official, 73
Permanent Court of Arbitration
(1899), 262
permanent embassies, origins of, 6–7
Persia, growth of European diplomacy
in, 108
Peter I, tsar, later emperor, of Russia,
49, 54, 174
assumes title of emperor, 66–7
and incorporation of Russia in
European diplomacy, 70–1
and training of Russian diplomats,
89
Philip I, the Fair, king of Castile, 10
Philip II, king of Spain, 11, 15, 17,
28, 133, 152
Philip IV, king of Spain, 165
Philip IV, king of France, 205
Philip V, king of Spain, 78
Philip Augustus, king of France, 1
physiocrats, in France, free trade and
European union, 229–30
hostile to conventional diplomacy,
230–1
stress secondary nature of foreign
policy, 231–2
Picquigny, meeting at (1475), 10
Pins, Jean du, French diplomat, 14
Pitt, William, the elder, British
statesman, 76
Pitt, William, the younger, British
statesman, 175

Romanovskii, colonel, Russian
    soldier, 131
Rome, centre for exchange of news, 13
    abuse of diplomatic immunities in,
        55–6
    expenses of diplomats in, 85–6
Roscher, W.G.F., German economist,
    270
Roseberry, Archibald Philip Primrose,
    earl of, British statesman, 262
Ross, bishop of, 25
Rossignol, Antoine, French
    cryptographer, 43
Rouillé, Antoine-Louis, French
    statesman, 44
Rousseau, Jean-Jacques, Swiss political
    philosopher, 150
Rumbold, Sir Horace, British
    diplomat, 121–2
Russia, surveillance of foreign
    diplomats, 14
    first contacts with western Europe,
        28–9
    difficulties of travel, 37–8
    maintenance of ambassadors of in
        London, 48–9
    maintenance of foreign diplomats,
        49
    importance of ceremonial, 61–2
    incorporation in European
        diplomacy, 69–71
    foreign office, 74, 75, 77, 111, 117
    training of diplomats, 89–90, 127–8
    teaching of oriental languages, 91–2
    recruitment of diplomats, 121–2
    control of foreign policy, 146–7
    and 1917 revolution, 148
    and balance of power, 174–6, 184–5
    fear of declines in later nineteenth
        century, 185–6
    place in schemes of European union,
        215, 224

Russo-Japanese war (1904–5), 130
Ryswick, peace congress (1697),
    precedence at, 65

St Petersburg, convention of (1868),
    251
Saint-Pierre, Charles Iréné Castel de,
    abbé, French political writer, peace
    scheme, 221–2
Saint-Simon, Claude-Henri de, comte,
    French utopian socialist, and
    European union, 241–2
Sainte-Beuve, Charles-Augustin,
    French critic, 199
Salisbury, Robert Cecil, marquess of,
    British statesman, and international
    arbitration, 262
Sartorius, Johann Baptist, German
    political writer, and international
    organisation, 239
Saunders, George, British journalist,
    140
Savona, meeting at (1507), 10
Savoy, duke of, appoints permanent
    ambassador, 6
    duchy of, uncertain international
        position, 59–60
Say, Horace, French economist, 246
Sazonov, S.D.Russian statesman,
    146
Schmoller, Gustav, German
    economist, 270
*Secretaria Apostolica,* in Rome, 73
secretaries to diplomats, 86–7
*secretarius intimus,* of popes, 73
Selim III, Ottoman sultan, 72, 106
Seven Years War, 172, 175, 181
Seymour, Sir George Hamilton, on
    importance of dinners, 126
Sigismund, king of Hungary, 7–8
Sigismund I, king of Poland, 10, 32
Simancas, archive at, 21

United Netherlands, *see* Dutch Republic
United States of America, and balance of power, 199
growing activity in international affairs, 200
belief in constructive aspects of war, 272–3
Universal Peace Congresses, 249
Universal Postal Union (1874), 251
Utrecht, peace congress at (1713), 101
precedence at, 66
and balance of power, 164

Vattel, Eméric de, Swiss international lawyer, on balance of power, 165
Vatican, archives of, 252
Vauban, Sebastien le Prestre, seigneur de, French soldier, on overseas empires, 171
Venice, official secrecy in, 14
demands reports from diplomats, 23
sensitivity about international standing, 49, 59
diplomatic privileges in, 56
claims to hold balance in Italy, 151
Vergennes, Charles Gravier, comte de, French statesman, 95
*Verband für internationale Verständigung*, in Germany, weakness of, 250
Versailles peace conference (1919), power of allied leaders at, 149
and creation of League of Nations, 287–8
Vienna peace settlement (1815), use of arbitration, 254
Viète, Francois, French cryptographer, 22
Vigenère, Blaise de, French cryptographer, 22
Villars, Claude Louis Hector, French soldier, 66
Visconti, Filippo Maria, duke of Milan, 7
Viskovaty, I.M., Russian official, 74
Vives, Juan Luis, Spanish humanist, appeals for peace and mediation, 210–11
Volapuk, synthetic language, 253
Voltaire, François Arouet de, French writer, hostility to war, 231

Waldersee, Albrecht von, German soldier, 130
Wallachia, hospodar of, 71
Walpole, Horace, British writer, 55
war, believed to be becoming less violent, 166–7, 251, 270
seen in middle ages as inevitable, 204
attacked by Voltaire, 231
and economic and technological change, 243
efforts to regulate, 251
seen as essential to progress, 270–3
underestimates of popular readiness for, 278–9
War of Devolution (1667), 161
War Propaganda Bureau, in Britain, 140
Werder, August von, German soldier, 130
Whitelocke, Bulstrode, English diplomat, 51, 60
Wicquefort, Abraham de, Dutch writer, 47, 57
William of Orange, stadtholder of the United Netherlands, 30
William I, king of Holland, 104
William II, emperor of Germany, 140, 188, 262
and control of foreign policy, 145–6
William III, king of England, 65
Wilson, Woodrow, American president, 148